Educational Leadership and Music

A volume in
New Directions in Educational Leadership:
Innovations in Research, Teaching, and Learning
Noelle Witherspoon Arnold, *Series Editor*

Educational Leadership and Music

Lessons for Tomorrow's School Leaders

edited by

Terri N. Watson
The City College of New York

Jeffrey S. Brooks
Monash University

Floyd D. Beachum
Lehigh University

INFORMATION AGE PUBLISHING, INC.
Charlotte, NC • www.infoagepub.com

Library of Congress Cataloging-in-Publication Data

A CIP record for this book is available from the Library of Congress
http://www.loc.gov

ISBN: 978-1-68123-855-5 (Paperback)
      978-1-68123-856-2 (Hardcover)
      978-1-68123-857-9 (ebook)

I dedicate this work to my mother, Theresa J. Watson. Thank you for your unwavering love and support. I am because you are.
— Terri N. Watson

To the members of Team Rainbow: Melanie, Holland, Bronwyn, Clodagh, and Jürgen—We are the music makers, and we are the dreamers of dreams.
— Jeffrey S. Brooks

This work is dedicated to George Suggs, Patricia Oates, Chester Beachum, Jr., and all of those family members who are no longer with us. You are not forgotten.
— Floyd D. Beachum

CONTENTS

"PLAYING THE CHANGES"

Building Strong Communities Through Innovation and Improvisatory Leadership

Mitchell Robinson
Michigan State University

The real power of music lies in the fact that it can be "true" to the life of feeling in a way that language cannot; for its significant forms have that ambivalence of content which words cannot have.
—Susanne Langer, 1942

Music expresses that which cannot be said and on which it is impossible to be silent.
—Victor Hugo, 1864

The notion that music may provide lessons for educational leadership is a powerful one and offers rich possibilities for school leaders willing to think in creative ways about their practice. For me, the true power of music is found in its ability to help us express ourselves when our feelings are complicated, and sometimes contradictory. As Jeffrey Brooks points out in his chapter on the band Ministry, conflict and tension in music are often great sources of productivity, but are generally avoided in education circles: "In

Educational Leadership and Music, pages xi–xvi
Copyright © 2017 by Information Age Publishing

education, it is particularly interesting to reflect on the oft-espoused value of having consensus before moving an initiative forward. Ministry reminds us that at times great results can come from working under great pressure" (Brooks, this volume, p. 51).

I have found that tension can indeed be a source of creative energy in my work as an educator and school administrator, and have studied this idea in my own scholarship. My dissertation research focused on the nature of the relationships present in complex, nonhierarchical organizational structures, specifically examining the metaphor of "tensegrity." Tensegrity is a contraction of "tensional integrity," and was first popularized by the American architect and engineer R. Buckminster Fuller (1895–1983). Tensegrity is a structural concept "based on principles of continuous tension and discontinuous compression. For Fuller, the concept manifested his philosophy that nature uses tension primarily and compression secondarily, whereas humans often misguidedly do the reverse" (Robinson, 2005, p. 12).

Rather than avoiding tension, structures designed as tensegrity arrays absorb and distribute forces, using them "to mechanically 'tune' the whole system as one" (Ingber, 1998, p. 56). Educational leaders can reconcile the presence of tension and conflict in their institutions by reorienting how they view the inevitable conflicts that arise in the daily course of their practice. Rather than perceiving these points of tension as undesired sources of friction, conflicts among coworkers can be viewed as opportunities for forging new understandings.

Judge (1998) suggests a three-step process for channeling creative tensions in a productive fashion:

1. Understanding and ordering differences.
2. Observing a degree of sensitivity regarding diversity when ordering differences.
3. Basing differences on an underlying unity of mission.

While school leaders who follow Judge's advice should notice improved levels of communication, they may not notice a decreased level of disagreement. Embracing creative tension as an engine for productivity and diversity of thought is often frustrating and time consuming. It does offer, however, the promise of better and more creative results than a simple quest for consensus.

This approach to conceptualizing differences as a positive aspect of school leadership is conducive to enhanced levels of risk-taking, and expanded horizons for personal and professional growth. It also offers a sense of empowerment for school personnel who can provide the necessary counterbalance to the natural inequities in power, resources, and prestige often found among the members of a school community.

Floyd Beachum suggests another perspective on the relationship between conflicting constructs in his chapter on the group Public Enemy. Beachum identifies the two principles that characterize the group's music and career, unity and critique, resisting the urge to present these concepts as simplistic notions, and providing fulsome explanations of each idea from a critical stance. The chapter concludes with this probing and insightful analysis.

The hip-hop music industry in general began to overemphasize material pursuits over the pursuit of economic social freedom (Dyson, 2004; West, 2008). West (2008) further indicated that,

> the recording industry is so interested in pacifying, distracting, and ensuring that the strength, grace and dignity of young people is not affirmed. They would rather keep them locked into a narcissistic, materialistic, and individualistic orientation.... *The legacy of Public Enemy is a continuous fight to emphasize the former and eliminate the latter.* (p. 127, emphasis added)

Both Brooks and Beachum remind us that nothing about educational leadership is simple or uncomplicated, and that much of what we deal with as leaders is paradoxical as well as idiosyncratic. The unique nature of leadership in schools requires a more complex and multifaceted approach to responding to situations and issues than that followed in other professions, an approach based on the recognition of multiple realities, diverse contexts, inequitable power relationships, and ever-changing conditions.

School leadership also requires a Janus-like sense of perspective, looking simultaneously forward and backward to establish a sense of historically-informed context. As Terri N. Watson notes in her chapter on the R&B group Sister Sledge, "Historical analysis such as this is an underutilized tool in educational leadership research and can be used to expand our knowledge base in meaningful ways."

In a larger sense, music when taught well provides the "antidote" to many of the problems that pervade education and schooling in the "accountability era," among them an obsession with standardized testing, draconian teacher evaluation systems predicated on junk science (i.e., value-added measures), attacks on veterans (read: "expensive" teachers), and a narrowing of the curriculum to a barren educational menu of math and reading at the expense of music, art, physical education, and any other "non-tested" subject. Music making demands creativity, critical thinking, and collaboration—the very skill set that business leaders and corporate education reformers claim to value—and yet music is often a casualty of the reforms being forced into the schools.

As Soribel Genao alludes to in her lyrical chapter on Lauryn Hill, students, parents, teachers, administrators, and anyone challenging the corporate education reform agenda often wonder, "Who made these rules?

We're so confused." It is as if the rules are being made up as we go, that our goals as teachers and administrators are moving targets, and that those of us entrusted with the education of our children have little power to affect change on the profession to which we have committed our careers. Adrift in a sea of frustration ("It seems we lose the game before we even start to play"), I believe that music offers a powerful metaphor for school leadership that can provide a moral and ethical compass to guide school leaders' efforts in a time of near-constant turmoil and change.

As a former music teacher and school administrator and now as a music teacher educator, I see the real value of music as a metaphor for school leadership less in the products that we create as musicians, and more in the creative processes in which musicians engage when performing, improvising, arranging, and producing music in a multitude of ways. Stephen Jacobson identifies two characteristics of the jazz great Sonny Rollins that encapsulate the power of these processes: innovation and improvisation.

INNOVATIVE LEADERSHIP

Rollins had a rare ability to take existing musical material and by applying his prodigious talent and knowledge in fresh and innovative ways breathe new life into it. Jacobson offers the example of Rollins's reinterpretation of the tune "I'm an Old Cowhand, a song originally made famous by Bing Crosby and then Roy Rogers":

> Anyone familiar with the song will quickly recognize the beginning and end of this rather hackneyed piece of fluff, but what happens in between as Rollins deconstructs and then reconstructs the melody is nothing short of magic.

I would suggest that this "magic" was actually the result of countless hours of what jazz musicians refer to as "woodshedding"—the often tedious process of listening, transcribing, and practicing short "licks" and musical motifs, transposing these melodic ideas into new keys in order to develop one's technical skills, and then rearranging these "musical germs" into new and previously unimagined forms, styles, and genres.

Innovative school leaders will recognize the parallels to their own work: careful and attentive listening to the various stakeholders that contribute to their school communities, considering the merits and values of these contributions, and finding ways to honor these voices in the crafting of new policies and procedures that strengthen and advance student learning and growth. As Jacobson points out, innovative leadership is a blend of art, science, and craft—or, as musicians might conceive of it, feeling, thinking, and doing. Just as music teachers have nothing to apologize for in helping children learn how to "feel" more and better, innovative school leaders should not apologize for recognizing the importance of valuing the importance of "feel" (art), in addition to that of data (science) and expertise (craft) in building strong learning communities.

IMPROVISATORY LEADERSHIP

One of the "knocks" on improvisation is the notion that improvising involves simply "making stuff up." While there is certainly an element of spontaneity involved with musical improvisation, the idea that improvising does not require careful planning, preparation, and practice could not be further from the truth. For educators, part of the misunderstanding here comes from our confusion between the terms planning and preparing.

Just as with musical improvisation, pedagogical improvisation is based on deep and thorough knowledge of the material to be taught, and extensive study and practice of these materials. Improvisatory teaching also requires an immersive approach to lesson preparation and doesn't really allow for linear lesson planning or a teacher-centered instructional style (Snow, 1998).

The process of improvisatory music teaching becomes, in effect, a re-creation of the composer's compositional process—or the improviser's creative process. It also requires a "flattening" of the hierarchical structures often present in classrooms, and an egalitarian approach to cultivating a learning culture rather than an authoritarian style of classroom management.

For school leaders, improvisatory leadership relies on deep knowledge of one's learning community, a commitment to a "flat" administrative hierarchical approach that empowers all members to develop their own leadership skills and abilities, and the confidence to allow others to lead. Just as with jazz improvisation, taking these risks while "on the bandstand" can be frightening. But as any jazz musician will tell you, the only way to get better is to play with better players—and to challenge yourself by playing harder tunes with harder "changes."

Improvisatory school leaders "get better" by surrounding themselves with excellent colleagues, listening to these colleagues as they "play the changes" to difficult educational problems, and using their deep knowledge of educational leadership theories and practices to develop new and innovative approaches to school governance. Innovative and improvisatory school leadership, like music, promises to provide an "antidote" to the challenges we face as a profession, by responding with creativity, connectivity, and collaboration.

REFERENCES

Dyson, M. E. (2004). *The Michael Eric Dyson reader.* New York, NY: Basic Civitas Books

Hugo, V. (1891). *William Shakespeare, Part I, Book II, Chapter IV* (M. B. Anderson, Trans.). Chicago, IL: A.C. McClurg.

Ingber, D. E. (1998, January). The architecture of life: A universal set of building rules seems to guide the design of organic structures—from simple carbon compounds to complex cells and tissues. *Scientific American,* 48–57.

Judge, A. J. N. (1998). Living differences as a basis for sustainable community. *Transnational Associations.* Retrieved from https://www.laetusinpraesens.org/docs/quenchin.php

Langer, S. K. (1942). *Philosophy in a new key: A study in the symbolism of reason, rite and art.* Cambridge, MA: Harvard University Press.

Robinson, M. (2005). A tensegretic theory of school-college collaboration in music education. *Arts Education Policy Review, 106*(3), 9–18.

Snow, S. L. (1998). *Rehearsing in the choral context: A qualitative examination of undergraduate conductor/teacher planning processes and relationships to emergent pedagogical knowledge evidenced in teaching* (Doctoral dissertation). Michigan State University, East Lansing, MI.

West, C. (2008). *Hope on a tightrope: Words and wisdom.* Carlsbad, CA: Hay House.

INTRODUCTION

Terri N. Watson, Jeffrey S. Brooks, and Floyd Beachum

Over the past half-century researchers and practitioners in educational leadership have developed useful ways of examining and improving their practice. They have also routinely looked to the business community, the social sciences, and policy makers to frame their ways of approaching the complicated work of leading schools. Yet, while these technical knowledge bases have their utility, scholars have begun to recognize the importance of spirituality, emotional intelligence, and the arts as important foundations of leadership practice (English & Ehrich, 2016). This has led to the recognition and realization that insight, information, and inspiration cannot only be gleaned from the aforementioned sources, but also from arts and specifically music. Music is therapeutic. It promotes creativity, reflection, and communication. In this light, we set out to understand how music has impacted professors of educational leadership and practitioners in the field.

There is a kind of magic that comes with music. It is that tune playing in the background, it is that song you sing when you are happy, it is that lyric that you keep singing to yourself over and over without realizing that your mouth is moving. Thus, music plays an integral part of our lives in very obvious and less apparent ways. West (2008) wrote, "Music has been our most powerful creative expression" (p. 114). West uses music to metaphorically analyze himself and the world around him. He even describes himself as "an aspiring bluesman in a world of ideas and a jazzman in the life of the mind" (p. 114). His appeal to these unique musical forms displays their greater applicability past only being of entertainment value. Similarly, Beachum and McCray (2011) noted that "music is more than an avenue for entertainment only" (p. 6). They used history, education, and music to trace the course of African Americans from slavery to the 21st century. These three components were critical to their analysis because they all occurred concurrently and frequently intersected. Thus, the historical time period in which one lives impacts educational attitudes and is also influenced by musical expression. Dyson (1997) used Black music as a tool of analysis to critique society's contempt for Black youth and its preoccupation with nostalgia. At the heart of his analysis, Dyson wrote:

> For our nostalgic true believers, it translates into the notion that the best in black music happened to coincide with their own youth. At the same time, they associate vice, or limitation, or smallness of vision, with the aesthetic form most alien to them ... We should adjust our evaluations of music based on the sorts of achievement that are possible, even desirable, in a given period. (p. 132)

How many times in our lives have elders criticized and demonized the music of younger generations? Furthermore, how many times have elders, professionals, and school leaders criticized and demonized kids and youth culture? Educators constantly reflect on a supposed "Golden Age" of education where students were orderly, respectful, and obedient (and coincidently culturally homogeneous). By using music for analysis we discover that "educators should recognize how their past experiences can coincide with the experiences of their students and not always conflict with them. In this way, educators should examine the ways in which collective memories can help them build closer relationships with their students" (Beachum & McCray, 2011, p. 123). Thus, music has many different academic, social, and educational applications. This is the essence of the book you are reading now.

In this book we considered new territory for educational leadership by looking to music for lessons and inspiration that may inform the next generation of schools leaders. Each chapter focuses on an artist or group whose work serves to refine, extend, and challenge our thinking in regards to educational leadership. You will find a vast array of musical forms of expression analyzed and described by an equally diverse collection of educational leadership scholars and practitioners. There may be some who question the academic appropriateness or relevance of a text such as this one. Our response is that part of our ongoing mission should be to break ourselves out of academic silos and forge meaningful connections between seemingly disparate disciplines. Furthermore, educational leadership stands to gain more by drawing from the arts and specifically musical influences. Finally, music is an obvious part of most of our lives; why not explore the ways in which it impacts us on an academic level and not just a personal level? In sum, we ask that as you read the chapters of this book, you reflect on your own musical tastes and favorite artists. Think about how music has influenced your life in various ways. As you reflect, keep in mind what West (2008) noted about blues and jazz:

> What is distinctive about using blues and jazz as a source of intellectual inspiration is the ability to be flexible, fluid, improvisational, and multi-dimensional—finding one's own voice, but using that voice in a variety of different ways. (p. 114)

We encourage you to listen to your music effectively, reflect deeply, and find your voice.

REFERENCES

Beachum, F. D., & McCray, C. R. (2011). *Cultural collision and collusion: Reflections on hip hop culture, values, and schools.* New York, NY: Peter Lang Publishing.

Dyson, M. E. (1997). *Race rules: Navigating the color line.* New York, NY: Vintage Books.

English, F. & Ehrich, L. C. (2016). *Leading beautifully : Educational leadership as connoisseurship.* New York, NY: Routledge.

West , C. (2008). *Hope on a tightrope: Words and wisdom.* Carlsbad, CA: Hay House, Inc.

CHAPTER 1

LEADERSHIP AS JAZZ

Critical Servant Leadership and the Music of John Coltrane

Judy Alston
Ashland University

The year was 1965 and the average cost of a new house was $13,600; the average income per year was $6,450; gas per gallon was 31 cents; the average cost of a new car was $2,650; a loaf of bread was 21 cents; and the average rent per month was $118 (peoplehistory.com). The year saw many changes and innovations—educationally, politically, musically, and socially.

- *Educationally:* The Elementary and Secondary Education Act (ESEA; 1965) provided federal funds to help low-income students. The Higher Education Act increased federal aid to higher education and provided for scholarships and student loans, and established a National Teachers Corps. And Project Head Start, a preschool education program for children from low-income families, began as an eight-week summer program.

Educational Leadership and Music, pages 1–10
Copyright © 2017 by Information Age Publishing
All rights of reproduction in any form reserved.

- *Politically:* The Immigration and Nationality Act of 1965, also known as the Hart-Cellar Act, abolished the National Origins Formula and resulted in unprecedented numbers of Asians and Latin Americans immigrating to the United States. President Johnson signed the 1965 Voting Rights Acts into law guaranteeing the rights of African Americans to exercise their right and duties in elections. The war in Vietnam began and Edward H. White, II, conducted the first American spacewalk.
- *Socially:* Dr. Martin Luther King, Jr., led a civil rights march from Selma to Montgomery, Alabama, which became known as Bloody Sunday. Malcolm X was assassinated at the Audubon Ballroom. The Watts riots erupted in California.
- *Musically:* Five Motown releases reached No. 1 on the top 10 pop charts including "I Can't Help Myself" by the Four Tops, "Stop in the Name of Love" by the Supremes, and "My Girl" by the Temptations. Top 40 singles included "(I Can't Get No) Satisfaction" by the Rolling Stones, "Unchained Melody" by The Righteous Brothers, "Help" and "Yesterday" both by The Beatles, and soul brother number one James Brown had a double hitter with "Papa's Got a Brand New Bag" and "I Feel Good." Music historian Andrew Grant Jackson (2015) in his book *1965: The Most Revolutionary Year in Music* chronicled what was:

> a ground-breaking year of creativity fueled by rivalries between musicians and continents, sweeping social changes, and technological breakthroughs...Never before had popular music been so diverse. Soul and funk became prime forces of desegregation.... *1965* is a fascinating account of a defining year that produced some of the greatest songs, albums, and artists of all time. (Jackson, 2015)

THE ARTIST: JOHN COLTRANE

Indeed, 1965 was a year filled with breakthroughs on many fronts. One such breakthrough came in the ultimate opus *A Love Supreme* released by one of the world's musical geniuses, John William Coltrane. Born on September 23, 1926, in Hamlet, North Carolina, he was destined to leave an indelible mark in American musical and spiritual history.

Coltrane was raised in the African Methodist Episcopal Zion (AMEZ) church where his father and grandfathers were ministers. His parents were also singers and musicians, and he began playing the saxophone at age 13.

In 1939, Coltrane's father, grandparents, and uncle died, leaving the household to be run by his mother, Alice, who found work as a domestic. Financial struggles defined this period for Coltrane, and eventually his mother and a few other family members moved to New Jersey in the hopes of finding a better paycheck. Coltrane, however, remained in North Carolina, living with family friends until he graduated from high school. (John Coltrane, n.d.)

In 1943, he moved to Philadelphia where he studied music at Granoff Studios as well as the Ornstein School of Music.

Coltrane entered the Navy in 1945 and was assigned reserve status, as were many African Americans at that time. According to Lewis Porter in *John Coltrane: His Life and Music,* only limited numbers of Black men served as seamen after 1942. The Navy was segregated, and Coltrane was sent to boot camp at the Black section of Sampson Naval Training Center in upstate New York. He spent one year in the Navy band while stationed in Hawaii. In 1949, Trane (as he became known) signed on to work with Dizzy Gillespie. He went on to work with Duke Ellington for a brief period, and then on to the Miles Davis Quarter.

Over his early life Trane developed a heroin addiction, which was the reason for being let go from both Ellington and Davis's bands. He began his solo career in 1957 and was finally clean from the addiction; this was also a period of spiritual transformation. Of this period, Coltrane said:

> During the year 1957, I experienced, by the grace of God, a spiritual awakening, which was to lead me to a fuller, richer, more productive life. At that time, in gratitude, I humbly asked to be given the means and privilege to make others happy through music. I feel this has been granted through His grace. All praise to God. (Coltrane, 1965)

By 1960 Coltrane had his own band, a quartet that included pianist McCoy Tyner, bassist Jimmy Garrison and drummer Elvin Jones. The group, known as the John Coltrane Quartet, produced some of jazz's most enduring albums including *Giant Steps* (1960) and *My Favorite Things* (1961). The latter album especially catapulted Coltrane to stardom. Yet it was the 1965 *A Love Supreme* that is Coltrane's most acclaimed record. Trane was awarded two Grammys for performance and jazz composition. One of the greatest saxophonists to ever live and a revolutionizer of jazz music, Trane died from liver cancer on July 17, 1967, in Huntington, New York.

Coltrane's legacy continues to live on in his music and his influence on those who follow jazz and other musical genres. Moreover, his spiritual influence is still alive and well in the form of the Saint John Coltrane African Orthodox church located in San Francisco. Founded in 1971, the mission of the church is to paint the globe with the message of *A Love Supreme*, and in doing so promote global unity, peace on earth, and knowledge of the one true living God (www.coltranechurch.org/#mission). Furthermore, as Price (2011) stated of the legacy of Trane:

In the realm of Black music, John Coltrane stands boldly and authoritatively as a 21st century prophet whose expressions gave meaning, whose communication provided direction and whose sound rang forth as an antidote to a prolonged 20th century period of chaos and turmoil for Blacks in the U.S. (p. 159)

THE WORKS AND THE FRAME: LEADERSHIP AS JAZZ

The dictionary defines jazz as "a type of music of Black American origin characterized by improvisation, syncopation, and usually a regular or forceful rhythm, emerging at the beginning of the 20th century" (Merriam-Webster, n.d.). It is our only original living art form. Furthermore, Jason West (2012) noted:

> Jazz music started in the Black ghettos of New Orleans at the end of the 19th century. In the 1920s jazz moved up river to St. Louis, then to Chicago and New York as African Americans migrated north in search of a better life. The 1930s saw the evolution of swing bands like those lead by Duke Ellington and Count Basie. At the same time great soloists emerged, virtuosi like Louis Armstrong, Coleman Hawkins, and Lester Young. In the 1940s bebop hit, personified in the music of Charlie Parker and Dizzy Gillespie.

Max DePree (1992) draws a compelling parallel between leadership and jazz in the text *Leadership Jazz*. He sees them both as art forms wherein freedom and technique, improvisation and rules, inspiration and restraint must be both precisely and expertly blended.

While leadership has been proficiently defined in many ways over the centuries, one form of leadership fits its combination with jazz, and that is the image of the jazz band as an expression of servant leadership. DePree stated, "The leader of the jazz band has the beautiful opportunity to draw the best out of the other musicians" (p. 9). In the case of leadership and spiritually awakened Coltrane, I would purport that this is not the Greenleaf version, but the version 2.0 as noted by Alston and McClellan (2011)—critical servant leadership, wherein critical spirituality (Dantley, 2003) is added to the analysis. The focus of critical servant leadership is to critique and destroy undemocratic power relations blended with spiritual reflection. For the leader, this requires the most personal of soul work, which requires spiritual intelligence, i.e., "navigating the pathways of transformation. It is the art and practice of inner and outer evolution. It is learning how to progressively live fully in body, mind, and spirit" (Anderson, 2011, p. 16). That is exactly what jazz does.

This chapter will focus on two of Coltrane's works in relation to critical servant leadership and spirituality with four ethical considerations (care, justice, responsibility, and conviction, see Figure 1.1): the well-known *A Love*

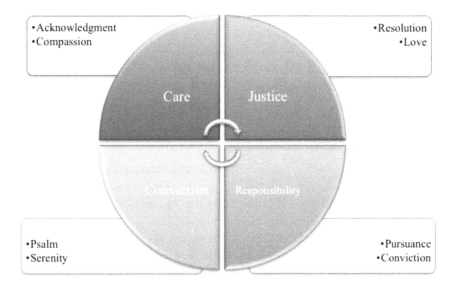

Figure 1.1 Critical servant leadership model in Coltrane.

Supreme and the lesser known yet critically acclaimed *Meditations*, which has been referred to as the spiritual follow-up to *A Love Supreme*. These two albums are quintessential Coltrane as he traverses this spiritual journey. Each of the albums are divided into four movements, with *Meditations* having a 12-minute introductory preamble.

ETHIC OF CARE: ACKNOWLEDGEMENT AND COMPASSION

Coltrane's opening in *A Love Supreme* with the first movement, "Acknowledgement," is to pay honor to the existence of and truth of a higher being. This aligns with the first movement in *Meditations*, "Compassion" or concern for and honoring the sufferings of others. For those of us in education, the higher being is relatable to the masses and is coiled in the idea of the "greater good," something larger than ourselves (Alston, 2015). Thus acknowledgement and compassion are perfect places to begin; they function as facets for empathy and care.

This ethic of care is one that is steeped in benevolence and compassion (Gilligan, 1982). For the critical servant leader, exercising care on the personal level is of the utmost importance. In the essay "The Ethic of Compassion," Dalai Lama talks about the importance of respect and compassion for others. He feels that, "Our feelings toward others depend very much on their circumstances" (Lama, 1999, p. 132). This also rings true for the

empathy
care

leader needs self care + self compassion

leader on a personal level. You cannot serve others if you are empty. Self-care and self-compassion are critical for a successful and effective leader. As Asbill (2015) stated: "Cultivating balance in your own life and compassion for self and others is key to being a leader that empowers others, and that can sustain your personal leadership role."

ETHIC OF JUSTICE: RESOLUTION AND LOVE

justice = fairness + impartial

In tandem with the ethic of care should always be the ethic of justice; they should not be mutually exclusive. While an orientation toward justice is concerned with fairness and impartiality, it works through the lenses of resolution and love (care). Resolution can be defined as "firmness of purpose or the expression of an opinion or intention" (Resolution, n.d.). Resolution coupled with love fortifies the ethic of justice. In the music Coltrane begins the second movement of "Resolution" with a building in its intensity as it moves toward changes within the traditional melody, an embracing of the other (love and care).

can't have ethical leadership w/o justice — leader in relationship w/ others spread justice

The ethic of justice is a part of the clarion call of the critical servant leader. Through praxis, the critical servant leader brings about transformation by liberating others from injustice and orienting themselves through love and resolution away from what Siddle Walker and Snarey (2004) refer to as biases and partial passion, and toward universal ethical principles. DePree (1992) simply says that ethical leadership withers without justice. This ethic of justice requires the leader to be in a relationship with those around and in the organization so that it will intersect with the common good. It is here where the concept of grace abounds with love and pursuance, particularly as the critical servant leader leads change and transformation. DePree (1992) noted that we should not underestimate the power of grace.

grace

- It's important that we focus more on what we need to be than on what we need to do. In so doing, leaders do transform people's lives.
- The quality of our relationships is key to establishing a positive ethos for change. Long-lived and productive relationship spring up from a soil rich in covenants and trust.
- Leadership see that organization's capacity to change depends to a great degree on effective followership.

leaders 1st open themselves

- When unusual people and ideas are welcome, there is an ethos for change. To persuade their organizations to be open and vulnerable to unexpected results, leaders first open themselves. (DePree, 1992, pp. 142–143)

ETHIC OF RESPONSIBILITY:
PURSUANCE AND CONSEQUENCE

The ethic of responsibility is a Weberian concept that "acknowledges value obligations, but assumes the absence of any given hierarchy of values and the inevitability of value conflict as the context of moral endeavor" (Starr, 1999, p. 407). For the critical servant leader, I would offer that it is your responsibility to do the work when placed in the position of leader with positional power, and this is done via the lanes of pursuance and consequence.

Pursuance is the act of trying to achieve something or the carrying out of a plan. This aligns with Weber's notion of social action as overt action as well as the failure to act and passively acquiesce (Alston, 2015). Pursuance is about the manifestation of an ethic of responsibility and has to be a personal endeavor for the critical servant leader. It is also here that the lens is turned inward with a particular deconstruction of leadership preparation programs where it often found that the voices and experiences of the marginalized are not heard in the discussion of leadership theories, concepts, and research in general. The critical servant educational leader is called to be the champion for and pursuer of justice.

It is in this space of responsible leadership where leaders build solid and enduring ethical relationships. De Bettignies (2014) noted that responsible leadership has five dimensions that must be considered on the individual, the organizational, and the societal level:

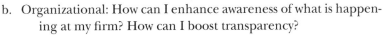
5 dimensions of moral leadership

1. *Awareness*
   a. Individual: How can I know myself better?
   b. Organizational: How can I enhance awareness of what is happening at my firm? How can I boost transparency?
   c. Societal: How can I increase my awareness of what is happening in the world around me?
2. *Vision*
   a. Individual: How do I envision myself in five years?
   b. Organizational: How do I envision my firm in 5 or 10 years?
   c. Societal: What is my vision for the planet 5 or 10 years from now?
3. *Imagination*
   a. Individual: Could I see myself being a different person, a different manager, a different leader?
   b. Organizational: Could my corporation have different values and another corporate culture?
   c. Societal: What kind of society do we want to leave to the grandchildren of our grandchildren?

4. *Responsibility*
   a. Individual: Though I cannot fix everything that is wrong with the world, how can I maintain and extend my own sense of responsibility as a leader?
   b. Organizational: How can I account for the negative externalities of my firm's behavior and build responsibility and sustainability in my corporate strategy and at all levels of its implementation?
   c. Societal: Instead of privatizing gains and externalizing losses, how can I ensure that my firm has a net-positive impact on society?
5. *Action*
   a. Individual: How can I cultivate the strength of character that will inspire trust and walk the talk?
   b. Organizational: How can I develop the courage to take action and give voice to my values, while inspiring others at all levels in the organization to do the same?
   c. Societal: How can I contribute to building a social environment where no one cops out, passes the buck, or dreads the risk of action? (De Bettignies, 2014, pp. 14–16)

ETHIC OF CONVICTION: PSALM & SERENITY

Coltrane's final movements in both *A Love Supreme* and *Meditations* are nestled in the sacred. One critic noted of Coltrane's "Serenity" that it "Closes an album of excitement with peacefulness and delicacy, something that John Coltrane more than likely felt himself when he discovered something above humanity" (Sputnik, 2007). This is the essence of the ethic of conviction. According to Weber, this ethic of conviction enables space for the leader to be able to choose autonomously not only the means, but also the end; "this concept of personality finds its 'essence' in the constancy of its inner relation to certain ultimate 'values' and 'meanings' of life" (Weber, 1903/1975). It is a space of mindfulness that opens up greater possibilities that are found in the sacred space of psalms and serenity. Dunoon and Langer (2011) stated:

> Mindfulness has a dynamic quality. When we are mindful, we notice what is new or different in the particular context, whether in the external environment or in our own reactions and responses. We allow ourselves to openly receive different signals, including signals that are faint or at odds with our previous experience. The accent is on perceiving directly, without immediately analyzing, categorizing, or judging. Ideally, we are able to just notice and hold an observation and to stay with uncertainty as to its meaning and significance. Noticing is not only characteristic of a mindful orientation, but noticing begets mindfulness. When we let ourselves take in new information

rake in new info and experience

and experience we are more likely to be grounded in the present, sensitive to context, aware of change and uncertainty, and attuned to possibility. (p. 1)

Critical servant leaders who understand this relationship with mindful leadership are stronger in their ethic of conviction, which ultimately allows them to become much more effective leaders because they realize that their leadership is about service to others so that they can then lead with authenticity.

CONCLUSION

Coltrane's work in both *A Love Supreme* and *Meditations* are journeys in spirituality and becoming, both qualities of the critical servant leader. Bolman and Deal noted,

> The search for soul and spirit always has been central to the human experience, despite a modern tendency to shunt it aside. More and more people are realizing that solipsistic faiths like careerism or consumerism can never provide adequate spiritual anchors. If you try to ignore basic spiritual questions, sooner or later they will knock on your door, usually at inconvenient moments. When your world is crashing around you, it's nice to have something to cling to. (Bolman & Deal, 2002)

Thus, the critical servant leader employs elements of spirituality with the ethical considerations of care, justice, responsibility, and conviction to manifest leadership at its best.

REFERENCES

Alston, J. A. (2015). Leadership as soul work: Living, leading, and loving the work. In C. Boske & A. F. Osanloo (Eds.), *Living the work: Promoting social justice and equity work in schools around the world.* (pp. 395–404). London, England: Emerald.

Alston, J. A., & McClellan, P. A. (2011) *Herstories: Leading with the lessons of the lives of black women activists.* New York, NY: Peter Lang.

Anderson, B. (2011). *The spirit of leadership.* [White paper]. Retrieved February 16, 2016, from https://leadershipcircle.com/wp-content/uploads/2011/05/07_SpiritOfLeadership.pdf

Asbill, D. (2015). *Being a leader is an inside job: The importance of self-care.* [Blog]. Retrieved February 29, 2016, from http://www.musicforall.org/blog/2015-mfa-summer-symposium/being-a-leader-is-an-inside-job

Bolman, L. G., & Deal, T. E. (2002). Leading with soul and spirit. *The School Administrator.* Retrieved February 2, 2016, from http://www.aasa.org/School AdministratorArticle.aspx?id=10442

Coltrane, J. W. (1965) *A love supreme* [Liner notes; LP]. Santa Monica, CA: Impulse Records.

Dantley, M. E. (2003). Critical spirituality: Enhancing transformative leadership through critical theory and African American prophetic spirituality. *International Journal of Leadership in Education, 6*(3), 3–17.

de Bettignies, H. C. (2014). *The five dimensions of responsible leadership.* Retrieved February 29, 2016, from http://knowledge.insead.edu/responsibility/the-five-dimensions-of-responsible-leadership-3685

DePree, M. (1992). *Leadership jazz.* New York, NY: Dell.

Dunoon, D., & Langer, E. (2011). Mindfulness and leadership: Opening up to possibilities. *Integral Leadership Review.* Retrieved March 1, 2016, from http://integralleadershipreview.com/3729-mindfulness-and-leadership-opening-up-to-possibilities/

Elementary and Secondary Education Act, 20 U.S.C. §§ 236–244 (1965).

Gilligan, C. (1982). *In a different voice: Psychological theory and women's development.* Cambridge, MA: Harvard University Press.

Immigration and Nationality Act, 8 U.S.C. § 1151 (1965).

Jackson, A. G. (2015). *1965: The most revolutionary year in music.* New York, NY: Thomas Dunne.

John Coltrane. (n.d.). In *Bio.* Retrieved from http://www.biography.com/people/john-coltrane-9254106

Lama, D. (1999). *Ethics for the new millennium.* New York, NY: Riverhead Books.

Price, E. G., III, (2010). The spiritual ethos in black music and its quintessential exemplar, John Coltrane. In L. L. Brown (Ed.) *John Coltrane and black America's quest for freedom.* (pp. 153–172). New York, NY: Oxford University Press.

Resolution. (n.d.). In *Merriam-Webster.* Retrieved from https://www.merriam-webster.com/dictionary/resolution

Siddle Walker, V., & Snarey, J. (2004). *Race-ing moral formation: African American perspectives on care and justice.* New York, NY: Teachers College Press.

Sputnik Music. (2007). *John Coltrane* Meditations *review.* Retrieved March 1, 2016, from http://www.sputnikmusic.com/review/12522/John-Coltrane-Meditations/

Starr, B. E. (1999). Essays: The structure of Max Weber's ethic of responsibility. *Journal of Religious Ethics, 27*(3), 407–434.

Weber, M. (1903/1975). *Roscher and Knies: The logical problems of historical economics,* (G. Oakes, Trans.). New York, NY: Free Press.

West, J. (2012). *What is jazz? Good question...* Retrieved February 18, 2016, from http://www.allaboutjazz.com/what-is-jazz-good-question-by-jason-west.php

CHAPTER 2

PUBLIC ENEMY, EDUCATION, AND LEADERSHIP

Muse-Sick or Mess-Age?

Floyd D. Beachum
Lehigh University

CONTEXT

When I heard Public Enemy's music for the first time, it was the late 1980s. The album was called *Yo! Bum Rush the Show.* This group's sound was very different from other rap at the time. First, it was the voice of a hype-man (Flavor Flav) talking at the beginning of songs and then came the booming voice of the MC (Chuck D). In addition, the music in the background had distinct hard beats and unexpected samples from different sources. I saw the group in concert and it was a musical and visual experience. This group featured three people: Chuck D, Flavor Flav, and Professor Griff. There was one DJ, Terminator X, and a paramilitary group on stage (The S1Ws) doing different military maneuvers and also carrying guns (I did not know that they were fake guns at the time). Furthermore, their music was loud, unyielding, and they preached a message of Black self-respect, knowing one's history, and

Educational Leadership and Music, pages 11–17
Copyright © 2017 by Information Age Publishing
All rights of reproduction in any form reserved.

political defiance. The group was called Public Enemy, and they impacted my worldview the same way they impacted the world of music.

ORIGINS

The members of Public Enemy are from Long Island in Roosevelt, New York. In the late 1970s to early 1980s, hip-hop was still in its infancy and Roosevelt was a place for middle class African Americans who in many cases had migrated from the more congested urban boroughs of New York City. Two brothers, Hank and Keith Shocklee, would throw parties at a place called Spectrum City. This is where Adelphi University graphic design student Chuck D would come to the party and eventually rock the microphone. The Shocklee brothers convinced Chuck to begin rapping more formally at Spectrum City. In addition, Chuck and the brothers realized that they were all interested in politics and issues facing the African American community. Chuck D recounted a story in which he was posting flyers of Malcolm X to promote cultural awareness, when a young man came along and asked, "Who is Malcolm 10"? They realized that they needed to teach through their music.

MEMBERS

Public Enemy consisted of members Chuck D, Flavor Flav, Terminator X, Professor Griff, and the S1W. Chuck D was the main MC, voice, and leader of the group. He was known for his bombastic rap delivery and direct style. Flavor Flav was the hype man and secondary MC. He represented disorder, spontaneity, and the unexpected. His flamboyant personality contrasted well with the hard straight-forward style of Chuck D. Before Public Enemy was signed to the label Def Jam, they did not want to sign Flavor Flav. They did not understand his purpose in the group. Chuck D famously forced Def Jam to take Flavor Flav as well as the rest of the group (Hale, 2011). Professor Griff was the group's minister of information and leader of the S1W (Security of the First World). According to Chuck D, the S1W "represents that the Black man can be just as intelligent as he is strong. It stands for the fact that we're not third-world people, we're first-world people; we're the original people" (Ridenhour & Jah, 1997, p. 82). Public Enemy's logo famously pictures a young Black male with his arms folded (B-Boy) within crosshairs. The symbol captures the defiant nature of hip-hop youth and how they are targeted by American society. Furthermore, it also acknowledges the way in which Black people have been targeted since their inclusion in the

Constitution as three-fifths of a human being (Hale, 2011). Terminator X became the group's DJ and thus completed the group.

Public Enemy also had another unique and innovative feature in that they were backed up by a creative production team known as the Bomb Squad. They consisted of Eric "Vietnam" Saddler, Hank Shocklee, Keith Shocklee, and Chuck D. Their sound focused on the sampler, an electronic device that allowed the user to take samples of different sounds and music and add it to one record. The Bomb Squad used multiple samples, and with the mixing of their DJ, they created an entirely new sound. This sound as well as their politically-charged lyrics would propel them into hip-hop icons.

EARLY YEARS

After the group was created and signed to Def Jam (with label mates like Run-DMC, LL Cool J, and the Beastie Boys) they began working on their first album. This first album was called *Yo! Bum Rush the Show* (1987). This album was an experiment with new musical sounds from the Bomb Squad as well as the constant contrasts in voice and tone of Chuck D and Flavor Flav on the vocals. While this first album was bold and new, it was overshadowed by the incredible success of Eric B and Rakim and their hip-hop classic album *Paid in Full* (1987). This album used well-placed James Brown samples, innovative music and scratching, and Rakim's lyrical delivery (Hale, 2011). Trying to compete in the shadow of *Paid in Full* forced Public Enemy to go back and work on the next album in order to create a new sound, one that would dominate hip-hop. They succeeded with a classic album called *It Takes a Nation of Millions to Hold Us Back* (1988).

SUCCESS

Public Enemy captured the hearts and minds of urban youth with a new sound and message, which are represented in one of their signature songs, "Rebel Without a Pause" that appeared on the *It Takes a Nation of Millions to Hold Us Back album.* This song is known for a blaring and unrelenting siren that continues throughout. This same album also featured hits like the incredibly up tempo "Bring the Noise" and the politically charged "Prophets of Rage." The group's third and most commercially successful album was titled, *Fear of a Black Planet* (1990). This album featured hits like, "Welcome to the Terrordome," "911 is a Joke," and the theme song for the movie *Do the Right Thing* (1989): "Fight the Power." Public Enemy was one of the first rap groups to enjoy international success and was one of the first groups to release MP3 only albums at the time. They also were innovators who fused musical forms like rap and heavy metal into rap metal. Public Enemy collaborated with thrash-metal band Anthrax and released a new version of the song "Bring the Noise" in 1991. The song appeared on albums for both groups and the two groups even went on tour together.

CONTROVERSY

Public Enemy was a group that was purposefully and meaningfully steeped in controversy. The group was unapologetically Black, they espoused pro-Black themes, quoted Black leaders and thinkers, and sought to educate their audiences with these messages. In their early days when Black radio stations primarily played R&B music, Public Enemy fought to get more mainstream airplay. In the song "Don't Believe the Hype" Chuck D even states, "I declared war on Black radio." He was calling out radio stations that were too afraid to play the political themes and messages in Public Enemy's music. In 1987, the group clashed with mainstream politicians when controversial Arizona governor Evan Mecham canceled the Dr. Martin Luther King Holiday in the state because it had not been properly authorized. In response, Public Enemy wrote the song "By the Time I Get to Arizona" where in the video the group assassinates the governor of Arizona (a character much like Governor Mecham) by remote car bomb.

The group's greatest controversy occurred in 1989 in an interview with group member Professor Griff. He was interviewed by David Mills, a journalist from the *Washington Times*. In this interview he stated that around the world the group that caused the most wickedness was Jewish people. This comment caused a firestorm of criticism for Professor Griff and the entire group. Chuck D and Griff both issued apologies, and for a time Griff was dismissed from Public Enemy. He would later be reinstated in the group. Years later, Griff explained that his words were taken out of context and that he was thrown under the bus at the time due to public pressure on the group (Griff, 2009).

Another form of controversy occurred in 2006 when group member Flavor Flav became the star of a reality show titled *Flavor of Love*. This show featured Flav as an eligible bachelor who had 20 women compete for his companionship while all living in a large house. It featured an elimination ceremony at the end of each episode. This was viewed by many as a course of action that was against the original intent and purpose of the group Public Enemy. While Public Enemy promoted knowledge of Black history, self-love, and social consciousness, *Flavor of Love* was characterized by some as misogynistic (Hale, 2011). This venture into reality television could possibly have caused some people to question the legacy of the group.

LEADERSHIP LESSONS

There are at least three leadership lessons that we can learn from examining Public Enemy. First is the all-important idea of unity as a primary theme in their work. The group realized early that they needed to do something in their music to help unify Black America, and also the world in general. They have received such broad support that the unification message applies across race-ethnicities, social class, and even countries. In educational leadership, we face a similar challenge as in many cases it seems like the setup is student versus teacher, teacher versus administration, school versus community, and so on. These arrangements create situations where common ground is difficult because of mistrust, hard feelings, and imbalances in power and authority (Beachum & McCray, 2011; Brooks, 2012; Frattura & Topinka, 2006). Successful schools start from a place of unity where students have a voice, teachers are empowered, administrators are respected, and communities are involved (Green, 2015; McCray & Beachum, 2014). Critics have accused the group of seeking to divide and segregate, but that is not the case (Stapleton, 1998). To promote Black awareness and pride does not have to come at the expense of other groups. Similar tactics have been used to limit ethnic studies programs, Black History courses, and the examination of gender identity in K–12 schools (Banks, 1993; Zamudio, Russell, Rios, & Bridgeman, 2011). The tactic tries to claim that by isolating these areas, we are segregating and not being inclusive. However, these topics can create a greater sense of unity if they involve all students and have general support (Banks, 1993; Beachum & McCray, 2011, Villegas & Lucas, 2002). A major problem is that the people who need to discuss these topics (people with the most power and privilege) are usually the biggest critics who also spend their time fighting against these issues (social justice and social equity). Public Enemy ran into similar problems as their influence grew.

Second is the notion of critique. Public Enemy brought a bold and scathing critique of social problems and policy. This was done at great risk to their album sales and success as a group. West (2008) said the following about Richard Wright, Ralph Ellison, and James Baldwin: "They were taking risks. They were willing to be pushed into the danger zone intellectually and existentially" (p. 126). He was also talking about Public Enemy who did the same in their music and actions. In educational leadership, there is a great value in critique (Starratt, 1991). Ryan (2006) elaborated on critique when he wrote:

> Being critical means becoming more skeptical about established truths. Being critical requires skills that allow one to discern the basis of claims, the assumptions underlying assertions, and the interests that motivate people to promote certain positions. Critical skills allow people to recognize unstated, implicit,

and subtle points of view and the often invisible or taken-for-granted conditions that provide the basis for these stances. (p. 114)

These critical skills are important in educational leadership because they allow school leaders to "engage in a liberated mindset, virtually free from the confusion of misinformation, stereotypes, and stigmatization" (Beachum & McCray, 2011, p. 58). When one critiques themselves then they can increase their own critical consciousness. This critical consciousness can then help the school leader ask bigger questions about their students, teachers, communities, etc. Villegas and Lucas (2002) wrote,

> Awareness of the pervasiveness and longevity of the inequities in schools and of the structures and practices that perpetuate them can be disheartening for prospective teachers [and administrators]. But it is essential that they recognize these realities. If they see schools through the rose-colored glasses of the meritocratic myth, they will unwittingly perpetuate inequities. (p. 58)

The problem is that critique involves risk. It can make some people upset, it can challenge conventional thinking, it can make people uncomfortable forcing them to work or think harder. This should be the natural role for the educational leader in schools and at the same time the natural role for us in a democratic society. Public Enemy reminded us of this duty.

LEGACY

As the 1990s progressed, hip-hop music changed from an emphasis on artists like Public Enemy to more artists like Snoop Dogg, Dr. Dre, Tupac, and others. Some may argue that the message in the music changed in early 1990s from Public Enemy's "Fight the Power" to "Gin and Juice" (Kitwana, 2002). This was not necessarily a criticism of West Coast rap because as Dyson (2007) reminds us:

> The political economy of crack precipitated the rise of gangsta rap on the West Coast. At its beginning, some gangsta rappers were just as eager to narrate the immoral consequences of state-sponsored domestic terror—through police brutality and racial profiling—as they were to glorify guns and gangs. (p. 84)

The hip-hop music industry in general began to overemphasize material pursuits over the pursuit of economic social freedom (Dyson, 2004; West, 2008). West (2008) further indicated that, "The recording industry is so interested in pacifying, distracting, and ensuring that the strength, grace and dignity of young people is not affirmed. They would rather keep them locked into a narcissistic, materialistic, and individualistic orientation" (p. 127). The legacy of Public Enemy is a continuous fight to emphasize the former and eliminate the latter. The group was innovative with their stage show, lyrics, sound, and political edge. They were controversial, willing to take on Black radio, urban problems, and politicians. And they are legends: after almost 30 years, the group still tours together spreading their socially conscious messages. Dyson (2007) may have best captured the legacy of Public Enemy when he wrote, "At their best, socially conscious rappers tackle thorny social problems and perhaps inspire those who engage in action. Such a role for the artist should not be downplayed, underestimated, or even undervalued" (p. 70).

REFERENCES

Banks, J. A. (1993). The canon debate, knowledge construction, and multicultural education. *Educational Researcher, 22*(5), 4–14.

Beachum, F. D., & McCray, C. R. (2011). *Cultural collision and collusion: Reflections on hip-hop culture, values, and schools.* New York, NY: Peter Lang.

Brooks, J. S. (2012). *Black school, white school: Racism and educational (mis)leadership.* New York, NY: Teachers College Press.

Dyson, M. E. (2004). *The Michael Eric Dyson reader.* New York, NY: Basic Civitas Books.

Dyson, M. E. (2007). *Know what I mean? Reflections on hip-hop.* New York, NY: Basic Civitas Books.

Frattura, E. M., & Topinka, C. (2006). Theoretical underpinnings of separate educational programs: The social justice challenge continues. *Education & Urban Society, 38*(3), 327–344.

Green, T. L. (2015). Leading for urban school reform and community development. *Educational Administration Quarterly, 51*(5), 679–711.

Griff, P. (2009). *Analytixz: 20 Years of conversation and enter views with Public Enemy's Professor Griff.* Atlanta, GA: Rathsi.

Hale, J. (2011). *Public Enemy: Prophets of rage.* London, England: BBC.

Kitwana, B. (2002). *The hip-hop generation: Young blacks and the crisis in African American culture.* New York, NY: Basic Civitas Books.

McCray, C. R., & Beachum, F. D. (2014). *School leadership in a diverse society: Helping schools prepare all students for success.* Charlotte, NC: Information Age.

Ridenhour, C. & Jah, Y. (1997). *Fight the power: Rap, race, and reality.* New York, NY: Dell.

Ryan, J. (2006). *Inclusive leadership.* San Francisco, CA: Jossey-Bass.

Stapleton, K. R. (1998). From the margins to mainstream: The political power of hip-hop. *Media, Culture, and Society, 20,* 219–234.

Starratt, R. J. (1991). Building an ethical school: A theory of practice in educational leadership. *Educational Administration Quarterly, 27,* 185–202.

Villegas, A. M., & Lucas, T. (2002). *Educating culturally responsive teachers: A coherent approach.* Albany, NY: State University of New York Press.

West, C. (2008). *Hope on a tightrope: Words and wisdom.* Carlsbad, CA: Hay House.

Zamudio, M. M., Russell, C., Rios, F. A., & Bridgeman, J. L. (2011). *Critical race theory matters: Education and ideology.* New York, NY: Routledge.

CHAPTER 3

KEEPING THE BEAT

Why Music Drives Leadership and Life

Ira Bogotch
Florida Atlantic University

Louis M. Ruccolo
School Board of Broward County

---

*As those with long memories tell it, in other times the sun was the lord of music,
until the wind stole music away. Ever since, birds console the sun with
concerts at the beginning and end of the day.*
—Eduardo Galeno, *Children of the Days* (2013).

I had just graduated with a master's degree in ESL from Teachers College
(TC), Columbia University and had taken a part-time job in mid-Manhattan
teaching adult English as a Second Language (ESL). It was my very first
paid gig as a teacher. On day two or three, I brought my tape recorder to
class and put on a cassette of Peter, Paul and Mary singing, *Leaving on a
Jet Plane.* At TC, I had taken a professional development workshop with
Carolyn Graham, author of *Jazz Chants,* where I learned how to use rhythms
and tempo to assist second language learners in not only learning new vocabulary, but also practicing oral sentence phrasings. This was just one of
the many innovative teaching strategies taught by my university professors.

Educational Leadership and Music, pages 19–32
Copyright © 2017 by Information Age Publishing
All rights of reproduction in any form reserved.

While I was playing the song and teaching the lesson, the school's director walked by my classroom and heard music coming through the door. He opened it and asked me to step outside the room right away. I remember his exact words: "We hired you to teach, not play with the students." At the end of that first week, I was out of a job. The year was 1976, decades before accountability and standardization had come to dominate instructional methods. Yet even then, back in the day, the distinction between work and play ruled the minds of school leaders, favoring the former over the latter.

Fast forward over the subsequent generations of school reforms into the 21st century, and the playing of music, drawing and painting, doing ceramics, and dance are all becoming lost arts in schools. The definitions applied to literacy and numeracy, which should be inclusive of musical metrics and rhythms of life, have been driven out by prescribed curricula that ignore the passions of teaching and the joys of learning. To be clear, this is not true in all schools or for all families in the United States. Wealthy and upper middle class families have never relied on schools alone (be they public, private, or parochial) for teaching children art and cultural mediums. Instead, these families and communities willingly pay extra for private afternoon, afterschool, and weekend music, art, and dance lessons. Many large public school districts around the country have opened magnet schools devoted to the performing and visual arts; but these schools are highly selective, and like charter and private schools require active parent involvement: at a minimum to get students to auditions, and if necessary provide daily transportation to and from school.

The essay you are about to read happened in real time and owes it beauty to teachers and musicians, notably Louis Ruccolo, Jeffrey Lee, and Nicole Yarling (the "and friends"). Yet for our purposes here, narrative and research have been spliced together for exposition and creative effect. The story begins with a jazz concert held on June 16, 2015, that was sponsored by the South Florida Jazz Society. It featured the Clayton Brothers: saxophonist Jeff, bassist John, John's son Gerald on piano, and two other amazing musicians, Terrell Stafford on trumpet and flugelhorn along with a young drummer, Obed Calvaire. Before the concert began, Jeffrey Lee, owner of Resurrection Drums in Hollywood, Florida, was called up on stage to tell the audience a story. It was of Obed's journey from a middle school student in inner city Miami to his becoming a world renowned jazz drummer. But what makes any story fascinating are the possibilities; that is, how people and circumstances can come together to make something meaningful and exciting in life. And that includes as the central figure in this story, a middle school math teacher, Louis "Marty" Ruccolo, who is a former chef and musician. Marty was sitting in the first row as Jeff told the story, which I found so compelling that I knew I had to retell it and share it with those who were not present at the concert. It's a story of how Marty was instrumental in Obed's rise to fame.

How often is a middle school math teacher the hero of a story? You don't have to tell me. I'm a professor of educational leadership and I know firsthand how teachers as leaders are often ignored or forgotten. So once I heard the story, it was my responsibility to learn more and share. Being a professor, I also feel obliged to weave peer-reviewed research into the narrative even as you and I know (as educators) that no amount of research will change people's minds regarding the place of music in the public school curricula. As an educator, you either feel the rhythm or you don't. It is our aim here for readers to feel the rhythm whether you play music or not.

MEET THE LEADERSHIP TEAM

Music concretely connects people through relationships. This is not an abstract concept, not when it comes to music. According to Louis "Marty" Ruccolo,

> Music is experiential, in the moment; learning is hard to express or create, but we can learn and model the emotional connection and 'commonplaceness' [that] music has and move it towards what leadership needs in order to be effective and connected. Not everyone plays music; but everyone listens to music.

How powerful are musical connections? Are they powerful enough to bring people together from different races, genders, socioeconomic statuses, and ages? Yes. In conversations, Marty frequently referred to Obed Calvaire not just as his adopted son, but also as his friend, despite their dramatic differences in race, culture, SES, and especially age. Most readers are aware that teachers are told explicitly not to blur relationship lines with their students and certainly not to be their friends. Yet when it comes to music, according to Marty,

> relationships are supreme, and move and provide possibilities beyond the people involved–energy/chemistry. I have worked with hundreds, maybe thousands of students, I recognized that I had a connection with Obed that required me to be more involved in helping him in and out of the school setting.

Musical relationships were made evident even before the evening's formal performance began. As I approached the auditorium on the NOVA Southeastern University campus in Davie, Florida, a group of youngsters were setting up folding chairs in front with their musical instruments close by. How nice, we would be treated to music before the real music!

Choreographing this outside performance was an African American woman who was everywhere, checking for sound, adjusting the video lighting and angles, managing every important aspect that goes into a performance, however informal. She occasionally shouted to one of the young musicians to warm up in place or practice a particular note. Realizing that her audience was gathering, she turned to us and simply said, "I've been in music all my life," and then turned her attention back to the teens.

For the next 30 minutes of so, Nicole Yarlings' students entertained the outdoor audience still waiting to be admitted into the auditorium. Between songs, she would praise one or more of the musicians and explain that both she and they were there to show the power of music by giving the teens a purpose and a joy. She made it clear that her work on behalf of children and music was how she voluntarily was giving back to both society and her profession, performing the music of jazz. At the end of the session, Yarling told the audience how they could help, with money of course, to keep the many voluntary Saturday workshop sessions going in Broward and Miami-Dade counties. It should be noted that all the teens were wearing T-shirts with the initials JECC, which stands for Jazz Educators Community Coalition. Please look it up online.[1] Just as the youngsters finished their last song, the auditorium doors swung open. The audience, including the teens who had just played outside, began to take their seats.

FROM THE BEGINNING

The announcement on the PA system at Thomas Jefferson (TJ) Middle School, an inner city school in Dade County, said, "Please welcome to our staff, Mr. Melton Mustafa, our new band director." No way, thought Marty. Melton Mustafa was and still is a jazz legend, and someone Marty had played with in his past musician days. As soon as Marty had a planning period break, he raced across campus to the band room expecting to meet and greet *the man* himself. Instead, a much younger man welcomed him at the door. Marty said, "I'm here to see Mr. Melton Mustafa." The young man replied, "That's me, I'm Melton Mustafa, Jr." Quickly overcoming his disappointment, Marty welcomed the legend's son to T. J. Middle. They talked music, and by and by Marty told him that he played the drums. In fact, Marty had a drum set in his special education math class to help his students hear "the math in their heads."

T. J. Middle was located in Miami Gardens, Miami, where Louis "Marty" Ruccolo was teaching special education mathematics in one of the school's many portables. "One day, during jazz band, Melton invited me to the band room asking if I could play 'fast swing' for his aspiring music students." While Marty played, they listened to the kids trying to imitate that beat. Obed was on bass. A few months after that, Marty was in Resurrection Drums to buy drum sticks when a young Haitian boy approached him and said "Hi Mr. Ruccolo, remember me, I was playing bass when you sat in with us at T. J.?" After that Obed would come to Marty's homeroom or they would meet in the band room and play and talk about drums, music, grooves, licks, etc. The first time they played drums together on a drum pad in Marty's classroom, Marty knew Obed was special. Looking back, it was a purely intuitive flash, true knowing, only realized years later upon reflection, and that he was witnessing a high level of undeniable and prescient talent! That was the moment. In music everything happens in a moment, especially in jazz. From that day on, the middle school student named Obed Calvaire would be on drums, for Marty knew then and there, "Obed was a natural." The question was how would Obed be able to continue to develop his talents?

Like most of the kids at T. J. Middle, Obed came from a home with few resources, none to spare for drum lessons. So Marty took it upon himself to bring him on Saturdays for lessons at Jeff's place, Resurrection Drums, located then in Hallandale. Marty, who lived in Hollywood first drove to North Miami to pick up Obed and then they drove together to Broward County; Marty paid for his lessons, and then drove Obed home before he himself returned to Hollywood. This went on throughout middle school. Every Saturday, this four hour round-trip routine was repeated.

ON STAGE

Jeff Lee knew he had just a few minutes before the Clayton Brothers were to perform with Obed Calvaire on drums. In fact, it was Jeff who arranged for a custom built drum set to be on stage for Obed. Marty was sitting in the first row and had no idea what Jeff was going to say to the audience. The idea was to introduce and welcome Obed Calvaire back to South Florida where his musical career had started, in large part because of Marty, Jeff, and Melton.

After four songs, each lasting about 15 minutes with enough time for Terrell, Jeff, Gerald, John and Obed (the quintet) to lose the rhythm and then creatively find their way back inside the improvised solos, the Clayton Brothers took a much needed break. I lost count of the number of bottled waters consumed on stage.

John Clayton served as the emcee and spoke with the same variable notes and tonal quality as he had coaxed from his standup bass. He not only praised each member of the band, but communicated a warmth and appreciation for what they individually and collectively were doing. That appreciation could be seen on the faces of each of them in mutual admiration for their musical gifts. When relationships mesh, good feelings can be felt within and shared with the audience. It's as close to what a spiritual oneness with the audience feels like. Between one of the songs, John spoke about a new project in which the quintet would share with online viewers the group's composing and creating processes (ArtistShare; http://www.artist-share.com/v4/Home/ArtistProfiles/40/ArtistShare-Profile-John-Clayton). Why this is so significant is that jazz is not always the most popular or accessible of the many different musical genres, and what the Clayton Brothers were attempting to do was unique, something that both educators and politicians often talk about but rarely demonstrate: true transparency. How fitting a metaphor for citizens of Florida where the government by law is supposed to operate in the sunshine.

LEADERSHIP IN A NEW *MUSICAL KEY*

Today, Louis "Marty" Ruccolo is a transition supervisor in the Broward County Public Schools responsible for partnering with community-based programs to assist students to transition into vocational training, paid employment, technical colleges, apprenticeship programs, community colleges, and universities. Marty's job is to facilitate students with disabilities transition into adult life. "I think of my responsibilities in Transition Services as well as being the drummer in the band as a de facto 'conductor.' In both, you have to orchestrate and multitask, oftentimes behind the scenes."

He is today a professional-career world away from teaching math in an inner city middle school in Miami–Dade. Yet Marty's leadership can be directly traced to working at T. J. Middle under the direct supervision of an assistant principal. Marty described him to me as his educational mentor/father. Why this fact is so important is that this school administrator deliberately allowed Marty to set up and play his drums in class. That's right, what supervisor today with all the accountability pressures to raise test scores would allow a public school teacher to set up his drum set in a classroom? The administrator took a risk because of Marty's feel for how children learn and how his love for them let him learn. It was not just the drums that were the instrument, Marty's being with the children became the instrument as well.

[He, the AP] was "always very supportive of me and what I did, once commenting on my future 'Lou, you will affect public policy in education, if you so desire.'"

What this administrator (not named here because he has retired and relocated) did became the role model for Marty's own evolving leadership philosophy when he arrived at the district level in Broward County. As a nontraditional teacher, Marty was outside "the warp and woof" of school administration. He was and still is "not one of them," but he had the courage and know-how to engage with school board members and superintendent-level administrators.

To do good, if not great work, you don't ask for permission, especially when

> I'm creating (jamming), I don't have the time nor the trust in the vision of my supervisors to have to explain what I am doing, i.e., transition.... They just need to trust me like school board member Mrs. Bartleman has: Her support is essential to my success, and underscores the need for people to recognize creative thinkers in organizations and take a chance on supporting them before they know if they will be successful, based on their ideas. It's so "in the moment" like playing music, but that is where the magic happens, so awesome to be around. Mrs. Bartleman has been instrumental for me as I navigate and create, based on vision, through this giant and dense bureaucracy. Broward Schools' leadership needs people who recognize "out of the box," and what change can ensue from support of these ideas: [the key is] to have to explain, re-explain and re-re-explain for leaders to make a decision on something they know nothing about is unreasonable and unfair and time consuming. I'd rather be forgiven than forbidden, and conduct my activities with determination and conviction based on the students' needs.

Marty's musical leadership philosophy is that life is rhythm (confirmed by neuromusic research; Chen, Penhue, & Zatorre, 2008). Rhythm, meter, rhyme schemes from sonnets to haiku, all connect to spatial thinking and math. That Marty was quick to mention names of those who have supported him, is evidence that music leadership is not a solo activity, but rather builds upon relationships. Music contextualizes the meaning of relationships. In music, you can hear, feel and see if the relationships are working well or not. Bands form almost as quickly as they break up. It could be because of personalities, egos, or different musical philosophies or sensibilities. To play together over an extended period of time requires strong ties. It's like being married, only more so. The point is that musical relationships are not clichés or built upon abstractions. They are felt realities dependent on the quality of the performance. And music—especially drumming—is the glue. So it was with Marty's relationship with Obed, Jeff's relationship with Marty, and Nicole's relationships with her kids: all real, passionate, creative, and meaningful.

INTERMISSION

Musicians, like all artists, are judged after each and every performance. They are authentically accountable. To open the creative process to the public builds relational trust, the opposite of fear. For music, it cannot be otherwise as the music comes from inside the artist. It's spiritual more than cognitive. And while the drummer guides the band, it is very different from how external authorities are driving K–12 public education. Even when musical artists cover one another's songs, their signature styles are always evident in the delivery. An aphorism attributed to the late great Ornette Coleman: "It's perfectly O.K. to repeat a phrase, just don't say the same thing." Who would have thought Lady Gaga and Tony Bennett were a musical match? In this sense, music models teaching and learning, improvisation, creativity and transparency. Over the past quarter century, you can count on one hand the number of K–12 school reforms that have put professional (i.e., artistic) judgment and creativity at the center of the enterprise. More typically, reforms that are developed outside school systems are imposed upon teachers and principals with the admonition to implement with fidelity. How unlike jazz! My mind goes back to the brouhaha caused by Professor Robert Slavin of *Success for All*, who charged that the lack of positive results in Miami-Dade, Florida, was because teachers did not follow instructions with fidelity. A comparison of the students' performance on the reading subtest of the Florida Comprehensive Assessment Test, Norm Referenced Test component, generally showed no difference in the scores of students in schools implementing the Success for All program and those attending comparable MDCPS schools (http://oer.dadeschools.net/sfasummary.pdf).

Of course music, particularly rock music, loves to parody school and the school administration: think Alice Cooper (*School's Out*) and Pink Floyd (*Another Brick in the Wall*). Songs filled with sarcasm and satire. Not only has public education ignored contextual and cultural questions (i.e., different genres and individual student needs), it has also ignored the progressive and aesthetic ideas of John Dewey, Maxine Greene, and Elliot Eisner favoring instead a narrow-minded, passionless, test-centered curriculum for today's public school children. What is stopping education and educators from being more like music and musicians?

THE ART OF PLAY VERSUS THE "SCIENCE" OF WORK

In the second half of the concert, the music reached higher highs, ending in a five minute drum solo by Obed Calvaire, a fitting tribute on his return to southeast Florida. But when music ends, the relationships created by the music with the audience continue, whether it be humming to oneself or singing out loud, walking to a new beat, or just smiling and feeling good. For too many researchers, when the music ends they turn directly to published research for understanding, affirming, or confirming the effects of music on learning. What happened to trusting one's feelings? What happened to professional judgment? Today, most educational practitioners and policymakers deem the playing of music and its salubrious effects on children and adults to be outside the curricular needs of students (recall my first job experience described in paragraph one). Not only are aesthetic research findings ignored, marginalizing art and music, but when discussed as extracurricular activities, they fall precipitously into the pejorative category of play.

What every musician knows for certain from performative experiences, and what researchers know from brain research, is that music is the rhythm of life. The evidence is abundantly clear that music matters in peoples' lives. Neuromusical science has a large database of more than 533 research studies (Edwards, 2008) catalogued and ready for synthesizing or a meta-analysis. The effects can be seen on PET scans and MRI imaging. The overwhelming evidence indicates that music is clearly visible, forming unique clusters on our brains at all ages of life. Citing from one of the database abstracts by Pavlygina, Sakharov, & Davydov, 2008), who contrasted brain responses in subjects listening to classical (Mozart) music and rock (Rolling Stones) music:

> Rock music listening showed more global brain responses than classical music listening did. However, [all] music listening increases the intensity of the brain activation. (Pavlygina, Sakharov, & Davydov, 2008)

Another researcher conducted a two-part research fMRI design testing both actions (motor systems from tapping out the rhythms) and perceptions (auditory systems, just listening). The findings reported that

> certain sub-regions of the PMC may be sensitive to the rhythm of the musical excerpt because PMC activity showed an increase as the rhythms increased in difficulty. However, brain activity in the mid-PMC region was seen during each trial, which researchers suggest, may be due to humans never truly being able to passively listen to music *since rhythms are involved in almost every part of daily life*. (Pavlygina et al., 2008, n.p., emphasis added)

For more than a century, however, pedagogy has been guided by "science" (i.e., best evidence, randomized controlled trials) over intuition and professional judgments (Lagemann, 2000). Professor James Catterall (2014), cofounder of the Center for Research on Creativity, says in his online blog:

> What children would miss most in a musically reduced or barren environment are the musical experiences that music education brings to them.... The biggest loss may simply be the chance to participate in a guided way with music— to learn how music is made, to try making music, to learn about the infinite

ways that music comes to us and to learn about music's connections to events and eras of our history. (Catterall, 2014)

Moreover,

> The losses…will surely visit children from low-income families disproportionately. [T]he big losers will be the children who would have developed a personal passion for music if they had benefited from an effective school music program. These are the young musicians who perform in school orchestras and bands when they reach sufficient proficiency and otherwise grow to place music near the center of their lives in school. (Catterall, 2014)

One of the very first discussions on play and work for preK–12 education (Johnson, 1907) stated: "Play involves the hardest of work, a greater output of energy than drudgery" (p. ix). The play versus work debate is too often framed as a zero-sum game by curriculum designers. Yet listen to two in-house resident professors at Harvard who recently wrote that, "If you want your child to succeed in college, the play-based curriculum is the way to go" (Christakis & Christakis, 2010). And so it continues, arguments favoring and opposing play and games without each side listening to one another or to the music.

UNDERSTANDING WHY:
PINK FLOYD'S *ANOTHER BRICK IN THE WALL*[2]

Why has research evidence not had the desired results described by those cited in the previous section? Marty described how career administrators would often misperceive his leadership style, seeing him as belligerent and arrogant. He wondered why career educators, many of whom I have had in my university graduate classes, might be so afraid of emotion and passion, spirituality, so much so that school has been easy fodder for satirists. One of the most well-known satirical rock songs was written by Roger Waters in 1979 as a member of Pink Floyd. In his semiautobiographical song *Another Brick in the Wall* (https://www.youtube.com/watch?v=YR5ApYxkU-U), school is shown to be a bureaucratic factory demanding conformity and ridiculing creativity, using images of a teacher's physical and verbal abuse. While the criticism targets specific instructional methods and systems, the key image is of a math teacher ridiculing a student for writing poetry in his class, a stark contrast between Water's math teacher who serves as another brick in the wall and our protagonist, Louis "Marty" Ruccolo. The most quoted verse, first sung by the band and then repeated chorally by the Cambridgeshire School for Boys (ages 13 to 15) in Islington, England, reads:

We don't need no education
We don't need no thought control
No dark sarcasm in the classroom
Teachers leave them kids alone
Hey! Teacher! Leave us kids alone!
All in all it's just another brick in the wall.
All in all you're just another brick in the wall.

For Waters, and sadly for too many readers, the rote learning and mono-chromatic delivery of lessons is meant to produce faceless, social clones who may learn mathematical formulae, yet who cannot produce an origi-nal, imaginative thought. Yet as all commentators have noted, the line "We don't need no education" is a double negative and literally means the op-posite, that is, "We do need education" (http://www.songfacts.com/detail. php?id=1696). But even that obvious of a message was too subtle for some societies as Pink Floyd was banned from performing in a number of coun-tries around the world.

MUSIC IS MATH IN YOUR EARS

School leaders do work inside bureaucratic systems that are becoming more and more prescriptive and standardized. It is becoming harder, therefore, to accommodate the diverse needs of all children beyond the single out-come measures of student achievement as test scores. A philosophy of sci-entific management, which was initiated at the turn of the 20th century by Franklin Bobbitt, a curriculum theorist, has been superimposed onto many public schools in the 21st century. Subject-by-subject progression plans were then and now put in place to measure the progress of students, teach-ers, and administrators, all this to ensure effective and efficient employees in school organizations.

Is it blowing in the wind to say that music has never been more needed in our schools? How do we as educators and musicians motivate through teachable moments and build real relationships with students so that the curriculum is aligned with our everyday lives in and out of school? How do we make music (or art, dance, athletics, poetry, etc.) the rhythm of school life regardless of the subject matter? The narrative retold here calls on mu-sic to bring passion and joy back to learning. How do we redesign schools as places where teachers and students are free to discover and explore new genres and themes, and where social justice actions make a tangible differ-ence in students' lives beyond good teaching and moral leadership? (Bo-gotch, 2014).

KEY LEADERSHIP LESSONS:
SECRETLY, EVERYONE WANTS TO PLAY DRUMS

1. *Filling holes in the system:* Schools in the image of corporations "do more with less" and function as "mean and lean" machines. Without resorting to sarcasm and double negatives, we need a return to educational ideals. This musical narrative, more accurately a counternarrative, elevates the concept of play as disciplined hard work that transforms learning from drudgery to joy. It describes how musicians serve as educational volunteers and educational mentors to our children. The emergence of Obed Calvaire as an artistic drummer does not happen without people like Marty, Jeff, Nicole, and friends who all extended their day jobs to educate him and others. What Nicole Yarling does every Saturday is fill the "holes in the school system" by bringing music to underserved populations, including young adults in detention centers. What Jeff Lee does with band camp for high school marching bands throughout the school district gives these students purpose, direction, and discipline by playing.

2. *The reluctant leader:* Job descriptions do not tell the whole story of what it means to be an "on-the-job" educator. Many talented teachers say, "I never wanted to be a leader." What they typically mean is that they don't want to do the managerial work of a school or district administrator. They would rather stay close to the children. And yet, the paradox is that these are the very individuals we need to lead bureaucratic schools and transform school systems artistically into places for creativity and joy, not careerism through fear, distrust and intimidation. We have lost our way. We have lost leadership. In Marty's educational career, he moved from being an inner city math teacher to district-level transition supervisor. But he did so never forgetting the lessons from his supervising assistant principal. He is, in his own words, a reluctant leader who is not afraid (for his job) to speak the truth.

3. *Problem solving:* The power of music itself aids in problem solving. Music helps to develop ears, react spontaneously, it allows us to figure things out and put them together; in short, how to think, alone and with others. Music requires listening skills so as to learn with students. Music requires trusting your inner self and finding your soul. It is powerful and mindful, not a fad or a business.

4. *The rhythms of life:* The evidence is conclusive: Music is aligned with the rhythms of life, and today's schools are out of tune. Musicians practice, practice, practice, and if there is a band member out of tune, that band member is either brought in line by the drummer

or is dismissed. The standards established by musicians professionally are far more exacting than the current leadership and teaching standards for principals and teachers. There are no justifiable defenses (other than due process) for mediocrity or incompetence. To paraphrase Ehrich and English (2016), we need a cosmological shift away from scientism, behaviorism, and structural-functionalism as the dominant paradigm in schools, so as to re-center education and schools around the arts.

5. *Redressing wrongs:* The history of jazz, in particular, is replete with musicians who have had to leave the United States in order to play regular gigs and fulfill their potential. Despite our national rhetoric, the United States is not as inclusive as it strives to be ideally. Whether it is self-exile or systematic marginalization, there are individuals and groups who must struggle disproportionately in order to achieve recognition or success. We remain a nation in progress with an unfinished agenda. We must learn to continually improvise our solos while playing collectively with others in the band. We must redress the wrongs of society within our schools through music and art.

Let's begin today to write a new playlist for school leadership.

NOTES

1. Their Facebook page is https://www.facebook.com/permalink.php?story_fbid=672808466089976&id=137200529650775.
2. Pink Floyd's producer, Bob Ezrin, had the idea for the chorus. He used a choir of kids when he produced Alice Cooper's "School's Out" in 1972. Ezrin liked to use children's voices on songs about school.

REFERENCES

Bobbitt, F. (1918). *The curriculum.* Boston, MA: Houghton Mifflin.

Bogotch, I. (2014). Educational theory: The specific case of social justice as an educational leadership construct. In I. Bogotch & C. Shields, (Eds.). *International handbook of educational leadership and social (in)justice.* Dordrecht, The Netherlands: Springer.

Catterall, J. (2014, February 25). *The consequences of curtailing music education* [Blog]. Retrieved from http://www.pbs.org/wnet/tavissmiley/tsr/dudamel-conducting-a-life/the-consequences-of-curtailing-music-education/

Chen, J., Penhune, V., & Zatorre, R. (2008). Moving on time: Brain network for auditory-motor synchronization is modulated by rhythm complexity and musical training. *Journal of Cognitive Neuroscience, 20,* 226–239. (in Cerebral Cortex record 522)

Ehrich, L. & English, F. (2013). Towards connoisseurship in educational leadership: Following the data in a three stage line of inquiry. In S. Eacott & R. Niesche (Eds.), *Empirical leadership research: Letting the data speak for themselves, untested ideas* (pp. 165–198). New York, NY: Research Center.

Graham, C. (1978). *Jazz chants.* Oxford, England: Oxford University Press.

Johnson, G. E. (1907). *Education by plays and games.* Boston, MA: Ginn.

Lagemann, E. (2000). *The elusive science: The troubling history of educational research.* Chicago, IL: University of Chicago Press.

Pavlygina, R. A., Sakharov, D. S., & Davydov, V. I. (2008). Interhemispheric EEG interrelations in recognition of masked visual images accompanied by music, *Human Psychology, 34*(4), 397–404.

CHAPTER 4

WHICH SONG DO YOU HEAR?

Using Music As Artmaking to Explore Social Justice and Equity in Schools

Christa Boske
Kent State University

Jay Liedel
Stark County Educational Service Center

Although authors were asked to focus on music that inspires us as scholars who promote humanity in K–12 schools, Christa wanted to share the first tellings of utilizing music as a means of transforming the way students think about social justice and equity in schools as a praxis for the Leading for Social Justice course at Kent State University. She asked one of the students with whom she worked to co-author this chapter, because Jay collectively composed music as a means of addressing social justice issues facing children who receive special education services. This original work was showcased at a public art gallery in Akron, Ohio, for the 2014 Leading for Social Justice art exhibit, "Be the Voice for Those Who are Unheard," in which more than 175 people attended the free public one-night event.

Educational Leadership and Music, pages 33–46
Copyright © 2017 by Information Age Publishing
All rights of reproduction in any form reserved.

In this chapter, we begin by providing a context for Jay's music as artmaking to engage children in social justice oriented work. Second, we examine the role music and experience play for Jay in understanding and promoting this significant work in schools, especially when considering the power of voice as a means to promote social action for marginalized populations. Third, we describe the process of music making as artmaking for the Leading for Social Justice course and provide readers with access to this original song available on YouTube. Next, music as artmaking is explored in preparing school leaders and children to engage in social justice and equity oriented work to encourage arts-based pedagogies to promote social action. We describe how to integrate music as artmaking to provide educators and school leaders with opportunities to examine, understand, and respond to wider societal issues of systemic oppression. Finally, we conclude with recommendations to explore music as artmaking as pedagogical and andragogical approaches to teaching social justice to deepen student understanding of social justice and equity-oriented work.

CREATING AND IMPLEMENTING THE LEADING FOR SOCIAL JUSTICE ART EXHIBIT

In 2008, Christa's colleagues at Kent State University asked her to create a course in which students examined justice issues in a K–12 leadership course. In 2009, she created the Leading for Social Justice course and piloted the course for aspiring and practicing school leaders in the spring of 2010. Due to the overwhelming positive responses from students, the educational administrative team (EDAD) decided to not only make this course a requirement, but to make this course the first course students register for EDAD program at Kent State University as a foundation for understanding what it means to lead K–12 schools in meaningful ways.

Throughout the years, candidates have continued to engage in readings to deepen their understanding of social justice and equity through several arts-based pedagogies, including artmaking. Graduate students begin the course by engaging in the following practices: dialogue critically with peers, teachers, families, community activists, and school leaders; reflect on their understandings through audio/video reflections; facilitate the creation of an equity audit team (i.e, children, families, teachers, school leaders, and community members); conduct/present a schoolwide/districtwide equity audit; examine injustices that K–12 populations face in U.S. schools; choose one social justice issue students perceive as pertinent and research the issue; create a metaphor, translate the metaphor into artmaking with the guidance and support of a community artist; and utilize their new ways of knowing and responding to injustices facing school communities through an original artmaking submission showcased in a public leading for social justice art exhibit.

The art exhibit is an opportunity for the general public to engage with children, teachers, school leaders, community activists, and professional artist mentors around issues of social justice and equity facing K–12 U.S. public schools. Each submission is accompanied by a research-based abstract. The abstract provides viewers with an in-depth understanding of a specific social justice issue, research supporting this significant concern, descriptions regarding the artmaking, and opportunities to engage in social action aligned with the artmaking. All of the submissions, if sold, benefit nonprofit organizations aligned with each social justice issue. For the purpose of this chapter, we focus on Jay's artmaking submission for the 2014 exhibit. The theme for the exhibit was: Be the voice for those who are unheard. Each exhibit theme emerged from students in the course working together to analyze themes throughout their reflections, critical community dialogue, and equity audits. Next, students analyzed these possible themes from their learning, and worked together to identify the title of the exhibit. After a theme had been voted upon, a graphic artist worked with the students to create possible graphics to advertise the exhibit.

JAY'S CO-AUTHORED MUSIC EXHIBITION

Throughout the Leading for Social Justice course, Jay worked with students and families at his school. He served children diagnosed with emotional and behavioral challenges. Many of the children were sent to Jay's school because they were intellectually and socially ostracized by their neighborhood school communities due to their diagnosis. Jay was committed to deepening his understanding of social justice and equity issues facing the children he served. He initiated an equity audit team comprised of teachers, family members, and school leaders in an effort to deepen their understanding of the lived experiences of those they serve. They discovered through surveys, focus groups, and written narratives that children within their school community often expressed feeling socially isolated, hopeless, and incapable of learning.

As a result of collecting students' narratives and engaging in a school-wide equity audit examining the experiences of children who lived on the margins due to their emotional and behavioral diagnosis, Jay decided to promote the injustices the children felt through artmaking. He utilized the children's first tellings as lyrics and his musical talents to create an original song. Jay's artmaking focused on the following social justice stance: Children identified with emotional disturbance (ED) often do not receive appropriate resources to support their learning. His metaphor was: Students labelled as ED are a song with two parts. Jay wrote and presented the following research-based art abstract as well as co-created an original song showcased at a public art gallery:

> Some students attend school and present with such challenging behaviors that at times, they may disrupt the learning environment. How do schools that serve children understand what is meant by challenging behaviors? This understanding plays a critical role in how schools promote student learning, especially for children diagnosed with social, emotional, and behavioral challenges. Often times, these students are labeled as emotionally disturbed (ED) and receive special education services. Unfortunately, some children identified as emotionally disturbed are often under identified (Forness, Freeman, Paparella, Kauffman, & Walker, 2012). It is estimated that identification appears restricted to less than the bottom tenth of all children in need (Forness et al., 2012). Yet as White, Asian, and Hispanics may be under-identified, Black students are often over-identified (May, Forness, McCabe, & Hough, 2004).
>
> These stats are significant in that in America, we know where you go to school matters with regard to what type of education you experience; and students who have been identified as emotionally disturbed, have significantly worse outcomes as adults (Conroy, Dunlap, Clarke, & Alter, 2005). Also, Black students who struggle in school are susceptible to what has been described as the school-to-prison pipeline (Wilson, 2014). Students who are identified as ED have higher mobility rates (i.e., moving from school to school; Malmgren & Gagnon, 2005), and are likely to be placed in alternative schools (or separate facilities). Much debate, yet little data, exists to support why students identified as ED are placed in alternative schools isolated from their peers and neighborhood schools (Hoge, Liaupsin, Umbreit, & Ferro, 2014).
>
> Throughout special education, resources are linked to the terms free *appropriate* public education (Fan, 2014). My artmaking focuses on injustices experienced by students who are labeled as ED. Unfortunately, they do not often receive the appropriate support and resources they need. Essential resources for students identified as ED are often advocates who will champion their causes. These advocates include educators who truly understand the nature of educational challenges facing this populations of young people receiving special education services. However, deepening understanding and empathic responses toward children faced with emotional, behavioral, and social challenges may be quite elusive. Promoting "best practices" for children with complex histories is not a simple textbook practice. School leaders and teachers must begin by knowing our children, believing in them, and supporting them throughout their learning. Unfortunately, the historical stigma associated with special education or mental illnesses, and when presented with challenging behaviors, people tend to respond to the children I serve with a lack of empathy, patience, and understanding (Corrigan, Watson, Byrne, & Davis, 2005).

Social psychology suggests all human behaviors occur in the context of relations with others and their environment (Baron, Byrne, & Suls, 1989). In many cases, students act out in socially inappropriate ways related to their traumatic histories and lived experiences. In some cases, students experience serious abuse and neglect, and yet for others, living with a mental illness may cause trauma. Either way, it is important we see beyond inappropriate behaviors and learn to know our children as human beings versus being defined by their struggles.

The first step is to understand the need for educators to ask "What's wrong with you?" and focus on the whole child by asking, "Tell us about you." This way, the child is afforded spaces to share strengths, talents, and lived experiences. As educators, we know early and positive intervention is effective when working with young people who display inappropriate behaviors (Conroy et al., 2005). I focused on the power of positive intervention and ways of knowing in my artmaking. Often times, people (including educators) struggle to perceive children with emotional disturbances in a positive light. They are often perceived as "troublemakers," "burdens on society," and "blamed" for societal ills; however, for those who work with children diagnosed with emotional challenges, it is essential for teachers, students, and school leaders to understand this perception of "children as problems" creates barriers. These barriers often stop us from "knowing our children" and thus providing them with the necessary supports to learn and grow.

We welcome you to listen to our original song titled, "Which Song Do You Hear?" as a way to showcase students' brilliance beyond their label of emotional disturbance. Our students should never be defined by their aggression or outbursts because they are human beings with goals, dreams, and strengths. Our artmaking showcases the voices of "real" children who are "labelled" as emotionally disturbed. They have feelings. They are human beings. Our children are valuable assets to the community. They should be valued, honored, and cherished. Please, let's listen to the whole song (https://www.youtube.com/watch?v=bXyifu-hyuw) and reflect on the power of their first tellings in an effort to better serve all children, especially those who live on the margins due to their emotional health.

WHAT INSPIRES JAY AND HIS MUSIC AS ARTMAKING?

Like many individuals, Jay is influenced by a large array of artists and styles. He utilizes music as a way to become more aware of social problems. The music becomes a pathway for general audiences to deepen their understanding of the experiences of marginalized populations. Therefore, in general, Jay is inspired by artists who seek to engage their audience in honest dialogues regarding the human condition. The everyday experiences of disenfranchised populations, especially those who attend schools, prompts him to write music that touches the lives of thousands of people caring for people who often live on the margins due to race, class, ability, geographic location, gender, sexual orientation, and other dimensions of diversity. Overall, Jay has been influenced by politically driven punk rock artists (e.g., Minor Threat, Fugazi, The Clash, Gang of Four, Dead Kennedys, Black Flag, and Bad Religion) determined to shine a light on the influence of societal racism, bigotry, and working class people.

Jay cannot remember a day when he did not identify as a musician. His musical roots began during childhood. When he reached adolescence, Jay sought out an outlet for expressing his thoughts and beliefs. He wanted to share his thoughts and convictions in a public forum via various performance spaces and venues. Throughout his music, Jay strives to explore many aspects of the human experience; specifically, he incorporates lessons of history throughout his work. Jay respects artists who are most often those who influence his work with students he serves as a special education teacher. For him, music as artmaking is a means of investing in the children and families he serves.

For the 2014 exhibit, Jay was keenly aware of central messages throughout the music and promotion of social justice work in schools. The original song is rooted in a revolutionary ideology focusing on the challenges marginalized groups and individuals encounter in Western society; and in the case of the students he serves, children who are identified with emotional/cognitive/physical challenges. The original song illustrates their deficit-laden experiences and disrupts these oppressive beliefs/attitudes with their hopes, aspirations, and dreams. Jay and the children discussed the extent their lived experiences and understandings play a significant role in addressing issues of social justice and equity. They shared their negative experiences and discussed how to navigate these oppressive social and institutional structures. Together, they critically analyzed the extent these negative beliefs influenced their capacity to believe in themselves as learners, reach their goals, and develop a strong sense of self. Their co-created lyrics represent their first tellings and spaces for voice. As Jay continues to work with his students, he maintains his success in using music to engage students in sharing their voice. Their capacity to engage in music as artmaking is based on his credibility as a nurturing, thoughtful, serious educator.

In an effort to live the music that Jay co-created with his students, he recognized how often schools and society tend not to open their hearts to children with learning differences, especially children with emotional challenges. Because society often struggles to see the children Jay works with as equal due to their learning differences, music becomes a quiet triumph in promoting culturally responsive practices and policies in schools. Jay understands this work as being aligned with empowerment and giving voice to others. The music Jay and his students co-created seeks to expose issues relating to social injustices and inequities they face. The music, inspired by punk rock, becomes relevant and transformative because Jay understands the contexts in which his students live. He keeps the big picture in mind—his inspiration to advocate for those who are marginalized—but he also understands the everyday experiences of his children's lives as he walks their walk as an educator.

By utilizing music as artmaking, Jay promotes this democratically inclusive pedagogy for promoting voice, social justice, and equity for those he serves. He asks his students to share their lived experiences, dreams, ambitions, and challenges they face. After interviewing students and speaking with their families, Jay works with students to identify what they deem most significant in their lives. He utilizes their storied lives and first tellings as the lyrics. And in turn, their lyrics inspire the instrumentals. Together, they create music. Jay and the children co-titled, "Which Song Do You Hear?" The song captures the myriad of experiences his children face as students with learning differences. Jay posted the song on YouTube with photos from the 2014 Leading for Social Justice exhibit.

Jay recognizes the extent music influences not only his sense of self as a social justice leader, but as a pathway to promoting voice for his students. Together, they utilize music to increase awareness and understanding of the realities that often impinge upon students he serves to succeed and attain their goals.

CAPTURING STORIED LIVES

Because educators lead storied lives, peoples' ways of knowing and responding to the world are essential to deepening our understanding regarding how people think and learn. Their lives and how they respond to their new understandings are of interest to us as educators in K–12 schools and in preparing school leaders. As authors, we contend the intersectionality of learning, teaching, and leading plays a significant role in understanding the influence of experience of music through artmaking to promote social justice and equity work in schools. Understanding the role of experience provides a starting point to better understanding people, their understanding of relation of self to others, and to their school community. And in regards to music as artmaking, understanding the lived experiences of students with learning differences.

Both of us are fans of documentaries, because stories provide people with a deeper understanding of their lives. Documentary film inspires us to explore the power of experience through voice. For Jay, this inspiration encouraged him to consider documentary film through music by capturing their lived experiences. In essence, he believed artmaking as music encouraged his students to explore their lived experiences as children who were often deemed "socially, emotionally, and cognitively deficient." Collaboratively creating music affords students to dialogue about how others perceive them, reflect on the impact of these perceptions, and interrupt deficit-laden beliefs by promoting their understanding of self. Jay believed artmaking through music would be a powerful experience for their voices to be heard in a new, vital context with students. He wanted them to understand they were not alone in understanding and experiencing the world as "outcasts."

The process of translating their lived experiences into music was twofold: (a) Jay correlated the music to the emerging themes from courageous conversations with whom he worked, focusing on ways in which children were defined by their behaviors; and (b) Jay provided spaces for students to interrupt deficit-laden beliefs by sharing their dreams, ambitions, and hopes, which were similar to other children their age. Music acted as a culturally responsive bridge providing listeners with opportunities to not only hear the lived experiences of the children he served, but to feel their passion, aspirations, and hope.

The process began with Jay meeting children from four K–12 classrooms in his building. He shared the purpose of the Leading for Social Justice art exhibit. Jay asked for volunteers and contacted their families for support. Jay explained he wanted to create an original song about their lives. He emphasized the significance of their voices throughout the song. Jay shared what he learned through the course about disenfranchised populations, and how often children with learning differences are defined by their behaviors, versus all of the talents they bring with them to school. After facilitating conversations with all of the children about their lived realities, Jay asked children how they wanted their experiences shared: individually, in pairs, or small groups. Children noted their preferences. Jay respected how they wanted to be digitally recorded and worked with them accordingly.

Jay asked students the following: "Have you ever felt people attempt to define you by how you act? If yes, how so?" Children shared responses ranging from, "We attend school in separate places," because "we have all been in trouble" in their public schools. Some high school students stressed how often adults "never bothered to ask us why we act the way we do." Others emphasized how often adults "just give us consequences" without taking time to understand the context of their behaviors. Jay asked students to elaborate on behaviors associated with their anger and frustration, because most of the students shared feelings of anger and frustration as the foundation for their "troublemaking" behaviors. They explored experiences supporting their anger as well as ways they may express their anger in school. Jay also asked children to consider other aspects of their sense of self, including their aspirations and dreams. Most of the children identified specific goals they wanted to achieve, their hopes for a viable future throughout their academics, as well as opportunities for vocational training.

After engaging in meaningful dialogue with the students he serves, he asked them to capture what they deemed most significant to their development as young people. In an effort to mirror their compelling stories, Jay chose to use a fuller, electric sound for a specific section of the song. In this section, students shared their understandings of how others may perceive them. Jay felt the strong electric sound reflected the often negative perceptions of the children's behaviors. When students explored their aspirations, hopes, and dreams, Jay intentionally chose "a more stripped, acoustic sound." Jay believed the contrast between how children felt about themselves versus how others perceived them drew attention to the children's resilience and promotion of humanity. The chord progressions and phrasing highlighted the power of individual voice. The music attempted to interrupt deficit-laden beliefs by reframing their personal narratives through sound. Music became a bridge, encouraging the listener to feel tension between "hard, loud, raw electric sounds" aligned with the pervasive degradation children faced with "soft, acoustic" sounds aligned with children's imaginary possibilities. Jay purposely chose chord progressions and phrasing to highlight individual voices and atmospheric space.

Once Jay collected all of their narratives, students were invited to review and approve the final edit of the song. Jay worked individually with each student to independently edit their part of the song. Children were directly involved in promoting their authentic self through song. Their understanding of self and capacity to edit their narratives played an integral role throughout the process. Students determined the sound bites, the order in which narratives were shared, as well as the overall production of the song. Jay emphasized the need for those who did not participate in sharing their narratives to engage in the editing process. He invited all of the students to play a role in producing the song. When their original song was ready for production, the children took great pride in their collaborative work. Jay found it interesting to watch their expressions throughout the process when they heard their own voices. For many of the children, they had never heard their own voice. The power of recording their personal narratives through song was a powerful experience, and one in which they had never been afforded or considered. Their authentic voices were embedded throughout the song, which they believed solidified their lived experiences as children with learning differences.

Jay invited students' families to listen to the song and their children's voices. All of the families requested copies of the song as well as the YouTube link highlighting the Leading for Social Justice art exhibit. One of the students and his family were able to attend the event. They expressed their pleasure and excitement about the artmaking process to Jay. They shared their appreciation for Jay's commitment to incorporating children's voices in an effort to share the lived realities of children with learning differences.

We received feedback regarding their original song from those who attended the event. Several people who listened to the song made comments such as: "I think it's commendable of the teacher to involve the students like this . . . I never saw anything like this before"; "The song made me teary-eyed . . . I was moved by what the students said . . . so often people just overlook children in schools like that"; "So powerful . . . I mean, really . . . it was interesting to hear what upsets the students . . . and then to hear their aspirations . . . we forget we are talking about children . . . very sad on our part"; "I work with children in special education, and I can say firsthand how often my kids are overlooked or judged because they are in my class"; "Their words kept this real . . . very real . . . I never stopped to think about the fact how many children are predisposed to our assumptions and biases . . . it's terrible, but I think I do what the teacher said in his description . . . I'm guilty of this . . . we . . . need to change"; and "We forget that attending a school like that doesn't mean something is wrong with a child . . . it's about supporting their learning . . . they reminded us to look at what is in their hearts . . . powerful song." Jay noted many of the attendees were touched by hearing the voices of the children. One attendee, who received special education services as child, said to Christa, "Their voices just shine right through . . . it was incredible . . . and made me think of how often people thought less of me just because I worked with the special education teacher . . . and I had so much more to offer, but no one seemed to be interested in that . . . just what they thought was wrong with me." Jay conversed with some of the audience members who related how difficult it is to "see the whole child" when children "engage in troubling behaviors." They stressed how important the song was to encourage people, especially educators, to consider how often children receiving special education services are perceived as "less capable" or "less than" children who do not receive such services. These audience members believed this original song deepened people's ways of knowing and encouraged them to rethink their assumptions about children with social and emotional challenges.

We explained to attendees the significance of integrating artmaking with a social justice focus in K–12 schools as well as higher education. The space affords children and adults spaces to understand ways of knowing social justice. Artmaking, and in Jay's case making music, requires those who engage in this work to authentically, collectively, and directly work with students. Throughout this dynamic interaction, students learn to socially interpret, deconstruct, and reconstruct issues they face within K–12 schools, practices, and policies.

The children's lived realities, including social, political, and economical are at the forefront of every dialogue. Together, they explore lived realities both inside and outside of school. Creating these authentic spaces to deepen understanding of self, disparities across social circumstances, and discrimination throughout the wider society is essential in promoting and sustaining moral and legitimate discourses regarding what it means to educate children holistically.

ARTMAKING AS RECONCEPTUALIZING IMAGINARY POSSIBILITIES

Although social justice and equity have been the focus in educational administration literature over the last 15 years (see Anderson, 2010, Boske, 2010, 2014; Bogotch, 2002; Capper, Theoharis, & Sebastian, 2006; Dantley & Tillman, 2010; Furman & Gruenewald, 2004; Shields, 2004), there is a need for those who engage in social justice pedagogies and curriculum studies to better understand what knowledge is of most worth to those who engage in this work in schools. Artmaking, and in considering Jay's collaborative music, widens the scope of what it means to engage in leading for social justice. Those who immerse themselves in artmaking move beyond deepening their historical awareness of what it means to educate children to political agendas and school practices that often perpetuate injustice. Unfortunately, a more narrow scope of what is often taught in preparation programs may ignore significant scholarship from women, queer voices, people with learning differences, people of color, Indigenous voices, and other marginalized populations, as well as imaginative possibilities to actively engage in practices and policies to interrupt and dismantle injustices. Artmaking provides spaces to reconceptualize what is possible in creating a more socially just society.

For social justice to be understood as practical, it must be embedded in the work of those interested in promoting and sustaining what is possible. Those who engage in this work must engage in discourse beyond their school communities. There is a need to not only understand the lived realities within local contexts, but deepen awareness of larger structural influences, such as economics, socially constructed ideologies, as well as unjust practices and policies that impact oppression. Acknowledging these influences is simply not enough to address injustices. Those engaged in this work need spaces to reconceptualize dominant mental models in an effort to reconstruct ways to interrupt prevailing ideologies, often keeping disenfranchised populations on the margins. Jay's collective artmaking through music was a call to action not only for the children he served, but for educators, community members, and the wider society. Their message was very real: promoting humanity and a need for change. Experiencing music as artmaking to deepen their understanding of social injustices was inherent in students' embodied experiences as well as Jay's experiences as an aspiring school leader. Both Jay and his students were transformed.

They not only deepened their understanding of injustices faced by children receiving special education services, but in utilizing artmaking as a process of deepening understanding of self and becoming activists; thus, they advanced their social justice goals to promote humanity and democratic practices in schools, especially for children with learning differences.

For Jay and his students, music as artmaking provided a guide to understanding their lived experiences, decisions made on their behalf, and capacity to disrupt oppressive attitudes/beliefs regarding their success. The artmaking process also promoted their goal to change how audience members understood what it meant to identify as a child with emotional challenges. Jay and the children wanted audience members to understand that what schools say and do matters, especially for children receiving special education services.

As more scholars examine the influence of artmaking in promoting social justice and equity-oriented work, those interested in this work may want to investigate the extent music as artmaking encourages self-transformation; the extent these new understandings influence what it means to promote social justice-oriented work; and the imaginative possibilities artmaking offers in creating leaders for social justice and equity. For Jay, he utilized music as artmaking as a call to action for his children, school community, and educators-at-large. Through this artmaking process, Jay's new sense of self transformed the way in which he understood those he served, as well as reinforced the need to promote his children's capacities to disrupt deficit-laden beliefs and attitudes often aligned with students receiving special education services.

PREPARING SCHOOL LEADERS TO LEAD FOR SOCIAL JUSTICE THROUGH MUSIC AS ARTMAKING

There is an urgency to deepen understanding regarding ways to prepare school leaders to address issues of social justice and equity in U.S. public schools. An increased attention to arts-based principles centered on understanding sensory ways of knowing may be considered. Because artmaking is recognized as an experiential mode of inquiry, music as artmaking may reveal insights and ways of understanding that impact an individual's capacity for knowing what it means to lead for social justice and equity. Utilizing artmaking for making sense of lived experiences through sensory exploration creates spaces for school leaders to consider their actions and reflect upon their impact. Specifically, we explored how music as artmaking shifts their sensemaking, which is a formal curricular decision grounded in the recognition of rich meanings and imaginative possibilities embedded in non-text-based, sensual understandings.

Music as artmaking provides the field of educational leadership with a means to consider arts-based principles as critical pedagogical considerations. These pedagogies may provide new ways of knowing about social justice and equity in K–12 U.S. schools and recognize the need for new curricular visions for school leaders to embody this work. These curricular visions may provide new ways of conceptualizing social justice and equity work in the field of educational leadership as well as for those being served in K–12 school communities. As we progress in the field of educational leadership and social justice, we will continue to understand ways to analyze artmaking as music as well as artmaking in diverse mediums. This challenge involves developing new methods of analysis, as well as new methods of dissemination throughout schools. And with the proliferation of online journals and social media, music as artmaking may be more accessible, especially for marginalized populations. As we continue to explore the implications of music as artmaking in more diverse and dynamic forms of engagement, a continuation of this inquiry may become more relevant when considering the implications of arts-based pedagogies to promote social justice-oriented work.

REFERENCES

Anderson, G. L. (2010). *Advocacy leadership: Toward a post-reform agenda in education.* New York, NY: Routledge.

Baron, R. A., Byrne, D., & Suls, J. (1989). Attitudes: Evaluating the social world. *Social Psychology* (pp. 79–101). Boston, MA: Allyn & Bacon.

Bogotch, I. (2002). Educational leadership and social justice: Practice into theory. *Journal of School Leadership, 12*(2), 138–156.

Boske, C. (2010). I wonder if they had ever seen a black man before? Grappling with issues of race and racism in our own backyard. *Journal of Research on Educational Leadership, 5*(7), 248–275.

Boske, C. (2014). Critical reflective practices: Connecting to social justice. In I. Bogotch & C. Shields (Eds.), *International handbook of social [in] justice and educational leadership* (pp. 289–308). New York, NY: Springer.

Capper, C., Theoharis, G., & Sebastian, J. (2006). Toward a framework for preparing leaders for social justice. *Journal of Educational Administration, 44*(3), 209–224.

Conroy, M. A., Dunlap, G., Clarke, S., & Alter, P. J. (2005). A descriptive analysis of positive behavioral intervention research with young children with challenging behavior. *Topics in Early Childhood Special Education, 25*(3), 157–166.

Corrigan, P. W., Watson, A. C., Byrne, P., & Davis, K. E. (2005). Mental illness stigma: Problem of public health or social justice? *Social Work, 50*(4), 363–368.

Dantley, M., & Tillman, L. (2010). Social justice and moral transformative leadership. In C. Marshall & M. Oliva (Eds.), *Leadership for social justice: Making revolutions in education* (pp. 19–33). New York, NY: Pearson.

Fan, D. (2014). No idea what the future holds: The retrospective evidence dilemma. *Columbia Law Review, 114*(6), 1503–1547.

Forness, S. R., Freeman, S. N., Paparella, T., Kauffman, J. M., & Walker, H. M. (2012). Special education implications of point and cumulative prevalence for children with emotional or behavioral disorders. *Journal of Emotional & Behavioral Disorders, 20*(1), 4–18.

Furman, G., & Gruenewald, D. (2004). Expanding the landscape of social justice: A critical ecological analysis. *Educational Administration Quarterly, 40*(1), 47–76.

Hoge, M. R., Liaupsin, C. J., Umbreit, J., & Ferro, J. B. (2014). Examining placement considerations for students with emotional disturbance across three alternative schools. *Journal of Disability Policy Studies, 24*(4), 218–226. doi: 10.1177/1044207312461672

Malmgren, K., & Gagnon, J. (2005). School mobility and students with emotional disturbance. *Journal of Child & Family Studies, 14*(2), 299–312. doi: 10.1007/s10826-0055058-0

May, Y., Forness, S. R., Judy, H., McCabe, K., & Hough, R. L. (2004). Parental etiological explanations and disproportionate racial/ethnic representation in special education services for youths with emotional disturbance. *Behavioral Disorders, 29*(4), 348–358.

Shields, C. (2004). Dialogic leadership for social justice: Overcoming pathologies of silence. *Educational Administration Quarterly, 40*(1), 109–132.

Wilson, H. (2014). Turning off the school-to-prison pipeline. *Reclaiming Children & Youth, 23*(1), 49–53.

CHAPTER 5

THE EVOLUTION
OF A REVOLUTION

Leadership Lessons
From Al Jourgensen and Ministry

Jeffrey S. Brooks
Monash University

People change and grow over the course of their lives—some more so than others. Looking at the dramatic evolution of industrial music pioneer Al Jourgensen and his band Ministry offers an opportunity to learn lessons both through an examination of themes in the music and from the ways that Jourgensen works with—and against—other people and himself to create a unique sound. Specifically, this chapter will look at three dynamics related to Jourgensen and Ministry and consider their import for school leaders: (a) conflict may yield better results than coexistence, (b) allow yourself and your organization to evolve, and (c) surround yourself with creative and talented people. Further, an analysis of themes in Ministry's music reveal a set of tensions that may help leaders better understand certain issues in their own practice: (a) passivity versus activism, (b) authenticity versus

Educational Leadership and Music, pages 47–54

hypocrisy; and (c) creativity versus conformity. This chapter explores each of these in turn, but I begin with a brief history of the band.

MINISTRY: FROM SYNTHPOP SENSITIVITY TO SKULL-CRUSHING INDUSTRIAL METAL

Ministry was born in 1981 by its founder and sole continuous member, Al Jourgensen. From 1981–1984, Ministry was a synthpop band that played light synthesizer tunes in the style of new romantic band like Visage, Eurythmics, Heaven 17, and Soft Cell. The band's first album, *With Sympathy*, included dance songs with catchy hooks about love, longing, and uncertainty. Jourgensen sang in an affected English accent, and with bandmate Stephen George the duo wore teased-up hair and dressed in the New Romantic fashions of the day. The album peaked in the *Billboard* Top 200 at number 94, and it looked like there was a future for the band in the music industry. Everything looked positive—to everyone but Jourgensen himself. Jourgensen was unhappy, began to act unruly, insulted audiences, and played badly on purpose at shows. Around this time he also began a life-long love-hate affair with drugs and alcohol, heroin and cocaine being at the heart of his addiction. This was also the beginning of Jourgensen's now infamous violent and erratic behavior, a pattern that apparently spared no one. He assaulted bandmates, threatened managers, and abused those few loved ones in his life. Jourgensen was upset that their recording label, Arista, had forced them to take on an unauthentic dramatis persona in order to sell records—He wanted to explore and create a new sound, a new look, and a new form of music, but label executives demanded spandex and synthesizers. George had enough and soon left the band leaving Al to adopt an edgier sound, a different look, and to explore political topics. The 1985 release of the album *Twitch* was the beginning of a transformation. Ministry's sophomore effort was the first Ministry album created in Jourgensen's style. *Twitch* showcased a sound that incorporated elements of the growing industrial music movement of the mid 1980s (which also included bands like Skinny Puppy, Front Line Assembly, and Laibach[1]) such as extensive use of samples from films and political speeches, heavy bass, machine gun-like drums, distorted vocals, and textured production. Many of these acts shared a connection with Wax Trax! Records, a Chicago-based label that acted as a hub for the creation and distribution of this new sound. Ministry was the most successful Wax Trax! band, and they quickly gained a large underground following (Reed, 2013).

The Ministry sound evolved further when Blackouts bassist Paul Barker joined Jourgensen as primary collaborator. The Barker-Jourgensen partnership saw the introduction of guitars as a central part of Ministry, and their albums *The Land of Rape and Honey* (1988) and *The Mind Is a Terrible Thing to Taste* (1989) are considered by many to be groundbreaking tours de force that defined a wholly new musical genre: industrial metal. These critical successes helped them gain a large underground following, which peaked when Ministry released its most commercially successful album, *Psalm 69: The Way to Succeed and the Way to Suck Eggs* (1992). The success of the album boosted by the videos for "NWO" and "Jesus Built My Hotrod" being put in heavy rotation on MTV, and a headliner slot on the high-profile 1992 Lollapalooza tour, meant that Ministry had arrived in the American mainstream. The band's sound and look during this period influenced many bands who went on to greater commercial success than Ministry, including Nine Inch Nails, Marilyn Manson, Rammstein, Rob Zombie, Tool, and Korn.

Despite their growing sales, Ministry's sound continued to evolve, this time into a darker, more dense and layered production with complicated rhythms, droning walls of guitar and distorted vocals. The dense, droning style of the 1996 heroin-fueled album *Filth Pig* alienated some of the fans the band had won from mainstream exposure, and sales started to slide. Subsequent releases *Dark Side of the Spoon* (1999) and *Animositisomina* (2003) were still big hits among the Ministry faithful, but the band's days in the mainstream spotlight were over.

In 2004, the ongoing conflict about Ministry's direction finally meant that Barker left Ministry. Jourgensen recruited new musicians and released a series of three albums that attacked and critiqued then-President George W. Bush: *Houses of the Molé* (2004), *Rio Grande Blood* (2006), and *The Last Sucker* (2012). Barker's departure lead to yet another dramatic change in Ministry, and the band took on a thrash metal sound with much more simple production than previous works. As of 2016, the band was a revolving group of musicians with only Jourgensen as a constant. Despite threatening constantly to retire the band, they released a few more albums and have toured extensively in recent years (Connelly, 2014; Jourgensen & Widerhorn, 2013; Reed, 2013; Ministry Discography, n.d.).

MINISTRY: A PERSONAL RELATIONSHIP

My own relationship with Ministry began in the mid-1980s, shortly after the 1986 release of the *Twitch* album. To me their music was a revelation, characterized by an overall aggression and angst that moved my soul in a way nothing else had. Songs like "Just Like You," "We Believe," and "Over the Shoulder" allied social consciousness to an intensity that somehow made me simultaneously feel and think in a new way that encouraged critical consciousness and heightened my awareness of social justice. Ministry's lyrical themes, such as hypocrisy, authenticity and speaking truth to power, continue to inform and inspire me to this day. I've seen Ministry live three times, the first of these being an infamous 1990 Merrillville, Indiana, concert that was recorded for their *In Case You Didn't Feel Like Showing Up (Live)* album and concert film. I also saw them in 1996 on the Filth Pig tour and most recently in 2015 at a small club where I now live, in Melbourne, Australia. I've followed the band through most of their transformation, and while the music hasn't evolved to my taste, I always find something creative and poignant in the music that compels me to reflect on my life in some small or profound way. Although Jourgensen has given many interviews proclaiming his disdain for touring, they are one of those bands best appreciated through a live performance where the full force of their music and message are on display. When choosing a band to focus on for this chapter, Ministry was the first that came to mind partially because I felt that they had taught me important lessons that I wanted to pass on to the many people who may never listen to their music, and partly because I wanted to think through what those lessons actually were in an effort to make sense of their place in my life. The subsequent sections of this chapter relate these analyses and connect them with concepts germane to educational leadership.

LEADERSHIP LESSONS FROM THE WAY
THAT MINISTRY CREATES MUSIC

While Jourgensen is the heart of Ministry, the band has also featured a constantly changing slate of collaborators. Barker was the main partner during the band's heyday, but at various times Jourgensen worked with members of bands like Nine Inch Nails, Killing Joke, Anthrax, R.E.M., Fugazi, Front 242, Cabaret Voltaire, Skinny Puppy, and Prong, as well as singer-songwriter Chris Connelly. Typically, artists would come to Jourgensen's studio and play or sing part of a song with no other musicians. Jourgensen-the-producer would then kick in and build songs from various pieces of this vast musical catalogue. He would find a drum track that he liked, then add in a bassline, guitar riff, effects, samples, and finally vocals when the song was nearly finished. In the end, a Ministry song was created from small works of many artists recorded at various times, in some cases these had been recorded many years ago. This meant that artists were often confused about what they were doing, and surprised when their work appeared later as part of a Ministry record. The process was chaotic, and probably only made sense to Jourgensen and the few artists he worked with for an extended amount of time (Connelly, 2014). Still, it gives leaders some food for thought, with three main lessons rising above others.

CONFLICT MAY YIELD BETTER RESULTS THAN HARMONY

Famously, Jourgensen is difficult to work with. He is known for having a violent temper and for having a singular taste and vision for a song. He often argues with members of the band, and in Ministry's early days he was known to demand perfection during their complicated live performances (Connelly, 2014), which coordinated as many as 10 musicians delivering intricate individual parts in perfect harmony and unison. Ministry seldom creates or performs in a relaxed state, and there is certainly little room for debate when it comes to engineering and creating a song or album. Jourgensen not only invites tension and animosity, he creates it (Jourgensen & Weiderhorn, 2013). While this certainly isn't advice that every leader should embrace, it does compel us to remember that people do not always do their best work when they are relaxed and comfortable; some will thrive under pressure (Okoroma, 2007). In education, it is particularly interesting to reflect on the oft-espoused value of having consensus before moving an initiative forward. Ministry reminds us that at times great results can come from working under great pressure.

ALLOW YOURSELF AND YOUR ORGANIZATION TO EVOLVE

As of 2016, Ministry has existed for 35 years. Jourgensen and colleagues have released 13 studio albums, 6 live albums, and 14 remix and compilation albums. Importantly, over the band's life their sound has evolved dramatically. They began as a New Romantic synthpop band, became a force of innovation in the industrial music scene, and morphed again into a thrash metal outfit. It would have been easy to stick with the winning formula of their Gold and Platinum album era (Ministry Discography, n.d.), but that did not fulfil the artistic vision and sensibilities of their leader. Ministry, as a band, has never been afraid to experiment with new instruments, with new technology, and with new personnel; and so too should educational leaders. The band changed immensely, alternately attracting new fans and alienating old ones. This has at times been to the benefit and at times to the detriment of album sales, concert ticket sales, and positions in the chart, but they have never been afraid to take a risk (Carpenter, Pollock & Leary, 2003).

SURROUND YOURSELF WITH CREATIVE
AND TALENTED PEOPLE

Ministry songs often have one thing in common: a savage intensity delivered by top-notch musicians. The artists who have moved into and out of the band are for the most part highly accomplished members of other groups—many of which are more commercially successful than Ministry. But they are all happy to temporarily put their own work on hold to briefly collaborate with mad genius Jourgensen. The fact that he commonly invites new ideas to his creative world ensures a continuous stream of creative thought and innovation. Leaders would do well to get the best possible thinkers and doers into their work for collaboration, even if it is short-lived. Both leaders and collaborators will learn something from the experience (Waugh & Streib, 2006).

THEMES IN MINISTRY'S MUSIC: LESSONS FOR LEADERS

While the previous section focused on Ministry's process, it is also worthwhile to turn attention to the themes they have dealt with in their lyrics: rage, hypocrisy, politics, fear, lies, and many other themes. These are too varied and detailed to go into in such a brief chapter, but I will briefly explore a set of tensions that runs through the band's catalogue. Being cognizant of these themes may help leaders better understand certain issues in their own practice

PASSIVITY VERSUS ACTIVISM

Ministry songs such "Breathe" and "Burning Inside" explore thoughts and feelings related to understanding and fighting for what one believes, instead of letting life pass you by. In these and other songs, Jourgensen implores listeners to cast a critical eye at the world around them, create works that speak to those perceptions, hold others accountable who take advantage of others, and be active participants in their life rather than blithely resigning oneself to one's fate—especially when they see injustice around them. This orientation toward social justice is a lesson all leaders should take to heart. They would do well to heed this advice and act when they identify an injustice against those around them (Brooks & Brooks, 2015; Brooks, Normore, Jean-Marie, & Hodgins, 2007; Jean-Marie, Normore, & Brooks, 2009).

HONESTY VERSUS HYPOCRISY

Jourgensen has long been obsessed with truth and lying, and these themes show up in most of the band's albums. The Bush Trilogy of albums are full of songs about the ways that politicians deceive their followers for personal gain (Jourgensen & Wiederhorn, 2013). "No W," "The Great Satan," and

"The Last Sucker" all decry misleadership in the form of lies and deceit. Leaders should use such anthems to remember that leadership is nothing without a moral and ethical core manifested in word and deed (Bok, 1978; Normore & Dorscher, 2007; Starratt, 2004).

CREATIVITY VERSUS CONFORMITY

Many Ministry songs caution listeners to be vigilant against conformity and the insidious ways that people accept dominant norms without critiquing them, lessons that educational leaders have taken to heart via the works of scholars such as Paulo Freire, Peter McLaren and Catherine Marshall. "Filth Pig," "Dead Guy," "Never Believe," and "Supermanic Soul" stand out as songs that explore this particular tension. Creativity is at the heart of personal expression, and for Ministry it is their lifeblood. The band has always blazed new trails in terms of innovative music, and leaders would do well to nurture creativity in their own work and in their organizations (Afshari, Siraj, & Ghani, 2011).

SUMMARY: MINISTRY'S PROCESSES AND MUSIC SUGGEST THE IMPORTANCE OF AUTHENTIC AND PRINCIPLED LEADERSHIP

Reflecting on lessons from Ministry as a band and also in terms of the content of their creative output has been a useful exercise. On the one hand, it made clear many themes that related to authenticity, quality, and creativity that are underrepresented in mainstream educational leadership literature. The band's catalogue is full of lessons for leaders whether in principle or process. It is perhaps atypical to look to musicians for inspiration or guidance on matters of leadership, but on reflection they are often able to teach in three minutes what authors and researchers take hundreds of pages to explain. I found great value in this exercise and hope that readers likewise are able to take away interesting and useful lessons, and that they are compelled to also think critically about the ways that various forms of art inform their worldview and work.

NOTE

1. To be sure, these bands were part of a second or third wave of industrial music, which began with industrial/experimental artists like Throbbing Gristle, Kraftwerk, SPK, and Cabaret Voltaire.

REFERENCES

Afshari, M., Siraj, S., & Ghani, M. F. A. (2011). Leadership and creativity. *Australian Journal of Basic and Applied Sciences, (5)*10, 1591–1594.

Bok, S. (1978). *Lying: Moral choice in public and private life.* New York, NY: Pantheon Books.

Brooks, J. S., & Brooks, M. C. (Eds.) (2015). *Urban educational leadership for social justice: International perspectives.* Charlotte, NC: Information Age.

Brooks, J. S., Normore, A. H., Jean-Marie, G., & Hodgins, D. (2007). Distributed leadership for social justice: Influence and equity in an urban high school. *Journal of School Leadership 17*(4), 378–408.

Carpenter, M.A., Pollock, T.G., & Leary, M. (2003). Governance, the experience of principals and agents, and global strategic intent: Testing a model of reasoned risk-taking. *Strategic Management Journal, 24*, 803–820.

Connelly, C. (2014). *Concrete, bulletproof, invisible & fried: My life as a Revolting Cock.* Philadelphia, PA: Shipwrecked Industries.

Jean-Marie, G., Normore, A. H., & Brooks, J. S. (2009). Leadership for social justice: Preparing 21st century school leaders for a new social order. *Journal of Research on Leadership in Education, 4*(1), 1–31.

Jourgensen, A., & Wiederhorn, J. (2013). *Ministry: The lost gospels according to Al Jourgensen.* Boston, MA: Da Capo Press.

Ministry Discography. (n.d.). In *Wikipedia.* Retrieved May 14, 2016, from https://en.wikipedia.org/wiki/Ministry_discography

Normore, A. H., & Paul Doscher, S. (2007). Using media as the basis for a social issues approach to promoting moral competency in university teaching. *Journal of Educational Administration, 45*(4), 427–450.

Okoroma, N. (2007). Administrative stress: Implications for secondary school principals. *Educational Research Quarterly, 30*, 3–20.

Reed, S. A. (2013). *Assimilate: A critical history of industrial music.* New York, NY: Oxford University Press.

Starratt, R. (2004). *Ethical leadership.* San Francisco, CA: Jossey-Bass.

Waugh, W. L., & Streib, G. (2006). Collaboration and leadership for effective emergency management. *Public Administration Review 66* (special issue), 131–140.

CHAPTER 6

THE POTENCY
OF LOVE AND THE POWER
OF A THOUSAND

Reflections on Gustav Mahler
and Leadership for Social Justice

Katherine Cumings Mansfield
Virginia Commonwealth University

PRELUDE

In 1988 at the Republican National Convention, George H. Bush accepted his party's nomination for the upcoming presidential election. During his acceptance speech, Bush spoke about the importance of leadership and service. Since trying to change the world on one's own was not just overwhelming to think about, but impossible to do, Bush encouraged citizens to come together in collaborative service and a vision for peace.

> For we are a nation of communities, of thousands and tens of thousands of ethnic, religious, social, business, labor union, neighborhood, regional and other organizations, all of them varied, voluntary and unique ... a brilliant diversity spread like stars, like a thousand points of light in a broad and peaceful sky. (Bush, 1988)

Educational Leadership and Music, pages 55–66
Copyright © 2017 by Information Age Publishing
All rights of reproduction in any form reserved.

Bush's "Thousand Points of Light" speech was mocked by some, but affirmed by others; while for me, neither reaction was induced. Rather, I immediately heard the opening passage of Gustav Mahler's, *Symphony of a Thousand*: "Veni, creator spiritus! Mentes tuorum visita! (Come, creator spirit! Visit our souls!)" This was not the first time—nor would it be the last—that music would speak to my heart, inform my mind, and guide my personal and professional decision making. In fact, some of my other scholarship (Mansfield, 2014, 2016) has been inspired by two very different genres of music: classical baroque (George Frideric Handel's, aria "Every Valley") and contemporary pop ("The Cool Kids," by Echosmith).

The purpose of this chapter is to share how Gustav Mahler's background and artistic choices have influenced my thinking on social justice leadership. In the first section, I will give a short overview of Mahler's personal life and career in terms of: (a) his background, experiences, and beliefs, which channeled the main themes of his work; (b) some of the struggles Mahler experienced as a leader; and (c) his eventual recognition as a bridge builder. In the second section, I will reflect on my experiences as an educator and researcher, along with the leadership literature. Similar to the prior section, I submit: (a) the significance of one's positionality and how experiences and beliefs inform one's work; (b) some of the struggles leaders face as they lead for social justice; and (c) the importance of becoming a bridge builder between community and school.

VERSE I: REFLECTIONS ON GUSTAV MAHLER

Past as Prologue

The impressions of the spiritual experiences gave my future life its form and content . . .
If I weren't the way I am, I shouldn't write my symphonies.

—Gustav Mahler[1]

Gustav Mahler was born in 1860 in what is now known as the Czech Republic. His family was part of the German-speaking minority among native Bohemians. Later in life, he lived in Austria and was considered an outsider among the German majority. Also, whether he lived in Europe or the United States, his Jewish heritage was always an issue, despite the fact that he converted to Catholicism to secure employment. Hence, Mahler described himself as "perpetually homeless, an outsider supreme: everywhere an intruder, never welcomed." In addition to ethno-cultural rejection, Mahler grew up in humble economic circumstances: his grandmother was literally a beggar. Moreover, his home life was complete mayhem and devastation. Besides mourning the death of six of his siblings at an early age, he was estranged from his father, who physically abused his mother (Murray, 1998).

Mahler's experiences as an outsider followed him all his life, especially in terms of how others perceived his compositions. A deep love of philosophy and history permeated his work. For example, Mahler's music was preoccupied with the weighty questions of life, such as: "If God exists and He is kind, how can cruelty and malice exist among His creation?" Each of his symphonies is an incarnation of his search for ontological truth. According to Michael Tilson Thomas (n.d. a, b), for both Mahler, and audience alike, his music demanded candid self-reflection, with Mahler's earlier experiences critical to how he shaped his distinctive creations. Michael Murray (1998) noted:

> Death and thoughts of death were the constant companions of Mahler's youth … this torment and morbidity may be attributed the composer's nervous tension, his sense of the ironic, and his lifelong search for meaning amid life's absurdities and tragedies. (p. 2)

His music was all about contrasts and the capriciousness of life. It was at one moment innocent and sentimental, and the next grotesque and shocking, then back again (Hepokoski, 1992). According to Murray (1998) and Oron (2009), Mahler's symphonies were not only autobiographical, but lengthy and complicated, and the public was unprepared to welcome or comprehend music that advocated an explicit worldview.

In addition to seeking answers related to the nature of being as experienced in the earthly realm, Mahler was also constantly thinking about the mystical: the nature of reality in the spiritual realm after death. His compositions sought to trouble over his many questions and invited audience members to do the same. His spirituality was closely connected with nature and he believed life's mysteries should be explored and could be explained by using all ontological approaches known to us (Hepokoski, 1992; Murray, 1998; Oron, 2009). *Symphony No. 3* is an excellent example of Mahler's search for answers. This symphony is split into major sections with subtitles translated as: (a) what the flowers of the meadow tell me; (b) what the animals in the forest tell me; (c) what humanity tells me; (d) what the angels tell me; and (e) what love tells me. While Mahler was obsessed with death, he was also captivated by the concepts of mercy and resurrection, and believed in the healing power of love and music (Hepokoski, 1992; Murray, 1998).

A Controversial Leader

I cannot exchange one sensible word with anyone.

—Gustav Mahler

It is difficult to say whether Mahler experienced resistance from those with whom he worked because he was demanding, disrespected for his unorthodox compositions, a covert Jew, or all of the above. Concerning Mahler's compositions, Oron (2009) posits,

> Mahler's juxtaposition of material from both "high" and "low" cultures, as well as his mixing of different ethnic traditions, often outraged conservative critics at a time when workers' mass organizations were growing rapidly, and clashes between Germans, Czechs, Hungarians, and Jews in Austro-Hungary were creating anxiety and instability.

While his coworkers loathed him for his severe perfectionism, his contemporaries revered him as a primo conductor whose vision, discipline, and high standards raised the performance and profile of both the Vienna Opera and Vienna Philharmonic (Murray, 1998). In these most prestigious positions, he was renown for his mastery readings of Mozart, Wagner, and Beethoven and his ability to expand a formerly routine repertoire as well as raise artistic standards. (Hepokoski, 1992; Oron, 2009; Murray, 1998)

In terms of his creative output Mahler would remain an outcast. His music was called heretical, reactionary, too emotional, overly demonstrative, and excessively demanding on the listener (Steinberg, 1994). Bluntly put, audiences during the Romantic Era wanted to be entertained, but expected well-mannered restraint. They wanted to feel better after engagement. After all, troubling over both the ghastliness and splendor of life (and death) is not necessarily pleasant.

Mahler's Pièce de Résistance

A symphony must be like the world. It must contain everything.
—Gustav Mahler

Mahler's 8th symphony premiered in Munich in 1910 and was "one of the most spectacular events of musical Europe" (Hepokoski, 1992). When Mahler introduced his magnum opus to the world, he was in ill health and had less than a year to live. Mahler's 8th was a huge spectacle for a number of interrelated reasons. First, it was the first symphony on record to treat the human voice as a musical instrument that was "played" throughout, from beginning to end. Secondly, it required a massive marshalling of forces, including two huge adult choirs, one children's choir, eight vocal soloists, and ensembles such as brass players positioned throughout the venue. In addition, an enormous orchestra—triple the customary size—led to the re-title, Symphony of a Thousand.

Mahler's *Symphony of a Thousand* did not just involve the unconventional composition and configuration of the performers, but also the eccentricity of the selected texts and musical styles. The core message behind the composition was the disruption of binaries, suggesting a different reality that included an all-embracing unity that most were either unable or unwilling to accept. For example, Mahler jarred the audience with his attempts to integrate stylistic and conceptual disunities: voice versus orchestra, cantata versus symphony, old-school counterpoint versus modern sonata, sacred versus secular, and masculine versus feminine (Hepokoski, 1992). Through both the materiality of the performers and the metaphysical nature of the score, Mahler purposefully set out to communicate concepts of diversity (without essentialism) and inclusion (without assimilation). Thus, through the use of elements that most considered irreconcilable, inconsistent, and/or disjointed, Mahler aimed to communicate difference as invaluable; how differences can come together into a coherent whole that was far greater than the sum of its parts. His overall message was that seemingly relentless divisions (e.g., masculine versus feminine) could be healed in our present world and fulfill his idealistic vision of reconciliation and peace (Hepokoski, 1992).

Mahler believed that bringing together the principal agents of healing such as love (both spiritual and physical), unearned grace, and forgiveness the redemptive power of music would contribute toward resolving human antipathies. His assembling of the masses was symbolic of "a new, healed community of the whole, one that has finally transcended division at all levels, and one with which the audience was to identify" (Hepokoski, 1992). Mahler considered the literal act of being present, whether performing as a member of the collective or contemplating as one of many spectators, as potentially a healing act in and of itself. He envisioned the *veni, creator spiritus* motive as an "embrace of the wild heterogeneity within as if with a vast pair of arms" (Heposki, 1992). Today, Mahler is recognized not only as a musical giant, but as a bridge between the classical and modern age of music that, indeed, has the potential to heal the world.

VERSE 2: REFLECTIONS ON LEADING FOR SOCIAL JUSTICE

Positionality and Path

The point is not to take the world's opinion as a guiding star but to go one's way in life and working unerringly, neither depressed by failure nor seduced by applause.

—Gustav Mahler

When I first began studying Mahler and his works, I was captivated by his story and empathized with the pain and loneliness of his outsiderness. I, too, had grown up in difficult financial circumstances and was also estranged from my father for the same reasons Mahler was. Like him, I moved from place to place and never felt I belonged anywhere or really had a home. I knew what it was like to be considered a "loser." Some of the most humiliating situations included being beat up at school for being a "Polack" and being told by a school counselor that I "wasn't college material."

Fast-forward to today and now I am a university professor. But, I have never forgotten the embarrassment of being considered inferior by both peers and educators, nor the mortification of sitting with empty pockets and a growling belly every day during lunch in middle school. But the past has made me who I am. My background has directly impacted my career choices, which has centered around issues of equity and access for historically-marginalized people. And through the years, in addition to appreciating the productivity of past marginalization, I have also come to understand the privileges I have experienced as a White person. It was important for me to learn what Norton (2004) referred to as the manifold ways all people have various levels of both privilege and marginalization.

Personal experiences of marginalization have the potential to inspire social justice advocacy (Merchant & Shoho, 2009). For some, inspiration also springs from their religious faith. For example, DeYoung (2007) studied the lives of people he referred to as mystic activists from Buddhist, Christian, and Muslim faiths, and how their interpretations of ancient scriptures fueled their embrace of reconciliation and social justice. In addition, they adopted a worldview that emerged from the margins of society, and they recognized difference while embracing a common humanity.

A hallmark of these leaders was the merging of their faith with their intellectual and political pursuits. In addition, mystic activists learned to see the world through the eyes of the oppressed as well as the privileged. Seeing both sides enabled access to a variety of people and multiple ways to fight oppression. Whether emanating from past marginalizing experiences, one's private faith and spirituality, or a deep and profound commitment to social justice based on professional standards or political and philosophical values, the inspiration described by those committed to social justice work is often difficult to explain, but includes an inner drive to help and serve others (Mansfield, 2013).

In addition to reflecting on one's relative privilege and oppression, as well as source of inspiration, it is also important for educators to understand the multiple contexts of students' lives and view the nested contexts of schools as permeable membranes (Dantley & Tillman, 2009). In doing so, leaders more readily recognize ways their leadership practices may or may not reproduce marginalizing conditions.

Battling the Status Quo

The call of love sounds very hollow among these immobile rocks.
—Gustav Mahler

For me, teaching is a calling and a labor of love. I consider myself lucky that my first principal approached his work similarly. During the 3 years we worked together, we (and other "radical" teachers) implemented progressive policies and inclusive programs. Unfortunately, he was replaced by a man who let it be known that the only reason he was there was to make more money. During initial conversations he called me "naïve," remarking that the color and class divide in gifted programs "was just the way things were," and that I should "forget about trying to change the inevitable."

My experiences strongly resonate with Brooks and Miles (2008) and Theoharis (2007); that is, taking an explicitly activist stance while developing the school culture strengthens the chances that educational equity, access, and achievement in diverse contexts can be cultivated. But what is an educator to do if social justice efforts are thwarted by immobile rocks such as teachers and parents (and even principals)?

Researchers (DeMatthews & Mawhinney, 2014; Theoharis, 2007) have pondered similar questions and have made some interesting discoveries. For example, Theoharis studied principals committed to social justice, the challenges they faced, and their approaches to enduring enormous pressure. He found that these principals faced resistance from inside and outside the school, and experienced difficulty countering negative attitudes and combating the tenaciousness of the status quo, making change an arduous undertaking. Consequently, these principals were plagued with a persistent sense of discouragement and experienced strain on their physical and mental health. The principals coped two ways: by using proactive strategies such as developing supportive personal and professional networks, or employing negative strategies such as increasing alcohol use. In response, Theoharis (2007) called on leadership preparation programs to fill a much-needed gap by helping budding leaders develop skills to not only enact social justice, but develop resilience that would help them manage resistance.

Becoming a Bridge Builder

You must renounce all superficiality, all convention, all vanity, and delusion.
—Gustav Mahler

Authentic bridges can't be superficial. It's impossible. A phony bridge is no bridge at all, but a mirage that leads to nowhere (or off a cliff). Similarly, to do social justice work in educational spaces, one must abandon shallowness and pretension and "walk the talk" (Dantley & Tillman, 2009). Authenticity is one of the sterling characteristics of those who carry the social justice banner. I can't think of anyone who enjoys working with a leader who is fake; nor, can I imagine any community that prefers educational researchers who are selfish and eager to take advantage of research participants.

This may seem hyperbole, but for more than 100 years, North American First Nations have criticized researchers for being condescending, disrespectful of culture, uniformed about issues that are important to Indigenous communities, and neglecting mutual benefit (Brugge & Missaghian, 2006). This has led many to conclude that most researchers are self-centered, self-interested, and difficult to communicate with. Some have referred to researchers as having "White man's disease" (p. 495).

Julie Laible (2000) exhorted both educational leaders and researchers to examine intentions, attitudes, thoughts, and feelings before entering any community or school setting. For Laible (2000), researching the "other" was an unethical undertaking that could not be reconciled with her spirit and faith. Laible (2000) found Lugones' (1987) work on coupling world traveling with loving perception a thought-provoking alternative to her usual way of researching nondominant communities. Further, similar to how "outsiders" have, out of necessity, developed elasticity in shifting between majority and minority communities, Lugones (1987) claims that those in the dominant culture can, and should, willfully exercise this same flexibility as they travel from the mainstream to the outsiders' world. Laible (2000) and Lugones (1987) believed these efforts encouraged cross-cultural and cross-racial loving. Similarly, Cree scholar Shawn Wilson (2013) demands that before serving or researching the other, one must first ask oneself, "Am I demonstrating love in my actions?" Like Laible (2000) and Lugones (1987), Wilson views the concept of love as grounded in relational accountability and the most fitting approach to bridging cultures.

In addition to educational research, the concept of bridging cultures is also an important construct in the leadership literature. For example, according to Collins (2001), leaders of highly successful organizations are courageous and determined while also being modest and humble. Indeed, an individual whose leadership is enduring has learned to subordinate one's ego to a higher cause

(Covey, 2002). Research specific to educational leadership speaks to the importance of bridging cultures within and outside of schools. School principals working for social justice have been described as a bridge (Khalifa, 2012; Merchant & Shoho, 2005), boundary spanner (Green, 2015; Miller, 2009), cultural worker (Cooper, 2009), and cross boundary leader (Green, 2015). In addition to spurning egotism and operating in isolation, educational leaders who are true bridges understand that they cannot possibly do what is best for students without consulting with community stakeholders (Khalifa, 2012).

Coda

To judge a composer's work, one must consider it as a whole.
—Gustav Mahler

I can really appreciate Mahler's quote. He did not want to be remembered by an individual composition, but rather how his work fit together over the trajectory of his career. It reminds me of my current educational post: I would not want to be judged on a single article; rather I would like my body of work to be considered for its overall impact and/or potential.

Many parallels can be made between my reflections on Mahler and my thoughts on the leadership literature. Both Mahler and social justice workers aim to push the status quo and transgress false boundaries set up by "the establishment." Relatedly, both Mahler's music and leading schools for social justice require courage, critical self-reflection, and an openness to consider both the beauty and the tragedy of our particular contexts. Like Mahler, our work is—more often than not—autobiographical. And controversy seems to be the order of the day for all those who whose magnum opus aims to disrupt binaries, embrace diversity, and labor for inclusion.

It is interesting to me that Mahler did create what is considered his magnum opus, and he was acknowledged by the public for—at the very least—its astonishing size. It was not until decades after his death, that future readers of his music would reintroduce him to the world. And, finally the world—in that time and in that place—was open to Mahler's revolutionary philosophy and how it was conveyed through his music. Likewise, our life's work is in the hands of future readers—whether our labor regenerates or perishes with us. To be sure, most of us would like to leave some sort of positive legacy. But the truth is, we may never see the fruits of our labors. But like Mahler, we press on anyway with the belief that we were not born in vain, and that working together by the thousands, our "ardent labors of love" have made a difference.

Fortunately, something always remains to be harvested. So let us not be idle.
—Gustav Mahler

NOTE

1. Gustav Mahler's quotes included in this chapter are used so often in artistic communities that they are rarely referenced with a particular book or historical artifact. I direct the reader to some helpful resources that show various interpretations of many of Mahler's well-worn quotes:

> Hepokoski, J. (1992). *Gustave Mahler: Symphony No. 8* [CD], Hamburg, Germany: Deutsche Grammophon.
> Murray, M. (1998). *Mahler Symphony No. 3* [CD], Cleveland, OH: Telarc International.
> Oron, A. (2009, May). *Gustav Mahler* (composer, arranger). Retrieved October 1, 2015, from http://www.bach-cantatas.com/Lib/Mahler-Gustav.htm
> Steinberg, M. (1994). *Gustav Mahler. Symphony No. 2 in C minor* [CD]. London, England: Decca Records.
> Thomas, M. T. (n.d.a). Gustav Mahler: Legacy. In *PBS Keeping Score* [Television series episode, Season 3, Part 2]. Retrieved from http://www.pbs.org/keepingscore/mahler-legacy.html
> Thomas, M. T. (n.d.b) Gustav Mahler: Origins. *PBS Keeping Score* [Television series episode, Season 3, Part 1]. Retrieved from http://www.pbs.org/keepingscore/mahler-origins.html

REFERENCES

Brooks, J., & Miles, M. T. (2008). From scientific management to social justice ... and back again? Pedagogical shifts in the study and practice of educational leadership. In A. H. Normore (Ed.), *Leadership for social justice: Promoting equity and excellence through inquiry and reflective practice* (pp. 99–114). Charlotte, NC: Information Age.

Brugge, D., & Missaghian, M. (2006). Protecting the Navajo people through tribal regulation of research. *Science & Engineering Ethics, 12*(3), 491–507.

Bush, G. (1988, August 18). *Address accepting the presidential nomination at the Republican National Convention in New Orleans.* Retrieved January 15, 2016, from: http://www.presidency.ucsb.edu/ws/?pid=25955

Collins, J. (2001). *Good to great: Why some companies make the leap . . . and others don't.* New York, NY: Collins.

Cooper, C. W. (2009). Performing cultural work in demographically changing schools: Implications for expanding transformative leadership frameworks. *Educational Administration Quarterly, 45*(5), 694–724.

Covey, S. R. (2002). *Seven habits of highly effective people: Restoring the character ethic.* New York, NY: Simon & Schuster.

Dantley, M. E., & Tillman, L. C. (2009). Social justice and moral transformative leadership. In C. Marshall & M. Oliva, (Eds.), *Leadership for social justice: Making revolutions in education* (2nd ed.; pp. 19–34). New York, NY: Allyn & Bacon.

DeMatthews, D., & Mawhinney, H. (2014). Social justice leadership and inclusion: Exploring challenges in an urban district struggling to address inequities. *Educational Administration Quarterly, 50*(5), 844–881.

DeYoung, C. P. (2007). *Living faith: How faith inspires social justice.* Minneapolis, MN: Fortress Press.

Green, T. L. (2015). Leading for urban school reform and community development. *Educational Administration Quarterly, 51*(5), 679–711.

Hepokoski, J. (1992). *Gustav Mahler: Symphony No. 8* [CD]. Hamburg, Germany: Deutsche Grammophon.

Khalifa, M. (2012). A re-new-ed paradigm in successful urban school leadership: Principal as community leader. *Educational Administration Quarterly, 48*(3), 424–467.

Laible, J. C. (2000). A loving epistemology: What I hold critical in my life, faith, and profession. *International Journal of Qualitative Studies in Education, 13*(6), 683–692.

Lugones, M. (1987). Playfulness, "World"-travelling, and loving perception. *Hypatia, 2*(2), 3–19.

Mansfield, K. C. (2014). Creating smooth spaces in striated places: Toward a global theory for examining social justice leadership in schools. In I. Bogotch & C. Shields (Eds.), *The international handbook on social [in]justice and educational leadership,* (pp. 37–50). New York, NY: Springer.

Mansfield, K. C. (2013). I love these girls, I was these girls: Women leading for social justice in a single-sex public school. *Journal of School Leadership, 23*(4), 634–657.

Mansfield, K. C., & Alexander, Q. (2016). The cool kids. In K. C. Mansfield, A. D. Welton, & P. L. Lee (Eds.) *Identity intersectionalities, mentoring, and work-life (im)balance: Educators (re)negotiate the personal, professional, and political* (pp. 53–64). Charlotte, NC: Information Age.

Merchant, B. & Shoho, A. (2005). Bridge people: Civic and educational leaders for social justice in an urban community. In C. Marshall & M. Oliva (Eds.), *Leadership for social justice: Making revolutions in education* (2nd ed.). Boston, MA: Allyn & Bacon.

Miller, P. M. (2009). Boundary spanning in homeless children's education. *Educational Administration Quarterly, 45*(4), 616–630.

Murray, M. (1998). *Mahler Symphony No. 3* [CD]. Cleveland, OH: Telarc International.

Oron, A. (2009, May). *Gustav Mahler (composer, arranger).* Retrieved October 1, 2015, from http://www.bach-cantatas.com/Lib/Mahler-Gustav.htm

Steinberg, M. (1994). *Gustav Mahler. Symphony No. 2 in C minor* [CD]. London, England: Decca Records.

Theoharis, G. (2007). Social justice educational leaders and resistance: Toward a theory of social justice leadership. *Educational Administration Quarterly, 43*(2), 221–258.

Thomas, M. T. (n.d., a). Gustav Mahler: Legacy. *PBS Keeping Score* (Season 3, Part 2). Retrieved August 3, 2015, from http://www.pbs.org/keepingscore/mahler-legacy.html

Thomas, M. T. (n.d., b) Gustav Mahler: Origins. *PBS Keeping Score* (Season 3, Part 1). Retrieved August 3, 2015, from http://www.pbs.org/keepingscore/mahler-origins.html

Wilson, S. (2013, October). *Why is using an indigenist research paradigm an Indigenous survival necessity?* Speech presented at the 2013 Conference of the American Indigenous Research Association, Pablo, MT. Retrieved from http://american-indigenousresearchassociation.org/conference/2013-conference-report/

CHAPTER 7

BEYOND ROPAR BAR

Transcultural and Transformative Collaborations of the Australian Art Orchestra and the Young Wagilak Group

Leon R. de Bruin
Monash University

The Australian Art Orchestra (AAO) is a portable orchestra that meets the demands of the new millennium's explorations in improvised music. Exploring the meeting points between disciplines and cultures, musicians of the AAO imagine new musical forms that reflect the energy and diversity of 21st century Australia. Initially conceived as a contemporary jazz orchestra, it draws inspiration from Australia's vibrant local contemporary music scene and significant cultural diversity, "exploring the interstices between the avant-garde and the traditional, between art and popular music, between electronic and acoustic approaches, creating works that traverse the continuum between improvised and notated forms" (AAO, 2016). Central to this is an ongoing dedication to nurturing dialogues with artistic collaborators in India, Korea, China and Indonesia, as well as with deepening its connection with Australian indigenous cultures. The Orchestra is

Educational Leadership and Music, pages 67–77
Copyright © 2017 by Information Age Publishing
All rights of reproduction in any form reserved.

commissioned to create music perspectives committed to the notion of a future in which truly new music that integrates Asian and Western influences is part of the cultural fabric of our region.

Establishing a reputation for the breadth and quality of its ambitious cross-cultural collaborations, Crossing Roper Bar (CRB) is a visionary exploration of the musical traditions of Australia's first people by the Australian Art Orchestra in collaboration with the Indigenous Australian Young Wagilak Group.[1] The Wagilak speaking songmen of South East Arnhem Land, Northern Territory, are custodians of one of the oldest continuously practiced cultures on Earth. Their songs are performed regularly in Ngukurr, Numbulwar, Groote Eylandt and surrounding areas where the strong Wagilak musical culture is admired. The Australian Art Orchestra began collaborating with the Young Wagilak Group in 2005. Based on an equal exchange of knowledge that began as a dialogue centered on music, CRB developed into a process of collaborative composition that retains the beauty and dynamism of both traditions. The Young Wagilak Group have worked closely with the AAO to create a contemporary interpretation of Wild Blackfella, a song cycle, which traces the journey of an ancestor through his country as he recounts lived histories, places, and events. A marriage of the ancient with the new, CRB is an exploration of ancestral spirits, country, ceremony, musical leaders, improvisers both indigenous and arrived, and of the power of music in building enduring bridges across cultures, time and place.

UNDERSTANDING THROUGH COLLABORATION

Rehearsals between the two groups occurred in both Ngukurr and Melbourne that established the beginnings of understanding each culture's musical meaning. Initial collaborations were characterized by imitation and a musical ebbing back-and-forth between the distinct groups. Continued interaction produced a refined understanding, sensitivity, and depth of awareness of each other's ways of being, making, and representing musically. Members of the AAO engaged in understanding the complexities of the Wagilak way, and the Wagilak grew to understand the processes, freedoms, and dialogic interplay of a Western art music improvizing ensemble. Over several meetings, the AAO investigated the rich and complex tenets that construct the Wagilak song forms. To do this, they immersed themselves in an understanding of the Wagilak people: their customs, their beliefs, and their hermeneutics of society and culture.

According to Aboriginal belief, all life as it is today (human, animal, bird and fish) is part of one vast unchanging network of relationships that can be traced to the Great Spirit ancestors of the Dreamtime. An Aboriginal understanding of the world, the Dreamtime is the beginning of knowledge, from which came the laws of existence and of survival. The Dreamtime is not simply a reciting of historical events, of retelling of religious significance and greatness. It is something directly experienced as it is encountered in the present; an encounter between a life and its existential animation as a life within a history, society, ecology, and body of knowledge.

The Wagilak identity is thus born into a world of tradition, history and culture, where *gurrutu* (kinship), *rom* (law, correct living), and hermeneutic systems of understanding and languages shape worlds. Wagilak came to be through ancient actions of Djuwalpada who danced when he founded the Wagilak homeland at Ṇilipidji, and Wagilak today dance this narrative when performing *manikay*. Ben Wilfred, Wagilak elder, speaks of this birth from the land:

> *Manikay* bin coming out of that ground. Comes from that ground at Ṇilipidji. *Manikay* is for country, for leading new generation. *Manikay* is for using in funeral, *wata* [wind], smoking [purification ceremony]. Learn about country. *Manikay* means spirit for the country, and songs; where he walked, Wild Blackfella [Djuwalpada]. *Manikay* means for the land and for the ground, tree, no matter what animal. Everything. *Manikay* means for the countryside and for land, land and sea—no matter where you go. (Benjamin Wilfred in Curkpatrick, 2013, p. 78)

Ancestral law is carried into new contexts through engaging and dynamic interaction in performance. Deep knowledge of *manikay* is shrouded in secrecy and preserved by wise elders who ultimately regulate its transferral, and the most restricted (*ŋärra*) interpretations held by senior men are the *ŋaraka* (bones) of a clan (Curkpatrick, 2013, p. 79). Highly protected and veiled, "only shortly before old men [and women] know they are going to die will they reveal to their successors the full extent of the meanings of what they have stored and guarded in their memories" (Williams 1986, p. 24). Likewise, only as Sambo Barabara[2] [Wagilak elder] was nearing death did he pass over to current elders Benjamin and Daniel Wilfred the authority to continue to perform Wagilak *manikay*: "Sambo come in my dream and give me that clapping stick" (Benjamin Wilfred in Curkpatrick, 2013, p. 79).

In ceremonial performance, *manikay* is a woven tapestry of sound, of dance movements, designs, images, language and time, past and present. Transmitting social, cultural, legal and religious "expressions of hereditary identities, knowledge and values" (Corn 2002, 17), manikay brings to life the cultural expression and celebration of tribal ancestors, country, law and congress. Manikay is an expression of these themes and influences, layered through generations building on the ancestral footprint of what has gone before. Through performance and iteration, congress and interaction, manikay continually evolves and progresses, replenished and rejuvenated by each new relationship and 'maintaining vitality and authenticity through the passing from leader to leader of successive generations of Wagilak elder' (Caruana & Lendon 1997, 26). Benjamin Wilfred, an elder and leader of the Wagilak retells a story of learning, ownership and renewal:

> All my grandfathers and my in-laws, they are all gone now. All our grandfathers, father's fathers, all passed away. We are the only people that know the culture and the secret singing. Only us mob now. Andy [Peters] is the only elder in the Wagilak clan. This is me talking, [Benjamin] Miyala. I'm doing this recording for all my children to listen and learn, and move along with our culture. And we always think about bush tucker when we are walking. I'm the only person that knows the traditional songs. All the rest are gone. This is for you mob; you mob got to listen properly, learn and carry on. Only then can I stop. (Benjamin Wilfred in Curkpatrick, 2013, p. 40)

Yolngu[3] advocates for the sharing of culture through a bicultural approach between autonomous Yolngu cultural systems of Arnhem Land (Morphy & Morphy 2013). The Yolgnu seek difference as a way of perpetually revitalizing their culture; difference is seen as complementary (Yunupingu, 1993). For the musicians of the AAO, the CRB project avails an opportunity to engage in intercultural music making that gives further meaning to their music-making and life-long learning as improvisers. The AAO musicians bring vast knowledge of jazz and improvised music and embarked upon this exploration of the Yolngu cultural system with respect and inquisitiveness. Both entities combined with a willingness to collaborate, to absorb and be absorbed in the essence and meanings of newfound dialogic discourse. As George Lewis explains:

> In performances of improvised music, the possibility of internalizing alternative value systems is implicit from the start. The focus of musical discourse suddenly shifts from the individual, autonomous creator to the collective. (Lewis, 2002, p. 234)

The CRB project challenges music making in several ways. Through interaction, space is given to individual voices in open engagement that allows personal articulation of ideas, narratives and feelings. Yet, central to CRB is the resonance and unity of the collective. The improvised collective is a paradox to these musicians: every player must lead and every player must follow and respond to both the immediate situation and a sense of greater musical development or course of events. Effective improvisation requires fluidity and flexibility of response, a musical reflex shaped from our past histories and experiences elicited "in the moment." Far beyond the demands implicit in genre-specific jazz performance, the CRB collaboration synthesises in performance both groups' histories and stories, shaping new forms, structures and vocabularies. A vehicle for articulating possibilities of equality, freedom and agency, in which "artists sought to mediate social and individual necessity, to bring them into an ever-dynamic state of equilibrium" (Saul, 2003, p. 19). The ongoing innovative "action that propels the possibilities of jazz is conspicuous in both the creative, transformative thought of its practitioners and the diasporic intercultural and collaborative possibilities evident in the genre's evolution." (de Bruin, 2016a, p. 94).

Cross-cultural collaborations are delicate situations, demanding for the AAO sensitivity and willingness to explore a truly shared music meeting point. By interrogating theories of intercultural engagement, these musicians questioned their personal assumptions about meaningful collaboration, and respectful, artful music making. Leader Paul Grabowsky elaborates:

> In an age where the term "world music" has come to disguise a multitude of musical crimes and in which sampling technology has resulted in wide spread looting of cultural artefacts, reducing everything to the status of the "found object," the onus on our creative team has been to approach the composition process as a partnership. (Grabowsky in Curkpatrick, 2013, p. 310)

Thus, in the creating of *CRB*, traditions of both cultures play with and against each other, sorting between past and present, individuality, and interplay. Collaboration between different individuals and cultures is enacted through a positive and productive tension, allowing unique voices to emerge as the collaboration evolves through new manifestations.

It is not only collaborative processes at play in the formation of this CRB collaboration. The demands upon the individual in embarking on self-reflective practice, a self-interrogation of one's history and perspective that is at the core of both sets of musicians' fulfilling of the projects' possibilities. AAO musician Tony Hicks elaborates on his journey of intercultural engagement and dealing with the musical implications he and the collective saw in this collaborative venture. Hicks explored his own development in great detail. Tracing his decades-long improvising interactions, an enduring and pervasive goal for him remains the liberation of performance from old "codes of production," that seek to allow "for more contextually sensitive contributions within a range of unconventional music making contexts" (Hicks 2011, p. 65). Development reflected on 2009 and 2011 CRB recordings confirm Hick's process of evolution. He elaborates further on the musical processes inherent in the CRB project:

> Musically, this project [CRB] forced a further redefinition of my improvisation conceptions and musical philosophies by revealing the habitual nature of Western musical constructs such as tonality and temperament. A new language was required that could express the raw power and transcultural potential of this collaboration. Improvisation can exist to drive evolving creative

processes, leading to profound creative transformations and the development of new languages.' (Hicks 2011, pp. 2–3)

Transformative experiences through collaboration were experienced from both AAO and Wagilak musicians. Manikay song subjects discussed and rehearsed in workshops originated from the collaboration, but were not exclusively a result of the collaboration. AAO musician Tony Hicks recalls an example of the unexpected cultural processes experienced while on tour with the group in 2008:

> Well, the first thing that I knew was that they said, "We have to go to the beach." We're in Broome, it's six o'clock in the morning: "There's a new song!" "Where's the new song come from?" "I dreamt it. My grandfather gave it to me, last night." (Tony Hicks quoted in Curkpartick, 2013, p. 174)

Through collaborative work in rehearsals, the organizing and sorting out of responses to melodic and rhythmic complexity sometimes captured unexpected and new levels of communication. Wagilak musician Daniel Wilfred responds to such a moment.

> That song came from nowhere, that Malka one. Him really fast! I don't know what's going on there, we bin follow you mob. That's from you, wawa (my brothers). New one. That's the Malka. New one. Manyyak (good)! Followed you mob beat. That sound comes from the bass. New song, for you mob. Manymak! That music come in from nowhere, even for the didj. (Daniel Wilfred quoted in Curkpartick, 2013, p. 236)

The first performances in July 2005 placed the Wagilak group singing first, answered by a solo improvisation by an AAO member. The manikay song was then performed by the full orchestra. Though triumphantly acclaimed, these performances provided reflection of the musicians on the processes involved, and the communicative power with which this collaboration resonated with both Indigenous and immigrant audiences around Australia.

> We did that with seriousness of purpose, albeit total ineptitude. I was talking to one of the elders this morning and he said it was enormously significant that we did that last night. It was a sign to them that we were willing to go wherever, do whatever, be whatever. (Paul Grabowsky; Australian Broadcasting Commission 2005)

> I'm really, really excited. It nearly made me cry one time because professional musicians are actually playing the music from the people, rather than musicians arranging music for didj or clapsticks. (Archie Roach; Australian Broadcasting Commission, 2005)

As coparticipants, the musicians share in the responsibilities, endeavor, and possibilities of outcomes. Through conversation with another individual or culture, perspectives are transformed because we do not exist on our own. To "reach an understanding in a dialogue is not merely a matter of putting oneself forward and successfully asserting one's own point of view, but being transformed into a communion in which we do not remain what we were." (Gadamer 2006, 371). This cross-cultural musical experience created by the Wagilak and the AAO reveal a unity and commitment expressed through the creative act: we are one, not rhetorically but in fact. CRB represents possibilities of transformative cultural renewal and vitalization that illuminates the past in the present together in unique experience that shapes the future.

IMPLICATIONS FOR ORGANIZATION AND LEADERSHIP

The AAO and Wagilak collaboration in CRB is an astounding approach of creative music making, capturing the diversity and engagement possible between Indigenous and non-Indigenous Australians. The collaborative artistic efforts of the AAO and Wagilak to absorb and breathe the inherent complexities of each other's' histories beyond mere superficial interaction offers compelling insights into the developing of personal relationships, languages, and understandings, from which deeper engagement can facilitate transformative change. The experiences of this collaboration offer much to understanding interpersonal relationships; the distribution of leadership, knowledge, and shared engagement in activity within communities of practice (Wegner, 1998), and of the developing of productive, collaborative conversations that potentially shift our own situated understandings of heritage and/or culture.

DISTRIBUTED LEADERSHIP

The dynamics within an improvised music collective compels the distribution of leadership (Brookes & Grint, 2010) and the evolving conceptualizations of the division of labor that develop through shared understandings (Timperley, 2005). Rather than the attribution of specific leadership roles or responsibilities to individuals, distributed leadership concerns the practice of leadership that is shared, collective, and extends leadership practice that builds the capacity for change and improvement.

In this highly creative, dynamic and productive setting, leaders' practice (both as thinking and activity) can be viewed as distributed across various situations of leadership that emerge and weave through interaction with other people, context and environment. In the CRB project we observe cross-cultural collaboration that organically evolves leadership practice as distributed, and conceptualized from within the organization. The CRB project offers critical reflection and comparison to current leadership practice and perspectives, challenging prevailing notions of shared experience, collaboration, and interactive discourse. Distributed leadership mobilizes leadership expertise at all levels within an organization that generates further opportunities for change and builds the capacity for improvement. Based on levels of trust, transparency, and mutual respect, the emphasis of distributed leadership is upon interdependent interaction and practice rather than individual and independent actions associated with those with formal leadership roles or responsibilities. (Leithwood, Mascall, & Strauss, 2009). We can draw from the CRB collaboration that organizational influence and decision-making is governed by the interaction of individuals rather than individual direction, privileging all perspectives and forms of knowledgeability (Wenger, 1998). Distributed leadership is about collective influence and shared knowledge and intelligences; it is not just some accidental by-product of high performing organizations, but rather is a contributor to organizational success and improved performance (Hargreaves, Boyle, & Harris, 2014). The implication revealed from this musical collaboration is that those in formal leadership roles have a key role to play in creating the conditions for distributed leadership to occur. They have to create the opportunities for others to flourish and lead.

DISTRIBUTED KNOWLEDGE

The CRB project reveals that through relationships we co-construct knowledge that facilitate the expansion of distributive cognition and organization (Harris, 2009; Spillane, Halverson, & Diamond, 2001, 2004). It opens a space within which we can reflect on the ways in which we have been made, and challenges us to reflect on the cultural conditions within which new self and social understandings might emerge. Distributing knowledge and leadership can nurture the active cultivation and development of leadership abilities within all. Distributed knowledge that is gained from purposeful and focused collaboration develops skills that are acquired and refined in context and draw directly on the personalized experiences of the organization. The distribution of knowledge can initiate innovation through a focus on action and culture building. Metacognitive strategizing beyond the individual that include shared regulatory processes constructively unite and align organizational thinking and connectivity (de Bruin 2016b; Hadwin, Järvelä, & Miller, 2011).

Effective learning from ongoing, dynamic, and shared knowledge production can propel an organization to powerful, transformative acts.

Shared knowledge and accountability in leadership holds the potential for the act of creating a sharing of visions and aims that facilitate a "fusion of horizons" in our educational organizations and communities of practice (Gadamer, 2006; Wenger, 1998).

DISTRIBUTED UNDERSTANDINGS

Exceptional organizational performance is not a random event, but is instead achieved through careful planning, design and "discipline" (Collins & Hansen, 2011). It requires organizational alignment, mutual understanding and flexibility, rather than rigidity, prescription or coercion. By engaging in dialogue with tradition on respectful and critical terms, we are positioned to examine our own prejudices that may be entwined with our situation. Discerning a reality of multiple perspectives, our situation gives us the possibility of grounding understanding and beginning the process of reaching greater understandings through dialogue. The ongoing evolving musical unification of the AAO and Wagilak encourages perspectives and possibilities beyond the short-term in producing meaningful and lasting collaborative practice.

This significant creative, organizational and artistic synergy between AAO and the Wagilak musicians compel us to continue to learn, adapt, and move toward more fundamental forms of collegiality and empowerment that are endemic within effective organizations. It challenges us to act critically to existing formalistic and constraining aspects of leadership and organizational practice. Such collaborations encourage us to explore knowledge-based networks both intra and interorganizational that expand concepts of affinity and connectivity.

For organizations seeking improved performance and better outcomes, the challenge is to create the conditions where professional knowledge and skills are enhanced, where effective leadership exists at all levels, and where all members feel valued and are working interdependently in the collective pursuit of better learner outcomes. The transformative collaborations of the AAO and Wagilak demonstrate that visionary leaders and the educational systems they create must facilitate fundamental change, not inhibit it. This profound musical collaboration reveals that through developing mutual understanding, trust in shared processes and a confluence of goals, transformative rewards can far exceed conventional practices and yields. As Michelangelo stated, "The great danger for most of us is not that our aim is too high and we miss it, but that it is too low and we reach it" (Isaacson, 2007, p. 106). It is time to set our sights higher.

NOTES

1. Recent accolades awarded to the AAO and Wagilak Group collaboration signify the importance of *CRB* as a part of jazz histories. These include: *Best Jazz Ensemble* 2010, Australian Bell Jazz Award; *Best Jazz Group* 2011, New York City Jazz Record.
2. The Wagilak clan (or *mala*'group') referred to is one particular patri-lineage within the greater Wagilak linguistic and cultural grouping. The *bapurru* (father's group) is descended directly from Sambo (Djambu) Barabara, whose *wananaraka* ('bone country'; clan estate) is at Ŋilipidji, South East Arnhem Land. The majority of this group currently reside in the town of Ngukurr, NT.
3. Yolngu society is divided into two moieties: Dhuwa and Yirritja. The Wagilak *manikay* series represents one of dozens of repertoires across Arnhem Land. While the songs tell of the foundation of the estate at Ŋilipidji and *wagilak* public law, the series ties into larger Dhuwa moiety narrative sequences, linking together related estates and clans, parliamentary ringitj (embassies) and sacred sites across the region in a complexity of intercultural relations.

REFERENCES

Australian Art Orchestra. (2016). *Homepage.* Retrieved from http://www.aao.com.au/about/

Brookes, S., & Grint, K. (2010). A new public leadership challenge? In S. Brookes, & K. Grint (Eds.), *The new public leadership challenge* (pp. 1–5). Basingstoke, England: Palgrave MacMillan.

Caruana, W., & Lendon, N. (1997). *The painters of the Wagilag Sisters story 1937–1997.* Canberra, Australia: National Gallery of Australia.

Collins, J., & Hansen, M. (2011). *Great by choice.* New York, NY: Harper Business Press.

Corn, A. 2002. *Dreamtime wisdom, modern-time vision: tradition and innovation in the popular band movement of Arnhem Land, Australia.* (Doctoral dissertation). University of Melbourne, Australia.

Curkpatrick, S. J. (2013). *Conversing tradition: Wägilak manikay 'song' and the Australian Art Orchestra's* Crossing Roper Bar (Doctoral thesis). Australian National University. Retrieved from http://static1.squarespace.com/static/53754972e4b000acb0692aca/t/53a8b66ce4b009ec0771d7fd/1403565676419/Samuel+Curkpatrick_Conversing+Tradition+Mar14.pdf

de Bruin, L. R. (2016a). *Expert practitioner voices: A phenomenological inquiry into teaching, learning, and collaborating in musical improvisation.* (Doctoral dissertation). Monash University, Melbourne, Australia.

de Bruin, L. R. (2016b) Expert voices in learning improvisation: shaping regulation processes through experiential influence. *Music Education Research Journal.* Retrieved from http://www.tandfonline.com/eprint/AE8UQqvAwKP86K9cnhna/full

Gadamer, H. G. (2006). *Truth and method.* London, England: Continuum.

Grabowsky, P. (2012, October). Comment: Art is a river. *The Monthly*. Retrieved January 25, 2013, from http://www.themonthly.com.au/comment-art-river-paul-grabowsky-6474

Hadwin, A. F., Järvelä, S., & Miller, M. (2011). Self-regulated, co-regulated, and socially shared regulation of learning. In J. Zimmerman & D. H. Schunk (Eds.) *Handbook of self-regulation of learning and performance* (pp. 65–84). New York, NY: Routledge.

Hargreaves, A., Boyle, A., & Harris, A. (2014). *Uplifting leadership*. San Francisco, CA: Jossey-Bass.

Harris, A. (2009). Distributed leadership and knowledge creation. In K. Leithwood, B. Mascall, & T. Strauss. (Eds.) *Distributed leadership according to the evidence* (pp. 253–266). New York, NY: Routledge.

Hicks, T. (2011). *The path to abstraction: a practice led investigation into the emergence of an abstract improvisation language.* (Master's dissertation). School of Music, Victorian College of the Arts and Music, The University of Melbourne, Australia.

Isaacson, L.S. (2007). *The principal's purpose: A practical guide to moral and ethical school leadership*. New York, NY: Eye on Education.

Leithwood, K., Mascall, B., & Strauss, T. (2009). *Distributed leadership according to the evidence*. London, England: Routledge.

Lewis, G. (2002). Improvised music after 1950: Afrological and eurological perspectives. *Black Music Research Journal 22*, 215–246.

McLaughlin, M. (2005, August 2). *Orchestra collaborates with top end musicians* (TV). Retrieved August 22, 2011, from http://www.abc.net.au/7.30/content/2005/s1428683.htm

Morphy, H., & Morphy, F. (2013). Anthropological theory and government policy in Australia's Northern Territory: The hegemony of the 'mainstream.' *American Anthropologist 115*(2), 174–187.

Saul, S. (2003). *Freedom is, freedom ain't: Jazz and the making of the sixties*. Cambridge, MA: Harvard University Press.

Spillane, J. P., Halverson, R., & Diamond, J. B. (2001, April 23–28). Investigating school leadership practice: A distributed perspective. *Educational Researcher*.

Spillane, J. P., Halverson, R., & Diamond, J. B. (2004). Towards a theory of leadership practice: A distributed perspective. *Journal of Curriculum Studies, 36*(1), 3–34.

Timperley, H. S. (2005). Distributed leadership: Developing theory from practice. *Journal of Curriculum Studies, 37*(4), 395–420.

Wenger, E. (1998). *Communities of practice: Learning, meaning, and identity*. Cambridge, England: Cambridge University Press.

Williams, N. (1986). *The Yolngu and their land: A system of land tenure and the fight for its recognition*. Stanford, CT: Stanford University Press.

Yunupingu, M. (1993). *Voices from the land*. Sydney, Australia: Australian Broadcasting Commission Books.

CHAPTER 8

TUPAC SHAKUR

A Lesson in Critical Reflection, Truth-Telling, and Advocacy

David E. DeMatthews and James Coviello
University of Texas, El Paso

Tupac Amaru Shakur (1971–1996) was an American rapper, actor, and poet born in East Harlem, New York. Foreshadowing his eventual political inclinations, Afeni Shakur named her son after Túpac Amaru II, a Peruvian revolutionary who led an Indigenous rights movement and uprising against the Spanish Empire in 1780. Afeni and a young Tupac moved frequently, going from East Harlem, to Baltimore, and finally settling in Marin City, California. Prison, Black revolutionaries, and the arts were the common elements that followed Tupac throughout these early formative years. In 1971, Afeni Shakur, a member of the Black Panther Party, was acquitted of more than 150 charges about one month before Tupac's birth. His godfather, Elmer "Geronimo" Pratt, was a high-ranking Black Panther who was convicted of murder. His stepfather, Mutulu Shakur, spent 4 years in prison after helping his sister, Assata Shakur (also known as Joanne Chesimard), escape from prison after being convicted of shooting a New Jersey State

Educational Leadership and Music, pages 79–89
Copyright © 2017 by Information Age Publishing

Trooper. Tupac, though, avoided these troubles in his youth. At age 12, he was cast in the play *A Raisin in the Sun* and performed at Harlem's famed Apollo Theater. When he moved to Baltimore, he enrolled in the Baltimore School for the Arts where he studied music, poetry, ballet, and dancing. There he began rapping and developed a lifelong friendship with (eventual) famed classmate Jada Pinkett Smith.

In 1991 at the age of 20, Tupac's professional music career began with the release of his first solo rap album, *2Pacalypse Now*. Over the next 5 years, he would release five more albums and act in critically acclaimed films like *Juice* (1992) and *Poetic Justice* (1993). At the time of his death, Tupac had appeared in four movies and released six albums. To date, he has now sold over 75 million records. Traces of Tupac's music and poetry can be found in the work of current mainstream rappers like Jay-Z, 50 Cent, and Kendrick Lamar. He is still one of the world's most recognized music artists and remains a cultural icon. Besides his immense commercial success, his racial and political commentary still resonates with youth and, increasingly, with scholars and social justice advocates around the world (Dyson, 2006).

The type of social unrest and political activism that was ongoing in the 1990s, when Tupac was at the height of his celebrity, would sound awfully familiar to the contemporary observer: infamous incidents of police brutality, turmoil in an economically depressed inner city, increasing recognition of inequities in marginalized communities, and pushback from established political elites. Both authors of this chapter grew up in the shadows of New York City during the late 1980s and 1990s and vividly recall numerous instances of police brutality. Tupac's music provoked his listeners to think deeply about race and class, especially during a time of provocative and incendiary events: the 1991 Crown Heights riots in New York; the beating of Rodney King and subsequent Los Angeles riots; the brutalization and sexual assault of Abner Louima by New York police officers; and the 1999 murder of Amadou Diallo, where police fired 41 shots at an innocent and unarmed man. In the current era of increasing civil rights agitation and the Black Lives Matter movement, which has been spurred on by the murders of Alton Sterling, Philandro Castille, Trayvon Martin, Eric Garner, Freddie Gray and the protests in Ferguson, Missouri and Baltimore, Maryland, the advocacy of an artist like Tupac rings tragically familiar. In one sense, his message is still fresh and strongly valid in the current political and social context; yet in another sense, there is a certain sadness that many of the issues he brought to light and so powerfully fought against have still not changed for the better.

DESCRIPTION AND BRIEF ANALYSIS OF WORK/IMPACT

It is difficult to encapsulate the total impact of Tupac's work. It can be controversial, vivid, and at times contradictory. His message was critical of White supremacy, a racist criminal justice system, and the endemic and structural poverty in urban Black communities across the United States. His music portrays "thug life" as glamorous, provocative, and hyper-masculine, but also desperate and self-destructive. Tupac initially described and defined thug life in multiple ways, including how young Black males felt life was hopeless and angry or as a term to describe maintaining a sense of pride and strength despite lacking opportunity and wealth. Tupac also used thug life as a backronym ("The Hate You Gave Little Infants F*** Every"), meaning that how the urban Black community is treated by society will negatively impact everyone in society. In a Los Angeles Times interview with reporter Chuck Philips (1995), Tupac said:

> I just wanted to rap about things that affected young black males. When I said that, I didn't know that I was gonna tie myself down to just take all the blunts and hits for all the young black males, to be the media's kicking post for young black males. I just figured since I lived that life I could do that, I could rap about that. (Phillips, 1995)

Tupac's words highlight a wholehearted desire to give voice to marginalized young Black males in American society and to depict their lived experiences.

While critics attacked Tupac's image and artistry before and beyond his death, fans and critical scholars attempt to make sense of the urgency, ferocity, and anger in his critique of society. Within the African American community and in war- and conflict-torn countries around the world, Tupac is regarded as a truth teller and poet. Youth and adults of all races throughout the world can draw important connections between their own personal or community struggles and Tupac's messages. Critical scholars recognize the power, relevance, and insightfulness of Tupac's critique as well as his lived experiences. Michael Eric Dyson (2006) notes, Tupac "spoke with brilliance and insight as someone who bears witness to the pain of those who would never have his platform" (p. 17).

When it was released, *2Pacalypse Now* generated significant controversy in the national media and in many political circles. Tupac's lyrics on that album were a social commentary on life in the inner city, where young African American men, women, and children were subjected to violence, brutalized by the police, and victimized by broken schools, poverty, gangs, and drugs. In one of his first solo hits, "Brenda's Got a Baby," Tupac delves deeply into this topic, describing a 12-year-old girl who lived in the ghetto, could not read, and was molested and impregnated by her cousin (Shakur,

1991). Brenda is scolded by her mother, runs away, and begins to sell drugs to survive. After being robbed and beaten, Brenda becomes a prostitute to earn money. She is ultimately murdered on the street, leaving her child an orphan. The cycle of poverty and pain continues.

Another track from *2Pacalypse Now*, "Trapped," focused on the impact of violence, police brutality, racial oppression, and mass incarceration. Tupac describes how feelings of anger and rage had built up in racially-segregated Black communities as a result of police brutality, leading to feelings of hopelessness and hyper-masculinity:

> Tired of being trapped in this vicious cycle
> If one more cop harasses me I just might go psycho
> And when I get them, I'll hit'em with the bum rush
> Only a lunatic would like to see his skull crushed
> Yo if you smart you'll really let me go "G"
> But keep me cooped up in this ghetto and catch the uzi,
> They got me trapped. (Shakur, 1991, track 2)

He would continue to explore various social, cultural, gender, and political issues in such songs as, "Keep Ya Head Up," "Unconditional Love," "Dear Momma," and "To Live and Die in L.A." These songs included dichotomous imagery of hope and hopelessness, violence and peace, Black love and melancholy, and materialism, sexism, and spirituality.

In 1993, Tupac released his second solo album, *Strictly 4 My N.I.G.G.A.Z.*, which included the track, "Keep Ya Head Up." In this socially conscious song, Tupac explores race and gender in a song dedicated to Latarsha Harlins, a 15-year-old girl killed by a Los Angeles shop owner (Williams, 2015). This song presents a multilayered analysis of racism and sexism while promoting the ideas of Black beauty, love, and feminism. He specifically calls upon men to treat women and children with love and respect: "And since we all came from a woman, Got our name from our women, I wonder why we take from our women, Why we rape our women, do we hate our women?" (Shakur, 1993, track 11). At the same time, Tupac recognizes the top-down oppression of U.S. society. In the second verse, he criticizes the hypocrisy of the U.S. government: "You know it's funny when it rains it pours, They got money for wars, but can't feed the poor." In the song's third verse, Tupac sends a message of hope to single mothers, recognizing the importance of their daily struggle to raise their children in a challenging situation. He says, "I know you're fed up ladies, but please, you gotta keep ya head up." Yet, not all of Tupac's songs are so socially conscious. On the same album he glorifies sexism in "I Get Around" and violence and revenge in "5 Deadly Venomz." Tupac's combination of songs on *Strictly 4 My N.I.G.G.A.Z* and other albums highlights his emphasis on various social ills as well as his complicated, dichotomous, and often conflicted artistry.

In his third album, *Me Against the World,* Tupac called for critical consciousness and hope in the face of life's difficulties:

The message I stress: to make it stop study your lessons, don't settle for less,
Even a genius asks his questions, be grateful for blessings
Don't ever change, keep your essence
The power is in the people and politics we address. (Shakur, 1995, track 3)

In what was perhaps his most commercially successful album, in 1996 Tupac released his fourth studio album titled *All Eyez on Me.* Although criticized for moving away from socially conscious topics, Tupac still found ways of weaving such topics in songs that appear more geared toward wider popular success. One of the more popular singles from that album, "How Do You Want It," revolves around sexually and violently explicit themes, yet Tupac still found a way to slip in brief references to politicians in his takedown of a critic: "Instead of tryin' to help a n**** you destroy a brother, Worse than the others, Bill Clinton, Mr. Bob Dole" (Shakur, 1996a, track 5). He later comments on his past issues with the establishment: "They wanna censor me, they'd rather see me in a cell, Livin' in hell, only a few of us'll live to tell." Although the album's overall tone was certainly less politically charged, Tupac had a unique ability to pepper even "radio friendly" songs with these types of themes.

Tupac's fifth album, *The Don Killuminati (The 7 Day Theory),* was written and recorded in the week following his release from federal prison. This was the first, though not the last, album to be released after his death. Coincidentally dark and emotional, the album's release date was pushed up after Tupac's murder in Las Vegas in September 1996. A less well-known (it is the 11th track on a 12-track album), but a no less impactful song from the album is "Hold Ya Head," a dark three-verse lament on the devastating effects of violence and the criminal justice system on young Black men. The chorus, sung in the style of a funeral hymn, pleads with the listener, asking, "How do we keep the music playing, How do we get ahead, Too many young Black brothers are dying, Living fast, too fast" (Shakur, 1996b, track 11). Over the course of his short career, Tupac also collaborated with other influential rappers and musicians, including Dr. Dre, Snoop Dogg, and K-Ci & Jo-Jo.

Twenty years later, these same themes of systemic injustice and violence are still relevant in today's political and social context. Tupac's career was cut short by legal problems, a prison sentence for sexual assault, and multiple shootings. On September 7, 1996, Tupac was shot and killed in a drive-by shooting after leaving a Mike Tyson fight in Las Vegas, Nevada. His death was less than 2 years after he was shot five times in the lobby of a New York recording studio. Incredibly, the immense popular success of Tupac's music continued after his death. Of his 10 studio albums, six were released after his death. Tupac had three albums that topped the *Billboard* charts after he died and more number one albums awarded after his death than when he was alive. His long and prolific posthumous career, including collaborations with Elton John, Eminem, Nas, Bone Thugs-n-Harmony, T.I., and Scarface (as well as his popularity), might have fueled a phenomenon similar to that of another popular music figure: Elvis Presley. Like Elvis, reported sightings of Tupac continued for years after his untimely death. The reasons are complex, but one reason might be the dearth of the kind of unique voices that Tupac provided in a genre that soon turned further away from these "songs-with-a-conscience." Regardless of the reason, the popularity of his music, even years after his death, is a testimony to the immense impact he had on the consciousness of U.S. popular culture.

Powerful political figures, angered by Tupac's music and message, sought to condemn what they considered to be vulgar, violent, and misogynistic lyrics. President George H. Bush, President Bill Clinton, Vice President Dan Quayle, Senator Bob Dole, former Secretary of Education Bill Bennett, and civil rights activist C. DeLores Tucker were just some of the leaders who believed Tupac's music should be censored and removed from the radio and record stores (Pareles, 1995). In 1992, Quayle even claimed that the *2Pacalypse Now* album was responsible for the death of a Texas state trooper because the murder suspect was allegedly listening to the album when he was pulled over (Broder, 1992). The trooper's family filed a lawsuit against Shakur claiming the album incited violence.

In spite of his detractors, Tupac's supporters and fans recognized the power of his work and artistry. His voice became the voice of an entire generation that had found truth in what he had spoken. For many wealthy and middle-class White adolescents, Tupac presented vivid imagery of a more complex, inequitable, and violent world. Tupac's notions of resistance and social commentary continue to resonate, having been adopted as topics of study at major universities such as Harvard University and the University of Arizona. For African American youth and those growing up in high-poverty urban communities, Tupac's work was partly a cathartic release of frustration with the status quo and provided a voice for their experiences. Numerous African American scholars have studied the meaning and impact of Tupac's work and how his lyrics have stimulated social and political thought as well as revolutionary behavior (Keeling, 1999). Internationally, Tupac's work has inspired millions of young and disenfranchised youth. In the 1990s, Tupac's work was widely popular in the Balkans and specifically Sarajevo and Kosovo, as the region was immersed in war, economic depression, and other sociopolitical challenges. His stature and impact continues to grow beyond his death, as Arnold (2006) notes:

Since his death, Tupac has become an international martyr, a symbol on the level of Bob Marley or Che Guevara, whose life has inspired Tupacistas on the streets of Brazil, memorial murals in the Bronx and Spain, and bandanna-wearing youth gangs in South Africa. (p. 79)

In Germany, a large statue of Tupac has been erected in front of a contemporary art museum. In a 2013 *National Public Radio* (NPR) interview, a Libyan-American rapper spoke about Tupac in Libya: "I think Tupac really represented struggle. He represented trying to come up out of your environment and be something bigger, exceeding expectations and, you know, that's something that all youth in Libya can relate to" (Martin, 2013).

LESSONS AND INSPIRATIONS

School leaders have a variety of responsibilities associated with administrative tasks, accountability, and testing while also ensuring schools are safe and orderly. However, organizational effectiveness and student learning outcomes are not sufficient leadership goals. There must be a larger, more socially conscious set of aims that school leaders adopt. The music and messages of Tupac Shakur serve as a clarion call for school leaders to adopt a critical stance toward injustice. "Tupac was angered by the political and economic system since it systematically hindered his community's progress. He wanted his people to recognize all of the injustices so they could break out of the negative cycle in the ghettos" (Iwamato, 2003, pp. 48–49). He was a student and voice of his community who understood the lived experiences of nonrecognition and cultural domination, the inequitable distribution of resources, and the lack of opportunities to participate in democracy, holding government accountable, and empowering people to feel that they have ownership over their lives. His critique centers on power asymmetry between his community and mainstream White America, and how injustice spreads through all aspects of community life. Tupac's commentary is reflective of other political philosophers and social justice scholars who conceptualize justice as "dismantling institutionalized obstacles that prevent some people from participating on a par with others, as full partners in social interaction" (Fraser, 2010, p. 16). This commentary and emphasis on social justice is central to school leaders and the roles they can play to support their schools and communities in addressing systemic injustices.

School leaders must understand the impact of systemic poverty, community violence, the school-to-prison pipeline, and other sociopolitical issues that plague marginalized communities. To do so, they must be critically reflective and identify not only internal problems (e.g., budget shortfalls, teacher shortages, run-down campuses in disrepair, limited classroom technology, segregated classrooms, Euro-centric curricula), but also out-side-of-school factors related to poverty, healthcare, housing, hunger, and employment (Berliner, 2013). Only by understanding these outside-of-school factors can school leaders recognize justice is not simply about nar-rowing achievement gaps, improving test scores, or creating more inclusive classrooms, but about empowering students, teachers, families, and com-munities to organize and act on the behalf of all children and the commu-nity as a whole (Anderson, 2009; DeMatthews, Edwards, & Rincones, 2016; Khalifa, 2012).

Almost 15 years ago, Larson and Murtadha suggested the field of ed-ucational leadership could learn a great deal from social justice leaders outside of education like Dr. Martin Luther King, Jr., Gloria Steinem, and Nelson Mandela. They acknowledged the field's failure to more deeply con-sider how social justice leadership outside of education "might enhance leadership theory and practice in education" (Larson & Murtadha, 2002, p. 150). By looking beyond schools and rejecting self-deceptive rational-izations about what principals can and cannot do, Larson and Murtadha pose an important question for social justice leadership in education: "A person should be able to enjoy good health, good nutrition, and adequate shelter. If school leaders recognized the importance of these capabilities to the education and development of children and families, what would they do?" (Larson & Murtadha, 2002, p. 154). Similarly, Tupac's work challenges dominant beliefs and advocates for comprehensive change, as well as pub-licly engages in candid discussions about race, ethnicity, social class, and other marginalization conditions.

Tupac's work also emphasizes themes of hope, love, and perseverance. These themes are also highly relevant to educational leaders and reflect what Anderson (2009) calls a "politicized notion of leadership ... that ac-knowledges that schools are sites of struggle over material and cultural resources and ideological commitments (Anderson, 2009, p. 13). Tupac's music prompts school leaders to act as public intellectuals and activists, re-think and reform organizational structures and curricula, model critical re-flection, and engage the community in public and candid discussions about the marginalizing conditions confronting their communities (Brooks, 2012). We conclude with four research-based actions for school leaders that reflect Tupac's critical commentary, social activism, hope, and love.

- School leaders must recognize various forms of oppression, engage in "problem-posing" activities, and challenge students, teachers, families, and communities to rethink what is stopping them from achieving their full potential (Freire, 2000). This must include an examination of seemingly race-neutral policies and practices, such as student discipline policies, special education identification and placement, and student advising (Beachum, Dentith, McCray, & Boyle, 2008; DeMatthews, 2016).

- School leaders must identify the untapped potential in their communities, access the cultural and community resources, and galvanize the community to act on behalf of the school and its students (Green & Gooden, 2014; Yosso, 2005).
- School leaders must challenge teachers to recognize their own implicit biases and engage in leadership practices that encourage both teachers and students to exercise their own agency and political power as citizens and lifelong learners (Anderson, 2009; Howard, 2003).
- School leaders must inspire the creation and adoption of culturally relevant curricula that provides a counternarrative to racism and other forms of discrimination that are rooted in student empowerment and the healthy development of identity (Beachum et al., 2008). This requires leaders to address broader cultural and political issues in their schools, including how teachers are treated, professional development opportunities, and the discourses around accountability, testing, and state-mandated curricula (Ylimaki, 2012).

In sum, Tupac's legacy is educative because his work highlighted a flawed, prejudiced, and unjust society. The ferocity and candor of his lyrics gave voice to disenfranchised people around the world and enabled millions to question the status quo of social, economic, cultural, and political injustice. For Tupac, education was a tool for awakening and bringing about social change, but also a tool for dreaming. School leaders must also recognize the injustices within their schools and communities, speak with candor and courage, and engage in advocacy and leadership actions that allow students to build a positive self-identity, dream bigger and bolder than before, and overcome whatever social, political, and economic challenges that lie ahead. Of course there are significant challenges for engaging in such leadership, but as Tupac notes, "If you can make it through the night, there's a brighter day" (Shakur, 1996, track 9).

REFERENCES

Anderson, G. L. (2009). *Advocacy leadership: Toward a post-reform agenda in education.* New York, NY: Routledge.

Arnold, E. (2006). From Azeem to Zion-I: The evolution of global consciousness in bay area hip hop. In D. Basu & S. J. Lemelle (Eds.), *The vinyl ain't final: Hip-hop and the globalization of Black popular culture* (pp. 71–84). London, England: Pluto Press.

Beachum, F. D., Dentith, A. M., McCray, C. R., & Boyle, T. M. (2008). Havens of hope or the killing fields: The paradox of leadership, pedagogy, and relationships in an urban middle school. *Urban Education, 43*(2), 189–215.

Berliner, D. (2013). Effects of inequality and poverty vs. teachers and schooling on America's youth. *Teachers College Record, 115*(12), 1–26.

Broder, J. (1992, September 23). Quayle calls for pulling rap album tied to murder case. *Los Angeles Times.* Retrieved from http://articles.latimes.com/1992-09-23/news/mn-1144_1_rap-album

Brooks, J. S. (2012). *Black school, White school: Racism and educational (mis) leadership.* New York, NY: Teachers College Press.

DeMatthews, D. E. (2016). Effective leadership is not enough: Critical approaches to closing the racial discipline gap. *The Clearing House: A Journal of Educational Strategies, Issues and Ideas, 89*(1), 7–13.

DeMatthews, D. E., Edwards, D. B., & Rincones, R. (2016). Social justice leadership and family engagement: A successful case from Ciudad Juárez, Mexico. *Educational Administration Quarterly.* doi: 0013161X16664006.

Dyson, M. E. (2006). *Holler if you hear me (2006).* New York, NY: Basic Books.

Fraser, N. (2010). *Scales of justice: Reimagining political space in a globalizing world.* New York, NY: Columbia University Press.

Freire, P. (2000). *Pedagogy of the oppressed.* New York, NY: Bloomsbury.

Green, T. L., & Gooden, M. A. (2014). Transforming out-of-school challenges into opportunities: Community schools reform in the urban Midwest. *Urban Education, 49*(8), 930–954.

Howard, T. C. (2003). Culturally relevant pedagogy: Ingredients for critical teacher reflection. *Theory Into Practice, 42*(3), 195–202.

Iwamoto, D. (2003). Tupac Shakur: Understanding the identity formation of hypermasculinity of a popular hip-hop artist. *The Black Scholar, 33*(2), 44–49.

Keeling, K. (1999). "A homegrown revolutionary"? Tupac Shakur and the legacy of the Black Panther Party. *The Black Scholar, 29*(2/3), 59–63.

Khalifa, M. (2012). A re-new-ed paradigm in successful urban school leadership principal as community leader. *Educational Administration Quarterly, 48*(3), 424–467.

Larson, C. L., & Murtadha, K. (2002). Leadership for social justice. *Yearbook of the National Society for the Study of Education, 101*(1), 134-161. doi:10.1111/j.1744-7984.2002.tb00007.x

Martin, M. (2013, March 20). Tupac encouraged the Arab Spring. *National Public Radio.* Retrieved from http://www.npr.org/2013/03/20/174839318/tupac-encouraged-the-arab-spring

Pareles, J. (1995, June 11). Rapping and politicking: Show time on the stump. *New York Times.* Retrieved by http://www.nytimes.com/1995/06/11/arts/pop-culture-view-rapping-and-politicking-show-time-on-the-stump.html

Philips, C. (1995, June 11). Tupac Shakur: I am not a gangster. *Los Angeles Times.* Retrieved from: http://www.latimes.com/local/la-me-tupac-qa-story.html

Shakur, T. (1991). "Trapped." On *2pacalypse now* [CD]. Santa Monica, CA: Interscope Records.

Shakur, T. (1993). "Keep ya head up." On *strictly 4 my n.i.g.g.a.z.* [CD]. Santa Monica, CA: Interscope Records.

Shakur, T. (1995). "Me against the world." On *me against the world* [CD]. Santa Monica, CA: Interscope Recoards.

Shakur, T. (1996a). "How do you want it." On *all eyez on me* [CD]. Los Angeles, CA: Death Row Records/Interscope Records.

Shakur, T. (1996b). "Hold ya head." On *the don killuminati (The 7 day theory)* [CD]. Los Angeles, CA: Interscope Records.

Williams, B. (2015, Jun 22). 7 Tupac songs that still resonate with Black America today. *Huffington Post*. Retrieved from: http://www.huffingtonpost.com/2015/06/16/tupac-songs-black-america_n_7596448.html

Ylimaki, R. M. (2012). Curriculum leadership in a conservative era. *Educational Administration Quarterly, 48*(2), 304–346.

Yosso, T. J. (2005). Whose culture has capital? A critical race theory discussion of community cultural wealth. *Race, Ethnicity and Education, 8*(1), 69–91.

CHAPTER 9

INSIGHTS FROM THE FLOW OF THE TEACHA'

Considering Hip-Hop in Education

Sean Dickerson, Omar J. Salaam, and Adrian Anthony
University of South Florida, Tampa

The popularity of hip-hop culture and its influence on varying aspects of society cannot be ignored, especially when considering the multiplicitous facets of youth culture. According to a survey of youth culture by Cohen, Celestine-Michener, Holmes, Merseth, and Ralph (2007), 58% of Black, 45% of Hispanic, and 23% of White youth listen to rap music every day. When considering the percentage of youth who report listening to "some" rap music, Cohen et al. (2007) found the numbers to be 97%, 88%, and 81%, respectively. With so much attention given to a specific component of youth culture, there is little wonder why scholars have increasingly sought out spaces for hip-hop in education as "a line of flight" (Wallin, 2010, p. 2) from hegemonic Eurocentric models of curriculum and pedagogy. The Eurocentric perspective centers and therefore privileges whiteness at the expense of other cultures "to protect White privilege and advantage in education, economics, politics, and so forth" (Asante, 1991, p. 171). Those who

Educational Leadership and Music, pages 91–100

ascribe to the Eurocentric paradigm may not value the creation of space for hip-hop in education.

The divergence of opinions on how to best utilize educational space continues. As such, school educational leaders in urban environments are consistently being asked to balance competing demands from various interested parties (i.e., parents, teachers, communities, special interest groups, districts, states, and the federal government). Meanwhile, schools continue to promote a Eurocentric curriculum that often fails to connect to students' cultures and identities (Kim & Pulido, 2015; Serpell, Hayling, Stevenson, & Kern, 2009). Further, school disciplinary policies (i.e., zero tolerance) and the application of harsher disciplinary penalties for those students already on the margins of school culture—Black and Brown students in particular—only seem to exacerbate the school and student disconnect by the strengthening of the school-to-prison pipeline (Giroux, 2003; Hall & Karanxha, 2012; Losen & Skiba, 2010; Rocque & Paternoster, 2011). In order to disrupt many of the negative linkages between schools and students, researchers and practitioners (see Ballingall, 2016; Emdin, 2009; Hill, 2009; Khalifa, 2013; McNeil, 2016; Morrell & Duncan-Andrade, 2002; Stovall, 2006) call for the creation of a space for hip-hop culture within educational contexts.

School leaders are uniquely positioned to influence the creation of space for students to deterritorialize and break away from Eurocentric paradigms of being, by using various forms of hip-hop culture. Khalifia (2013) found principals to be in the best position to implement and oversee changes in how schools forge an inclusive culture. In working toward an objective of disrupting inequities for students considered to be on the margins (Theoharis, 2010), leaders who choose to include hip-hop as a line of flight from hegemonic curriculum and pedagogy should be sound in their own decision for choosing to include hip-hop culture. As it stands, students who embrace the cultural identity of hip-hop are often seen as at odds with mainstream discourse. This discourse, oftentimes, perceives hip-hop culture as disruptive, anti-intellectual, and befitting only for leisure, among other negative correlations (Akom, 2009; Prier & Beachum, 2008; Williams, 2008). In urban school communities where students are more likely to identify with hip-hop culture, school leaders face the challenge of creating educational space for hip-hop with a teacher population that may not identify with and/or relate to the culture.

The purpose of this chapter is to analyze the work of Lawrence Kris "KRS One" Parker, also known as the Teacha' and connect his insights to the work of educational leaders. A hip-hop icon and leader of multiple socially conscious movements within hip-hop, KRS One's knowledge and experience in forging lines of flight from dominant ideologies across hip-hop can serve as a guide for educational leaders. We give particular attention to his lyrics on the track "Hip-Hop Knowledge" (KRS One, 2001). The reflective rap song examines and chronicles KRS One's lines of flight as an artist, a leader, and an activist within the hip-hop movement. Seeking best-case academic and socioemotional outcomes for all of their students, school leaders may find themselves navigating similar lines of flight at different points in their respective careers. As such, insights from the Teacha' may help school leaders determine a trajectory in activating a line of flight from the hegemonic Eurocentric model of education in order to connect schools with students and students with schools. Here we neither demand nor defend the decision of school leadership in utilizing hip-hop in educational spaces. Instead, our overall aim is to encourage leaders to purposefully interrogate their own meanings for considering hip-hop in school.

This chapter begins with an examination of how KRS One answered the initial call for change to the crisis surrounding hip-hop in the later part of the 1980s. We then consider the notion of inclusivity as it relates to the personal affinity of school leaders' own perspective of hip-hop. Lastly, we articulate what school leaders can learn from the Teacha' as they consider creating a line of flight from the hegemonic Eurocentric model of curriculum and pedagogy.

ANSWERING THE CALL

As an artist, KRS One (knowledge reigns supreme over nearly everyone) came onto the hip-hop scene as a battle rapper in the South Bronx area of New York in the early to mid-1980s. While traversing between the streets and homeless shelters of the city, he met social worker and deejay, Scott "DJ Scott La Rock" Sterling (Parker, 2009). They hit it off immediately and soon formed the hip-hop group Boogie Down Productions (BDP). KRS One and La Rock released their first album, *Criminal Minded* in 1987. The album was a representation of urban environments during the 1980s wherein economic opportunities were scarce and poverty, drugs, and violence were in abundance.

Despite the fact that as a neophyte to the rap game KRS One wanted to interject "a line of flight" from the established narrative of rap music, he admittedly felt the pressure to conform. His early lyrical flow had flashes of the socially conscious perspective, but the dominant narrative of aggrandizing capitalism, belittling fellow African Americans, and otherwise denigrating already marginalized groups of people could also be heard on BDP's first album. Further, when sharing details about the making of "Stop the Violence: Overcoming Self Destruction," a hit song found on BDP's second album, KRS One stated,

> What most people don't know is that Scott co-wrote ["Stop the Violence"] with me, but we just didn't get a chance to put it out because the industry wanted rap artists to say "Yo man" and all that other sh—. (George, 1990, p. 33)

Unfortunately, most people do not know about the contributions of Scott La Rock on "Stop the Violence" because he was shot and killed on August 27, 1987.

During a concert at the Nassau Coliseum on September 10, 1987 where KRS One was one of the performers along with Kool Moe Dee and Doug E. Fresh, several concert attendees were robbed and stabbed and one man died as a result of his injuries (George, 1990). This melee prompted rap music and artists to be denigrated by society at large due to the underlying bravado and glorification of nihilistic behaviors found in rap music and videos. Soon after, a call went out to move hip-hop culture beyond the territorial reach of the dominant narrative encompassing hip-hop.

Reflecting on this tumultuous period of time over the track "Hip-Hop Knowledge" (KRS One, 2001), KRS One flows, "The call of the order was to avoid the slaughter...in 1988 there was no debate, we had to end the hate. The name of the game was stop the violence and unity, knowledge and self-reliance." Although the deaths of both DJ Scott La Rock and the concert attendee were a result of a larger crisis in urban America, this marked a shift in how KRS One thought about the influence of hip-hop in society as a whole. To answer the call of the order, KRS One made a shift from being a hip-hop artist to an artist-leader of what would become known as the Stop the Violence Movement. A highlight of the movement was the collaborative song "Self Destruction" featuring 14 prominent hip-hop artists. However, answering the call came at some cost to KRS One as he began to experience external pressure, namely the "sting of a more powerful corporation manipulating and trying to hold its space in the music industry by pushing us little guys around" (Murphy, 2012, p. 33), and the internal sting from other hip-hop artists who did not see the value of the movement.

In creating the title song for the movement, record industry executives forbade the artists signed to their label from performing on the song. Executives went as far as threatening artists who went against the corporate call with dropping them from the label (Murphy, 2012). Some artists acquiesced to the call of record companies—Run DMC, according to KRS One, was told by Def Jam executives not to participate—while others like LL Cool J, given a similar directive from the same record label, stood with KRS One and recorded their contributions to the movement despite the potential personal consequences to the artists' own career (Murphy, 2012). In addition to the overarching corporate battle with the movement, there was also an internal battle within the hip-hop community. The Teacha' summarized this conflict on "Hip-Hop Knowledge" as follows:

We tried to talk about the state of humanity but all these other rappers got mad at me. They called me Captain Human, another message was sent, Self Destruction don't pay the f__kin rent. Remember that? Nobody wanted conscious rap. It was like, where these ballers at? Where can they call us at? All was wack. Hip-hop culture was fallin flat and that was that.

Working to publicize a line of flight back to hip-hop's more foundational component of socially conscious critiques aimed at sociopolitical conditions, KRS One felt the dismissive and exclusionary attitude from within the hip-hop culture by his peers in lieu of the more widely accepted destructive model of hip-hop.

In an attempt to accede to his peers, KRS One put out rap music that was considered contradictory to his movement for hip-hop to become more socially conscious. Recording a remixed version of "Step Into A World" with Sean "Puff Daddy" Combs—who was for a time considered the face of commercialized hip-hop in pursuit of profits—KRS One was considered to be a contradiction to that which he once condemned, hip-hop culture (Hamilton, 2007). The backlash received by the Teacha' left him contemplating his role in creating a line of flight from the prevailing narrative territorializing the hip-hop industry that held concerns of profits over the development of people.

YOU LIKE IT CAUSE YOU CHOOSE IT

Foundational elements of hip-hop are steeped in critical discourse in an effort to speak truth to power and call attention to substandard and inequitable conditions found in many urban communities. The Teacha' considers nine elements inclusive of hip-hop culture: break dancing, emceeing, graffiti art, deejaying, beatboxing, street fashion, street language, street knowledge, and street entrepreneurialism (KRS One, 2001). While many incorrectly confuse rap music and hip-hop as synonymous, rap music is only one component of hip-hop culture. Rap music, one of the first expressions of hip-hop culture during the early 1970s, is expressive storytelling spoken with syncopated rhythms in a poetic manner (Ginwright, 2004). This provided the connection between the words of those leading the empowerment of African Americans to African American youth being inspired to speak those words into the content of hip-hop culture. To explain, when KRS One states that he is "not White or Red or Black, [but] Brown and from the Boogie Down" (Parker, 1988), he further clarifies that he is definitely speaking to the experiences of African Americans whether described as the physical color of black or brown.

Personal affinity toward specific aspects of culture and knowledge, places emphasis on what those in decision-making roles view as valuable. KRS One's own affinity toward unity, knowledge, and self-reliance through incorporation of different philosophies into his world of hip-hop is exhibited through his lyrics, speeches, and writings (see *The Science of Rap* (1995), *Ruminations* (2003), and *The Gospel of Hip-hop: First Instrument* (2013). KRS One's most popular lyrical expression of his philosophy is contained in the song "My Philosophy" and is on the second album from BDP, *By Any Means Necessary* (1988). Moreover, in "Hip-Hop Knowledge," the Teacha' further points out the influence of philosophy with the flow: "Started studying philosophy full-time. To have a full heart, full body, full mind." Understanding KRS One's affinity toward studying life from a philosophical perspective that encourages self-development, there is little wonder why his body of work is dominated by socially conscious critiques. He likes it, because he chooses it.

However, choosing a particular form of hip-hop to include in an educational space can create the perception of excluding other aspects of the same culture, for better or worse. No different than the selection of KRS One for the development of this chapter, the affinity of the authors toward issues of social justice in and outside of the educational space places underlining values above that of other hip-hop elements. In this case, personal affinity toward socially conscious rap music leaves other aspects of hip-hop culture outside these pages. School leaders considering using elements of hip-hop to find culturally relevant connections may find themselves examining similar concerns of inclusion and exclusion when faced with the demands of meeting students in a common space.

LEARNING FROM THE INSIGHTS

Being a school leader is part artistry (Cranston & Kusanovich, 2014; Kaimal, Drescher, Fairbank, Gonzaga, & White, 2014). Creating solutions to long-standing problems in communities that feel pushed to the margins or have taken the blame for general societal shortcomings can take more than following every procedure as written, if it is indeed written. The call for leaders to be flexible in how they approach the context of the communities they serve advances priorities that may not be the same for every school. Therefore, solutions to the issues of the community may fall into that of unconventional when compared against other solutions to similar problems. A lack of connection between schools and students is not a new problem that has only recently made itself known to those interested in the issue. As student populations become more diverse and teacher/administrator bodies remain nonreflective of the ongoing changes, cultural connectivity will remain a concern for educators, students, parents, and communities (Amatea, 2009; NCES, 2011). The solution may come from a leaders' ability to create space where others may not be able to see the vision. As exemplified by the Teacha', leaders moving to a more inclusive approach may not be well-received by their colleagues, but they should stand strong in their convictions.

Research suggests that school leaders should take a more active role in creating community collaboration that not only improves outcomes for students, but also improves outcomes for the community (Brown & Beckett, 2007; Khalifa, 2012). As KRS One gleaned from the Stop the Violence Movement, it was easy for the existing structure (record industry) to single out artists with threats of dropping them from the label if they participated in the making of the song "Self Destruction." Additionally, conflict can arise from within the peer group of leaders for reasons that can range from disbelief that youth culture has value in the educational space to potential inabilities of key personnel to manage and oversee a new line of flight from the traditional model.

In this light, usage of each of the aforementioned nine elements of hip-hop may not be useful in everyday instruction. School leaders looking to be inclusive are faced with the challenge of determining what is and is not included in this new space. Placing emphasis on determining which aspects of hip-hop culture should or should not be included in educational spaces offers an opportunity for not only clarity on the part of the leader, but teachers and students can understand the parameters of this new educational space. Although the establishment of parameters to inclusivity by the school leader does not equate agreement for neither teachers nor students, it does offer a framed space to have critical dialogue on what it means to be inclusive. From the perspective of the Teacha', not every aspect of the nine elements of hip-hop culture has value in uplifting those it reaches.

Furthermore, while not every instructional staff member is likely to have familiarity with hip-hop culture, professional development centered in the topic will provide an opportunity to familiarize all staff with a better understanding of hip-hop culture and its validity in regards to its usage in education (Irby, Hall, & Hill, 2013). All instructional staff have a familiarity with Eurocentric lines of thinking in regards to education based on its historical usage in America. Instructional staff members who have reached the minimum requirement of achieving a bachelor's degree in education have experienced enough success within the Eurocentric curriculum that their methods of teaching are in line with the dominant practices. In order to teach from the aspect of another culture, an understanding of that culture must be at the roots of instructional development resulting from professional development. In so doing, it must be also understood that this should not be viewed as a transition from Eurocentric paradigms into hip-hop culture, but a blurring of the lines between the two with a respect for both. As the Teacha' explains, "When one doesn't learn about the other ones culture, ignorance swoops down just like a vulture" (KRS One, 1989).

In this case, teachers who want to engage and connect with students should look to learn about youth culture that is relevant to them (Sealey-Ruiz & Greene, 2011). Each culture affects the other in various ways, which should be analyzed within professional development sessions among instructional staff as well as during instruction when teachers are working with students.

Regardless of instruction being from a Eurocentric viewpoint or with the usage of hip-hop culture, involvement of student's viewpoints adds to the validity of instruction. Students must not feel they are being patronized. Connecting with students where they are is of the utmost importance and the best way to make sure of doing so is to directly engage students with their views on the topics at hand in class daily (Milner, 2010). Staff members who do not feel an intimate connection with hip-hop culture must be honest with that fact when attempting to integrate hip-hop culture into their lessons. These teachers must directly engage with staff members with an understanding of hip-hop culture to foster a better connection with the culture and just as importantly make efforts to directly connect with students as an interest is shown in better understanding their culture. In the end, there will be some teachers that students view as not having an understanding of where they come from or the experiences they have in daily life outside of school. But for those same students to be aware that those same teachers have made an effort to better understand them and their culture will bring more connectivity between schools and students. The hope is that this evolution or line of flight from the traditional model enables schools and students to better connect within the educational space and thus enable schools to answer the call for more relevant connections in education going forward.

Although not a guarantee of success—in this case cultural connectivity—an insight from the Teacha' is that a movement is stronger with collaboration than it is for those that go at it alone. School leaders considering hip-hop in education can benefit from creating a collaboration among teachers and administrators that support hip-hop culture as a line of flight from the Eurocentric curriculum and pedagogy model. While the effort can be put forth on the strength of one, a collaborative approach offers support and space for improvements to be made in making a culturally relevant connection. With so many elements to consider, our intent is not to discourage school leaders from using hip-hop culture in their schools, but to encourage leaders who are considering hip-hop in education to do as the Teacha' has done: utilize knowledge in hip-hop to spark collaborative movement toward cultural connections.

REFERENCES

Akom, A. A. (2009). Critical hip-hop pedagogy as a form of liberatory praxis. *Equity & Excellence in Education, 42*(1), 52–66.

Amatea, E. (2009). *Building culturally responsive family-school relationships.* Boston, MA: Allyn & Bacon.

Asante, M. K. (1991). The Afrocentric idea in education. *The Journal of Negro Education, 60*(2), 170–180.

Ballingall, A. (2016, September 6). Hip-hop education turns young rapper into a science genius. *The Star.* Retrieved from https://www.thestar.com/news/gta/2016/09/06/hip–hop-education-turns-young-rapper-into-a-science-genius.html

Brown, L. H., & Beckett, K. S. (2007). Building community in an urban school district: A case study of African American educational leadership. *The School Community Journal, 17*(1), 7–32.

Cohen, C. J., Celestine-Michener, J., Holmes, C., Mereseth, J. L., & Ralph, L. (2007). *The attitudes and behavior of young Black Americans: Research summary.* Chicago, IL: University of Chicago Center for the Study of Race, Politics, and Culture.

Cranston, J., & Kusanovich, K. (2014). More drama in school leadership: Developing creative and ethical capacities in the next generation of school leaders. *Canadian Journal of Educational Administration and Policy, 151,* 1–33.

Emdin, C. (2009). *Urban science education for the hip-hop generation.* Rotterdam, The Netherlands: Sense.

George, N. (1990). *Stop the violence: Overcoming self-destruction.* New York, NY: Pantheon Books.

Ginwright, S. A. (2004). *Black in school: Afrocentric reform, urban youth & the promise of hip–hop culture.* New York, NY: Teachers College Press.

Giroux, H. A. (2003). Racial injustice and disposable youth in the age of zero tolerance. *Qualitative Studies in Education, 16*(4), 553–565.

Hall, E., & Karanxha, Z. (2012). School today, jail tomorrow: The impact of zero tolerance on the over-representation of minority youth in juvenile system. *PowerPlay, 4*(1), 2–30.

Hamilton, P. (2007, May 24). *Lessons from the Teacha KRS-One educates.* Retrieved from http://exclaim.ca/music/article/lessons_from_teacha_krs-one_educates

Hill, M. L. (2006). Using Jay-Z to reflect on post-9/11 race relations. *The English Journal, 96*(2), 23–27.

Irby, D. J., Hall, H. B., & Hill, M. L. (2013). Schooling teachers, schooling ourselves: Insights and reflections from teaching K–12 teachers how to use hip-hop to educate students. *International Journal of Multicultural Education, 15*(1), 1–18.

Kaimal, G., Drescher, J., Fairbank, H., Gonzaga, A., & White, G. (2014). Inspiring creativity in urban school leaders: Lessons from the performing arts. *International Journal of Education & the Arts, 15*(4), 2–22.

Khalifa, M. (2012). A re-new-ed paradigm in successful urban school leadership. Principal as community leader. *Educational Administration Quarterly, 48*(3), 424–467.

Khalifa, M. (2013). Creating spaces for urban youth: The emergence of culturally responsive (hip-hop) school leadership and pedagogy. *Multicultural Learning and Teaching, 8*(2), 63–93.

Kim, J., & Pulido, I. (2015). Examining hip-hop as culturally relevant pedagogy. *Journal of Curriculum and Pedagogy, 12*(1), 17–35.

KRS One. (1989). You must learn. On *Ghetto music: The blueprint of hip-hop* [CD]. New York, NY: Jive Records.

KRS One. (2001). Hip-hop knowledge. On *The sneak attack* [CD]. New York, NY: Entertainment One Music.

Losen, D., & Skiba, R. (2010). *Suspended education: Urban middle schools in crisis.* Montgomery, AL: Southern Poverty Law Center.

McNeil, E. (2016, June 20). English teacher's hip-hop curriculum gets students writing. *Education Week.* Retrieved from: http://www.edweek.org/tm/articles/2016/06/20/english-teachers-hip-hop-curriculum-gets-students-writing.html

Milner, H. R., IV (2010). *Start where you are, but don't stay there: Understanding diversity, opportunity gaps, and teaching in today's classrooms.* Cambridge, MA: Harvard Education Press.

Morrell, E., & Duncan-Andrade, J. M. R. (2002). Promoting academic literacy with urban youth through engaging hip-hop culture. *The English Journal, 91*(6), 88–92.

Murphy, K. (2012, March 29). *Full clip: KRS One runs down his catalogue ft. BDP, Run-DMC, LL, DJ Premier, Diddy, Nelly and more.* Retrieved from http://www.vibe.com/2012/02/full-clip-krs-one-runs-down-his-catalogue-ft-bdp-run-dmc-ll-dj-premier-diddy-nelly-and/self-destruction/

National Center for Educational Statistics (NCES). (2011, April). *Digest of education statistics, 2010.* Retrieved from http://nces.ed.gov/pubs2011/2011015_2a.pdf

Parker, K. (1988). My philosophy [Recorded by Boogie Down Productions]. On *By all means necessary* [CD]. New York, NY: Jive/RCA Records.

Parker, K. (2009, February 19). *KRS One: "I am hip-hop."* Retrieved from http://www.krsone.biz/BIOGRAPHY.html

Prier, D., & Beachum, F. (2008). Conceptualizing a critical discourse around hip-hop culture and Black male youth in educational scholarship and research. *International Journal of Qualitative Studies in Education, 21*(5), 519–535 doi:10.1080/09518390802297805

Rocque, M., & Paternoster, R. (2011). Understanding the antecedents of the "school-to-jail" link: The relationship between race and school discipline. *Journal of Criminal Law and Criminology, 101*(2), 633–666.

Sealey-Ruiz, Y., & Greene, P. (2011). Embracing urban youth culture in the context of education. *Urban Review, 43,* 339–357.

Serpell, Z., Hayling, C. C., Stevenson, H., & Kern, L. (2009). Cultural considerations in the development of school-based interventions for African American adolescent boys with emotional and behavioral disorders. *The Journal of Negro Education, 78*(3), 321–332.

Stovall, D. (2006). We can relate: Hip-hop culture, critical pedagogy, and the secondary classroom. *Urban Education, 41*(6), 585–602.

Theoharis, G. (2010). Disrupting injustice: Principals narrate the strategies they use to improve their schools and advance social justice. *Teachers College Record, 112*(1), 331–373.

Wallin, J. J. (2010). *A Deleuzian approach to curriculum: Essays on a pedagogical life.* New York, NY: Palgrave Macmillan.

Williams, A. D. (2008). The critical cultural cypher: Remaking Paulo Freire's cultural circles using hip-hop culture. *International Journal of Critical Pedagogy, 2*(1), 1–29.

CHAPTER 10

THE LEADERSHIP IDENTITY DILEMMA

Franz Schubert and *Winterreise*

Lisa Catherine Ehrich
Queensland University of Technology

Fenwick W. English
University of North Carolina at Chapel Hill

Most leaders face the problem of establishing their own identities as unique in their age and context. Standing apart from other potential leaders of their times is especially a problem with political leaders who are often competing for the same followers or sponsors (Gardner, 1995). Musicians, composers, artists and poets also face the problem of identity. If contemporaries are well-established and have built up large reputations, the search for a unique identity can be daunting. A leader cannot afford to live in the shadow of a contemporary rival or colleague and expect to find lasting recognition. It is the same with poets, musicians, philosophers, and composers.

Educational Leadership and Music, pages 101–114
Copyright © 2017 by Information Age Publishing
All rights of reproduction in any form reserved.

One of the best known works dealing with the problem of identity and influence in the arts is Harold Bloom's (1973, 1997) classic *The Anxiety of Influence: A Theory of Poetry.* In this work Bloom posits that every established poet has to first be inspired by and then distance himself/herself from the individuals who had originally inspired them.

This chapter is about the case of the Austrian composer, Franz Schubert (1797–1828). Schubert lived and worked at the same time as Beethoven. If he had not found a way to dissociate his work from Beethoven, he would not be considered "the greatest song composer in history" (Kapilow, 2011, p. 117) nor would he be considered one of the greatest composers of all time. His output was prolific as he produced more than 600 songs, nine symphonies, 35 chamber works, six masses, 17 operas, 22 sonatas for piano, and hundreds of piano pieces (Kapilow, 2011, p. 118) during his 31 years of life.

This chapter will begin by introducing Schubert, his life, and the broader context in which he developed his music. It then identifies some of his greatest pieces of music and discusses more fully the *Winterreise* (Winter Journey), a set of 24 songs by Schubert set to the poems of Wilhelm Müller. The final part of the chapter draws lessons and inspirations from the life of Schubert for contemporary educational leaders. Here we apply ideas from Harold Bloom's (1973, 1997) *The Anxiety of Influence* thesis to understand how Schubert carved out a distinctive place for himself and his music in a context and age of musical composition unparalleled in the Western landscape. Of critical importance was the relationship between Schubert and Beethoven. Bloom's central ideas are then considered in relation to the struggles school leaders face as they are influenced by their predecessors yet strive to make their own way within their professional field. The chapter concludes with a return to the themes within the *Winterreise* by drawing parallels between the winter journey and the school leadership identity journey. It also comments upon the ability of great leaders to connect to potential followers by appealing to familiar themes and metaphors in their lives (Gardner, 1995). Of particular importance in this regard is Schubert's pragmatic combination of what may be thought of as "high" and "low" art. Schubert's pragmatism was aimed at the total human experience, for as Schusterman (2000) notes, "For anything to have human value, it must in some way serve the needs and enhance the life and development of the human organism in coping with her environing world" (p. 9). One of Schubert's gifts was his ability to transcend these cultural differentiations because his music as art "keeps alive the power to experience the common world in its fullness" (Dewey, 1987, p. 138).

OVERVIEW, LIFE, AND TIMES OF FRANZ SCHUBERT

Franz Schubert was born in 1797 in Vienna and lived there most of his short life. He was said to have inherited from his father a great love of music, and an artistic spirit/disposition from his mother. His father was a school teacher and gave his son, Franz, and his other children a solid musical education (Bevan, 1998). A turning point in Schubert's education occurred in 1808 when he was selected to attend the exclusive Imperial and Royal Seminary due to his singing prowess and musical knowledge. It was here that he received a well-rounded education (Baker, 1997) as well as advanced musical lessons that enabled him to nurture his great talent (Woodford, 1978). He stayed at the seminary for 5 years, after which time he moved back to the family home. On his father's recommendation, he attended teacher training college and taught for a couple of years in his father's school. During his early years as a teacher, he composed many musical works and also mixed with a close circle of friends (Woodford, 1978). After a couple of years of teaching, Schubert left the profession for good and concentrated on music. He worked as a composer and musician, and was supported (both emotionally and at times financially) by close friends. Unlike so many of his peers, Schubert was considered one of the first "freelance" composers; other composers were employed by the church or had wealthy patrons (Bostridge, 2015, xi). Although Woodford (1978) says that Schubert received little public recognition of his genius during his life (except by his close circle of friends), Bostridge (2015) claims Schubert's music was well-known, performed by great instrumentalists of the day, and second only to Rossini in popularity.

The period of time in which Schubert lived was one of significant economic and political turmoil (Great Composers, 1989). During his lifetime, Schubert witnessed the ideals of the French Revolution (1788–1799) and the Napoleonic wars that saw Austria at war with France. Napoleon Bonaparte occupied Vienna in 1805 and 1809. While Austria was viewed as a relatively stable country by 1815, a police state was enforced in 1819 that meant heavy censorship of books, words, and music. In 1820, Schubert and some of his friends were arrested for suspected revolutionary activity, but all were released except for one member of the group who was imprisoned and then exiled. Apart from this incident, Schubert managed to be largely unaffected by the wider political activities within Vienna (Woodford, 1978) and reaped the benefits of living in a city that was considered the center of music in Europe. Music could be heard in homes where many families owned a piano or other instruments, in the streets, in inns, and in coffeehouses. A very high standard of music was performed in salons to an intimate audience, and this is where Schubert performed some of his music. Vienna was also the home to other well-known and respected composers such as Beethoven and Haydn, both of whom were influential in his development (Woodford, 1978).

Schubert was said to have contacted a serious illness around early 1823. It is generally agreed that this disease was syphilis (Bevan, 1998, p.244). Between 1823 to the end of his life in 1828, he spent time in a hospital where mercury was used to treat this complaint. While it alleviated some symptoms, it also had a lot of side effects. Schubert was also said to have suffered from depression for more than 10 years, and this worsened at the height of his illness and its treatment (Bevan, 1998). According to Bevan (1998), Schubert's health deteriorated significantly during the last 2 years of his life. In letters he wrote to friends, he mentioned physical pain and feelings of weakness. Bevan explained this as Schubert had entered into the tertiary phase of the disease where there is "formation of tumours under the skin... also structural damage to bones, eyes, main arteries, the brain and locomotor nerves" (p. 246). It was in 1827 that Schubert completed the *Winterreise*. Bevan (1998) says that the piece probably gave an insight into his state of mind. Yet later in 1827, he composed instrumental music: *Impromptus D899* and *D935* and the *E flat piano trio D929*—all of these pieces showed little if any evidence of depression (Bevan 1998, p. 258). Bevan claims that during Schubert's last year of life (1828) even with continued symptoms of pain, giddiness, headaches, depression, and gastritis, he composed an enormous body of work. He was said to have composed music up until a couple of days before he died (Bevan, 1998).

DESCRIPTION OF GREATEST WORKS

> *Schubert's importance as a composer lies, in the end,*
> *in the irreducible magnificence and humanity of his music.*
> —Bostridge, 2015, p. 477

While Schubert's music straddles the Classical and Romantic periods, it has been described as quintessentially "human" (Great Composers, 1989, p. 109) since it expresses with sensitivity and poignancy a huge range of emotions. Gammond (1987, p. 126) described Schubert's music as

> melodious yet deeply expressive songs... There was a warm, even sentimental, side to this artist that endears his music to many: yet there are also darker shadows, as in the *Death and Maiden String Quartet* and the *Unfinished Symphony*.

According to Andras Schiff (1998), concert pianist and performer of Schubert's work, "Schubert's piano sonatas are unquestionably among the most sublime works ever written for the instrument" (p. 191). Schiff has only praise for Schubert's music when he says,

> In Schubert's music melody, harmony and rhythm co-exist in perfect equilibrium (p.197) . . . As a melodist, Schubert is in a class of his own. Endless melodies seem to burst out of his creative genius. Someone who has spent most of his life writing for the human voice will always think vocally, even when the music is purely instrumental . . . Schubert's treatment of harmony is miraculous, and he is the greatest master of modulations. (Schiff, 1998, p. 204)

Noteworthy is the point that while Schubert was incredibly gifted as a composer, he was not considered a virtuoso pianist like Beethoven, Chopin, or Liszt. According to Schiff (1998, p. 193), Schubert lacked the technique to play some of his own music, such as the *Erlkönig* and the *Wanderer Fantasy*.

Connoisseurs of music have identified the following works as among Schubert's best:

- *The Piano Quintet: Death and a Maiden*
- *The Trout*
- *Unfinished Symphony*
- *Erlklönig*
- *Winterreise*

Schubert was inspired to write music to accompany works written by internationally famous poets such as Goethe, Schiller, and Müller. For example the *Erlklönig* is a poem based on a Danish folktale by Goethe. It was Goethe more so than other poets who was seen to most inspire him (Kapilow, 2011). That Schubert was attracted to poetry is not unusual, as Schiff (1998, p. 207) likens Schubert's music or musical language to poetry because of "its rhetoric, punctuations, exclamations, questions, and quotations" (p. 207). Kapilow (2011) reminds us that when listening to Schubert's songs,

> it is crucial to understand that once a poem is set to music, its meaning is completely transformed. In a song, words no longer have a purely verbal meaning, and music no longer has a purely music meaning. At every moment, the music means something in the context of the poem that it could not mean by itself, and each word of the poem means something in the context of its musical setting that it could not mean by itself. Once music and poetry join forces, it is the combination that is meaningful, and it is the combination that is magical. (p. 119)

Of the *Winterreise*, Bostridge (2015) claims that Müller's words and Schubert's music were meant to come together as "their poetic methods were quite in tune" (p. 20). Moreover, Schubert was said to have been attracted to the story of the *Winterreise* because it concerned a man's winter journey where he leaves his home and wanders from village to village reflecting on his life. The songs describe the different emotions he feels: grief, despair and loneliness, longing for connection, and occasional feelings of hope (Bostridge, 2015). In many ways, the journey is an inner journey as the journeyman or wanderer seeks self-discovery and asks himself a series of existential questions: "Who am I?...Where can I find meaning in the world?" (Youens, 1993, p. xv). While there are many themes that wind themselves like thread through this rich musical tapestry, three are highlighted here. First, is alienation and estrangement experienced by the journeyman. Bostridge (2015) refers to the existential tone of the songs, the loneliness of the journeyman, and the emptiness of life without meaning (Bostridge, 2015, p. 28). Bostridge goes on to say that in the Winter Journey is

> a pre-echo of so much 20th century philosophy and literature . . . a connection with absurdism, existentialism, and a whole slew of other twentieth century isms; with characters out of Beckett, Camus or Paul Auster. Schubert's was an age in which, and perhaps for the first time, to be a human could seem very lonely in a metaphysical sense. (p. 32)

Second is beauty and the search for beauty in an austere and hostile world. It is a known fact that at the time of writing the music for the *Winterreise*, Schubert was dying. Yet as Harbison (1993) says, "the telling [of the Winter Journey] still brought him [Schubert] in touch with beauty" (p. x). The need to embrace beauty in difficult or ugly times is understandable, as beauty has been described as "the only true protest" (Ochs in Adler, 2011, p. 208).

Third and finally is the theme of death that permeates a number of the songs in the *Winterreise*, particularly, "The Linden Tree" and "The Hurdy-Gurdy Player." "The Hurdy-Gurdy Player" concerns an old beggar who plays the hurdy-gurdy, but is ignored by everyone. The wanderer approaches him and asks him, "Strange old man, shall I go with you? Will you grind your organ to my songs?" (Bostridge, 2015, p. x). While the song can be interpreted in many ways, one is to view the old man playing the hurdy-gurdy as representing death with the wanderer finally accepting his fate.

A review of the *Winterreise* published in *Theaterzeitung* in 1828 said,

> Schubert's mind shows a bold sweep everywhere, whereby he carries everyone away with him who approaches, and he takes them through the immeasurable depth of the human heart into the far distance, where premonitions of the infinite dawn upon them longingly in a rosy radiance, but where at the same time the shuddering bliss of an inexpressible presentiment is accompanied by the gentle pain of the constraining present which hems in the boundaries of human existence. (Bostridge, 2015, p. xii)

LESSONS

In the final part of this chapter, we distill some of the lessons that can be learned from Schubert's life and work for school leaders today. We undertake this analysis in two parts. First, we review the central ideas from Harold Bloom's (1973, 1997) *The Anxiety of Influence: A Theory of Poetry* thesis to understand the relationship between Schubert and Beethoven. This was a relationship of profound admiration on Schubert's part and one that created some anxiety, as he said, "I still hope to make something of myself, but who can do anything after Beethoven" (Schubert in Woodford, 1978, p.7). Second, we return to the themes evident within the *Winterreise*.

THE ANXIETY OF INFLUENCE: A THEORY OF POETRY

The central thesis of Bloom's work is that all art is greatly influenced by previous art. Bloom says that poor artists imitate other artists, while talented artists are those who "misread" them. This means that they take what they want or need from what has been before and use it in a unique way. In so doing, they "clear imaginative space for themselves" (Bloom, 1997, p.5) thus overcoming the anxiety of influence. Bloom (1997) argues that if Keats had not read Shakespeare, Milton, and Wordsworth, it is unlikely that he would have written odes and sonnets. While Bloom does not refer to the relationship between Schubert and Beethoven, Kapilow (2011) does. He says,

> Schubert, however, like several of the strongest Romantic composers, chose not to shy away from Beethoven's legacy. Though he may have initially found his voice through song, he ultimately neither ran from Beethoven's domain—chamber music, sonata and symphony—nor copied the master's approach. Instead, he remade these forms in his own image—creatively misread them—appropriating what he needed from Beethoven's compositional technique while redirecting that technique toward his own aesthetic ends. He immersed himself in Beethoven's world, yet emerged intact as Schubert. (p. 139)

A number of writers (Bostridge, 2015; Kapilow, 2001; Schiff, 1998) have gone to great pains to compare Schubert with Beethoven; not so much to diminish Schubert, but to revere his genius and acknowledge his original contribution to classical music. As alluded to earlier, while Schubert himself felt somewhat inadequate in comparison with Beethoven, he recognized that the performances of his songs (such as the *Winterreise*) had "created a new artform ... The manner in which Vogl sings and the way I accompany, as though we were one at such a moment, is something quite new and unheard of" (Bostridge, 2015, p. xix). Kapilow (2011) supports this when he says that Schubert's "great accomplishment was to take this genre [songwriting] and turn it into one of the central forms of the Romantic period, giving it an artistic prestige on the same level as that of opera or symphony" (p. 117)

Schiff (1998, p. 192) compares Beethoven and Schubert by saying that much of Schubert's music was left unfinished, unlike Beethoven's work that forms a logical cycle. Schiff says that Schubert's development as a composer can be understood in terms of three phases: early youth through to maturity until his death. This was similar to Beethoven, but unlike Beethoven he only had 3 to 4 years between phases since he lived such a short life. Another point of difference between Beethoven and Schubert noted by Schiff is that Schubert was said to have used the markings of *pp* and *ppp* on his music. These markings on music mean to play very softly (*pp* = pianissimo) or very very softly (*ppp*). These markings reflect "more distant ranges of the dynamic scale" (Schiff, 1998, p. 194). According to Schiff, Beethoven did not use these markings.

It is not known whether Schubert ever met Beethoven, but he was acutely aware of his domination of music in Vienna at the time, and he had attended the performance of Beethoven's *Fidelio* in May 1814. Schubert was one of the torchbearers at Beethoven's funeral (Baker 1997, p. 32). Schubert was also said to dedicate a piece of music, "Variations on a French Song" to Beethoven. The dedication read, to "Herr Ludwig van Beethoven by his worshipper and admirer Franz Schubert" (Baker, 1997, p. 66). On his deathbed, Schubert requested that he be buried near Beethoven. He was buried three graves away, but in 1863 remains of both men were exhumed, and today they are together in the Musicians' Grove of Vienna's new cemetery (Baker, 1997, p. 134)

According to Baker (1997, p. 32), Schubert's attitude to the music of Beethoven was one of ambivalence. While he was influenced by him and this is reflected in his symphonies that were considered grand in style like Beethoven's, he was said to be overwhelmed by the wildness of some of Beethoven's later works.

Bloom's central ideas are relevant to consider in light of the struggles school leaders face as they are influenced by their predecessors yet strive to make their own way within their professional field. Throughout history, leaders have been inspired by the lives of previous leaders, beginning with Alexander the Great who kept a copy of Homer's *Illiad* featuring the exploits of Achilles under his pillow at night. Julius Caesar was inspired by Alexander, Churchill by Carlyle's portraits of heroes as well as Mahatma Gandhi. U.S. President Harry Truman read *Plutarch's Lives* in the White House. President Barack Obama talked openly about the model of leadership provided by Abraham Lincoln. Previous Prime Minister of Australia, Paul Keating, was said to be greatly influenced by Winston Churchill. While leaders seek exemplars and models from previous times to inspire them and keep them going in times of adversity, they must also seek to find space among them to create their own legacy or else they will simply be imitators and shadows of those models. This is the nugget of Bloom's anxiety of influence thesis.

School leaders also have such exemplars of leadership such as mentors, colleagues, previous bosses, or university professors. As an example, the anxiety of influence notion can be understood in relation to a novice school leader who greatly admires an experienced leader/mentor and strives to emulate that person's practices and outlook. However, once the novice leader becomes more knowledgeable, confident, and experienced, he/she is no longer reliant on the leader/mentor for guidance or affirmation. The novice leader's independence signals not only a change in the dynamics of the relationship, but also the beginning of a journey whereby he/she seeks to follow his/her own unique path and make his/her own unique contribution to the field.

It is also possible that school leaders may seek exemplars less close to home, but from the worlds of politics, history, business, science, medicine, and law. Even as these very personal portraits may sustain and even guide them at times, they must create a unique space that is not an echo of them. Schubert's life provides an example of how a composer living in the same age as Beethoven could also create a distinctive place for himself as a genius judged on his own terms and not obliterated in Beethoven's shadow. Schubert's gift was that as a vocalist he found inspiration in songs and that he could write them to illustrate poems in an unparalleled manner, which utilized his talent as a melodist. Memory is enhanced with a singable melody. This is also part of his universal appeal. In a historical example, Jesus was remembered as a great teacher and his mastery of the parable as a form of storytelling was able to be recalled a hundred years after his death and then preserved in the gospels for all time (Crossan, 1991).

WINTERREISE AND BEAUTY

The *Winterreise* is a piece of art that uses Müller's words and Schubert's sublime music to tell the story of one person's life journey with its victories and defeats. Similarly, leadership can be described as a personal journey travelled by leaders who similarly face victories and defeats in the course of their professional and personal lives. Throughout the journey leaders develop a sense of personhood, time, and place, and seek meaning and purpose within a context that can at times be both hostile and welcoming. Bostridge's (2015) thoughts regarding the purpose and importance of art for human beings relates closely to the purpose and importance of leadership:

Art is created in history, by living, feeling, thinking human beings; we cannot understand it without grappling with its associations to and grounding in worlds of emotion, ideology, or practical constraint. Art is made from the collision between life and form; it does not exist in some sort of idealised vacuum. (p. 489)

Like art, leadership is a product of its context and history; it is created by leaders who are feeling and thinking beings both constrained by the context (i.e., external as well as internal pressures by a variety of stakeholders) and also at times empowered by it. Joseph Campbell said that, "Opportunities to find deeper powers within ourselves come when life seems most challenging" (in Kapilow 2011, p. 116). It was through one of the most challenging times of his life that Schubert created the *Winterreise*. It can be said that *Winterreise* was an existential and aesthetic response to Schubert's inner and physical struggles. Yet the power of *Winterreise* like other forms of music is that it is

well-suited to bringing us into contact with the basic conditions of our lives, such as dependency, vulnerability, mortality, the fragility of relations, and existential loneliness . . . [As a form of existential experience, music] . . . involves putting aside the tendency to conceal problematic human basic conditions, by breaking through the outside of being to bring us into the presence of its inside. (Pio & Varkøy, 2012, p. 104)

In other words, music reminds all of us, least not leaders, of our existential condition, our purpose, and our being in the world. Like all of the arts, it provides "a disposition for sympathetic awareness" (Stout, 1999, p. 33) since it heightens our perceptions and awakens a dialogue between ourselves and the world (Stout, 1999). Moreover, music allows us to not only see the world as it is but also how it might be. This notion is captured by Taylor (2015).

The arts [including music] can teach the rest of us to see better, to hear better—in short, to sense better and to better communicate what we sense. But it is more than just sensing better, it is about a qualitatively different way of paying attention to the world . . . (p. 53) . . . The arts can teach us to stay with our senses and not know and in that way to provide a balance to the dominance of the analytic approaches to our organizational worlds. (Taylor, 2015, p. 52)

For school leaders, the prevailing hegemonic approach to school leadership as dictated by policy reform is instrumental, narrow, reductive, and managerial in orientation (English, 2008; English & Ehrich, 2016). An alternative perspective of leadership is urgently warranted; one that is located in emotion, intuition, ethics, and aesthetics, which is a type of embodied knowledge created from sensory experiences (Hansen, Ropo, & Sauer, 2007). What is also needed is a "leadership of possibility" (Adler, 2011, p. 208) that embraces hope, imagination, aspiration, inspiration, and beauty. At the center of this new form of leadership is a call for leaders to "lead beautifully," since leading beautifully

> speaks to a quality of being—one honed through the development of self-mastery, and quickened through the congruence of one's acts with their "measured" expression. It also alerts us to the possibility of a leader's goals being directed towards the best of human purposes. (Ladkin, 2008, p. 40)

We have argued elsewhere (see English & Ehrich, 2016) that there is an urgent need for school leaders to embrace beauty as it offers an alternative way of thinking about educational leadership. Like artists who seek to see the world anew, school leaders will need a new set of eyes to see beyond the current bleak and dehumanized educational leadership landscape. This landscape is characterized by accountability regimes, standardization, testing rather than learning, and routinized joyless work. It is in this landscape that school leaders have been cast in the role of manager striving for efficiency and effectiveness, rather than artistic performer who is aesthetically aware and follows a more nuanced approach to human interactions.

If in the current context of schooling school leaders experience existential crises of despair and alienation from the human side of their work, it is highly understandable. If in the busyness of their daily lives school leaders succumb to their fate by taking the predictable, well-trodden managerialist path that lies ahead (like the wanderer who willingly follows the hurdy-gurdy man), then it is unlikely there will be any changes to the way school leadership is enacted or construed. It will continue to be an overwhelmingly rational and technical activity that denies its human side. What Schubert's *Winterreise* reminds educational leaders is that while the wintry landscape is likely to be austere and present many obstacles, the challenge remains for the journeyman/woman to maintain hope, seek meaning, purpose, and joy in what he/she does, and be resolute in the search for beauty.

CONCLUSION

The connection between music and leadership was noted as early as book seven of Plato's *Republic* when he noted that "Music educated the guardians by habits...a fine concord by song and fine rhythm by tune, and the words they used had in them qualities akin to these, whether the words were fabulous taken or true" (Plato, 1956, p. 320). In other words, music generated a sensitivity and an appreciation of beauty and balance. Music had a place in Greek educational development and thought, because the presence of harmony in music became the origination of mathematics in Pythagorean explanations of an ordered universe (Tiles, 1996, p. 329). The idea of appropriate preparation in order to become a leader rested within this contextual nexus of order and balance.

In addition to the issue of balance and order, which are essential to organizational life generally and schools in particular as places for the development of the young, music also has expressive qualities that deal with emotion. Langer (1942) believed that music contained a kind of "logical form" of emotion and articulated it as language cannot. This kind of isomorphism between emotion and music rests on a special kind of symbolism, which is metalinguistic. It may well be what Goleman (1998) discusses in dealing with emotional intelligence in leaders and how emotional states should be recognized as essential to an organization's viability and health (pp. 286–287).

In this chapter, we opened a small window into the life and works of classical music composer Franz Schubert whose *Winterreise* contained some of the most expressive and emotional symbols that linked life, love, life's journey, and death ever written in a musical score. It is a journey every human being must take and leaders are no exception. Irrespective of the musical taste of the reader, Schubert's legacy as a common benchmark of our own humanity links us all together across time, context, and culture because as Bourdieu (1984) states in his classic work *Distinction*:

> Music is the most "spiritual" of the arts of the spirit and a love of music is a guarantee of "spirituality." One only has to think of the extraordinary value nowadays conferred on the lexis of "listening" by the secularized (e.g., psychoanalytical) versions of religious language. As the countless variations on the soul of music and the music of the soul bear witness, music is bound up with the "interiority" (inner music) of the "deepest" sort and *all* concerts are sacred...Music is the "pure" art par excellence. (p. 19)

REFERENCES

Adler, N. (2011). Leading beautifully: The creative economy and beyond. *Journal of Management Inquiry, 20*(3), 208–221.

Baker, R. (1997). *Schubert: A life in words and pictures.* London, England: Little Brown.

Bevan, P. G. (1998). Adversity: Schubert's illnesses and their background. In B. Newbould (Ed.), *Schubert studies* (pp. 244–266). Aldershot, England: Ashgate.

Bloom, H. (1973). *The anxiety of influence: A theory of poetry.* New York, NY: Oxford University Press.

Bloom, H. (1997). *The anxiety of influence: A theory of poetry* (2nd ed.). New York, NY: Oxford University Press.

Bostridge, I. (2015). *Schubert's winter journey: Anatomy of an obsession.* New York, NY: Knopf.

Bourdieu, P. (1984). *Distinction: A social critique of the judgment of taste* (R. Nice, Trans.). Cambridge, MA: Harvard University Press.

Crossan, J. D. (1991). *The historical Jesus: The life of a Mediterranean Jewish peasant.* Edinburgh, Scotland: T & T Clark.

Dewey, J. (1987). *Late works of John Dewey.* Carbondale, IL: Southern Illinois University Press.

English, F.W. (2008). *The art of educational leadership.* Los Angeles, CA: Sage.

English, F. W. & Ehrich,L. C. (2016). *Leading beautifully: Educational leadership as connoisseurship.* New York, NY: Routledge.

Gardner, H. (1995). *Leading minds: An anatomy of leadership.* New York, NY: Basic Books.

Gammond, P. (1987). *The encyclopedia of classical music: An essential guide to the world's finest music.* London, England: Salamander Books.

Goleman, D. (1998). *Working with emotional intelligence.* New York, NY: Bantam Books.

Great Composers. (1989). *Great composers.* Sydney, Australia: Golden Press.

Hansen, H., Ropo, A., & Sauer, E. (2007). Aesthetic leadership. *The Leadership Quarterly, 18,* 544–560.

Harbison, J. (1993). Foreword. In *Schubert's Winterreise: A winter journey in poetry, image and song* (pp. ix–x), Madison, WI: University of Wisconsin Press.

Kapilow, R. (2011). *What makes it great? Short masterpieces, great composers.* Hoboken, NJ: John Wiley.

Ladkin, D. (2008). Leading beautifully: How mastery, congruence and purpose create the aesthetic of embodied leadership practice. *The Leadership Quarterly, 19,* 31–41.

Langer, S. (1942). *Philosophy in a new key.* Cambridge, MA: Harvard University Press.

Pio, F., & Varkøy, Ø. (2012). A reflection on musical experience as existential experience: An ontological turn. *Philosophy of Music Education Review, 20*(2), 99–116.

Plato. (1956) *The Republic.* E. H. Warmington & P.G. Rouse (Eds.; W.H.D. Rouse, Trans.). New York, NY: New American Library.

Schiff, A. (1998). Schubert's piano sonatas: Thoughts about interpretation and performance. In B. Newbould (Ed.), *Schubert studies* (pp. 191–208). Aldershot, England: Ashgate.

Schusterman, R. (2000). *Pragmatist aesthetics: Living, beauty, rethinking art* (2nd ed.). Lanham, MD: Rowman & Littlefield.

Stout, C.J. (1999). The art of empathy: Teaching students to care. *Art Education, 52*(2), 21–34.

Taylor, S. S. (2015). Leading to learn. *Journal of Leadership Studies, 9*(1), 52–55.

Tiles, M. (1996). Philosophy of mathematics. In N. Bunnin & E.P. Tsui-James (Eds.), *The Blackwell companion to philosophy* (pp. 325–357). Oxford, England: Blackwell.

Woodford, P. (1978). *The illustrated lives of the great composers: Schubert.* London, England: Omnibus Press.

Youens, S. (1993). A wintry geography of the soul: Schubert's *Winterreise*. In *Schubert's Winterreise: A winter journey in poetry, image & song* (pp. xi–xxii) Madison, WI: University of Wisconsin Press.

CHAPTER 11

THE MISSED EDUCATION

Leadership Lessons From Lauryn Hill's
Everything is Everything

Soribel Genao
Queens College, CUNY

Pedro "Dro" Genao
Mobile Moguls, LLC

Exclusively, there have been countless studies on the impacts of effective educational leadership and the impact music has on learning. While several weekly reports and studies indicate how leadership or music impacts learning skills and student achievement, rarely are these two areas connected. In this chapter, we explore the lyrics of "Everything is Everything" by Lauryn Hill (1998; for complete lyrics, see Appendix). The song was selected because of its lyrical connections to educational leadership and the effect on student achievement in urban schools. In linking the two areas, we also examine the continuous need for culturally relevant curriculum and leadership. Dunbar and Scrymgour (2009) explain that culturally responsive schooling (CRS) has gained momentum internationally where students of

Educational Leadership and Music, pages 115–125
115

culturally diverse backgrounds are a consideration. In addition, we posit how emotional intelligence and leadership styles influence student and teacher achievements. Understanding the aspects of culture via music can assist in the development of attaining a better grasp of the type of leadership styles for a 21st century school.

LEADERSHIP AND MUSIC

Historically, school leadership has been connected with the role and functions of school-management teams (Schleicher, 2012). More recently, however, it has been emphasized both in reports by international organizations and in academic works that leadership involves a common culture of expectations, in which everyone is accountable for individual contributions to the collective outcome (Leithwood & Louis, 2011). Depending on the situation, the roles of leadership may be defined and discovered differently. The claim that educational leadership makes a difference in different ways causes a critical analysis in understanding the complexity of leadership and the importance of avoiding one-size-fits-all preparation approaches to successful school leadership (Crow, 2007). While some leadership qualities or practices may have universal characteristics, other leadership qualities are culturally specific (Crow, 2007). Culturally responsive leadership, derived from the concept of culturally responsive pedagogy, involves those leadership philosophies, practices, and policies that create inclusive schooling environments for students and families from ethnically and culturally diverse backgrounds (Johnson and Fuller, 2014). In exploring the significance of culture, how can musical lyrics create the opportunities to learn about leadership and its styles?

Research on how music impacts student achievement is not due to one song, instrument, theory, or behavior (Weinberger, 1998; Fagen et al., 1997). A substantial body of literature has found that students enrolled in a comprehensive arts curriculum achieve higher scores on standardized assessment, specifically math, science, and English subtests on proficiency exams (Johnson & Memmott, 2006; Kinney & Forsyth, 2005). In addition, music is perhaps even more pervasive in popular Western culture than any other form of popular culture (Callahan & Rosser, 2007). As a result, music can be an initial point of relation when seeking to learn more about being culturally responsive as it applies to leadership theory and practice. It is at this point that we can make the case for how both leadership and music are greatly influential.

In understanding the influences of our emotional intelligences as we relate to both leadership and music, it is important to explore the biological influences that these two areas have in common as well. An emotionally intelligent school leads to less stress, burnout and job satisfaction among educators. Leaders are capable of teaching the relevance and importance of emotional intelligence at developed schools (Brackett & Rivers, 2014). These schools also tend to have more student engagement in the classroom and throughout the school. Students in emotionally supportive classrooms report greater interest, enjoyment, and engagement (Curby et al., 2009; Marks, 2000; Rimm-Kaufman, La Paro, Downer, & Pianta, 2005). As it relates to music, developing personal and social skills and increasing emotional sensitivity are key factors of emotional intelligence (Hallam, 2010). In both leadership and music, these experiences influence leadership styles based on biological and climate developments on how they choose to lead.

SELECTION OF SONG

As previously stated and compared, leadership and music are both influential and constantly developing. The same can be said about the process of our selection. As children of a Caribbean mother, we were constantly reminded that she arrived in the United States for better opportunities and always stressed the importance of an education. She also taught us to embrace our own culture and music before we embraced American culture and music. We were constantly trying to prove how similar our friends' American culture was to our mother. She, however, could not understand why we enjoyed songs about struggle and inequities as much as we did and wanted us to continue embracing any Caribbean sound, usually upbeat and reflecting joy.

In selecting our song, we felt compelled to find lyrics that were most related to our own experiences as students of New York City's public school system. We attended public schools on the Lower East Side of Manhattan during the 1980s and 1990s. In 1998, Hill dropped her first solo album, *The Miseducation of Lauryn Hill*, which established her as a major talent. It was this album that gave Hill the social and cultural responsibility to address audiences globally through her lyrics. Each song captivated a specific time and place in her life as well as the listeners. Each song spoke true to what was going on in the 1990s. One song in particular, grabbed the hearts of "everyone who struggled in their youth." That song was "Everything is Everything." This song was the soundtrack to many inner-city children living in and attending a school system confronted by the challenges of attaining academic success and/or safety. While the city is safer now, there are still some educational similarities in urban areas.

During this era in New York City, one representative study indicated that of the urban working class minority adolescents in a targeted high school during a 6-year period, 87% of 1,436 of adolescents enrolled in the ninth grade during one academic year had been suspended or expelled (Kozol,

1995). In addition, low-income, low-achieving and non-White students, particularly those in urban areas like New York City, found themselves in classes with many of the least skilled teachers (Lankford, Loeb, & Wycoff, 2002). These teachers, while prepared to teach subject content, were not prepared to teach students in high-poverty school districts. Lyrically tied to our song, both students and teachers experience "Everything is Everything"; this phrase communicates that current reality can't be changed so it should be accepted, followed by is it possible that song writers think about creating songs with leadership theories and perceptions in mind?

The mentioned correlation between the lyrics and leadership will continue to be examined as it pertains to the emotional intelligence and leadership styles that impact the influences more recently.

EMOTIONAL INTELLIGENCE
AND EDUCATIONAL LEADERSHIP STYLES

Daniel Goleman's (2011) introduction to emotional intelligence concluded that our view of human intelligence is too narrow and that a high IQ score does not guarantee future success. According to Goleman, childhood is "a special window of opportunity for shaping children's emotional habits." In addition, five leadership styles corresponding with the components were identified. These styles are based on a review on school leadership, educational governance and effectiveness, and the investigative theoretical framework developed by Pashiardis and Brauckman (2009). Utilizing Goleman's five components of EI and Pashiardis and Brauckman's five leadership styles, we will summarize the song as it relates to EI and leadership styles in Table 11.1.

EXPLORING LEADERSHIP THROUGH MUSIC
AND LYRICS AS A 21ST CENTURY LEADER

So how do we begin to learn this concept in the current educational climate? Like teachers and students, school leaders also have to practice differentiated leading styles to accommodate their settings and style. There are several concerns among researchers between such huge practical challenges and the limited problem-solving capabilities that are promoted by the prevailing educational practices (Scardamalia, Bransford, Kozma, & Quellmalz, 2012).

In "Everything is Everything" Hill states, "It seems we lose the game before we even start to play." These lyrics refer to the struggles inner city youth face due to inadequate resources they are born into. In other words,

TABLE 11.1	Components of EI and Leadership Styles		
Component	**Lyric Excerpts**	**Feelings**	**Leadership Characteristics**
Self-Awareness	"You can't match this rapper slash actress" "More powerful than two Cleopatras"	Confidence, Humor, and can impersonate others- learns to lead by following	Instructional representing leadership practices that enable achievement of instructional objectives
Self-Regulation	"My practice extending across the atlas" "I begat this"	Conscientious Adaptable	Structuring representing leadership practices that promote establishment and implementation of clear rules
Internal-Motivation	"Let's love ourselves and we can't fail" "To make a better situation"	Initiator Committed Perseverance	Entrepreneurial representing leadership practices that promote the involvement of external actors
Empathy	"Who won't accept deception, in—instead of what is truth" Sometimes it seems We'll touch that dream But things come slow or not at all"	Perceptive Proactive	Personnel Development representing leadership practices that promote training and development of teachers
Social Skills	"L-Boogie spars with stars and constellations Then came down for a little conversation"	Communication Influence Conflict Management	Participative representing leadership practices that promote cooperation and commitment.

how can they be part of the game when they were never taught to play? These are significant points because she made an impact through self-awareness and self-regulation components that provided the opportunities of instructional and structuring leadership to occur among school leaders. These leaders enable achievement of instructional objectives and create practices that promote establishment and implementation of clear rules. In recent years, urban educational leaders have been part of an uphill battle with meeting annual yearly progress (AYP), making sure the Common Core State Standards (CCSS) are being met, and that adequate resources are sustained to meet demands, in addition to be culturally responsive teachers and leaders. As a result, various stakeholders have increased their expectations from school principals demanding, for instance, higher academic results and performance standards (Taliadorou & Pashiardis, 2011). While their efforts are incremental, the expectations have not been as realistic. Moreover, school leaders are feeling the greatest pressures from superintendents and district and network leaders, while teachers are receiving pressures from one place (Genao, 2013). Hill asks, "Who made these rules? We're so confused. Easily led astray" As it pertains to education, leaders will share an empathetic component, which as per Goleman is highlighted as a vital component in leadership (Goleman, 2011), leading to a more perceptive and proactive understanding in personnel development. The struggle, however, is trying to understand that if the rules are set in place to assist everyone equally, then why does the achievement gap exist and the decrease in student achievement in low-income communities persist?

According to the 2012 Education Trust-West study, a low-income student is more than twice as likely to have a low-value-added ELA teacher as a higher-income peer, and 66% more likely to have a low-value-added math teacher. These patterns are even more pronounced with Latino and African American students, who are two to three times more likely—in math and ELA, respectively—to have bottom-quartile teachers than their White and Asian American peers. As a society that is positioned in developing a future of equitable attainment, there is still a need for the refinement of high-level innovative skills improved self-efficacy, and related characteristics as possible inventors of awareness. In order for this to occur, teacher and principal effectiveness are the two most significant school-based factors contributing to student achievement, and principal effectiveness alone accounts for 25% (Seashore Louis et al., 2010). Lyrically aligned in "But things come slow or not at all," Hill emphasizes that it is important to aspire for change, but change does not occur immediately or may not occur at all. Leadership is guiding an organization through a process of change, understanding and respecting people and practices, and managing variables as best as possible within an ambiguous environment (Sayeed, 2015).

A school leader's ability to assure that these changes run as smoothly as possible is a constant and increasing demand at times. A leader must have skills in the operation and implementation of the organization (Jogulu 2010). Applying an entrepreneurial leadership style can promote "Let's love ourselves and we can't fail—To make a better situation," a style that promotes the involvement of external actors. Providing that teachers and principals come together via internal motivation component, "Tomorrow our seeds will grow—All we need is motivation." Hill's final verse ends with "Now here this mixture, while hip-hop meets scripture/develop a negative to a positive picture." That statement is a confidence builder for leaders looking for motivation, looking from a ground-level point of view proving that sound can teach them to be better teachers and leaders. Changes in the education system are caused by policies and context (Bolivar-Botia & Bolivar-Ruano 2011). These changes are unavoidable as requirements are increasing. However, it is important that a continued effort to create an environment that will help every student learn be sustained and effective—even via music.

CONCLUSION

Teachers who aspire to become effective administrators are responsive to their classrooms and their colleagues. In response to her audiences, Hill shares "my practice extending across the atlas," which means that she has become globally known and can reach all across like an atlas. The comparison here is that the objective of a leader must encompass the building of a different culture by developing a model curriculum, effective teaching styles, and a respectful environment (Trubowitz, 2007). Culturally competent leaders promote communication and allow transparency and trust to be cultivated. These leaders acquire the social skills representing leadership practices that promote cooperation and commitment. If the educational leaders have not been adequately prepared to roll out mandates effectively, how will their teachers be able to so?

While linking educational leadership to musical lyrics to assist our schools and communities is not ideal, the universal impact of both is certainly important to note. Innovation and change is constantly pushed in education, and musical lyrics can push for more emotionally intelligent and innovative leaders.

APPENDIX

Everything Is Everything
by Lauryn Hill

Chorus
Everything is everything, what is meant to be, will be
After winter, must come spring change it comes eventually
Everything is everything, what is meant to be, will be
After winter, must come spring change it comes eventually

I wrote these words for everyone who struggles in their youth
Who won't accept deception in, instead of what is truth
It seems we lose the game before we even start to play
Who made these rules? We're so confused
Easily led astray let me tell you that

Chorus
Everything is everything, everything is everything
After winter must come spring, everything is everything

I philosophy, Possibly speak tongues
Beat drum, Abyssinian, street Baptist
Rap this in fine linen, from the beginning
My practice extending across the atlas
I begat this flippin' in the ghetto on a dirty mattress
You can't match this rapper slash actress
More powerful than two Cleopatras
Bomb graffiti on the tomb of Nefertiti
MCs ain't ready to take it to the Serengeti
My rhymes is heavy like the mind of sister betty
L boogie spars with stars and constellations
Then came down for a little conversation

Adjacent to the king, fear no human being
Roll with cherubims to Nassau Coliseum
Now hear this mixture where hip hop meets scripture
Develop a negative into a positive picture

Chorus
Now, everything is everything what is meant to be, will be
After winter must come spring change it comes eventually

Sometimes it seems, we'll touch that dream
But things come slow or not at all
And the ones on top, won't make it stop

So convinced that they might fall
Let's love ourselves, then we can't fail
To make a better situation tomorrow
Our seeds will grow, all we need is dedication

Let me tell you that
Everything is everything, everything is everything
After winter, must come spring, everything is everything
Everything is everything, everything is everything
What is meant to be, will be
After winter, must come spring change it comes eventually

REFERENCES

Bolívar-Botía, A., & Bolívar-Ruano, R. (2011). Schools principals in Spain: From manager to leader. *International Journal of Education, 3*(1), E5

Brackett, M. A., & Rivers, S. E. (2014). *Transforming students' lives with social and emotional learning: International handbook of emotions in education.* New York, NY: Routledge.

Callahan, J. L., & Rosser, M. H. (2007). Pop goes the program: Using popular culture artifacts to educate leaders. *Advances in Developing Human* Resources, 9(2), 269–287.

Crow, G. (2007). The complex landscape of successful principal practices: An international perspective. *International Studies in Educational Administration, 35*(3), 67–74.

Curby, T., LoCasale-Crouch, J., Konold, T., Pianta, R., Howes, C., Burchinal, M., & Barbarin, O. (2009). The relations of observed pre-K classroom quality profiles to children's achievement and social competence. *Early Education and Development, 20,* 346–372. doi: 10.1080/ 10409280802581284

Dunbar, T., Scrymgour, M. (2009, November). *Cultural competence in Aboriginal education services delivery in Australia: Some lessons from the Aboriginal health service sector.* AARE International Education Research Conference Canberra, Australia.

Fagen J., Prigot J., Carroll M., Pioli L., Stein A., & Franco A. (1997). Auditory context and memory retrieval in young infants. *Child Development, (68),* 1057–1066.

Genao, S. (2013). Meeting AYP: Affective or effective on school leadership. *Management in Education. 27,* 159.

Goleman D. (2011). *Leadership: The power of emotional intelligence.* Northampton, MA: More Than Sound.

Hallam S. (2010). The power of music: Its impact of the intellectual, personal and social development of children and young people. *International Journal of Music Education, 38*(3), 269–289.

Hill, L. (1998). Everything is Everything. On *The miseducation of Lauryn Hill* [CD]. Philadelphia, PA: Ruffhouse Records.

Jogulu, U. D. 2010. Culturally-linked leadership styles. *Leadership & Organization Development Journal, 31*(8), 705–719.

Johnson, L., & Fuller, C. (2014). *Culturally responsive leadership.* New York, NY: Oxford University Press. doi: 10.1093/OBO/9780199756810-0067

Johnson, C. M., & Memmott, J. E. (2006). Examination of relationships between participation in school music programs of differing quality and standardized test results. *Journal of Research in Music Education, 54*(4), 293.

Kinney, D. W., & Forsythe, J. L. (2005). The effects of the arts impact curriculum upon student performance on the Ohio fourth-grade proficiency test. *Bulletin of the Council for Research in Music Education, 164,* 35–48.

Kozol, J. (1995). *Amazing grace: The lives of children and the conscience of a nation.* New York, NY: Crown Publishers.

Lankford, H., Loeb, S., & Wycoff, J. (2002). Teacher sorting and the plight of urban schools: a descriptive analysis. *Educational Evaluation and Policy Analysis, 24*(1) 38–62.

Leithwood, K. & Louis, K.S. (Eds.; 2011). Linking leadership to student learning. San Francisco, CA: Jossey-Bass.

Marks, H. (2000). Student engagement in instructional activity: Patterns in the elementary, middle, and high school years. *American Educational Research Journal, 37*, 153–184. doi: 10.2307/1163475

Pashiardis, P., & Brauckmann, S. (2009). Co-LEAD PROJECT: Analysis and Interpretation of the Background Report: Nicosia, Cyprus.

Rimm-Kaufman, S., La Paro, K., Downer, J., & Pianta, R. (2005). The contribution of classroom setting and quality of instruction to children's behavior in kindergarten classrooms. *The Elementary School Journal, 105*, 377–394. doi: 10.1086/429948

Sayeed, D. (2015). *Change at a large urban district: Developing and operationalizing an ed tech standards and support system at Chicago Public Schools* (Doctoral dissertation). Harvard Graduate School of Education, Cambridge, MA.

Scardamalia, M., Bransford, J., Kozma, B.,& Quellmalz, E. (2012), New assessment and environments for knowledge building. In P. Griffin, B. McGaw, & E. Care (Eds.) *Assessment and teaching of 21st century skills* (p. 231–300) Dordrecht, the Netherlands: Springer.

Schleicher, A. (2012). *Preparing teachers and developing school leaders for the 21st Century: Lessons from around the world.* Paris, France: OECD

Seashore Louis, K., Leithwood, K., Wahlstrom, K., & Anderson, S. (2010). *Investigating the links to improved student learning.* Washington, DC: Wallace Foundation.

Taliadorou, N. & Pashiardis, P. 2011. Examining the relationship of emotional intelligence and political skill with effective educational leadership styles. *International Congress for School Effectiveness and Improvement, 30.*

Trubowitz S. (2007). *Creating a culture for learning: Educational psychology* (22nd ed.). Dubuque, IA: McGraw-Hill.

Weinberger, N. M. (1998). The music in our minds. *Educational Leadership, 56*, 36–40.

CHAPTER 12

IMPROVISATION AND LEADERSHIP

Lessons About Direction and Influence From Sonny Rollins

Stephen Jacobson
University at Buffalo

After 30 years of studying and preparing school leaders, I've learned a few things about what separates the most successful principals from others, and there are two key factors I'd like to focus on in this chapter: (a) direction (i.e., knowing who you are, particularly those core values that enable you to set a direction for others to follow); and (b) Influence (i.e., influencing others, in this case through improvisation, by constantly reflecting upon and practicing your craft until you become so proficient that you can readily improvise when difficult situations arise). In fact, you make improvisation such a regular part of your practice that even when things are going well you continue to tweak and challenge boundaries in order to find new meaning in your work. In this chapter, I argue that the confidence in craft exhibited by the regular use of improvisation, coupled with clearly defined core values,

Educational Leadership and Music, pages 127–135
Copyright © 2017 by Information Age Publishing
All rights of reproduction in any form reserved.

can generate genuine excitement among those with whom you work. As a result, colleagues become more attentive, listening and watching more carefully in order to follow your lead, recognizing in time that collectively going off script, or in the case of this chapter, the sheet music, may ultimately elevate their own skills, and perhaps even encourage them to take the lead or even solo. Those who study leadership, whether as a generic concept or specifically in schools, talk about its primary vectors being direction and influence (Leithwood & Louis, 2012). From my own work in preparing school leaders, I would suggest that it is knowing who you are that sets your internal compass (direction), and that the willingness and ability to improvise by taking calculated risks utilizing well-honed skills, influences the behaviors of those around you. Oftentimes, it is this facility with improvisation that gives others the confidence to follow your lead (Jacobson, 2015; Jacobson, Johnson, & Ylimaki, 2011; Minor–Ragan & Jacobson, 2014). Considering leadership as direction and influence (core values and improvisation) from the perspective of jazz (my favorite genre in music), one musician stands out (one who also happens to be my favorite musician regardless of genre), Sonny Rollins, known to many as the "Saxophone Colossus."

But before delving into the metaphorical relationships between two of Rollins's works and successful school leadership practice, let me provide a bit of background about the artist himself, so that the reader can connect the actions to the person, a person who believes, "You have to love what you are doing.... This is what is important to me, what I am trying to do with my life, to give it meaning" (from FAQ on Sonny Rollins' website: sonnyrollins.com).

THE MAN AND THE MUSIC

Born in 1930 in New York City, Theodore Walter "Sonny" Rollins grew up immersed in music in the renowned Sugar Hill neighborhood of Harlem. By the age of 16 he was already something of a prodigy on the alto saxophone but, in order to emulate his idol jazz legend Coleman Hawkins, he switched to the tenor sax, which was to become his signature instrument. Two other jazz giants who also had a profound influence on Rollins' music were saxophonist Charlie "Bird" Parker and pianist Thelonious Monk, who was to become Sonny's mentor during the early stages of his career (from Bio on Sonny Rollins' website: sonnyrollins.com).

By his early 20s, Sonny Rollins had already established himself as an important player on jazz's bebop scene, one who was influencing the work of others. As Miles Davis, in his 1989 autobiography, would later write about Sonny at this stage in his career, "He was a legend, almost a god to a lot of the younger musicians... He was an aggressive, innovative player who always had fresh musical ideas" (p. 134).

But the NYC jazz community of the early 1950s was enveloped in drugs:

> There was a lot of dope around the music scene and a lot of musicians were deep into drugs, especially heroin. People—musicians—were considered hip in some circles if they shot smack. Some of the younger guys like Dexter Gordon, Tadd Dameron, Art Blakey, J. J. Johnson, Sonny Rollins, Jackie McLean, and myself—all of us—started getting heavily into heroin around the same time. (Davis, 1989, p. 129)

Perhaps the most notable heroin addict in the jazz world at that time was Charlie Parker who, as mentioned earlier, was one of Sonny's idols. Unfortunately, as Miles Davis (1989, p. 130) remembered, "the idea was going around that to use heroin might make you play as great as Bird." For a while Sonny followed his idol down this path. But that path for many led to incarceration or an overdose and, as a result, began taking some of the most promising artists from the city's jazz community. In order to escape this downward spiral, Sonny opted to walk away from his newly found fame and he left NYC for a few years of personal introspection.

When he returned to the Big Apple in 1955, his reputation grew still further as other musicians and jazz critics became increasingly aware of his command of his instrument, especially as exhibited in his melodic invention and brilliant improvisation. During this period he began to record under his own name as a group leader, not just as a sideman, and he produced two works that I feel best exemplify the direction and influence of his leadership.

The first tune, "St. Thomas," comes from his 1956 album, *Saxophone Colossus* (one of his many nicknames); an exploration of calypso music derived from his family's Caribbean heritage. "St. Thomas" is supposedly based on a traditional English folk song called the "The Lincolnshire Poacher," which was reworked into a nursery song in the U.S. Virgin Islands. It is a song that Sonny's mother sang to him as a child, and is arguably his best known composition. It is a beautiful, life-affirming piece of music that exposes the soul of the man. Find a copy online and see if you can listen to "St. Thomas" without smiling and moving your body to the lilting rhythms. By reaching back to his childhood in order to examine who he was and where he came from, "St. Thomas" is a clear musical articulation of Rollins' core values of creative and persistent exploration of who he is and where he is going. As such, "St. Thomas" represents a wonderfully melodic statement of his musical and personal direction for a lifetime of work to come.[1]

The second song, "I'm an Old Cowhand (From the Rio Grande)," comes from a 1957 album of Sonny's called *Way Out West*. For this album Rollins put together a most unusual trio consisting of himself on tenor sax and two very experienced and accomplished musicians, Ray Brown on bass and Shelly Manne on drums. Purposefully omitting a piano, a staple instrument of most jazz numbers because it is used to establish a song's chord structure,

Sonny instead allowed himself to go "strolling" over the bass and drums in order to open up new improvisational possibilities. I believe this creative instrumentation demonstrates how a leader, through skillful improvisation, can influence those around him to take chances and find new meaning in an old standard. By all accounts, this was the first time Sonny had ever played with either Brown or Mann yet, as the album's linear notes indicate, the piece was completed in just one session. The song itself, "I'm an Old Cowhand," was a comic Johnny Mercer tune with the famous tag line, "Yippie yi yo kayah," originally sung by Bing Crosby in the 1936 Western musical film *Rhythm on the Range* and later covered by, among many others, Roy Rogers and even Lucille Ball and Vivian Vance in an episode of *I Love Lucy*. It is hardly the type of song that comes to mind when one thinks of jazz classics, especially from the bebop genre. Yet, guided by the inventive improvisational skills of Sonny Rollins and the enthusiasm of two other very talented musicians who were clearly eager to follow his lead, this rendition of "I'm an Old Cowhand" has found a unique place in the annals of jazz.

But even though works such as these had established Sonny as perhaps jazz's most talented and innovative tenor player, he chose once again to withdraw from performing between 1959 and 1961 because "...I felt I needed to brush up on various aspects of my craft. I felt I was getting too much, too soon, so I said, wait a minute, I'm going to do it my way" (from Bio on Sonny Rollins' website: sonnyrollins.com). And, yet again, in the mid 1960s, he took another hiatus from performing, this time to focus on his spiritual core, "I went to India and spent a lot of time in a monastery. I took some time off to get myself together and I think it's a good thing for anybody to do" (from Bio on Sonny Rollins' website: sonnyrollins.com). These breaks have served Sonny well, who at the time of this writing, is 87 years old and still playing. Among the recognitions he has received for a career that spans almost 70 years is a Lifetime Achievement Award from the National Academy of Recording Arts and Sciences in 2004, election to the American Academy of Arts and Sciences in 2010 and, in 2011, the Medal of Arts, the nation's highest honor for artistic excellence from President Barack Obama at the White House (from Bio on Sonny Rollins's website (Rollins, 2017).

CONNECTING THE MUSIC TO THE WORK OF SCHOOL LEADERS

Direction

In the early 1990s, I worked with a group of faculty members from the University at Buffalo (UB), in collaboration with superintendents from the four largest school districts in Western New York, to begin a process of redesigning UB's administrator preparation program (Jacobson, 1998). Called the Leadership Initiative for Tomorrow's Schools (LIFTS), the program designers made a conscious decision to move away from an almost exclusive focus on developing the types of discrete managerial skills (e.g., school business administration, personnel management, and law) believed necessary to prepare administrators, and moved instead to emphasizing interpersonal, relational skills needed by leaders to build productive school teams (Jacobson, 1990). One of LIFTS' central design features was a cohort-based learning environment in which aspiring school leaders worked together as a team in a 2-year program that balanced academic and practical experiences. I note with pride that this is one of several design features developed by LIFTS in the 1990s that are now recognized as key practices of exemplary preparation programs (Jacobson, McCarthy & Pounder, 2015).

During the intensive team building experiences of the LIFTS program's first summer, students were introduced to theories and research on leadership, change, and school improvement. Perhaps more importantly, they were also engaged in developing a personal educational platform: an articulation of those core values they hold dear, values that explain how they look at life and thus set the direction for their future leadership practices.

But getting students to recognize and articulate their core values turned out to be a harder task than we originally assumed. Through trial and error, we came to find in *The Right Mountain,* John Hayhurst's 1998 reflections on an expedition to Mount Everest, an excellent tool for surfacing what people truly value. Having done this now for almost 20 years, I believe that most often what provides the grounding for the development of a person's core values can be found in their childhood and family interactions. For example, I have had several students recognize that their valuing of integrity and commitment came from watching their parents sacrifice to make a better life for their children. They internalized these values and now have come to realize that these deeply held beliefs guide the decisions and actions they take as educators. In other words, their direction was set, both for themselves and for what they expect from others. Setting direction by identifying and articulating a vision, fostering the acceptance of group goals, and creating high performance expectations for students and adults is one of several core practices identified by Leithwood and Riehl (2005) as being necessary, albeit insufficient, for successful school leadership. I believe the core value of on-going self-exploration found in Rollins's "St. Thomas," which articulates his direction, is the musical equivalent of the educational direction setting our LIFTS students develop when they can finally and clearly articulate their own core values, whatever they might be. Hopefully, these values, and the direction they set, serve as the springboard toward a successful career as an educational leader, but this will happen only if these leaders can influence those with whom they work.

Influence

As noted at the start of this chapter, leadership depends on direction *and* influence, because it really doesn't matter what direction you set if you can't influence others to follow. Moreover, enabling others to follow depends upon creating conditions conducive to genuine engagement and not mere compliance. In his 2012 book, *Yes to the Mess,* Frank Barrett, an accomplished jazz pianist and professor of management, examined leadership through the lens of jazz improvisation and provided several conceptions of organizational behavior useful in understanding how improvisation can enhance leadership influence.[2] The first is innovation and guided autonomy, which Barrett describes as, "maximizing opportunities for diversity rather than insisting on unity...leaders give subordinates additional freedom to experiment and respond to the sort of hunches in which true innovation is often found" (Barrett, 2012, p. 116). Let's consider innovation and guided autonomy in terms of "I'm an Old Cowhand," which I would encourage you to listen to on YouTube so that you'll have a better idea of the points that follow.

I suspect that as soon as the song begins you'll recognize it, although it sounds rather spare with only three instruments and no vocals. About one minute in, the cowboy ditty begins to morph into something you'd expect to hear in a little dimly lit jazz club. After the trio briefly reintroduces the standard's refrain, they happily ride off into new musical territory. When Sonny takes a break, the bass and drums begin experimenting, and as Barrett (2012) notes, respond to hunches that lead to some innovative musical trades, which are the instrumental, back and forth conversations at the heart of jazz. When Rollins returns, he promptly takes the group back to the original tune, but just as quickly ventures off one last time and slowly rides off into the sunset, ending the number. Not only do we hear in this composition innovation and Rollins-guided autonomy among the three players, but also a second organizational conception: loose coupling and dynamic capability. As Barrett (2012) writes,

> A healthy group typically shifts from tight to loose coupling over time. Coordination is not achieved through static rules, but through the evolution of ties between participants, allowing for the emergence of surprising detours. There is strong enough interdependence to complete tasks and bring ideas to fruition, but the ties are not so tight as to be suffocating. (p. 119)

In just under six minutes, Sonny Rollins puts on a master class in how to use improvisation to direct and influence colleagues to join him in a rather unorthodox way of mining new meaning from an old standard. For a first time trio, these musicians sound like a healthy group, as defined by Barrett (2102), and their musical detours, which break static rules, are nothing short of surprising. Their strong interdependence enables the task to be completed successfully and a brilliant idea is brought to fruition; one that still delights almost 60 years on. Let's try a hypothetical crosswalk to school leadership using Rollins's "I'm an Old Cowhand" as the template. You're a principal new to a school that has recently experienced teacher layoffs due to district budget problems, so this year the size of the workforce is smaller than usual (no piano). You all know the standard arrangement of the school year, but this semester, because of changes in the composition of the group, it's going to have to be played differently. You wear your core values on your sleeve, you have personal integrity and a commitment to a quality education for all students, and a record of achievement to support your ability to succeed. But clearly, to make this school year a success, you'll need to improvise. You have set a clear direction and hopefully you have enough influence to encourage your teachers to follow your lead by giving them the freedom to experiment with programs and curriculum and not be afraid to take risks (innovation and guided autonomy). You also must recognize that your leadership cannot be characterized by static, suffocating rules, but instead by a level of mutual respect and interdependence so that our faculty's improvisation on the school year can be brought to fruition (loose coupling and dynamic capability).

But here's the rub, with all this in place, there's no guarantee that the school year will turn out to be a success, any more than when a jazz musician starts improvising are you assured that a great musical experience will follow. Even an improvisational giant like Sonny Rollins has had his off nights, sometimes notably so. Perhaps some of his band mates were fearful of taking risks or simply not proficient enough to follow Sonny's lead, or maybe Sonny was just not in sync with his band that night. Similarly, some teachers may lack the confidence or competence to follow the lead of an improvising principal or the principal is just not in sync with his or her teachers. Recall that Leithwood and Riehl (2005) found their core leadership practices to be necessary, but insufficient, for school success. So too then would be direction, influence and improvisation. Returning to our hypothetical situation, while the best intentions of the principal and faculty's improvisation may not reach fruition, important insights can still be gained—even if what not to do again. Does that mean the principal should forego improvisation in the future? Of course, not. It suggests reflection on the experience and then more practice of one's craft. If Sonny Rollins never had an off night, there would be nothing for him to work on, no reason to practice. But practice is central to Rollins's improvisation and his practice regime is legendary, oftentimes as much as 14 hours a day. Without regular practice, proficiency can be lost and without proficiency, creative improvisation is unlikely. Understanding this relationship between practice and improvisation is best explained by Sonny Rollins himself, who when asked,

"After all these years, what do you practice?" answered, "Everything—but in no particular order."

NOTES

1. To see how core values can sustain a lifetime of work, go to YouTube and look for Sonny Rollins playing "St. Thomas" at a gig in Detroit on August 31, 2012. At the time of the performance he is 83 years old, playing a signature tune first recorded almost 60 years earlier. Watch and feel how his direction drives his fellow musicians, must of whom are 40 to 50 years his junior, to explore with him the melodies of his childhood.
2. Barrett also identifies Sonny Rollins' work as perhaps the exemplar of jazz improvisation.

REFERENCES

Barrett, F. (2012). *Yes to the mess: Surprising lessons from jazz improvisation for leading in a complex world.* Boston, MA: Harvard Business School Press.

Davis, M. (1989). *Miles: The autobiography.* New York, NY: Simon & Schuster.

Hayhurst, J. (1998). *The right mountain: Lessons from Everest on the real meaning of success.* Toronto, Ontario, Canada: John Wiley.

Jacobson, S. (1990). Reflections on the third wave of reform: Rethinking administrator preparation. In S. Jacobson & J. Conway (Eds.), *Educational leadership in an age of reform* (pp. 30–44). New York, NY: Longman.

Jacobson, S. (1998). Preparing educational leaders: A basis for partnership. In S. Jacobson, C. Emihovich, H. Petrie, J. Helfrich, & R. Stevenson (Eds.), *Transforming schools and schools of education: A new vision for preparing educators* (pp. 71–98). Newbury Park, CA: Corwin Press.

Jacobson, S. (2015). Practicing successful and effective school leadership: North American perspectives. In P. Pashiardis & O. Johansson (Eds.), *Successful school leadership: International perspectives* (pp. 155–164). London, England: Bloomsbury.

Jacobson, S., Johnson, L. & Ylimaki, R. (2011). Sustaining school success: A case for governance change. In L. Moos, O. Johansson, & C. Day (Eds.), *How school principals sustain success over time: International perspectives* (pp. 109–125). Dordrecht, the Netherlands: Springer–Kluwer.

Jacobson, S., McCarthy, M., & Pounder, D. (2015). What makes a leadership preparation program exemplary? *Journal of Research on Leadership Education, 10*(1), 63–76.

Leithwood, K. & Louis, K. (2012). *Linking leadership to student learning.* San Francisco, CA: Jossey-Bass.

Leithwood, K. & Riehl, C. (2005). What we know about successful school leadership. In W. Firestone & C. Riehl (Eds.), *A new agenda: Directions for research on educational leadership* (pp. 22–47). New York, NY: Teachers College Press.

Minor–Ragan, Y., & Jacobson, S. (2014). In her own words: Turning around an under–performing school. In C. Day and D. Gurr (Eds.), *Leading schools successfully: Stories from the field.* (pp. 9–18). London, England: Routledge.

Rollins, S. (October, 2017). *Bio.* Retrieved from www.sonnyrollins.com.

CHAPTER 13

"A FAIRY TALE IN A SONG IS NO MESSAGE"

Leadership Lessons From Oliver Mtukudzi and the Black Spirits

Christopher B. Knaus
University of Washington Tacoma

As his tall, thin frame returned to the stage in one of his many global performances, Oliver Mtukudzi, affectionately known as "Tuku," reminded the Seattle, Washington-based audience in the early 2000s, "In Zimbabwe, if you do not have anything to say, you do not get to sing." Over soft acoustic guitar strums, Tuku shared that one must tell the stories of the community, to remind us that no one is worth more than anyone else. Honesty, he continued, is the primary responsibility of the storyteller, to speak out about injustice—however small—and to spread messages of hope. Upon his signal, his band, The Black Spirits, burst into a colorful arrangement of the song "Todii," a ballad about the devastation HIV and AIDS have wrought across Africa. Soon, the harmonies made the audience swoon, even as the band compelled listeners to consider, "What shall we do?" in the wake of such

Educational Leadership and Music, pages 137–148
Copyright © 2017 by Information Age Publishing
All rights of reproduction in any form reserved.

devastation (Mtukudzi, 1999). The soft lullaby built a crescendo between Shona and English, as Mtukudzi's voice filled the room with a meaningful depth. Tuku's sharp lesson about voice and the privilege of having something to say juxtaposes with soothing melodies that urge an awakening to the reality of global devastation. With a style that spans global issues, local indignations, and personal responsibility, Tuku reminds listeners to collectively unite because our children, our families, and our neighbors are dying around us.

While Mtukudzi had a calming, soothing effect on my own frustration with my introduction to the field of educational leadership, his music also influenced others around me. One powerful example came from my nephew, Liam, when he was a toddler. My elder sister was engaged in an increasingly violent tit-for-tat with her then husband. My 3-year-old nephew came crying into the living room and sat directly in front of the stereo that happened to be playing the *Tuku Music* album. As my nephew's tears turned to quiet sobs, he began to listen. I watched in awe as Tuku softly lulled his body into peace, and the tears quickly dried on his face. Twenty minutes later, my nephew reflected a solace the entire household needed; he went directly to the kitchen, where his parents continued to yell at each other, and hugged his mother. His healing arms immediately disrupted the tension and pain we all were feeling, and I knew then that Mtukudzi had a particularly compelling impact on listeners. Even without translating the lyrics, the music has a healing property that compels listeners to reflect on how we live. Years later, my high school students would refer to his songs as "Music that makes us want to be better people."

Mtukudzi combines his music and message with an intentional commitment to being himself, rooted within his historical, cultural, and linguistic context. His approach—and my own unique experience with his music and messages—models a leadership orientation to critical race theory, providing a focus on our most pressing issues. This chapter thus frames educational leadership lessons based upon Oliver Mtukudzi and his band, The Black Spirits, from my personal perspective.

TUKU MUSIC

Mtukudzi was born in Harare, Zimbabwe, in 1952. A tireless songwriter with more than 60 albums in his 40-year career, Mtukudzi spreads messages of empowerment, critical awareness, and global harmony, as well as lessons from elders. As an artist deemed to "assum[e] the role of a social commentator," Tuku's songs have been framed as "about various aspects of life . . . whether he is talking about love, death, poverty, democracy, or social justice" (Riber & Riber, 2004, p. 3). Sung primarily in Shona, his songs also include English and Ndebele; integrate traditional cultural instruments; South African, Zimbabwean, and Shona beats and rhythms; as well as call-and-response patterns. As a *griot*, Mtukudzi's impact extends well beyond cultivating audiences to dance or sing along, as Tuku models the importance of intersectional identities, through using multiple languages, storytelling from various perspectives, and through integrating historic and contemporary music forms. Indeed, he is seen as a regional leader because his storytelling is compelling both musically and lyrically, and because he has remained a voice of reason through a revolution and the subsequent national struggle. Mtukudzi talks about his lyrical inspiration for his messages while on stage and in interviews, clarifying that, "I live with the people, so I get most of my ideas from the community" (Mtukudzi, as cited in Nickson, 2000). He describes his orientation to music as something that "unites people. Music gives hope" (National Public Radio, 2013).

"UNITE, DON'T WASTE TIME"

My own introduction to Mtukudzi reflects the intensity of his music. To explain, I entered the PhD program at the University of Washington in the late 1990s, excited to learn about how educational systems—particularly educational leadership—fostered systems of oppression. I was especially eager to study how to transform such systems. By the end of my first few quarters of struggling with the distance of academia, I had grown increasingly frustrated. My own experiences growing up with poverty, violence, and neglect differed dramatically from the sprawling campus, old school architecture, professorial lectures, and expectations of scholarly writing by an almost all-White faculty who presented themselves as distinguished. Unlike most of my peers, many of whom were relatively well-paid professional educators (and/or were married to partners who had professional salaries), my meager graduate student stipend kept me at the poverty line. The classrooms, afterschool programs, and detention facilities in which I taught writing workshops were filled with people much more like me, and much less like those in an elite graduate program in educational leadership.

My doctoral experiences diverged from my own life, and no required readings remotely acknowledged my experiences as a student or educator. The writing styles, foundational educational leadership texts, theoretical perspectives, and sharp dismissal of anything related to poverty, race, or gender disparities disconnected abruptly from my realities and prompted me to again question my presence in higher education. Indeed, the very language of educational leadership reflected an underlying colorblindness that "purports to see deficiency as an individual phenomenon" (Ladson-Billings, 1999, p. 22). As I continued to read articles that did not question the notion that "someone has to fail in school" (Duncan-Andrade & Morrell, 2008, p. 2), I further distanced myself from what I saw as a field unprepared to address the realities of schooling rooted in racism and racial disparities (Gay, 2000). While I have since found a not-large-enough community of social justice-oriented, educational leadership scholars and practitioners, my doctoral program had so thoroughly isolated me and dismissed my personal experiences and commitment to social justice that I considering walking away from graduate school every single day.

One late night, after tossing a particularly colonial article onto the floor in disgust, I leaned back in my chair and turned up the music. I remember the song that was playing well: "Tsika Dzedu," by Mtukudzi (1999). I allowed myself to disengage from the hegemonic text, the academic jargon, and the intentional distance created by the field. And slowly the music entered my ears. From the first soft guitar strums to the beat breaks, transitions, and building of voices that crashed into harmonies layered upon harmonies, lulling listeners through repetitious crescendos, I was captured. This was music! Where had this been all my life? I hit repeat once, twice, three times. I was hooked. I knew this song had meaning; no one would take so much care to sing, to wail with such depth to the voices playing off each other. The colonial article long gone from my mind, I began to really listen to what Mtukudzi conveyed.

Tuku Music was both the name of the album I was listening to and what Mtukudzi's music is typically referred to, and it came at exactly the right time in my life. The song "Wake Up" on the album also had a particularly profound impact on me. A beautiful arrangement of plucky guitar riffs, soft percussion, soothing backup singers, and Tuku's raspy, yet soothing voice; "Wake Up" is a song about action. The first half of the song alternates between rhythmic cycles of repeating lyrics in Shona, musical interludes, and a chorus of "Wake up...open your eyes." This song pointed out to me how my own intellectualism was being lulled to sleep by the doctoral education I was receiving. I imagined Tuku singing to me, begging me to "Wake up, open your eyes." Yet the second half of the song transitions, and after Tuku's voice explodes with passion, the chorus shifts from "Wake up," to "Unite, don't waste time." In this shift, I heard Tuku specifically telling me to unite people, and I interpreted a collaborative approach as my social justice mission (Mtukudzi, 1999).

As I worked in deeply segregated urban schools, witnessing firsthand the negative impact racist school leaders and school systems had on students of color, I faced increasing difficulties in paying attention to academic articles that simply seemed unaware of what Derrick Bell (1992) explained as the permanence of racism. In contrast, Mtukudzi's music made the disjoint between the educational leadership field and student experiences impossible to ignore. Moreover, what I had planned as background music was soon foregrounded by its intensity and my growing desire to understand more of his Shona-informed messages. Tuku anchored me at a time when the insular confines of academe had lost me. Indeed, as I began my own transformation from teacher to educator, from student to mentor, and from writer to poet, Mtukudzi's balance of soothing melodies with complex, instrumental interplays, and to-the-point lyrical refrains guided my pathway. He was, in short, waking me up, calling me to action.

That following year, I discovered a range of critical race theorists, including Derrick Bell, Gloria Ladson-Billings, Daniel Solorzano, and Richard Delgado. They combined to advocate for a theoretical orientation that fit with my framing of what was needed in educational leadership. While critical race theory has been explicated extensively throughout the literature (see for example, Bell, 1998; Delgado & Stefancic, 2012; Ladson-Billings, 1999; Ladson-Billings & Tate, 2005), several tenets have been argued to have particular relevance for education. In brief, these include the aforementioned permanence of racism, race as a socially constructed phenomenon, a focus on the narrative voices of people of color, interest convergence (or the idea that systemic policies and practices are implemented only when they align to support White interests), and a critique of White liberalism (Knaus, 2014; Ladson-Billings, 1999).

Some 14 years after completing my own doctoral program, however, critical race theory has been minimally integrated into the educational leadership field. As Capper (2015) clarifies, "Few publications directly apply CRT to educational leadership as it relates to formal positions of authority (e.g., school principals or superintendents), and no publications identify implications for leadership practice guided explicitly by the CRT tenets" (Capper, 2015, p. 792). This absence perpetuates a colorblind approach throughout the entire field, and this absence fueled my need for something that reflected the dramatic racism I saw firsthand in schools.

Tuku's music came at exactly the right intellectual time for me. His commitment to storytelling, reflecting the importance of voices and experiences of oppressed communities of color (Delgado & Stefancic, 2012), provided a creative way for me to see how one could model the fostering of critical, culturally rooted voices through musically-informed storytelling. As I continued to search obscure music stores for his albums (which in the early 2000s, were incredibly difficult to come by), I gradually became exposed to more and more of his music. I eventually reached out to him, saw as many of his shows as I could, and chatted with him and his band members at every opportunity. I asked him how he learned to see himself as a model, if he saw himself as a leader, what drove him to continue his voracious creative productivity. Continually gracious, Mtukudzi laughed at my questions, and with humility responded that he was a storyteller. His job, his profession, was to observe the world around him, and to translate all of our social ills into music that would help us make sense of love and loss. But unlike traditional schooling, Tuku's approach to helping people see what is wrong in the world (and what we can do about everyday injustice) was and is through making compelling music. "If the people cannot hear the message," he told me once, "then it is not a good song" (Mtukudzi, personal communication, 2008). These themes, and the focus on crafting messages of despair in ways that audiences cannot refute, have guided how I continue to listen to Mtukudzi, and how I integrate his creative, affirming, simple messages and approaches into my own approach to transformative, race-conscious educational leadership.

JOINING THE STRUGGLE

In "Hariputirwe," Mtukudzi (2003) opens with a few guitar strums and then begins with women harmonizing the lyric, "Rina manyanga hariputirwe," a Shona idiom that roughly translates in English to "Nothing on earth can stay hidden forever." After a few bars, Mtukudzi comes in by softly reminding that "What you do in the dark, can be known in the day." He continues in English with "What you think is a secret, can be a gossip everywhere." He then slips back and forth between Shona and English, with backup singers repeating "Rina manyanga hariputirwe" as a refrain. The repetition of multiple ways of saying that what we personally do in the world will eventually come to light stuck with me when I first heard it. While a simple repeated lesson, I immediately translated this in my head to what is often framed as the foundational tenet of critical race theory, that racism is a permanent, normal part of society (Delgado & Stefancic, 2012; Ladson-Billings, 1999). Indeed, while many people might be surprised by the covert nature of systemic racism, and while many hide systems of racism, eventually the resulting disparities—and the underlying racial commitment to White supremacy—will come to light.

Mtukudzi conveys the importance of being present in the world across his many albums, and highlights both what goes on in his community, and "some of the things [the community] don't know they are doing" (Riber & Riber, 2004). In reflecting on the song "Gudo Guru," Mtukudzi described trying to convey the importance of modeling how *to be*. "If you are a father," he clarified, "your children will act like how you act" (Riber & Riber, 2004), and therefore, our role must be to recognize the world around us. In turn, I internalized this message of modeling to the notion of the permanence of racism, recognizing that as a White person, antiracism is a series of conscious actions to disrupt structural racism and the racism that people do not know they are doing. Regardless of whether or not we are being observed, leaders must model how we wish to be seen.

Tuku Music integrates this notion of modeling throughout the music. In talking about the song "Mutavara," which he wrote during Zimbabwe's revolution against Britain, its colonial ruler, Tuku asserted that they were "encouraging the youth to go out and join the struggle" (Riber & Riber, 2004). Because talking about revolution was not allowed, Tuku saw music as a way to reach the masses, while also keeping people safe. He clarifies that The Black Spirits were "talking about the feelings of the people, encouraging more and more youth to go out and fight... but you couldn't say that, so we used proverbs... that the regime couldn't understand" (Riber & Riber, 2004). While the meaning of the song "Mutavara" translates to "build the drum," Mtukudzi noted that it was sung in a dialect in the northern part of Zimbabwe, where the war had started. Mtukudzi suggested that those details led the people to understand "that beating the drum was 'take your arms and fight'" (Riber & Riber, 2004). In addition to the clear anticolonial message coded for those who would rise up, Tuku modeled knowing the idioms and language customs of the students we teach, an important recognition required to resist the "official master script" taught in schools (Ladson-Billings, 1999).

While being transparent about modeling the leadership attributes we would want our children to emulate—with a particular focus on knowing how to speak directly to the people in ways that can move them—Tuku identified additional constructs of racism. In "Kwawakabava" (Mtukudzi, 1997), for example, Tuku spoke more directly. An acoustic rendering of Black affirmation, Mtukudzi walks through a context of racism impacting Black children: "Your color is black, my son... Our color is black, my son... The color is black" (Mtukudzi, 1997). The song continues:

> Yes there are beautiful colors on the rainbow
> Yet your color is never on a rainbow
> Why then they say the color is beautiful
> Your color is beautiful
> Your color is beautiful
> Black is beautiful.

Tuku ends these lyrics with the repeated refrain, "Black is beautiful." In the album's liner notes (Mtukudzi, 1997), Tuku described "Kwawakabava" as a note to our children. He translates from Shona to clarify his message: "Don't forget your roots dear son. You can never transform yourself. You will always remain what you are... That can never be changed." His point was to recognize that Black people are beautiful, and that one must accept who they are despite the negative messages they will face.

"PLAY THE DRUM"

In 2007, Mtukudzi visited the high school I worked at in Berkeley, California. During his talk with students—an entirely Black and Latino student population—Mtukudzi repeatedly conveyed the importance of being who you are. One student asked him how he learned to know who he was, and Mtukudzi replied that he was "of many cultures, Ndebele and Shona, Zimbabwe, and Southern Africa," and that he was also "a son, a father, a musician, a storyteller, and an African" (Mtukudzi, 2007, personal communication). These multiple roles all meant that although he knew who he was, fundamentally, the world would see him as a Black man.

The high school students began to ask him what racism was like in Zimbabwe, and he told numerous stories about day-to-day life in Harare and in rural communities. He told of his growing up years, the dramatic changes brought on by revolution, and the contemporary struggles for basic resources. Weeks after Mtukudzi's visit, what stuck with students was his messages that antiblackness is experienced globally, and as he reminded them, "People are the same everywhere, we all have similar struggles, we all have pain, we all need to have joy." Mtukudzi shared that the experience of being Black may be different across the world, but "the experience of colonialism, of racism, is one that is shared" (Mtukudzi, 2007, personal communication).

In "Kucheneka" (which translates from Shona to "don't kill me"), Mtukudzi (2002) calls out global genocide and political violence. The song is filled with sharp guitar picks and an increasing intensity, broken only by the soothing embrace of the female backup singers, who respond occasionally to break the growing tension. The lyrics, translated from Shona, are direct and to the point:

When you kill me
don't kill me for the sake of it
when you kill me
you better eat me
why do you have to be so heartless

Why the malice?
Why the hatred?
Why the jealousy?
You should emulate
Those who are brave
Those who went before you
Those who love you
Those who make you what you are
Those who look after you.

I taught this song to both high school and undergraduate students as a demonstration of how music can build up meaning without needing to understand the language of the lyrics. Before offering translations, students made connections to systems of oppression, to racism that specifically targeted African Americans, Indigenous Americans, and Latinos. One college student argued that this song should have been sung to those implementing manifest destiny, essentially wiping out entire Indigenous American populations. In another school, a high school student suggested that the song reflected his own pathway from reacting violently against racist White peers to instead listening to his family, essentially offering a way to center "those who love you."

This recognition of racism—and of the need to validate and learn from our families and those who resist such racism—in both the music and lyrical content was attributed to Mtukudzi's intensity. As one high school student argued, "Tuku is so intense in the music, in his voice, that you know he must be talking about something important, and when you listen, you learn to apply your situation to his messages." Thus, while Tuku certainly centers an awareness of racism in his work, he does so through multiple and indirect ways, conveying nuances connected to resisting the racism that limits voice, that targets communities and nations of color. These indirect ways reflect Mtukudzi's lyrical approach that I link to critical race theory's storytelling tenet.

"A fairytale in a song is no message," Mtukudzi cautions in "Strange Isn't It" (Riber & Riber, 2004), over an arrangement of guitar, drums, and in harmony with several other singers on stage. Because of the obviousness of this message, I had high school students write responses to Mtukudzi prior to his visit to our classroom. One student shared this with Mtukudzi:

> A fairytale in a song is no message
> The messages we hear, we say we ignore
> Too focused on the beat and the hook to see the true meaning of the words, the nouns and verbs that confirm the stereotypes we trying to resist
> It ain't even dreams they are selling, we glorifying the path to the self-destruction of our community while claiming immunity and singing the lyrics like fools.

Mtukudzi was floored by the student's response. He said he was honored to have students interpret the lyrics and that once he put the song out there, he hoped people would make sense of his music in ways that made sense to them. "When you hear my song, and apply the lesson to your life," Mtukudzi clarified in our high school classroom, "then I have made a good song." The students then described the music they were typically exposed to, noting that most of the lyrics were offensive, degrading to women and people of color, and often they only appreciated the beats. As the student's excerpted quote indicates, offensive lyrics can become an unconsciously ignored part of a song, where they may find themselves singing along to lyrics they feel are deeply offensive. Mtukudzi reminded students that they can tell their own stories, but also that they had agency in choosing who and what plays in their ears.

The experience of hosting Mtukudzi at the high school was powerful for students and educators alike, particularly because his message of voice and storytelling reflected the students' experiences. These students had felt silenced both by their educational experiences and by the music they were exposed to, even as they often appreciated the beat, rhythmic flow, and cultural context of hip-hop. Yet Tuku offered them another lens, and shortly after his visit, students reaffirmed their own commitment to conscious hip-hop, seeking out local artists with messages of hope and healing. His impact on students intertwined with his commitment to the use of voice as a way of conveying what is happening in the world and reflecting the normalization of racism, while offering hope and agency that students had some control over messages they take in. The fact that Mtukudzi conveyed such depth through music entirely unfamiliar to the students, and often in a language they could not understand, exemplified his intentional storytelling approach that validated blackness in a way that resonated with students across the globe.

"I'M HERE TO PUSH A MESSAGE"

I once asked Mtukudzi if he would translate one of his songs for me, or at least let someone else translate, and he responded that if I really wanted to understand the words and the meaning, then I should learn not just Shona, but about Shona people. While his invitation to Zimbabwe was an honor, his deeper point was to urge me, and all people who listen to his music, to live multicultural ideals, rather than have someone translate other people's experience into our own. That Tuku graciously turned me down reflected my own early ignorance that his music was and is tied specifically to his message. Indeed, in "Messenger," Mtukudzi tells listeners to "Get me right get me straight I'm here to push a message" (1990/2011). In "Mean What You Say," Mtukudzi (2001) further vocalizes his belief that he serves as a messenger, singing, "That's why if I have a word, I say it loud, if I have a song, I sing it loud" (Mtukudzi, 2001). With much of this song in Shona, Tuku presents a dialogue between a grandson and a grandfather, and the multigenerational message reflects the importance of saying what you need to say as an orientation to life. From the stage, he repeatedly reminds that while he can introduce audiences to Zimbabwe, he is first and foremost a storyteller.

CONCLUSION

Oliver Mtukudzi and The Black Spirits have remained a force on the global touring circuit even beyond public shows, concerts, radio shows, and the occasional interview. Mtukudzi has continued to shed a light on difficult to navigate social issues, while modeling a multicultural blend of musical influences. I was personally exposed to his approach at exactly the right time in my life, and have integrated his work and critical race theory into my own leadership framework in order to both address the gaps in traditional educational leadership scholarship and advance a more multiculturally affirming notion of what education can be. Tuku reminds educators that we must be fully aware of our actions, and that in order to unite, we must first wake up and open our eyes.

AUTHOR'S NOTE

The author would like to thank Terri Watson and Jordan Gonzales for providing incredibly helpful comments and edits on previous drafts.

REFERENCES

Bell, D. (1992). *Faces at the bottom of the well: The permanence of racism.* New York, NY: Basic Books.

Bell, D. (1998). *Afrolantica legacies.* Chicago, IL: Third World Press.

Capper, C. A. (2015). The 20th year anniversary of critical race theory in education: Implications for leading to eliminate racism. *Educational Administration Quarterly, 51*(5), 791–833.

Delgado, R., & Stefancic, J. (2012). *Critical race theory: An introduction* (2nd ed.). New York, NY: New York University Press.

Duncan-Andrade, J., & Morrell, E. (2008). *The art of critical pedagogy: Possibilities for moving from theory to practice in urban schools.* New York, NY: Peter Lang.

Gay, G. (2000). *Culturally responsive teaching: Theory, research, and practice.* New York, NY: Teachers College Press.

Knaus, C. B. (2014). Seeing what they want to see: Racism and leadership development in urban schools. *The Urban Review, 46*(3), 420–444.

Ladson-Billings, G. (1999). Just what is critical race theory and what's it doing in a *nice* field like education? In L. Parker, D. Deyhle, & S. Villenas (Eds.), *Race is, race isn't: Critical race theory and qualitative studies in education* (pp. 7–30). New York, NY: Westview Press.

Mtukudzi, O. (1990/2011). Messenger. On *Chikonzi* [CD]. Johannesburg, South Africa: Sheer Sound.

Mtukudzi, O. (1997). Kwawakabava. On *Ndega Zvangu* [CD]. Johannesburg, South Africa: Sheer Sound.

Mtukudzi, O. (1999). Wake up. On *Tuku Music* [CD]. New York, NY: Putamayo World Music.

Mtukudzi, O. (2001). Mean what you say. On *Neria* [CD]. Johannesburg, South Africa: Sheer Sound.

Mtukudzi, O. (2002). Kucheneka. On *Vhunze moto* [CD]. New York, NY: Putamayo World Music.

Mtukudzi, O. (2003). Hariputirwe. On *Tsivo* [CD]. Johannesburg, South Africa: Sheer Sound.

National Public Radio. (2013). *Left alone: Oliver Mtukudzi sees music as therapy.* Retrieved from http://www.npr.org/2013/07/24/205149058/left-alone-oliver-mtukudzi-sees-music-as-therapy

Nickson, C. (2000). *Oliver Mtukudzi releases fairy tale of an album: Zimbabwean star's new Paivepo is biggest seller in nation's history.* Retrieved June 14, 2000, from http://www.mtv.com/news/1021391/oliver-mtukudzi-releases-fairy-tale-of-an-album/

Riber, J. (Director), & Riber, L. (Director). (2004). *Shanda* [DVD]. Harare, Zimbabwe: A Cross Culture and Tuku Music Production.

CHAPTER 14

BONO

Unapologetically Human

Ellyn Lyle
Yorkville University

Since gaining momentum in the 1950s, the rock music movement and the artists belonging to it have played an active role in influencing our understanding of the sociopolitical contexts in which we live (Bonastre, 2011). While there are multiple examples of rock's constructivist capacity, one artist stands out to me for both his public traction and his perseverance.

I confess I was not really a Bono fan. I knew very little about his music, even less about his humanitarian work, and associated him more with his antics than his efforts. Having grown up with music as a big part of my life, I did however like the aim of this collection: to explore the intersection of music and leadership. Not sure where to begin, I did some research to determine what musicians lived the values that I associated with leadership for social change: authenticity, tenacity, and compassion for the human condition. The results consistently brought me back to the lead vocalist of U2. Curiosity piqued, I followed the trail and found at the end of it a

Educational Leadership and Music, pages 149–156
Copyright © 2017 by Information Age Publishing
All rights of reproduction in any form reserved.

man who is far from above reproach, but absolutely transparent about his shortcomings:

> When you sing, you make people vulnerable to change in their lives. You make yourself vulnerable to change in your life. But in the end, you've got to become the change you want to see in the world. I'm actually not a very good example of that—I'm too selfish, and the right to be ridiculous is something I hold too dear—but still, I know it's true. (Tyrangiel, 2002)

In acknowledging his human fallibility, I think Bono and I both hope to mitigate distractions from his greater purpose: to showcase how music can be leveraged for social change.

THE FORMATIVE YEARS

Paul David Hewson was born in 1960 to a Catholic dad and a Protestant mum in deeply divided Northern Dublin. At age 12, after misalignment with a couple of religiously affiliated schools, Paul was enrolled in Mount Temple, Ireland's first nondenominational comprehensive high school. Hewson describes himself while at Mount Temple as wide-awake, head-strong, and experimental. In his 13th year, Paul's mother died suddenly, leaving him in the care of his father with whom Paul didn't have a happy relationship. Missing the nurturing presence of his mother and surrounded by sociopolitical and religious conflict, Paul was propelled by anger and confusion through most of his teen years. Less than an exemplary student, he found reprieve from these unhappy emotions in music and sought the company of those who shared his passion for performing (Black, 1997; Fry, n.d.; Jackson, 2001).

At age 14, Hewson responded to a call posted on his school bulletin board for musicians, and in doing so met his future bandmates: Larry Mullen, Jr., David Evans (later dubbed Edge), and Adam Clayton. The group was first named Feedback, and then The Hype, before eventually becoming U2. Playing publically at every opportunity, Hewson became known as Bono Vox (colloquial Latin for good voice). Soon shortened to Bono, his name would become known around the world (Assayas, 2005; Wikipedia, n.d.; Fry, n.d.; Jackson, 2001).

From his earliest days in music, Bono earned the respect of both fans and critics for his ability to captivate audiences with his music, as well as his passion for humanitarian causes. Making central the role of lived experience, he attributes using music to inspire change to growing up in a conflict-laden Ireland. A track called "Sunday, Bloody Sunday" (1983), on U2's third album, *War*, was the first of such songs to achieve international success. Detailing the continuing strife in his homeland, this song introduced a band and a man determined to bring consciousness to a global audience while calling for peace (Assayas, 2005; Frye, n.d.; Jackson, 2001).

During his nearly 40-year music career, there are multiple examples of songs that take up various causes ranging from famine and AIDS, to racism and war. This sociopolitical focus positioned U2 as a rock band with a social conscience and paved the way for its continued use of music to advance society. Given the sheer volume of tracks produced in almost four decades (approximately 250), it is difficult to select a single song that embodies the implications of his musical life as leadership. That said, "Ordinary Love," a song written for *Mandela: Long Walk to Freedom,* embodies important tenets of Bono's musical style and social leadership.

Ordinary Love

U2 members claim a longstanding friendship with Mandela, a friendship they say was born of Bono's humanitarian efforts in South Africa. Recorded at the end of 2013 for Mandela's cinematic biography, this song captures U2's classic sound as well as the lead singer's passion for the pursuit of peace. *RollingStone* described "Ordinary Love" as a song about "seeds of dreams," and says "U2 plays it perfectly: down to earth, while looking up" (Fricke, 2013).

In typical U2 fashion, "Ordinary Love" is metaphorically powerful yet compelling in its simplicity. The opening lyrics create an appealing aesthetic of the sea kissing the shore and skin being warmed by the sun, but then juxtaposes the ethereal with a reminder of lost beauty—beauty that we have forsaken. Drawing deeper on the implied neglect, the metaphor blooms as he chastises us for allowing ourselves to be thrown about at the whimsy of the sea, which leaves us worn but appearing polished. Alluding to Mandela, he points to what is achievable if we refuse to accept what is and how devotion to equity writes on humanity in an irreversible way. This tireless commitment to a better tomorrow is the essence of ordinary love, which the refrain maintains can elevate humanity if we are just tough enough and brave enough to embrace it. Understood this way, "Ordinary Love" condemns our indifference to the human condition, issues a call to action, and names that call to action as the very undergirding of what should be a baseline for conduct—not exceptional—ordinary.

Musical Life as Advocacy

While many artists use music to inspire others to action, Bono uses his craft to lead social change. He has been said to not only devote every free moment between studio sessions to humanitarian efforts, but also to take time from the band to make those efforts a priority. From the time of his youth, he has identified inequity and advocated change (Assayas, 2005).

In the band's early days, even predating U2, Bono used music to call for environmental responsibility in Ireland, to expose religious tensions, and call for peace. Soon after U2's formation, singles like "Sunday, Bloody, Sunday," began to top the charts with their explicit anticonflict messaging. By the mid-1980s, the band was developing a definite political flavor and found itself participating in high profile events such as Live Aid. It was shortly after this event that Bono expressed feeling deeply conflicted about having benefited from the concert aimed at overcoming famine in Africa. In an effort to live more authentically the causes he claimed to support, he and his wife Ali traveled to Ethiopia where they spent a month working with locals to develop infrastructure and improve living conditions. He claimed the experience wrote on his soul in such a way that once home he found the enduring perseverance of community-minded Ethiopians a humbling contrast with the selfishness of the developed world (Jackson, 2001).

Determined to continue support in Africa, and drawing great inspiration from Martin Luther King's historical messages about peaceful pursuits of change, Bono aligned himself with Artists United Against Apartheid and broadened his focus from famine to equality. His efforts earned him official recognition and gratitude from South African Archbishop Desmond Tutu. By the late 1980s, the frontman of U2 had the band performing benefit gigs for Amnesty International, which resulted not only in raising substantial funds, but also in tripling the organization's membership (Fry, n.d.; Jackson, 2001).

In the 1990s, in addition to his advocacy and efforts in Africa and Central America, he campaigned with Greenpeace against a nuclear power plant in Northern England. At this same time, in partnership with U.S. journalist Bill Carter, he helped turn the world's eye to the Bosnian conflict (Fry, n.d.).

Since the turn of the century, Bono has leveraged his musical stardom to rally numerous members of the public elite to participate in the efforts to end third world poverty and the AIDS epidemic. Specifically, he has served as spokesman for the Jubilee 2000 project, cofounder of DATA (Debt, Aid, Trade, Africa) in 2002, ONE Campaign to Make Poverty History (United States) in 2004, and Make Poverty History (United Kingdom) in 2005 (Fry, n.d.; Jackson, 2001).

In 2006 Bono cofounded RED, an initiative that lobbies large global organizations to market and sell specific product lines that commit a portion of their profits to the Global Fund to Fight AIDS, Tuberculosis and Malaria (Fry, n.d.).

Bono's advocacy has earned him several prestigious awards ranging from knighthood to Nobel Peace Prize nominations. He has made appearances in the Royal Court, at the Vatican, in Washington, DC, at the G8 Summit, and before the United Nations. He has been invited to the inner sanc-tums of presidents and religious leaders. Yet, despite his influence with the world's power brokers, he maintains that his greatest impact resides among the millions of ordinary people moved by his music and life to show love for humanity and work to make the world a better place (Fry, n.d.).

Musical Life As Embodied Leadership

Bali (2011) tells us that, "Across all domains and disciplines, leader-ship is about the human spirit and human endeavor, underpinned by core values that define character." This holds true in educational leadership where Bono's authenticity, tenacity, and compassion for the human condi-tion have interesting implications for viewing his musical life as embodied leadership.

At the heart of Bono's leadership is his ability to communicate a compel-ling vision, and inspiring others to join him, pursue that vision tirelessly (Bali, 2011; Stallard, 2014). Bono has demonstrated this capacity consis-tently for more than three decades. He uses his music to awaken people to the problems in our societies and nudges them out of their apathy toward social responsibility. Through his lyrics as well as his personal commitment to the causes to which he brings awareness, he encourages others to care about the human condition. His vigorous pursuit of these ideals has ac-corded him the respect of both fans and critics. This type of commitment is invaluable in the schools where we shape the minds and passions of future citizens and leaders (Leithwood, Day, Sammons, Harris, & Hopkins, 2006).

Bono also demonstrates authenticity, which is equally integral in earning the respect of those who look to him for leadership. Warren Bennis said, "Becoming a leader is synonymous with becoming yourself. It is precisely that simple and also that difficult" (Bali, 2011, p. 2). Bono is nothing if not real. His flaws are the subject of a range of publications and press releases (Browne, 2013). Under all of the egotism and pontificating, though, is a man committed to driving change. Schmidt (2012) reinforces this message when he argues that educative initiative must be built on the capacity to create space for agency in others so that they might expand their ability to enact those things they claim to hold dear thereby allowing them to live more authentically.

Closing this space between what we claim to hold dear and the ways in which we behave points to values congruence. Bono values peace and hu-man rights. He is responsible for raising millions of dollars to support these causes, has taken time from his own career to participate in the advance-ment of them, and has inspired hundreds of thousands of people to join the global efforts that advocate for them. Such stewardship is central to leader credibility. This is particularly important in schools where generational gaps pose divisiveness in empathy and understanding (Rinke, 2009; Van Damme, 2014).

Bono also values people. Not only those anonymous lives his causes aim to improve, but also those people who are in his more immediate circle. Bono's bandmates, for example, attest to his encouragement and reaffirmation of their worth. He publicly credits them as essential to U2 and splits the profits equally among the four longtime members as well as their manager (Black, 1997; Jackson, 2001; Stallard, 2014). In schools, we are responsible not only for valuing our colleagues, our students, their guardians, and the communities in which we find ourselves, but also teaching students to value themselves. Integral in this sense of self-worth is internalizing the responsibility to respect ourselves and others as we make our way in the world. Schmidt (2012) says, "One of the essential qualities of innovative leadership is the capacity to break the social deadlock often found in schools... [and] think of leadership as the ability to act with others" (p. 222).

When we value others, we create spaces where they are able to have an equal voice. Bono, in his insistence that his bandmates have equal voice in all decisions, models distributed power and shared leadership. He acknowledges that this style of decision making takes longer and is often frustrating, but he maintains that it is a necessary part of the path to excellence. Embracing this style of leadership, says Stallard (2014), creates a sense of unity and undergirds the ability to build a broader community.

A final leadership characteristic that Bono embodies is his adaptability to change. This trait is evident in the band's midcareer rebranding. While his advocacy was commendable in many regards, Bono's often politically charged sermonizing gave rise to many critics who condemned him for bombastic and egomaniacal self-righteousness (Fry, n.d.). In an effort to create a fresh persona, the band relocated to Berlin to gain some distance and revisit the intersection of their music and activism. The result was a more tempered but no less passionate presence in the pursuit of social equity. Educational leaders also must find the sweet spot of tempered passion so as to light a fire in the bellies of students and staff while protecting everyone from potentially damaging burns (Jean-Marie, 2010).

Bono's musical legacy viewed as embodied leadership suggests several ways of being that are integral to leading others. The ability to create, communicate, and pursue a compelling vision is central to successful leadership across contexts, including education. Authenticity and consistency between espoused and enacted values are also central to creating critical capacity to lead others. Similarly, demonstrating genuine appreciation for the value of others is an invaluable trait in educational leadership. Finally, resilience in the face of change is necessary in school's current climate of continuous fluidity.

CLOSING TIME

Bono, as the frontman of the iconic rock band U2 uses his music to make explicit the interconnectedness of the personal and the political, and the capacity of tenacity and conviction to inspire consciousness and change. The ideological coherence between his music and his sociopolitical activism lends a particular credibility to a man who otherwise may have been suspect by virtue of his career and occasional public antics. His enduring championship of social equity has positioned him as an exemplar of critical leadership, and in doing so has important lessons for educational leaders.

REFERENCES

Assayas, M. (2005). *Bono in conversation with Michka Assayas*. New York, NY: Riverhead Books.

Bali, V. (2011). *Leadership lessons from everyday life*. San Francisco, CA: Jossey-Bass.

Black, S. (1997). *Bono: In his own words*. London, England: Omnibus Press.

Bonastre, R. (2011). Beyond rock. Social commitment and political conscience through popular music in Australia 1976–2002. The case of Midnight Oil. *Coolabah, 5,* 54–61. Retrieved from http://www.ub.edu/dpfilsa/5bonastrecoola5.pdf

Browne, H. (2013). *The frontman: Bono (in the name of power)*. London, England: Verso.

Frick, D. (2013) U2: No ordinary love. *RollingStone.* Retrieved from http://www.rollingstone.com/music/songreviews/ordinary-love-20131202

Fry, M. (n.d.). *Bono biography.* Retrieved November 25, 2015, from http://www.atu2.com/band/bono/

Jackson, L. (2001). *Bono: The biography.* Frome, England: Butler & Tanner.

Jean-Marie, G. (2010) "Fire in the belly": Igniting a social justice discourse in learning environments of leadership preparation. In A. Tooms & C. Boske (Eds.), *Building bridges, connecting educational leadership and social justice to improve schools: Educational leadership for social justice* (pp. 97–119). Charlotte, NC: Information Age.

Leithwood, K., Day, C., Sammons, P., Harris, A., & Hopkins, D. (2006). *Successful school leadership: What it is and how it influences pupil learning* (Report RR800). Nottingham, England: University of Nottingham. Retrieved from http://webarchive.nationalarchives.gov.uk/20130401151715/http://www.education.gov.uk/publications/eOrderingDownload/RR800.pdf

Rinke, C. (2009). Exploring the generation gap in urban schools: Generational perspectives in professional learning communities. *Education and Urban Society, 42*(1), 3–24.

Schmidt, P. (2012). Critical leadership and music educational practices. *Theory into Practice Journal, 51*(3), 221–228.

Stallard, M. L. (2014, January). *Three practices CEOs should adopt from this rockstar* [Blog]. Retrieved November 15, 2015, from http://www.foxbusiness.com/business-leaders/2014/01/09/3-practices-ceos-should-adopt-from-this-rock-star/

Tyrangiel, J. (2002, February 23) Bono's mission. *Time, 15*(9). Retrieved November 15, 2015, from http://www.atu2.com/news/bonos-mission-1.html

Van Damme, D. (2014). *The ever-growing generation gap in the classroom. Education indicators in focus.* Retrieved from http://oecdeducationtoday.blogspot.ca/2014/03/the-ever-growing-generation-gap-in.html

Wikipedia. (n.d.). *Bono.* Retrieved November 25, 2015, from https://en.wikipedia.org/wiki/Bono

CHAPTER 15

KENDRICK LAMAR

An Authentic Leader in the Hip-Hop Community

Samuel Martin
St. Louis, Missouri

Heather Wynne
Westchester, New York

Carlos R. McCray
Fordham University

We got a young brother to stand for something!
We got a young brother that believe in the all of us!
Brother Kendrick Lamar! He's not a rapper, he's a writer, he's an author!
And if you read between the lines, we'll learn how to love one another! But you can't do that
Right on
I said, you can't do that—without loving yourself first
—Kendrick Lamar, 2015

This chapter examines the work of noted hip-hop artist, Kendrick Lamar. In his brief career, Lamar received 39 awards, and was awarded Best Rap

Educational Leadership and Music, pages 157–170

Album, Best Rap Performance, Best Rap Song, and Best Rap/Sung Collaboration at the 2016 Grammy Awards (Tsioulcas, 2016). Lamar introduced himself to mainstream music circles in 2011 with his debut studio album *Section .80*. In the ensuing years, Kendrick cemented his status as an elite emcee through his ability to capture the complexities of urban life via powerful narratives and insightful social commentary.

His second album, *Good Kid M.A.A.D. City* (GKMC) made him well-known in the hip-hop community. His single "Swimming Pools (Drank)," a reflective song describing the damaging effects of alcoholism, captivated the imagination, interest, and collective consciousness of the hip-hop community (Duckworth, 2012). A catchy chorus and hypnotic beat paved a path for Kendrick to communicate a poignant message. He made a club song that offered a scathing rebuke of the irresponsible alcohol consumption that is often synonymous with that lifestyle—and it is one of his most enduring songs. This is a consistent pattern in his work. He captures the audience's attention with the music and melody, and delivers lyrical content that critiques, conceptualizes, and comments on life in 21st century America. Morality is a consistent topic of his work, but he doesn't project a sense of self-righteousness. His music is so powerful because Lamar preaches without being pretentious.

Hip-hop music is a competitive genre of music by nature. Emcees compete with each other to determine who can sound the most unique while at the same time embodying the traditional traits of the average emcee. Kendrick's willingness to take risks has only increased his influence in the genre. The conceptual cohesion of *GKMC* hinted at the storytelling ability, knack for thematic moralizing, and his prodigious potential raising expectations for his third studio album. His adventurous spirit is most evident on his third and most recent album *To Pimp a Butterfly* (TPAB). *TPAB* is considered a contemporary classic because of its emotional rawness, conceptual depth, and lyrical dexterity (Carmancia, 2015; Hope, 2015; Kamier, 2015).

Overall, Kendrick's work has evidence of the traditional elements of West Coast rap, such as misogyny, materialism, and violence. However, what sets him apart from others is his exploration of traditional themes such as police brutality and masculinity, as well his willingness to touch on more taboo themes, such as mental health. His work challenges listeners to reflect on their own values and to then assess how those values impact their perception of self, perception of others, and ultimately how those perceptions influence their actions. It is this reciprocal process of transformation that makes Kendrick Lamar a leader that extends beyond hip-hop music into society as a whole.

FIVE LEADERSHIP THEMES FROM LAMAR'S MUSIC

Hip-hop culture is not only reflected in the lives of the students many educators serve, but also in the backgrounds of many of its leaders. Many current educators and certainly all future educators have matured as individuals and professionals in a world that celebrates the poetry of Tupac Shakur, recognizes Will Smith as a quality actor, and recognizes the mainstream financial success of Jay-Z. The hip-hop generation is no longer composed solely of young people, and by all accounts hip-hop has become mainstream, both musically and culturally.

Given the emotion and movement involved with music, individuals can develop their own leadership style from taking away musicians' concepts and themes (Hall, 2008). Hip-hop scholars have described the emcee as one who connects with the audience and uses that connection to communicate a message, which is similar to the role of an educational leader (Emdin, 2013). The relationship between hip-hop and educational leadership goes beyond simply listening to rap music. Several scholars have explored the connection between hip-hop culture and marginalized urban youth (Beachum & McCray, 2011; Bridges, 2011; Emdin, 2013; Hill, 2009; McCray, Beachum, & Yawn, 2015; Morrell & Duncan-Andrade, 2002; Petchauer, 2015). Hip-hop provides a foundation to begin a critical discourse in social justice education (Akom, 2009). It can provide meaningful principles such as motivation and values across primary and secondary students (Gause, 2008). The musical aesthetics include how individuals present themselves, process information, and communicate (Petchauer, 2015).

At its core, hip-hop culture creates a place for marginalized individuals to engage, express, and empower each other (Akom, 2009). It provides space for participants to disrupt traditional narratives (Baszile, 2009). Thus, it seems every educator should strive to be a hip-hop educator in order to connect better with his or her students. This chapter seeks to build upon that discourse by elucidating key principles found in the work of Kendrick Lamar in general and specifically within his latest album, *TPAB,* which can be applied to the field of educational leadership. The authors suggest five emergent themes from this album that are worth noting: authenticity, the power of vulnerability, empowerment, individualism, and double consciousness.

Authenticity

The foundation of all leadership is authenticity, and *TPAB* offers a straightforward and unapologetic narrative. Authentic leadership stems from the humanistic psychological aspect of self-actualization (Maslow,

1968; Rogers, 1959), and how, "through increased self-awareness, self-regulation, and positive modeling, authentic leaders foster the development of authenticity in followers," (Avolio & Gardner, 2005, p. 317). Kendrick is comfortable with his story and communicates this fact frequently. He takes pride in his Compton, California, upbringing and expresses appreciation for the lessons he learned from being reared in challenging circumstances. On the track "Home," Kendrick describes how his fame and fortune have allowed him to experience the world, but also how important it is for him to remain connected to his past.

In their essay "Discovering Your Authentic Leadership," George, Sims, McLean, and Mayer (2007/2011) describe authentic leadership as an orientation rooted in passionate, value driven action by leaders. Authentic leaders draw significant lessons from their life experiences to develop a strong sense of self that ultimately guides their leadership. Authentic leaders are in touch with their authentic self, practice their values, and reflect their principles in their daily actions (George et. al, 2007/2011). Though some may see it as shameful and embarrassing, Kendrick presents his autobiographical moments as triumphant and praiseworthy. His humility and genuineness strikes a chord with his audience and draws them in. Similarly, authentic educational leaders must be comfortable with themselves while empowering others to do the same (George et. al., 2007/2011). This in turn fosters confidence and inspirational thinking in the organizations they lead.

Vince, a high school building leader, is introduced in this vignette to help elucidate the discussion of the leadership lessons that compose this chapter:

> Vince has been charged with revamping a school wide transition program for incoming ninth graders. The faculty members responsible for implementing the program are split in opinion. Some are enthused about the change, others are against any changes, and the rest of the staff is indifferent. In leading a program with multiple, diverse perspectives, it is important for Vince to remain grounded and focused on his principles as a leader. He wants what's best for the students that his program will serve, and believes his teachers want the same. He can't allow himself to be swayed or distracted by minor conflict and personality differences. Vince began his first meeting by sharing an anecdote about a caring adult who positively impacted his high school experience.

In the scenario, Vince remained true to his personal values and principles as a leader. He explained the program through personal experiences so his staff could relate and connect to the reasons why he supported the program. He observed and offered feedback on the program while also navigating away from the politics in order to stay true to his professional self.

Vulnerability

The second lesson that one can draw from *TPAB* is the power of vulnerability. The academic study of leadership has long noted that effective leaders must be able to forge connections with the individuals they lead (Shamir & Eliam, 2005). Gone forever are the days when leaders barked commands indiscriminately and expected meaningful engagement from their people and quality results in return. Contemporary leaders must be skilled at the relational component of leadership as they are the managerial aspect of leadership (George et. al, 2007/2011). A key component of any relationship is vulnerability. Effective authentic leaders understand the importance of genuine, value based relationships and are able to use traits such as honesty and transparency to connect the people they lead.

In the song "u" (Duckworth, 2015), Kendrick opens up to his audience concerning his insecurities and regrets. He describes his battle with self-hate and suicidal ideation with stunning clarity and stark honesty. In a genre that prides itself on arcane concepts of masculinity and power, he offers a counternarrative. Scholars have utilized the counternarrative as an effective tool for amplifying a perspective or experience that has been historically marginalized (Decuir & Dixon, 2004). Educators employ counternarratives to directly challenge commonly held beliefs. Counternarratives are important for students to grow since they give an alternate viewpoint from commonly held beliefs (Kelly, 2013). His display of vulnerability doesn't make him weak, rather it makes him relatable. It makes him human. Educational leaders can increase the scope of their influence by embracing the concept of vulnerability.

It is important to define what vulnerability is and what it is not. Vulnerability is not having a confessional session with each of your followers. Vulnerability is honesty. Vulnerability is taking ownership of one's mistakes. Vulnerability is asking those you lead to hold you accountable. Effective leaders understand that establishing trust through transparency is critical to cultivating a followership (Avolio & Gardner, 2005; Norman, Avolio, & Luthans, 2010). To apply this lesson to daily life, Vince's tribulations of starting a schoolwide program will continue.

As a leader, Vince articulated a vision for the program and provided support for his program to be implemented within his building. This program was initiated since many students who have struggled academically due to hardship outside of school drop-out of high school by the end of their freshman year. However, three months after instituting the changes, the program was ineffective due to a lack of teacher support. Vince consulted with several key faculty members and asked for honest feedback. In opening himself up to critique, he realized that although his vision was clear to him, it was not clearly and consistently communicating to the faculty charged with implementing the program. He listened to the suggestions of the staff and made a decision to be responsive to their requests to have collaborative discussions regarding the direction of the program.

In this scenario, it would have been easy for Vince to dismiss the concerns of his faculty as short sighted and out of touch. However, this example highlights the power that leaders harness when they are vulnerable with the people they lead, and when they also provide a space for their voices to be heard and responded to with genuine feedback (Avolio & Gardner, 2005).

Empowerment

Empowerment can be defined as the act of connecting individuals to their agency to be instruments of change. Scholars have suggested that psychological empowerment serves as the impetus of organizational creativity (Conger & Kanugo, 1988; Spreitzer, Janasz, & Quinn, 1999). In order for an organization to thrive, its members must be invested in the vision and direction of the organization. Empowerment is critical to the engagement of members of the organization. The challenge for educational leaders is determining the most effective path for empowering teachers and staff while providing vision and direction for the individuals they lead.

Leaders who are committed to empowering individuals in their sphere of influence must be secure, confident, and outwardly focused. "By empowering others, a leader does not decrease his power; instead he may increase it" (Kanter, 1979, p. 328). This can be counterintuitive. It takes time and trust for leaders to learn how to share responsibility. In order to do so one must prioritize the long-term success of the organization over the short-term benefits of micromanagement. Scholars have described power as the ability to influence others (Bolman & Deal, 2013; French & Raven, 1959). Effective 21st century leaders are able to motivate and inspire others by harnessing referential power through the establishment of meaningful relationships.

As an artist, Kendrick's ability to impact his audience is rooted in his connectedness to his community and to his listeners. Listeners identify with his authenticity and vulnerability giving credence to his message of self-actualization. The message is simple: If Kendrick can face challenges and overcome, then you as a listener can overcome the challenges you face. He steps down from the pedestal of celebrity and embraces his humanity. Effective leaders position themselves as partners with the people they lead. We again come back to Vince, an authentic school leader implementing a schoolwide program to decrease his school's dropout rate:

Vince followed through with his efforts to collaborate with his 9th grade staff on a weekly basis. He provided financial resources to teachers leading the after school meetings so students can receive homework help before they go home. His meetings to 9th grade staff started with an inspirational Ted Talk or narrative to cultivate a sense of belonging and meaning toward mentoring the freshman class. Teachers were given an opportunity to discuss their hopes and fears in leading the students. Vince also put the teachers through professional development seminars aimed at identifying their leadership styles. Vince also spoke up about the freshman program to 10th through 12th-grade teaching staff and support staff. He encouraged his staff to speak with the 9th-grade team. Through this process, 9th-grade teachers were motivated and excited to make a difference in the freshman class.

Vince catapulted his program by giving teachers an opportunity to grow as professionals through continuing education seminars. Using Kanter's (1979) philosophy, Vince increased the power behind the program by instilling personal responsibility and change to the staff members running the program on a daily basis. The seminars and professional growth allowed the teachers to become leaders and would help foster ideas to improve the program.

Individualism

The next lesson that can be garnered from *TPAB* is individualism. Even in the eclectic world of hip-hop, Kendrick is seen as a unique individual. Vulnerability and authenticity lay the groundwork for individuals to embrace their individuality. Through Kendrick's authenticity and vulnerability, he is able to express his individualism in powerful ways. On the self-love track "i," Kendrick's chants detail the positive perspective that maintains despite the negativity and cynicism in the world (Duckworth, 2015). He asserts that loving yourself is a conscious choice.

For Kendrick, his positivity is rooted in his faith. He raps "illuminated by the hand of God, boy don't seem shy, I love my self" (Duckworth, 2015). This quote underscores the confidence that leaders have access to when one is comfortable with oneself. He also understands that the source of his confidence is rooted in his spiritual perspective. As an effective leader, Kendrick lives in the moment, but also understands that his message is bigger than the present moment and approaches his craft accordingly.

The individualism of effective leaders is manifested through their approach to leadership (Avolio & Gardner, 2005). Their principles provide a framework to handle the various situations they will encounter (Shamir & Eliam, 2005). Individualism also denotes how leaders interact with the members of their organization. An effective leader recognizes that autonomy is precious and sees oneself as a facilitator or conduit of great ideas. A leader who understands individualism encourages measured risk-taking and understands that the main difference between problems and opportunity is perspective. Furthermore, leaders who are comfortable with their individuality, embrace the character lessons they have learned from their past struggles, and dare their followers to embrace the unique experiences that contribute to their sense of self (Avolio & Gardner, 2005). Individuality is a key component of creating a culture that respects and honors creativity. Learning organizations are able to adapt because leaders provide opportunities and outlets for their members to grow.

Kendrick's sense of individuality is a tool for connecting with his audience and unifying individuals from diverse perspectives. He is unapologetic for his frank discussion of blackness, spirituality, and mental health even if it makes it difficult for some to completely grasp his work. Kendrick embraces his uniqueness and endears listeners with his honesty. Ultimately, individualism can be understood as the product of an authentic leader who embraces vulnerability. Leaders who are comfortable with their own individualism encourage and provide space for the members of their organization to embrace their sense of individualism. This lesson is showcased through Vince's dropout program after the implementation phase:

> The increase in teacher buy-in provided Vince with the confidence needed to embrace his unique perspective as a leader. The response to the changes Vince implemented has been largely positive. In fact, central office leadership took notice of the effectiveness of the 9th-grade program. The district has discussed replicating the program at the other district high schools. Even though Vince is excited about the expansion of the program, he has been careful to maintain the authenticity and sincerity that is essential to its effectiveness. As the program expands, it is essential that it reflects the principles that have guided its development up to this point. He understands the positive attention the program receives is beneficial, but recognizes the pressure 9th-grade staff members face with increased expectations.

Throughout the implementation process, Vince and his staff members continuously developed the program with their unique vision. Vince's past experiences, and the staff members' personal and professional visions shaped the foundation of service delivery. This 9th-grade program reflected the culture of the school, and the principles and values of Vince and his teachers. Without each stakeholder's individual input, the program may have looked completely different. Without Vince's individual perspective on leadership, the program might not have been as successful.

Double Consciousness

The final lesson that can be garnered from *TPAB* is the DuBoisan notion of double consciousness (DuBois, 1903). DuBois defined double consciousness as the double mindedness of the Black experience—a conflict between the authentic Black self and the American self. These two identities in perpetual conflict would not allow an individual to fully embrace one identity without forsaking the other. DuBois defines the veil "as this sense of always looking at one's self through the eyes of others, of measuring one's soul by the tape of a world that looks on in amused contempt and pity" (1903/1965, p. 215). Rath (1997) described double consciousness as both the awareness of double mindedness and as the act of navigating through two distinct worlds simultaneously. To this end, double consciousness is intellectual and experiential in nature.

It is clear that Kendrick negotiates a nuanced perspective of double consciousness; His work is not only about how he sees himself and his community, but also a critique of how outsiders view him and his community, the effect that perspective has on his audience, and how they in turn receive his message (DuBois, 1903/1965). On the song, "Institutionalized," Kendrick laments the expectations (or lack thereof) that society places on him and the difficulty he has escaping the consequences of those negative perceptions (Duckworth, 2015). As a young Black male, Kendrick understands that his life and music will be seen through a particular lens. On the track, "Blacker the Berry," he embraces the wholeness of his Black experience acknowledging that although he is viewed as flawed, it is important for to him affirm and celebrate the positive aspects of his identity (Duckworth, 2015). Shortcomings are not shameful, but are instead opportunities to display inner strength. He embraces the responsibility that comes with his platform as a Black male. The effects of double consciousness are long-lasting across marginalized students, which can affect academic achievement and their behavior (McCray & Beachum, 2011). Educational leaders must understand that their leadership is not only about how they view themselves, but also how students are impacted across racial groups, how staff members view their leadership approach, and the impact that has on their actual leadership outcomes.

Effective leaders are acutely aware of how they are perceived by others around them in their sphere of influence. They must be able to negotiate multiple relationships and diverse perspectives while providing steady leadership. Leaders who are unaware of how they are perceived are out of touch with their followers and struggle to lead their organizations effectively. In the decades following DuBois' original description of double consciousness, some scholars have noted its applicability beyond the traditional Black-White dichotomy (Logel, Iserman, Davies, Quinn, & Spencer, 2009;

Wallace, 2002). Double consciousness can be experienced across multiple aspects of identity, including but not limited to race, gender, class, orientation, and ability. The story of Vince and his program exemplifies this lesson.

Vince was delighted and excited that his program has gained support among his staff and has gained accolades across the school community. However, all of the hours of preparation and collaboration have put a strain on his personal life. He feels fulfilled within his school identity but has missed various life events that his three children have experienced with his wife. His oldest son won a Scholar Athlete Award for Cross Country, and he was unable to make the ceremony due to work demands. His youngest daughter started a community service club and he has not been able to support her service events. It is hard to balance his work and home life at times. It is also mentally demanding to have a leader persona at school, with a loving, doting father persona at home. In order to assist in this shift, he values his commute home alone. During this transitional time, he is able to listen to music and relax to the sounds of his car on his way home. He knows that improving and evaluating his identities across home and school is hard, but meaningful work. In order to succeed as a leader, Vince must constantly evaluate his external and internal demands while being a genuine, empowering leader at work and father at home. These stressors only serve as growth opportunities to make him a better man overall.

Identity is not manifested in a vacuum, and various personality factors impact one's leadership. Vince has to balance his identities as a middle-aged school building leader, husband, and father of three children. The middle-class Black male leader employed in an urban setting has to be aware of how his multiple identities impact his practice. Similarly, the White female leader in a predominantly Latino/a community has to be aware of how her audience perceives her through the lens of her multiple identities. Various identities may make some connections easier to forge and may make others more difficult. Awareness of these factors will allow her to be more purposeful in her interactions with members of her organization. Ultimately, double consciousness is not a luxury, but a necessity for effective leaders in the 21st century. Every individual in society holds various responsibilities and roles across their daily settings. It is imperative to assess all of one's roles to further grow and develop as a leader.

HOW KENDRICK LAMAR'S MUSIC CAN INFLUENCE SOCIETY

Music can help individuals grow and develop their sense of self through offering inspiration and the multiple perspectives artists may portray in their songs (Hall, 2008). Additionally, music is a powerful cultural agent influencing thoughts, attitudes, beliefs, and behavior. The platform that his music career provides cements his status as a leader. The lessons in authentic leadership we draw from the work of Kendrick Lamar can be applied practically through the lens of culturally relevant leadership (Beachum & McCray, 2012). This theory asserts that leaders must understand and acknowledge the culture in which they work, and align their practices with the needs and culture of the population they lead (Beachum & McCray, 2012). Further, culturally relevant leadership is promoted by having awareness of diversity and social justice within the school's community (i.e., liberatory consciousness), promoting positive attributes of what their diversity can bring (i.e., pluralistic insight), and by continuously reflecting and assessing their own practices (i.e., reflective practice; McCray & Beachum, 2011).

A clear strength of Kendrick's approach is his ability to connect with his audience. Kendrick uses music to serve as a motivation to initiate change in oneself and society, while staying culturally relevant through the use authentic language, conscientious lyrics, and relatable topics in his songs. By connecting with his audience on multiple levels within their cultural experience, Kendrick has transformed his role as an artist and increased his sphere of influence beyond the hip-hop community.

Likewise, educational leaders must be able to identify needs within their organizations, and act as agents of change while empowering others to do the same. Culturally relevant scholars assert that teaching practices must align appropriately with the student populations served (Beachum & McCray, 2008; Gay, 2000; Milner, 2006). In practice, a leader should be reflective toward not biasing their decisions toward the dominant cultural group, employ continuous reflection toward their behaviors and actions, and be mindful toward connecting across all student groups (Beachum & McCray, 2012; McCray, Wright, & Beachum, 2007; Villegas & Lucas, 2002). Adding this perspective, Vince's story will now conclude:

> The 9th-grade transition program was successful due to Vince's leadership style. He carefully addressed the needs of his students through a cultural lens, and maintained continuous collaboration with his staff members. He learned what the values of his school community were and worked to have those values reflected in the program. He was a genuine person and showed his vulnerability by changing his practices in response to constructive feedback. Throughout the process, Vince was able to refocus and empower his staff to instill value into the program he implemented. This in turn, influenced his faculty members to make a positive change for the school. Vince was also careful to recognize his different identities within and outside of his school environment. Vince embodied Kendrick's leadership qualities through his culturally specific lens, which led to school-wide success and collaboration.

Vince maintained his personal and professional self, in spite of challenges across school and home settings. He had an appreciation for the culture of his building, and understood the environment his students were exposed to. Through the student support program he led, Vince was able to initiate schoolwide change to improve the dropout rate of his freshman class. Throughout the process, he adjusted his service delivery to meet the needs of his team and most importantly was able to do so without sacrificing his authenticity. The program flourished because it was reflective of the school community, responsive to the cultural values of the building, and the perspective of multiple stakeholders were considered in the implementation of the program. Vince's challenges are not unlike the challenges many educational leaders face on a daily basis. Effective leaders must be sincere, principled individuals willing to engage and empower the people they lead. Ultimately, the principles discussed in this chapter are essential for any leader seeking to make a positive impact in their sphere of influence.

REFERENCES

Akom, A. (2009). Critical hip-hop pedagogy as a form of liberatory praxis. *Equity & Excellence in Education, 42,* 52–66. doi:10.1080/10665680802612519

Avolio, B., & Gardner, W. (2005). Authentic leadership development: Getting to the root of positive forms of leadership. *The Leadership Quarterly, 16,* 315–338. doi: 10.1016/j.leaqua.2005.03.001

Avolio, B. J., Gardner, W. L., Walumbwa, F. O., Luthans, F., & May, D. R. (2004). Unlocking the mask: A look at the process by which authentic leaders impact follower attitudes and behaviors. *The Leadership Quarterly, 15,* 801–823. doi:10.1016/j.leaqua.2004.09.003

Baszile, D. T. (2009). Deal with it we must: Education, social justice, and the curriculum of hip-hop culture. *Equity & Excellence in Education, 42,* 6–19. doi:10.1080/10665680802 594576

Beachum, F. D., & McCray, C. R. (2008). Dealing with cultural collision in urban schools: What pre-service educators should know. In G. S. Goodman (Ed.), *Educational psychology: An application of critical constructivism* (pp. 53–70). New York, NY: Peter Lang.

Beachum, F. D., & McCray, C. R. (2011). *Cultural collision and collusion: Reflections on hip–hop culture, values, and schools.* New York, NY: Peter Lang.

Beachum, F. D., & McCray, C. R. (2012). The fast and the serious: Exploring the notion of culturally relevant leadership. In J. L. Moore, III, & C. W. Lewis (Eds.), *African American students in urban schools.* (pp. 231–248). New York, NY: Peter Lang.

Bolman, L. G., & Deal, T. E. (2013). *Reframing organizations: Artistry, choice, and leadership* (5th ed.). San Francisco, CA: John Wiley & Sons.

Bridges, T. (2011). Towards a pedagogy of hip-hop in urban teacher education. *The Journal of Negro Education, 80*(3), 325–338.

Burns, J. M. (1978). *Leadership*. New York, NY: Harper & Row.

Caramancia, J. (2015, March 17). Emboldened, but not burdened by success. *The New York Times*. Retrieved from http://www.nytimes.com/2015/03/18/arts/music/kendrick-lamar-emboldened-but-burdened-by-success.html?_r=0

Conger, J. A., & Kanungo, R. N. (1988). The empowerment process: Integrating theory and practice. *Academy of Management Review, 31*, 471–482.

DeCuir, J. T., & Dixon, A. D. (2004). So when it comes out, they aren't that surprised that it is there: Using critical race theory as a tool of analysis of race and racism in education. *Educational Researcher, 33*, 26–31. doi: 10.3102/0013189X033005026

DuBois, W. E. B. (1903/1965). *The souls of black folk*. In J. H. Franklin (Ed.), *Three negro classics* (pp. 213–388). New York, NY: Avon Books.

Duckworth, K. L. (2012). *Good kid, m.a.a.d. city*. Santa Monica, CA: TDE/Aftermath/Interscope.

Duckworth, K. L. (2015). *To pimp a butterfly*. Santa Monica, CA: TDE/Aftermath/Interscope.

Emdin, C. (2013). Pursuing the pedagogical potential of the pillars of hip-hop through sciencemindedness. *International Journal of Critical Pedagogy, 4*(3), 83–99.

French, J. R. P., Jr., & Raven, B. (1959). The basis of social power. In J. M. Shafritz, J. S. Ott, & Y. S. Yang (Eds.), *Classics of organizational theory* (7th ed., pp. 52–64). Boston, MA: Wadsworth.

Gause, C. P. (2008). *Integration matters: Navigating identity, culture, and resistance*. New York, NY: Peter Lang.

Gay, G. (2000). *Culturally responsive teaching: Theory, research, and practice*. New York, NY: Teachers College Press.

George, B., Sims, P., McLean, A.N., & Meyer, D. (2007/2011). Discovering your authentic leadership. In Harvard Business Review (Eds.), *HBR's 10 must reads: On leadership* (pp. 163–178). Boston, MA: Harvard Review Press.

Hall, J. L. (2008). The sound of leadership: Transformational leadership in music. *Journal of Leadership Education, 7*, 47–68.

Hill, M. L. (2009). *Beats, rhymes and classroom life*. New York, NY: Teacher's College Record.

Hope, C. (2015). The overwhelming blackness of Kendrick Lamar's *to pimp a butterfly*. *The Muse*. Retrieved from http://themuse.jezebel.com/the-overwhelming- blackness-ofkendrick-lamars-butterfly-1691770606

Kamier, R. (2015). Kendrick Lamar's new album is critic-proof, and that's a good thing. *Fader*. Retrieved from http://www.thefader.com/2015/03/18/to-pimp-a- butterfly-commentary-proof

Kanter, R. M. (1979). Power failure in management circuits. In Shafritz, J., Ott, J., & Jang, Y. (2015). *Classics of organization theory* (pp. 320–339). Boston, MA: Cengage Learning.

Kelly, L. L. (2013). Hip-hop literature: The politics, poetics, and power of hip-hop in the English classroom. *English Journal, 102*(5), 51–56.

Lamar, K. (2015). i. On *To Pimp a Butterfly* [CD]. Hollywood, CA: Chalice Recording Studios.

Logel, C., Iserman, E. C., Davies, P. G., Quinn, D. M., & Spencer, S. J. (2009). The perils of consciousness: The role of thought suppression in stereotype threat. *Journal of Experimental Social Psychology, 45*(2), 299–312. doi:10.1016/j.jesp.2008.07.016

Maslow, A. H. (1968). *Toward a psychology of being.* New York, NY: John.

McCray, C. R., & Beachum, F. D. (2011). Capital matters: A pedagogy of self-development: Making room for alternative forms of capital. In R. D. Bartee (Ed.). *Contemporary perspectives on capital in educational contexts* (pp. 79–100). Charlotte, NC: Information Age.

McCray, C. R., Beachum, F. D., & Yawn, C. (2015). Saving our future by reducing school suspensions and expulsions among African American males. *Journal of School Leadership, 25*(2), 345–367.

McCray, C. R., Wright, J. V., & Beachum, F. D. (2007). Beyond brown: Examining the perplexing plight of African American principals. *Journal of Instructional Psychology, 34*(4), 247–255.

Milner, H. R. (2006). But good intentions are not enough: Theoretical and philosophical relevance in teaching students of color. In J. Landsman & C. W. Lewis (Eds.), *White teachers/diverse classrooms: A guide to building inclusive schools, promoting high expectations, and eliminating racism.* (pp. 79–90). Sterling, VA: Stylus.

Morrell, E., & Duncan-Andrade, J. M. (2002). Promoting academic literacy with urban youth through engaging hip-hop culture. *English Journal,* 88–92.

Norman, S. M., Avolio, B. J., & Luthans, F. (2010). The impact of positivity and transparency on trust in leaders and their perceived effectiveness. *The Leadership Quarterly, 21*(3), 350–364.

Petchauer, E. (2015). Starting with style toward a second wave of hip-hop education research and practice. *Urban Education, 50,* 78–105. doi:10.1177/00420 85914563181

Rath, R. C. (1997). Echo and narcissus: The afrocentric pragmatism of W. E. B. Du Bois. *The Journal of American History, 84*(2), 461–495.

Rogers, C. (1959). A theory of therapy, personality and interpersonal relationships as developed in the client centered framework. In S. Koch (Ed.), *Psychology: A study of science. Vol 3: Formulations of the person and the social context* (pp. 185–256). New York, NY: McGraw Hill.

Shamir, B., & Eilam, G. (2005). "What's your story?" A life-stories approach to authentic leadership development. *The Leadership Quarterly, 16*(3), 395–417.

Spreitzer, G. M., De Janasz, S. C., & Quinn, R. E. (1999). Empowered to lead: The role of psychological empowerment in leadership. *Journal of Organizational Behavior, 20*(4), 511–526.

Tsioulcas, A. (2016). Taylor Swift and Kendrick Lamar lead 2016 Grammy awards. *The record: Music news from NPR.* Retrieved from http://www.npr.org/sections/therecord/2016/02/16/466876001/taylor-swift-and-kendrick-lamar-lead-2016-grammy-awards

Villegas, A. M., & Lucas, T. (2002). *Educating culturally responsive teachers: A coherent approach.* Albany: State University of New York Press.

Wallace, D. L. (2002). Out in the academy: Heterosexism, invisibility, and double consciousness. *College English, 65*(1), 53–66.

CHAPTER 16

JILL SCOTT

A Champion of Affirmation and Empowerment: Lessons for Leaders on Mindfulness and Professional Self-Care

Patrice A. McClellan
Lourdes University

Public education is wrought with many misconceptions and negative judgments about the work performed in schools by caring professionals. Teachers, support staff, and principals' work in highly stressful and sometimes toxic environments to ensure children receive a quality education. Many of the accomplishments, accolades, and joyfulness brought to their profession often go unnoticed due to various agendas of stakeholders within and outside of the educational community. The agendas of politicians, community activists, parents, students, and teachers can often be at odds due to misunderstanding and misconceptions about the nature of the work teachers and principals perform on a daily basis. High-stakes testing is but one measure of accountability that puts constituents and stakeholders of public education at odds with teachers and principals.

Educational Leadership and Music, pages 171–183
Copyright © 2017 by Information Age Publishing
171

The national movement of high-stakes testing started in the 1980s, after the Civil Rights Movement and a solid decade of integration at the public school level (Dworkin & Tobe, 2014; Newsome, Christopher, Dahlen, & Christopher, 2006). In reports such as *A Nation at Risk* (1983) under the Reagan administration by the National Commission on Excellence in Education, angst about the effectiveness of public education began to fester. This report and those to follow in the Clinton, Bush, and Obama administrations cited the deficiency in science and mathematics of American students' ability to compete globally (Blake, 2008; Borek, 2008; Guthrie & Springer, 2004). These reports cited an increased need for accountability in schools, thus inherently blaming the teachers for the lack of competitiveness of students in comparison to their global counterparts.

The reform movement did not emerge by chance (Dworkin & Tobe, 2014). The changes during the Civil Rights Movement and desegregation were monumental to some, but caused conservative pundits, middle class/upper middle class White parents to mull over concerns regarding integration, diversity, and multiculturalism. The gains in integration were seen as gains that threatened those with more power, privilege, and property (Maslach, 2003; Maslach, Schaufeli, & Leiter, 2001). Thus, Berliner and Biddle (1988) labeled *A Nation at Risk* (1983) a product of a manufactured crisis (Berliner & Biddle, 1996) intended to weaken public schools (Berliner & Biddle, 1996; Dworkin & Tobe, 2014). The accountability/high-takes testing movement is based on misguided assumptions about public schools and the core premise of schools, teachers, and principals being broken. This movement assumes that teachers and principals cannot prepare students and/or adequately evaluate their success (McNeil, 2000). Therefore, the push for external motivation and assessment by politicians, businessmen, and external stakeholders. These value-laden assumptions lay a heavy burden (Friedman, 1993, 2002; Marshall, Brooks, & Brown, 2012) on school leaders that are having devastating effects on them as well as the students, families, and community members with whom they interact (Jacob, 2005; Smith & Syzmanski, 2013).

STRESS AND BURNOUT

It should come as no surprise that teachers and principals/school leaders are overworked, stressed, and on the brink of burnout. They face internal and external demands that far exceed their premonitions of their life's work as educators. Many who chose this line of work did so out of a calling to make a positive impact on future generations. Therefore, it's safe to say that many chose education as a calling over a career to advance for personal gain (Friedman, 1993, 2002; hooks, 1994; Newsome, Christopher, Dahlen, & Christopher, 2006).

Burnout is a crisis in the profession. It is widely known to exist, but rarely are there any methods to address the problem. It is mostly addressed with quick tips and day-long professional development seminars mainly due to the fact that intrinsic motivators are what can slowly chip away at its effects (Friedman, 1993, 2002; Marshall et al., 2012). There are various psychological and sociological approaches to understanding and defining burnout. Psychologists state burnout can be described as emotional exhaustion and a sense of loss of personal accomplishment in regards to a career (Friedman, 1993, 2002; Maslach, 2003; Maslach et al., 2001). It can also lead human service professionals and/or teachers to withdraw emotionally from their work, perform less effectively, and become more hostile to those they are supposed to help. Burnout is also characterized as questioning the value of one's work and sense of self (Pines, 1996; Pines & Aronson, 1988). Teachers and principals who experience burnout, inadvertently question their role as educators, their level of importance and/or expertise in their field, and may lash out at those entrusted in their care. Organizational studies scholars also reiterate that professionals often define themselves in terms of their work roles (Clegg, Hardy, & Nord, 2013). To be dissatisfied with the work and work demands reflects a discontent with and appraisal of their own worth as educators.

Much has been researched regarding teacher stress, workload, and burnout (Dworkin & Tobe, 2014; Supovitz, 2009; Wyn, Turnbull, & Grimshaw, 2014). However, the majority of research neglects the plight of principals who lead in these turbulent and toxic environments as well. Few studies (Carr, 1994; Klocko & Wells, 2015; Wells, 2013) detail how the principalship is hazardous to one's health due to the overwhelming demands placed on them. These research studies cite dealing with teacher stress negatively impacts the teacher/principal trust relationship. Stress and burnout of key personnel in schools creates an environment and breeding ground for distrust, apathy, and a "blame victim" mentality (Federici & Skaalvik, 2012). It is urgent to combat the effects of stress and burnout. Therefore, this chapter posits that professional self-care and mindfulness be embraced as a mandate of the work of leading schools (Collins, 2005; Hoy, Gage, & Tarter, 2006; Langer, 2000; Lewis & Ebbeck, 2014; Shapiro, Brown, & Biegel, 2007).

PROFESSIONAL SELF-CARE AND MINDFULNESS

School leaders/principals are all too familiar with stress. The emotional, physical, and psychological toll can be insurmountable and vary from day to day. Stress can have negative effects such as mood changes, apathy, and distrust, but can also have positive effects for some that compel them to action (Collins, 2005; Federici & Skaalvik, 2012). Stress needs to be minimized, but how shall leaders cope with stressful situations outside of their control?

Educators (teachers, principals, school counselors) in general are guided by a desire to help others. The cost of caring and the emotional investment may lead them to neglect their own personal self-care. Professional self-care is defined as an individual's ability to balance personal, occupational, and spiritual activities that promote rejuvenination of energy, harmonious interconnectedness, and overall health promotion (Newlin, Knafl, Melkus, 2002; Spitzer, Bar-Tal, Ziv, 1996; Ellis, 2000). Caring of self is inextricably linked to mindfulness. Mindfulness is defined as bringing ones's complete attention to what is happening in the present moment, cultivating awareness with the aim of helping people live each moment of their lives with intent, and enabling a greater awareness of "what is." (Langer, 2000; Lewis & Ebbeck, 2014; Raab, 2014).

Self-care and mindfulness have deep spiritual roots (Collins, 2005; Raab, 2014). They are an integral part of a person's life, including emotional, spiritual, and physical health. Caring for self and being mindful requires an intent, a decision, a level of self-awareness that promotes self-love, affirmation, health, and growth. Through examination of Jill Scott's empowering lyrics, it is hoped that the fire of the calling to teach and lead schools will overpower the negativity that surrounds the discourse of public education, thus combatting the negative effects of stress.

JILL SCOTT: LYRICIST, POET, AND CHAMPION OF EMPOWERMENT

Jill Scott was born in Philadelphia in 1972. She was an only child raised by her mother and grandmother. After years of abuse by her stepfather, Scott escaped through journaling and writing, chronicling the turmoil of her life, school, and neighborhood woes. Poetry became an outlet as her 8th-grade English teacher introduced her to the works of poetess Nikki Giovanni. At the juncture, Scott began her love affair with writing, poetry, and performing. Scott majored in English at Temple University with hopes of becoming a high school teacher—inspiring others as she was inspired. Delving more into the arts, Scott felt the confines of academia were stifling to her creativity. She dropped out of Temple to pursue her singing career. Shortly after, she formed a partnership with Scott Storch, a producer who had worked with artists such as Christina Aguilerra, Chris Brown, and Beyonce to name a few. Together they co-wrote "You Got Me" for The Roots, a Philadelphia-based rap group. The vocals she prepared on this song were replaced with

Eryka Badu, another songstress and neo-soul artist. Dealing with the turmoil, neglect, and rejection of that encounter, Scott went on to persevere, write, and journal. Writing and journaling helped Jill Scott to become an icon in the neo-soul community. Neo-soul is a genre of R&B soul music that pays homage, reminds one of, or directly samples old-school R&B artists of the 1970s and 1980s (Cunningham, 2010). The neo-soul designation is a continuation of R&B with a jazz swing and new age appeal that advances the genre and tradition of self-affirmation, self-acceptance, love, relationships, and social justice to name a few themes of songs.

By the late 1990s, Philadelphia had become the nexus for neo-soul musicians. During this time, Scott wrote and debuted her groundbreaking song "A Long Walk," which described a first date. Songs that mimicked everyday life with her soulful vocals made her a new sensation on the music scene. Scott's music incorporates jazz, poetry, modern R&B, and elements of hip-hop. Her music is liberating, empowering, and complete with raw emotion that encompasses the ups and downs of life. For this, it is fitting that her music be used to empower school leaders to persevere during tough times.

Hate on Me

The discourse on public education often does not have a positive tone. Although there are many success stories to tout, the national debate is rife with stories of failing schools, underpaid teachers, ineffective leaders, and so on. However, in this chapter public education is to be valued and supported with acts and words of affirmation.

The song "Hate on Me" by Jill Scott was released in 2007. The overarching premise of the song is that "haters" are those who will always find something wrong with what one is doing. Haters are often living examples of the old adage "misery loves company." This song, with its blues undertones and jazz upbeats starts off with:

> If I could give you the world, On a silver platter
> Would it even matter, You'll still be mad at me
> If I can find in all this, a dozen roses
> Which I would give to you, you'd still be miserable
> In reality
> I'm gon be who I be
> And I don't feel no faults, for all the lies that you bought
> You can try as you may, Break me down when I say
> That it ain't up to you, gon on do what you do

This verse speaks volumes to those working hard in schools. Their work goes unnoticed, unappreciated, and not rewarded. In fact, it may seem the more positive work is done, the more the scrutiny it invokes. Thus, the haters arise. Teachers, school leaders/principals, and other school personnel work from their hearts. They plan lessons with precision, hug the child that cries because mom and dad's argument scares him, keep a plastic bin of snacks for the hungry child, and even brushes the hair of the little girl whose mom was in a rush. The work of those in schools encompasses more than teaching children how to read, write, and do arithmetic. As seen from the examples, the work of those in schools is to care for the whole child; their social, emotional, and educational well-being. Yet, despite all of these efforts, the haters of public education see only 3rd-grade reading scores or high school graduation rates as signs of a successful education. These scores are important indicators, but should not be viewed without the proper contextual understanding of other factors that influence them and the environment in which they were learned.

The second verse of "Hate on Me" states:

If I gave you sanity
For the whole of humanity
Had all the solutions for the pain and pollution
No matter where I live
Despite the things I give
You'll always be this way
So go ahead and . . .

Hate on me

You cannot . . .
Hate on me
Cause my mind is free
Feel my destiny
So shall it be

In this verse, Jill Scott references providing solutions for the pain and pollution; but no matter what, a hater will always choose to see things from their perspective. Many decisions are made in regards to public education without consulting those on the front lines dealing with students, families, and communities. The high-stakes testing movement is but one example.

By chance if there was a paradigm shift in viewing public education, perhaps those with the vast experience of educating children and leading schools would be consulted. Imagine the destiny of children if those entrusted with their care were called to lobby meetings. Imagine a school with those decisions at the hands of the experts. It is definitely a possibility to be included in the decision making, but school leaders *must* do as Jill Scott says in the chorus; let the haters hate.

Hate on me hater
Now or later
Cause I'm gonna do me
You'll be mad baby

Go head and hate
Go head and hate on me hater
I'm not afraid of
What I got I paid for
You can hate on me . . .

By letting the haters hate, it frees up mental space, emotional energy, and time to do what is best for children and schools. The focus shifts from giving too much energy to the negative naysayers. Yes, schools have problems and sometimes a lot of them, but focusing on more positive efforts can change a mountain into a molehill. Practicing this simple, yet difficult task is being mindful and accepting haters for what they are: a distraction to the overall plan and purpose of education. At the end of the day, school leaders are mandated by the universe to live a good life, to care for themselves as they care for others. Ignore the haters, stay on task because children's lives matter.

Golden

Released in 2004 on her 3rd album. "Golden" peaked on American and U.K. singles charts and was also nominated for a Grammy Award for best R&B album. This song reflects her life experience of taking time for self-reflection and learning to be free of others judgements and living her best life. It is empowering on so many levels. Concepts such as freedom, strength, and joy are just a few ideals that educators could grasp hold. To take freedom, generally speaking in terms of being free to be yourself, and wear it proudly speaks to the teachers who desire for their students to be and do their best, or to that school leader who supports teacher expertise and is a champion for students and their families.

Letting joy unfold as one is "living life likes it's golden" can be a source of empowerment to educators as they assess the nature and purpose of their work, to practice self-care (Collins, 2005), and to be mindful about exuding confidence and joy during difficult times (Newsome et al., 2006). As stated previously, self-care (Collins, 2005) and mindfulness (Hoy et al., 2006; Langer, 2000; Raab, 2014) have huge spiritual undertones, as does this song. For example, the third verse states:

I'm holdin on to my freedom
Can't take it from me
I was born into it,

It comes naturally
I'm strumming my own freedom
Playing the god in me
Reverence in his glory
Hope he proud of me

Freedom, strength, and joy are self-care concepts (Collins, 2005; Lewis & Ebbeck, 2014; Raab, 2014), but are also strong themes in the liberation theology cannon (Cannon, 2006; Cone, 1997; Gutierrez, 1988), which places the experiences of the exploited and alienated at the center of an analysis when seeking solutions to problems. To care for self in this way requires a shift in how a school leader views their purpose in the profession. It requires one to put self first before others. There's an old adage that states, "One cannot give what one does not have." To neglect oneself depletes what is available to give to others. Rather than burn out and be stressed to the brink, recognition of the need to take a few moments to assess ones' reality is pertinent.

Blessed

To culminate the Jill Scott experience, the song titled "Blessed" is fitting for motivating teachers and school leaders. This song speaks to the complexity of the nature of their profession: experiencing the ups and downs of dealing with students and their families, sacrificing time that often conflicts with personal lives, and having the courage to acknowledge the stress of their work. The first verse:

This is the last take for the night
Understand it's kinda late
And I gotta get home to my son
'Cause he's so special to me
I mean I gotta see him
I need to breathe him
That's my baby don't call me crazy
I love the studio but I love him more

School leaders often pull long days and nights from attending open houses at school, parent-teacher conferences, to after-school events and activities. Jill Scott's first verse references a long day at the studio and wanting to go home and see her son. In this portion of the song, Scott clearly speaks to the love of her career, but the love of her family even more. Surely, school leaders feel the same. However, as with any profession, one has to prioritize work and life, painfully seeking normalcy from day to day

(Allison, 1997; Carr, 1994; Federici & Skaalvik, 2012; Hoy et al., 2006; Marshall, et al. 2012).

In the second verse, the lyrics elude to stress:

> I woke up in the morning feeling fresh to death
> I'm so blessed, yes yes
> I went to sleep stressed, woke up refreshed
> I'm so blessed, yeah yes
> Water in my face and everything is in its place
> Peace of mind even my grace
> I'm so blessed, yes yes yes

Unfortunately going to bed with stress, thinking of what wasn't accomplished and what needs to be done plagues many teachers and school leaders (Allison, 1997; Carr, 1994; Friedman, 1993). To wake up with peace of mind is challenging. Being blessed as Jill Scott exemplifies in her lyrics is a deliberate choice and requires a shift in thinking of situations and circumstances. Practicing self-care (Newsome et al., 2006) and mindfulness (Langer, 2000) also requires deliberate intention and awareness to be present, while acknowledging feelings, thoughts, and emotions regarding stressful situations at that time.

In the big scheme of things, school leaders are blessed in the spiritual, reciprocal sense. They are able to shape the minds and positively influence the next generations of thinkers, doctors, lawyers, teachers, and school leaders. Switching focus from the haters and the negative discourse about public education to a more appreciative tone aids in promoting a healthier environment in which children learn (Calabrese, 2002; Hoy et al.; 2006; Johnston, 2010; Lewis & Ebbeck, 2014). Monumental change begins with small steps (Senge, 1994). A small, yet challenging step is for school leaders to take back their power, by centering themselves as the catalyst for changing the environment within schools. By centering themselves and taking care of self, school leaders will be better equipped to handle the stress and complexities of dealing with students, parents, and the community.

PARADIGM SHIFT AND SPIRITUAL REJUVENATION

The overarching premise of this chapter is that school leaders rarely practice professional self-care (Lewis & Ebbeck, 2014; Shapiro et al., 2007; Wells 2013) during times of stress and adversity. This often leads to burnout and dissatisfaction with the job (Carr, 1994; Friedman, 2002; Wells, 2013). It is a fact that there are aspects of being a school leader that are beyond one's immediate control. However, through self-care and mindfulness practices, school leaders are hopefully empowered to be a catalyst for change within the school environment. But to do so will cause a paradigm shift in thinking. This is to care for the social, emotional, and physiological well-being of self before attending to the needs of others. This concept is often difficult to grasp because the education profession is centered on the needs of students, teachers, parents, and surrounding communities, inadvertently neglecting the well-being of its workers (Klocko & Wells, 2015).

Jill Scott, as many school leaders, wears multiple hats. She is an acclaimed singer, actress artist, poet, and parent. These roles culminate the totality of the person she is. Each role adds value to her outlook on life as she is adamant about self-care and setting aside time to journal and write about the joys and frustrations of life. In this way, she rejuvenates her spirit so that she is able to live her life's passion. As Jill Scott is intentional about rejuvenation, so should school leaders.

Professional self-care and mindfulness have spiritual roots grounded in Buddhist and Christian traditions (Collins, 2005; Langer, 2000; Raab, 2014). The concept of spirituality is often complex and controversial as it relates to school leaders and public education (Dantley, 2003b; Dantley & Tillman, 2010; Drath & Palus, 1994; Gibson, 2014). The complexity of spirituality is due in part because of peoples' sensemaking is shaped by cultural, social, economic, and religious life experiences (Cone, 1997; Dantley, 2003a; Gibson, 2014; Gutierrez, 1988; Tisdell, 2003). In an attempt to simplify the concept, spirituality is defined as a personal commitment to a process of inner development that ultimately realizes the interconnectedness between, self, others, and a higher power in an effort to construct knowledge, meaning, and purpose (Dantley, 2003b; Dillard, Abdur-Rashid, & Tyson, 2000; Fairholm, 1997; Fry, 2003).

To simplify does not negate the fact that spirituality is often contested and controversial, however, the goal of inclusion in this chapter is to empower school leaders to center themselves, rejuvenate their spirit, realign their purpose and/or calling as leaders, and practice forms of professional self-care in an effort to strive for success in schools. School leaders carry the heavy weight of student achievement, teacher satisfaction, and parent involvement to say the least. Striving for success in schools is an act of change.

The change must begin with that internal dialogue of accepting "what is" and doing as Jill Scott states: "Let the Haters Hate." There will always be naysayers, but having confidence and in being a change agent and responsible for the learning and teaching environment with the school within the school is living life like its golden. Allowing for purposeful attention to the environment within schools that will allow school leaders to connect on a deeper level with teachers (Hoy et al., 2006), students, and parents, and therefore, empowering others to do the same. Changing outlook and taking small monumental steps is akin to Jill Scott's stance on being blessed. By chronicling Scott's transformation through song, hopefully school leaders will be empowered to take intentional steps to impact schools and the environment in which teachers teach and students learn.

REFERENCES

Allison, D. G. (1997). Coping with stress in the principalship. *Journal of Educational Administration, 35*(1), 39–55.

Berliner, D. D., & Biddle, B. J. (1996). *The manufactured crisis: Myths, fraud, and the attack on America's public schools.* New York, NY: Perseus Books.

Blake, S. (2008). A nation at risk and the blind men. *Phi Delta Kappan, 89*(8), 601–602.

Borek, J. (2008). A nation at risk at 25. *Phi Delta Kappan, 89*(8), 572–574.

Calabrese, R. (2002). *The leadership assignment: Creating change.* Boston, MA: Allyn & Bacon.

Cannon, K. (2006). *Black womanist ethics.* Eugene, OR: Wipe and Stock.

Carr, A. (1994). Anxiety and depression among school principals: Principalship can be hazardous to your health. *Journal of Educational Administration, 32*(3), 18–34.

Clegg, S. R., Hardy, C., & Nord, W. R. (Eds.). (2013). *Handbook of organizational studies* (2nd ed.). Thousand Oaks, CA: Sage.

Collins, W. L. (2005). Embracing spirituality as an element of professional self-care. *Social Work & Christianity, 32*(3), 263–274.

Cone, J. H. (1997). *God of the oppressed.* Maryknoll, NY: Orbis Books.

Cunningham, P. L. (2010). There's nothing really new under the sun: The fallacy of the neo–soul genre. *Journal of Popular Music Studies, 22*(3), 240–258.

Dantley, M. E. (2003a). Critical spirituality: Enhancing transformative leadership through critical theory and African American prophetic spirituality. *International Journal of Leadership in Education, 6*(3), 3–17.

Dantley, M. E. (2003b). Purpose-driven leadership: The spiritual imperative to guiding schools beyond high-stakes testing and minimum proficiency. *Education and Urban Society, 35*(3), 273–291.

Dantley, M. E., & Tillman, L. C. (2010). Social justice and moral transformative leadership. In C. Marshall & M. Olivia (Eds.), *Leadership for social justice: Making revolutions in education* (pp. 19–34). Boston, MA: Allyn & Bacon.

Dillard, C. B., Abdur-Rashid, D., & Tyson, C. A. (2000). My soul is a witness: Affirming pedagogies of the spirit. *International Journal of Qualitative Studies in Education, 13*(5), 447–462.

Drath, W. H., & Palus, C. J. (1994). *Making common sense: Leadership as meaning-making in a community of practice.* Greensboro, NC: Center for Creative Leadership.

Dworkin, A. G., & Tobe, P. F. (2014). The effects of standards based school accountability on teacher burnout and trust relationships: A longitudinal analysis. In D. V. Maele (Ed.), *Trust and school life* (pp. 121–143). St. Bellaire, TX: Springer Science.

Fairholm, G. W. (1997). *Capturing the heart of leadership: Spirituality and community in the new American workplace.* Westport, CT: Praeger.

Federici, R. A., & Skaalvik, E. M. (2012). Principal self-efficacy: Relations with burnout, job satsifaction and motivation to quit. *Social Psychology of Education, 15*(1), 295–320.

Friedman, I. A. (1993). Burnout in teachers: The concept and its unique core meaning. *Educational and Psychological Measurement, 53*(4), 1035–1044.

Friedman, I. A. (2002). Burnout in school principals: Role related antecedents. *Social Psychology of Education, 5*(3), 229–251.

Fry, L. (2003). Toward a theory of spritiual leadership. *The Leadership Quarterly, 14*(2), 693–727.

Gibson, A. (2014). Principals' and teachers' views of spirituality in principal leadership in three primary schools. *Educational Management Administration & Leadership, 42*(4), 520–535. doi: 10.1177/1741143213502195

Guthrie, J., & Springer, M. (2004). A nation at risk revisited: Did "wrong' reasoning result in "right" results? At what cost? *Peabody Journal of Education, 79*(1), 7–35.

Gutierrez, G. (1988). *A theology of liberation: History, politics, and salvation* (15th ed.; C. Inda & J. Eagleson, Trans.). Maryknoll, NY: Orbis Books.

hooks, b. (1994). *Teaching to transgress: Education as the practice of freedom.* New York, NY: Routledge.

Hoy, W. K., Gage, C. Q., III, & Tarter, C. J. (2006). School mindfulness and faculty trust: Necessary conditions for each other. *Educational Administration Quarterly, 42*(2), 236–255.

Jacob, B. A. (2005). Accountability, incentives, and behavior: The impact of high-stakes testing in the Chicago Public Schools. *Journal of Public Economics, 89*(1), 761–796.

Johnston, J. G. (2010). *Thriving on collaborative genius: The art of bringing organizations to life.* Perrysburg, OH: Partners for Innovations.

Klocko, B. A., & Wells, C. M. (2015). Workload pressures of principals: A focus on renewal, support, and mindfulness. *NASSP Bulletin, 99*(4), 332–355.

Langer, E. J. (2000). The construct of mindfulness. *Journal of Social Issues, 56*(1), 1–9.

Lewis, A. B., & Ebbeck, V. (2014). Mindful and self-compassionate leadership development: Preliminary discussions with wildland fire managers. *Journal of Forestry, 112*(2), 230–236.

Marshall, J. M., Brooks, J. S., & Brown, K. M. (Eds.). (2012). *Juggling flaming chainsaws: Academics in educational leadership try to balance work and family.* Charlotte, NC: Information Age.

Maslach, C. (2003). Job burnout: New directions in research and intervention. *Current Directions in Psychological Science, 12*(5), 189–192.

Maslach, C., Schaufeli, W. B., & Leiter, M. P. (2001). Job burnout. *Annual Review of Psychology, 52*(1), 397–422.

McNeil, L. (2000). *Contradictions of school reform: Educational costs of standardized testing.* New York, NY: Routledge.

Newsome, S., Christopher, J. C., Dahlen, P., & Christopher, S. (2006). Teaching counselors self-care through mindfulness practices. *Teachers College Record, 108*(9), 1881–1900.

Pines, A. M. (1996). Burnout, existential perspectives. In W. B. Schaufeli, C. Maslach & T. Marek (Eds.), *Professional burnout, recent developments in theory and research.* Washington, DC: Taylor & Francis.

Pines, A. M., & Aronson, E. (1988). *Career burnout: Causes and cures.* New York, NY: Free Press.

Raab, K. (2014). Mindfulness, self-compassion, and empathy among health care professionals: A review of the literature. *Journal of Health Care Chaplaincy, 20*(1), 95–108.

Senge, P. M. (1994). *The fifth discipline: The art and practice of the learning organization.* New York, NY: Doubleday.

Shapiro, S. L., Brown, K. W., & Biegel, G. M. (2007). Teaching self-care to caregivers: Effects of mindfulness-based stress reduction on the mental health of therapists in training. *Training and Eduction in Professional Psychology, 1*(2), 105–115.

Smith, V. G., & Syzmanski, A. (2013). Critical thinking: More than test scores. *NC-PEA International Journal of Educational Leadership Preperation, 8*(2), 16–26.

Supovitz, J. (2009). Can high stakes testing leverage educational improvement? Prospects from the last decade of testing and accountability reform. *Journal of Educational Change, 10*(1), 211–227. doi: 10.1007/s10833-009-9105-2

Tisdell, E. J. (2003). *Exploring spirituality and culture in adult and higher education.* San Francisco, CA: Jossey-Bass.

Wells, C. M. (2013). Principals responding to constant pressure: Finding a source of stress management. *NASSP Bulletin, 20*(10), 1–15.

Wyn, J., Turnbull, M., & Grimshaw, L. (2014). The experience of education: The impacts of high stakes testing on schools, students, and their families. A qualitative study. In Whitlam Institute (Ed.), (pp. 1–35). Sydney Australia: University of West Sydney.

CHAPTER 17

FROM "SMOOTH OPERATOR" TO "YOUNG, GIFTED, AND BLACK"

Understanding Big Daddy Kane's Evolution as a Metaphor for a Praxis of Critical Care in Leadership

Alprentice A. McCutchen
Alexander Hamilton High School

Rosa L. Rivera-McCutchen
Lehman College CUNY

As with effective school leadership, musical trends have the power to shape the tenor of the music of their day, coaxing out critically conscious and emancipatory lyrics from the least likely of artists. One exemplar of this is none other than hip-hop artist Antonio Hardy, best known as Big Daddy Kane. In this chapter, we examine the evolution of Kane's early music that embodied greater sociopolitical awareness and reflected his own critical

Educational Leadership and Music, pages 185–195
Copyright © 2017 by Information Age Publishing
All rights of reproduction in any form reserved.

consciousness. We see the impact that the conscious hip-hop movement had on Kane as a metaphor for a praxis of critical care in educational leadership, wherein school leaders support members of their school communities, while simultaneously demanding more from them (Antrop-González, 2011; De Jesús, 2012; Rivera-McCutchen, 2012; Rolón-Dow, 2005).

KANE'S BEGINNINGS

One of the most well-remembered MCs of the golden era of hip-hop (1985–1992) and beyond, Kane was born and raised in Brooklyn, New York. He began his career as a ghostwriter for established artists such as the well-known Juice Crew, whose ranks included Roxanne Shante, Marley Marl, and close friend Biz Markie (Gonzalez, 1999; Hess, 2009). After achieving early success behind the scenes, in 1987 he wrote and collaborated vocally with the well-established Biz Markie for his debut single, "Just Rhymin with Biz." While still ghost writing for Biz Markie's first album, Kane's first solo single, "Raw," and album, *Long Live the Kane,* soon followed (Ex, 2003). With his use of varied lyrical styles, compelling confidence, and a burgeoning application of critical consciousness, Kane soon began to distinguish himself from the already notable lineup of golden era MCs (Gonzalez, 1999).

In addition to his unique lyrical presentation, Kane's "Huey Newton Badass Swagger" and "Custom Dapper Dan Suits" propelled him even further into the spotlight (Gonzalez, 1999, p. 107). With his first two albums, *Long Live the Kane* and *It's a Big Daddy Thing,* Kane (which stands for King Asiatic Nobody's Equal) cemented himself as an artist who would later be referred to as one of the most talented MCs in hip-hop's history (Gonzalez, 1999). After the release of his second album, *It's a Big Daddy Thing* in 1989, Kane would go on to make five more studio albums, star in several motion pictures, and capitalize on his sex appeal in several nude photo shoots, including Madonna's infamous 1992 photo essay book, *Sex* (Hess, 2009; Lazerine & Lazerine, 2008).

In the world of hip-hop and rap music, Big Daddy Kane found early success in defining himself in terms of his relationships with women. From his very first recorded song "Just Rhymin' with Biz," where he rhymed "gigolo, Romeo, Friday night spend money on a ho-tel," (Hardy, 1988a) Kane was comfortable professing his love for "the ladies." This was exemplified most noticeably on his first two album covers, both of which positioned Kane as a king in the company of attractive women who were pictured as servants and party companions in his limousine. Thus, Kane's artistry was interpreted within the hip-hop community through this narrow lens, with overwhelming attention given to the imagery and songs his record label chose to release as radio singles. Nevertheless, beneath the surface of radio spins and optics of his amours in magazine shoots, there was much more to him (Lazerine & Lazerine, 2008).

Growing up in Brooklyn, Kane had been heavily influenced by the Five Percent Nation, a youth-oriented offshoot of the Nation of Islam (Hess, 2009), which combined pseudo-Islamic theology with Black nationalistic rhetoric. His connection to the "Five Percenters," first as an adolescent and later as an adult, gave him a foundation for developing a sociopolitical consciousness about cultural achievements within the African diaspora, as well as issues of police brutality and racism (Lazerine & Lazerine, 2008). This critical mindset gave him a foundational knowledge that later allowed him to contribute to the golden age of hip-hop's culture of consciousness, using his music as a vehicle to encourage critical conversations about the experiences of people living in marginalized urban communities.

THE "B SIDE": KANE AS A CONSCIOUS RAPPER

Whereas Kane wrote and performed songs that reflected his love of women, and at times misogynistic undertones including "Smooth Operator," "I Get the Job Done," and "Pimpin Ain't Easy," that was not the totality of Kane's musical identity (Hess, 2009; Lazerine & Lazerine, 2008; Perry 2004). Eventually, several of his songs and identity conformed to the prevailing politically and socially conscious elements of the golden era of hip-hop (Chang, 2005; George, 1998; Fricke & Ahearn, 2001; Kitwana, 2002; Perkins, 1996) exemplified by artists like Afrika Bambaataa, Public Enemy, KRS-ONE, Poor Righteous Teachers, and Bran Nubians (Hess, 2009; Lazerine & Lazerine, 2008; Perry 2004). These artists drew from sociohistorical influences to fuel various forms of creative expression (e.g., music, dress, dance), and used hip-hop culture and music as a forum to shine a light on the devastating poverty that had never been fully addressed by the Great Society programs within Black and Brown urban communities. Along with tremendous cuts to school music and arts programs, community-based programs, and the crack and AIDS health epidemics, there was the persistent backdrop of racially motivated incidents and negative interactions with the police that extended from the 1960s and 1970s (Henderson, 1996). Consequently, codified epistemological frameworks such as the Five Percent Lessons and Afrika Bambaataa's (and his Zulu Nation's) Infinity Lessons emerged as templates for critical consciousness and to address these systemic challenges within Black and Brown urban communities. Through these lessons, young people of the post-Civil Rights Era were reminded of their historical connection to Africa and its sociopolitical, intellectual, economic, and spiritual greatness. These community corpora also shaped the lyrical messages and stylings of conscious hip-hop artists like KRS-One, Public Enemy, and others. Consequently, to be taken seriously, MCs like Big Daddy Kane were compelled to follow suit and embrace sociopolitical awareness, expression, and elevation.

Accordingly, although Kane was known more for his party tunes and smooth melodies typically released on the "A side" of singles records, he released a variety of "B side" songs that embodied the plight of urban youth and marginalized communities such as "Word to the Mother(land)," "I'll Take You There," "Another Victory," "Ain't No Stopping Us Now," "Children R the Future," and "Young Gifted and Black" (Bogdanov, 2003). Though these songs were not always released as B sides of popular singles records, we use the term to highlight that these tracks were not necessarily intended to garner commercial radio success. Rather, Kane wrote and recorded them in an effort to embrace a more conscious form of hip-hop while continuing to release radio friendly A-side singles. For example, "Ain't No Half Steppin" became a radio and video hit in the spring/summer of 1988. In the song, he demonstrated his boisterous style.

> My rhymes are so dope and
> The rappers be hoping
> To sound like me, so soon I'll have to open
> A school of emceeing, for those who want to be in
> My field in court
> Then again on second thought
> To have emcees coming out sounding so similar
> It's quite confusing for you to remember
> The originator, and boy do I hate a
> Perpetrator, but I'm much greater (Hardy, 1988a)

In "Ain't No Half Steppin," Kane clearly focuses on and flaunts his microphone skills. In a braggadocio style, Kane boasts that he could teach other MCs aspiring to achieve his level of greatness, all while warning them not to bother trying to copy his style.

In contrast to the boisterous tone of "Ain't No Half Steppin," Kane's 1988 "Word to the Mother(land)" reminds the listener of his ancestral roots in Africa. Debunking the persistent provincial depiction of Africa as the "backwards continent," Kane seeks a redefinition of the continent that would promote greater emotional pride and intellectual recognition of the diaspora and the land itself. Refuting the social construction of race in America, which historically asserted "Black" as inferior, inhuman, and threatening (Delgado & Stefancic, 2012), Kane wrote:

> Take a stand the fight for power
> Cause we've been here before the Mayflower
> Living superior abiding by nature

The history of the asiatic one paid the
Price to be paid in slavery
Like the name of Antonio was gave to me
But knowledge of self broke every shackle and chain
Now I declare myself as the Big Daddy Kane
The teacher, teaching a lesson to be heard
That's word, to the mother my brother
So discover the truth of one another
Cause here's the real deal upon our skin color
Lay down white, yellow, red or pink
But the color of Black is most dominant
The rising and sizing can never cease
<Marley Marl: what you gonna say now?>
Peace! (Hardy, 1988b)

In the face of hundreds of years of prevailing institutional racism internalized by people of the diaspora, Kane chose to contribute important words of pride to the critical consciousness brand of hip-hop through this song. In this verse, Kane evokes the seminal work by Dr. Ivan Van Sertima (1976) *They Came Before Columbus*, using a scholarly body of work to reinforce the line "Cause we've been here before the Mayflower" (Hardy, 1988b), and also an empirical reference to substantiate what he posited as the dominance of the African diaspora. Kane's invocation of this lyric, legitimized research like Van Sertima's among young and mature hip-hop audiences alike, while also contributing to the historical and psychological process of changing prevailing racial theory narratives. Further, lyrics like these catalyzed a sequence of events whereby listeners could unpack the lyric independently and also in conversation with others. They might then go so far as to seek out Van Sertima's text, and others like it, which might yield even further dialogue and reflection. This potential sequence of events and interactions that hopefully inspired further studies might raise self-esteem and self-love, underscoring Kane's belief that "knowledge of self broke every [mental, physical, and sociopolitical] shackle and chain."

Kane continued to be artistically compelled by the emerging culture of critical consciousness in hip-hop in the following year, 1989, with the Central Park Five rape case and the murder of Yusuf Hawkins in Bensonhurst, Brooklyn, providing a racialized social context (Henderson, 1996). In the early part of that year, he released "Young, Gifted, and Black." Although not filled line by line with the cultural and nationalist rhetoric of "Word to the Mother(land)," "Young, Gifted, and Black" was an obvious nod to the great Nina Simone's similarly named song, "To Be Young, Gifted, and Black." Also, the revivification of this title and its artist served as a bridge between the older generation and the "new school" around the familiar theme of redefining the dominant narrative of "blackness." The song begins with

Louis Farrakhan, leader of the Nation of Islam, speaking as an introduction to the song.

> So out of the mercy of Allah
> And the law written in our nature
> We call an individual into existence
> And when that individual comes, I make, no apologies
> For what I'm about to say (Hardy, 1989d)

Kane's use of Farrakhan, a prominent figure in the Black community and in the country as a whole, affirmed the cultural and spiritual viability of the African diaspora to Kane's listeners, and further legitimized his identity as a socially conscious artist. Like Nina Simone, he reminded his listeners of the power and majesty of blackness, countering the dominant images of Black men as drug addicts and/or dealers, social system dependents, or unintellectual, with this closing line: "With the knack to attract the pack, So just get back, I'm young, gifted, and Black."

This style is a stark contrast to the prevailing perceptions of Kane as a one dimensional MC with a materialistic and misogynistic focus. For example, the same album that produced "Young Gifted and Black," contained Kane's seminal song "Smooth Operator," which many might conclude was a reflection of his dominant persona:

> Now girls step up to this
> One simple kiss, and it's over Miss
> Sold to nice dreamers, high as the price seem
> Girlfriend, you been scooped like ice cream
> So just swing or fling a gathering try to cling
> 'Cause It's a Big Daddy Thing
> And I'm lovin' 'em right word is bond
> So just play Marvin Gaye and let's get it on
> I make it real good like Dr. Feelgood
> To make sure that my point is understood
> That when it comes to this there's none greater
> Sincerely yours, the smooth operator (Hardy, 1989c)

These lyrics and others on similar tracks led many to perceive that Kane was a rapper who was solely concerned with self-indulgence. Although that perception became part of Kane's legacy, it is not the totality.

As Kane produced party tracks, the critical consciousness movement within hip-hop compelled him to create B-side songs such as "Children R the Future." This song extended the message of "Young, Gifted, and Black" by dedicating every line of the song to youth. Kane rhymed,

And there are desires that we all want to achieve
But remember, respect is most greatest to receive
And we don't have to gain it by being TOUGH
Or selling our own kind that cooked white stuff
So bring your negative mind from out of the shade
Find your true self and let's all get paid (Hardy, 1989b)

Here Kane examines the realities of poverty and counters that dealing drugs is not a productive solution. Reminiscent of "Young, Gifted and Black," Kane's use of the phrase "our own kind" conveys nationalistic lessons of self-love, ancestral pride, and intellectual achievements to his youthful audiences. These pillars of self-esteem were given to Kane by those purveyors of the critically conscious hip-hop movement, and were designed to change mindsets and shape actions so that they might lead toward greater prosperity.

Likewise, on the *It's a Big Daddy Thing* album, the song "Another Victory" typified Kane's intention to think beyond his perceived identity and purpose, and moved toward speaking to larger societal concerns. Kane rapped,

When I'm cruisin' in my Volvo, cops harass me
They never ride past me, they hound me like Lassie
Wantin' to give me a summons or a ticket
Huh, I got a place for them to stick it (kick it)
They can't understand to see a Black man
Drivin' a car that costs 25 grand
The first thing they say is "Where'd you steal her?"
And then they assume that I'm a drug dealer
Huh, that just makes me wanna laugh
Cause now I'm a star and your son got my autograph
So all the cops on the highway gettin' me
My name ain't Keith, so could you please stop Sweatin' me (Hardy, 1989a)

In "Another Victory," Kane again used his position as an artist whose voice was respected by youth to bring awareness to external societal issues of racial profiling and Fourth Amendment violations in the form of illegal searches. Songs like these encompassed the theme of being "Young, Gifted, and Black," consistent with the messages espoused by a culture of critical consciousness within the golden age of hip-hop.

At the height of his fame, Kane released "Lean on Me," the title song from the 1989 film of the same name, which highlighted the controversial leadership style of a Newark, NJ, high school principal, Joe Clark. This track off the *It's a Big Daddy Thing* album further illustrated the themes during this era, projected through many of its cultural icons such as Boogie Down Productions, Rakim, and Public Enemy (Chang, 2005; Fricke & Ahearn, 2001; George, 1998; Kitwana, 2002; Perkins, 1996). Thus in 1989, in the wake of projects such as *It Takes a Nation of Millions to Hold Us Back* (Public Enemy), *By All Means Necessary* (Boogie Down Productions), *Follow the Leader* (Eric B & Rakim), and even *Straight Outta Compton* (Niggas With Attitudes), Big Daddy Kane continued to develop songs that spoke to the crisis in urban communities (Henderson, 1996; Lazerine & Lazerine, 2008; Watkins, 2011).

CRITICAL CARING IN LEADERSHIP

We draw important leadership lessons from examining the relationship between Kane's evolution from a straight up ladies' man to an artist whose lyrics reflected greater sociopolitical awareness. As noted earlier, Kane came of age among the Five Percent Nation and was not unfamiliar with critical issues facing young people of color who were economically, socially, and politically disenfranchised. However, it took the leadership of hip-hop greats like KRS-One and Public Enemy and their contributions to the genre to demand more from Kane. Though respected as a mainstream artist within the genre, conscious hip-hop expected more from him and pressed him to go further (Chang, 2005; George, 1998; Fricke & Ahearn, 2001; Kitwana, 2002; Perkins, 1996).

Likewise, educational leaders must be courageous enough to compel their school communities to move beyond traditional paradigms of teaching and learning to establish greater mechanisms for schools to work toward affecting the lives that students experience inside and outside of the building (Dantley & Tillman, 2010; Horsford, Grosland & Gunn, 2011; Shields, 2010). This type of leader recognizes the need for creating spaces for authentic student voices to address contemporary concerns on issues like police brutality, social relationships, as well as their perspectives on the (ir)relevance of much of what school offers them. To that end, school leaders must adopt a model of critical care that both supports and pushes teachers to move beyond their comfort zones to engage in liberatory practices (Antróp-Gonzalez, 2011; De Jesús, 2012; Rivera-McCutchen, 2012; Rolón-Dow, 2005; Valenzuela, 1999).

Caring as a theoretical construct has been frequently explored in the education research, most notably by Nel Noddings (2005), whose work has been extended by other scholars who theorize notions of "critical" caring as a more equity-focused approach (Antróp-Gonzalez, 2011; De Jesús, 2012; Rivera-McCutchen, 2012; Rolón-Dow, 2005; Valenzuela, 1999). This research suggests that students attending schools that adopt a critical care approach to schooling, particularly those serving historically marginalized low-income Black and Latina/o youth, are generally more successful. Specifically, the school actors who practice critical care are more likely to push their students to meet high standards, while also providing the necessary academic and socioemotional supports they need in order to be successful (Antróp-Gonzalez, 2011; De Jesús, 2012; Rolón-Dow, 2005). Further, the school actors' work with and for students is informed and shaped by recognition of the roles that institutional racism and classism play in the reproduction of educational inequalities.

Though recent research on leadership underscores how important it is for leaders to embrace an ethic of care (Louis, Murphy, & Smylie, 2016), what we draw from the example of Kane's evolution is that a model of critical care in leadership is even more essential. Conscious hip-hop moved Kane, by way of example, to connect with his roots and embrace his more conscious self through his music. Kane's trajectory focused on highlighting both problems and solutions concerning inner city and marginalized communities. As a result, Kane and other MCs such as Queen Latifah, Tribe Called Quest, and even Run DMC also used their platforms to contribute to the discourse of creating counternarratives of inner city and marginalized communities as well as the re-dress of perennial concerns.

Likewise, school leaders who adopt a critical care mindset expect more from both their students and from the teachers who teach them. It is a hard love, rather than a soft one. While critical care is concerned with the affective care of their students—and by extension the rest of the community, demonstrating unconditional love for each one—it also demands that everyone in the school must strive to do better with every expectation that they, in fact, will.

Big Daddy Kane's evolution as an artist as a result of the leadership within the conscious hip-hop movement is a powerful metaphor that can be applied in school leadership contexts. There is greatness in our schools. A leadership praxis centered on critical caring can unearth that potential by expecting more.

REFERENCES

Antrop-González, R. (2011). *Schools as radical sanctuaries: Decolonizing urban education through the eyes of youth of color.* Charlotte, NC: Information Age.

Bogdanov, V. (2003). *All music guide to hip-hop: A definitive guide to Rap and hip-hop.* Ann Arbor, MI: BackBeat Books.

Chang, J. (2005). *Can't stop won't stop: A history of the hip-hop generation.* New York, NY: St. Martin's Press.

Dantley, M. E., & Tillman, L. C. (2009). Social justice and moral transformative leadership. In C. Marshall & M. Oliva (Eds.), *Leadership for social justice: Making revolutions in education* (2nd ed.; pp. 19–34). Boston, MA: Pearson.

De Jesús, A. (2012). Authentic caring and community driven reform: The case of El Puente Academy for Peace and Justice. In M. Hantzopoulos & A.

Tyner-Mullings (Eds.), *Critical small schools: Moving beyond privatization in New York City public school reform* (pp. 63–78). Charlotte, NC: Information Age.

Delgado, R., & Stefancic, J. (2012). *Critical race theory: An introduction.* New York, NY: New York University Press.

Ex, K. (2003). Big Daddy Kane: Long live the Kane; It's a Big Daddy Thing, Biz Markie: Goin' Off. In O. Wang (Ed.), *Classic material: The hip-hop album guide* (pp. 36–39). Toronto, Ontario: ECW Press.

Fricke, J., & Ahearn, C. (2002). *Yes yes y'all: The experience music project oral history of hip-hop's first decade.* Cambridge, MA: Da Capo Press.

George, N. (1998). *Hip-hop America.* New York, NY: Penguin Books.

Gonzales, M. A. (1999). The Juice Crew: Beyond the boogie down. In A. Light (Ed.), *Vibe: A history of hip-hop* (pp.101–109). New York, NY: Three Rivers Press.

Hall, T. M. & Hardy, A. (1987). Just rhymin' with Biz. On *Biz is goin' off* and *Long live the Kane.* New York, NY: Cold Chillin' Records.

Hardy, A. (1988a). Ain't no half steppin.' On *Long live the Kane* [LP]. New York, NY: Cold Chillin' Records.

Hardy, A. (1988b). Word to the mother(land). On *Long live the Kane* [LP]. New York, NY: Cold Chillin' Records.

Hardy, A. (1989a). Another victory. On *It's a big daddy thing* [LP]. New York, NY: Cold Chillin' Records.

Hardy, A. (1989b). Children r the future. On *It's a big daddy thing* [LP]. New York, NY: Cold Chillin' Records.

Hardy, A. (1989c). Smooth operator. On *It's a big daddy thing.* [LP] New York, NY: Cold Chillin' Records.

Hardy, A. (1989d). Young, gifted, and black. On *It's a big daddy thing* [LP]. New York, NY: Cold Chillin' Records.

Henderson, E. A. (1996). Black Nationalism and rap music. *Journal of Black Studies, 26*(3), 308-339.

Hess, M. (2009). Brooklyn keeps on taking it: A conversation with Bushwick, Brooklyn's da beatminerz. In M. Hess (Ed.), *Hip-hop in America: A regional guide, east coast and west coast* (Vol. 1; pp. 47–74). Santa Barbara, CA: Greenwood Press.

Horsford, S. D., Grosland, T., & Gunn, K. M. (2011). Pedagogy of the personal and professional: Toward a framework for culturally relevant leadership. *Journal of School Leadership, 21*(6), 582–606.

Kitwana, B. (2002) *The hip-hop generation: The crisis in African American culture.* New York, NY: Basic Civitas Books.

Lazerine, D., & Lazerine C. (2008). *Rap up: The ultimate guide to hip-hop and R&B.* New York, NY: Grand Central Publishing.

Louis, K. S., Murphy, J., & Smylie, M. (2016). Caring leadership in schools: Findings from an exploratory analysis. *Educational Administration Quarterly, 52*(2), 310–348.

Perkins, W. E. (1996). The rap attack: An introduction. In W. E. Perkins (Ed.), *Droppin' science: Critical essays on rap music and hip-hop culture* (pp. 1–45). Philadelphia, PA: Temple University Press.

Perry, I. (2004). *Prophets of the hood: Politics and poetics in hip-hop.* Durham, NC: Duke University Press.

Noddings, N. (2005). *The challenge to care in schools: An alternative approach to education* (2nd ed.). New York, NY: Teachers College Press.

Rivera-McCutchen, R. L. (2012). Caring in a small urban high school: A complicated success. *Urban Education, 47*(3), 653–680. Retrieved from http://doi.org/10.1177/0042085911433522

Rolón-Dow, R. (2005). Critical care: A color(full) analysis of care narratives in the schooling experiences of Puerto Rican girls. *American Educational Research Journal, 42*(1), 77–111.

Shields, C. M. (2010). Transformative leadership: Working for equity in diverse contexts. *Educational Administration Quarterly, 46*(4), 558–589.

Valenzuela, A. (1999). *Subtractive schooling: U.S.-Mexican youth and the politics of caring*. Ithaca, NY: State University of New York Press.

Van Sertima, I. (1976). *They came before Columbus*. New York, NY: Random House.

Watkins, R. (2011). *Hip-hop: Redemption*. Grand Rapids, MI: Baker.

CHAPTER 18

FAITH AND LEADERSHIP

Elements of Fred Hammond's Life and Lyrical Influence on the Development of Educational Leaders

Jason McKinney and Kimberly Starks Berglund
University of Missouri

There are many challenges that come along with the title educational leadership, and when you are an African American in an educational leadership role, those challenges can be compounded (Lyons & Chesley, 2004). However, as we confront the challenges that come with these roles in educational leadership through the lens of developing scholars, we realize that one of our greatest strengths can be found in the lyrics of gospel music, which can console our heart, mind, and body. Gospel music is a core component of many within the Black faith community (West, 2008). The world-renowned gospel artist Fred Hammond's music contains critical elements of faith such as prayer, worship, and acts of praise. This chapter explores the positive influence of gospel music in the lives of Black graduate students/leaders linking the lyrics of Fred Hammond to times in their lives that have brought distress and life-changing moments. We will view valuable lessons within

Educational Leadership and Music, pages 197–205
Copyright © 2017 by Information Age Publishing
All rights of reproduction in any form reserved.

Hammond's songs that can inspire and encourage leaders to be empowered through the teams that they lead. We will close the chapter by incorporating organizational leadership frameworks by Bolman and Deal's (2013) theoretical model of ethics and spirit to view leadership through elements of gospel music lyrics.

WHO IS FRED HAMMOND?

Frederick William Hammond was born in 1960 and is a native of Detroit, Michigan. He is a pioneer in the gospel music industry. His journey began at an early age while growing up in the church. As a youth, Hammond looked toward music and his faith for strength and encouragement to make it through the hard times (Dempsey, 2000). Hammond's faith in God and his love for music would be the tools he would use to embark on an extraordinary musical career. Hammond's career began with an opportunity to play bass for the legendary gospel group The Winans, in which he gained recognition. In 1985, he became the founding member of the gospel group Commission, writing many of their songs. He developed his craft by producing, writing lyrics, and playing various instruments on 10 of their 12 albums up until his departure. Hammond ventured off on his own and formed the award-winning group Radical for Christ, writing a plethora of award-winning worship and praise songs including "No Weapon," "Running Back to You," "We're Blessed," "They That Wait on the Lord," "This is the Day," and his latest single, "The Lord is Good" from the upcoming album *Worship Journal*.

Even with a successful career, Hammond had his share of pain, loss, and difficult moments in his life. Hammond endured the passing of his mother and a painful divorce. Nevertheless, he remained strong and continued to press forward utilizing these life-changing events to write songs illustrating God's grace within his life, while encouraging and inspiring others to stay strong in spite their situation. Hammond's dedication to his craft, unwavering faith, strong work ethic, and moral values are components found in good leaders, and his lyrics contain elements and tenets that educational leaders can utilize to be successful and at peace. Kirk Franklin describes gospel singer Fred Hammond as "one of the most prolific worshippers of our time. Fred is my hero" ("Fred Hammond: Gospel," 2006, p. 49).

Gospel music has been an intricate element within Black culture that can be traced back to the Antebellum slavery era. According to Robinson-Martin (2009), these songs illustrated the conditions/situations that Black slaves faced while they looked toward God for strength to overcome by incorporating biblical scripture within the lyrics. Hammond writes his praise and worship songs in a similar way, by describing various situations within one's life, and informing his audience how God's grace is sufficient during those times of need. Some may get the Blues confused with Gospel Music due to the similarities in their rhythm and even the style of the lyrics. However, the late gospel legend Mahalia Jackson said, "Blues tells the world your troubles, but the Gospel tells the world your troubles and what the solution is" (Minowa & Glover, 2009, p. 267) . By incorporating various genres within his musical development, Hammond is able to deliver a message that encourages and hope to a broader audience.

Hammond's prayer, worship, and faith in his lyrics is a unique combination that touches the soul, by applying biblical principles through visual applications seen in everyday life. "God's hand is on it, and he is moving it," explains Hammond in a statement about the popularity of gospel music ("Why gospel music," 1998, p. 15). Hammond also believes that musicians have taken gospel music more seriously, and the producers value the music they produce. Hammond's music has given the Black community as well as other listeners hope. By presenting his listeners with lyrics based on biblical foundations, illustrated through practice and personal experience, he assures his listeners to stay encouraged during turbulent times.

Fred Hammond's albums often follow a theme with different perspectives of a similar problem, with a common solution. Moreover, his music offers his listeners multiple lenses in which to view how God and their faith are working in their lives. Gospel music is one element some Black graduate students use to minimize and cope with the daily stresses in their lives. Some of Hammond's work that speaks to coherent themes in our lives can attest how we were encouraged and inspired by his music through our educational journey. Gospel music is a crucial piece of cultural content that emerging scholars and educational leaders can utilize. According to Romans 1:1 (Holy Bible, 1996), Paul, a disciple of Christ, defines the gospel as "good news" and Hammond's music speaks to people by sharing the good news. Likewise, Ellison (1998) explains how one's faith through gospel music can pertain to life satisfaction and well-being.

HOW HAMMOND'S LYRICS INFLUENCED THE LIVES OF TWO DOCTORAL STUDENTS

One of this chapter's authors shares a candid moment that occurred during the fall semester of 2015 expressing how Hammond's song, "Jesus Be a Fence," gave her strength and courage:

> My PhD experience during this time challenged me both academically and mentally. I would never have thought that I would be on a college campus right in the midst of racial tensions. During this time, I had a lot of mixed emotions from the intense backlash my campus received, and how I should move forward through my educational leadership journey. As a graduate stu-

dent of color, I felt frustrated and saddened by the ordeal. The environment on our campus did not feel safe. By listening to Hammond's song "Jesus Be a Fence," it helped me realize that God's protection along the way will help keep me safe. The fence of protection in the lyrics gave me the strength, encouragement, and endurance to continue my journey as a graduate student for the remainder of that semester.

Facing these obstacles on a daily basis can drain a student of color's sense of self-worth, confidence to believe that he/she could obtain a degree, and become successful in the world. However, it is through gospel lyrics that empower, renew, and revitalize the dreams of some students of color to continue to strive to be great despite the obstacles that lie ahead. As a future educational leader, my goal is to remain encouraged and continue to press forward. Hammond's music along with his example also encourages me to aim toward shared visions and values through a professional learning community. According to Hilliard (2012), students along with educational leaders should have a systematic mindset so that they can be productive and successful leaders.

Today, I continue to listen to Hammond's song "A Song of Strength" for guidance and hope as I complete my last semester of coursework. Other songs such as "Celebrate" and "I Will Find a Way" encourage me as I approach my comprehensive exams and dissertation. The coherent themes in these songs give me the courage to complete papers and to continue my educational journey.

The other author of this chapter also shared his moments of hardship and how songs such as "No Weapon," "More of You," along with others by Hammond gave him strength and courage:

My PhD journey began in the fall of 2014, and since that time, I have encountered hardship within my personal life, in addition to becoming familiar with a new city and the educational system. My mother diagnosed with colon cancer two weeks after the fall semester began; she passed away at the beginning of spring semester 2015, and I lost my father in a tragic accident at the end of the 2015 fall semester. During life's challenges, I gained strength from my family, friends, and church, but the songs were, and continue to be, a key element from which I draw comfort. "No Weapon" offered encouragement during the diagnosis of my mother's cancer, reminding me to remain strong and stand by my faith. "More of You" gave me comfort after learning of my mother's passing, as the song speaks of just leaning and relying solely on the power and the mercies of God and living your faith in the midst of the situation.

As 2015 ended, I lost my dad in a tragic car accident, the day after the fall 2015 semester ended. During that time the song, "Please Don't Pass Me By" stayed on repeat as it reminded me once again that I am not alone in my situation. Now, two months have passed since my Dad's passing, and the song I play daily is, "This Is the Day," which encourages me to live life to the best of my ability, knowing that this is the day the Lord has made. Fred Hammond's songs have given the light of hope during some of the darkest times in my life and assisted in keeping my mind focused as an educational scholar and leader.

Fred Hammond's music has inspired many to press through to their goals despite the challenges of life and to be optimistic in everything they do. There are many lessons that educational leaders can learn by listening to Fred Hammond's lyrics to help them become a better leader.

SOUL AND SPIRITUAL CONCEPTS AND EDUCATIONAL LEADERSHIP ETHICS

Hammond's music can extend academic content and enrich the learning community. The lyrics in Hammond's music can also enhance the classroom environment and work in students' minds through meaningful learning (Antepenko, 2008). Both music and the lyrics in Hammond's songs can be essential components for creating a positive learning environment. Gospel music is influential in creating a relaxing atmosphere for educational leaders through times of tension (Taylor & Chatters, 1991). Furthermore, gospel music introduces and reinforces concepts through various networks that are important to educational leaders, such as hope, courage, encouragement, and endurance.

Many of Fred Hammond's songs have concepts that illuminate actions that can be a foundation to develop a bridge to connect and strengthen interactions with staff and leadership personnel as leadership exemplifies authority, but from a humble perspective. Some educational leaders forget that their staff members are not just merely numbers or robots, but they are human beings, and they must treat them as such with dignity and respect (Kouzes & Posner, 2007). Incorporating ethical policies within the organization, but also within the manner in which they interact with others, will ultimately make them a more efficient and approachable leader (Bolman & Deal, 2013).

An organization is a living organism with the actions performed by the human participants, who make it function similar to the church from a theological perspective (Davies & Dodds, 2011). Just as the human body needs all of its organs to function in a harmonious and healthy manner, so does an organization need its employees to simulate this within their interactions, and communication. According to Bolman and Deal (2013), there are four ethical frameworks within organizational ethics: faith, excellence, justice, and caring. However, the leadership contributions that align with these ethics are significance, authorship, power, and love.

SIGNIFICANCE

According to Taylor and Chatter (1991), faith plays a significant role in the daily lives of many African Americans, not just faith in God but in their abilities as well. Educational leaders must have faith and trust in their abilities/ training to make conscious and ethical decisions. The level of faith for some African Americans is uniquely connected to social networks in which church attendance, church membership, and religious affiliation are conducive to feelings of coherence, control of one's life, a sense of belonging, physical health, and self-esteem. Thus it is important that educational leaders receive and give support and encouragement, especially through natural settings and environments such as through music and faith. Significance is exemplified in the music of Fred Hammond as it offers support and encouragement, which musically models the desired behavior for educational leaders.

AUTHORSHIP

According to Bolman and Deal (2013), power and authorship share similar traits such as autonomy, space, and freedom, which are important in both. However, authorship has parameters set by the editor, or in this case the manager of the project/organization. Educational leaders can achieve this goal by ensuring the structural framework within their departments has authorship that offers space within the boundaries of the department giving their staff the ability to create something new and fresh. Bolman and Deal (2013) defined authorship as, "Trusting people to solve problems generates high levels of motivation and better solutions" (p. 579). However, for this to work the leader must clarify his or her expectations and objectives. With clarity can come autonomy to allow people to work freely toward the goals of the organization. For example, Hammond could not develop a live album without collaborating with his staff and band as their creativity expressed by the lead/bass guitar, drums, and background singers. Hammond allows them to be creative in developing their unique elements within the development of the greater project. Although Hammond is the executive administrator/ producer, he constantly illustrates that he is not the only one with creativity/ authorship, and in an organization the sum of the team is the greater power.

POWER

Power is an element that can corrupt the best of leaders if they do not have the proper mindset. Encouragement from other people helps to remind leaders that they must show humility in their position. Fred Hammond's music illustrates to us that even though one may have power over certain objects within the physical realm, there is a higher power that is even greater than our own. In a corporation, it could be the board of trustees, board of curators, or even a school board as all have the ability to overturn a decision made by an educational leader. That is why it is important for educational leaders to remain humble and ensure that their decisions are not prideful, jealous, or controlling, but rather made in the best interest of the organization and its staff and students. In reference to humility, Kouzes and Posner (2007) wrote, "Perhaps the best advice that we can give all aspiring leaders is to remain humble and unassuming—to always remain open and full of wonder" (p. 348).

Fred Hammond's lyrics in the song "I Will Trust" encourages us to value each human being as we value ourselves and to respect your teammates and trust their abilities, as they trust you. According to Bolman and Deal (2013), it is vital for leaders to develop strong team building environments within their corporations, similar to a family, expressing care and love for their co-workers in the manner in which they interact and support them. This type of framework and atmosphere within the workplace will develop a strong culture. However, the key is that the leader leads by example.

LOVE

To love is to illustrate how one individual/group cares for another, being open and having the willingness to help and support one another. Showing love and significance within one's leadership is a key component to developing trust, loyalty, and respect from your staff as it illustrates your concern for them, not just their position (Bolman & Deal, 2013). The essence of these perspectives is expressed in Fred Hammond's lyrics and can encourage us through difficult/joyous moments in our academic journeys. Educational leadership has its high and low moments; it is sometimes mellow or up-tempo, just like a song. Bolman and Deal (2008) wrote, "Through life's peaks and valleys, love holds people...together in a caring community" (p. 404).

According to Bolman and Deal (2013), an organization is similar to a temple, and temples need spiritual leaders. They are not speaking of promoting or advertising spirituality within the workplace, but in this reference they are utilizing the definition of spirit as a secular term. The Merriam-Webster's dictionary (11th ed.) defines *spirit* as the intelligent or immaterial part of man, which means vital principles living and the moral nature of humanity within our actions. Fred Hammond's music illustrates these elements. Bolman and Deal agree: "Music captures and expresses life's deepest and precious moments when people sing or dance together, they bond to one another and experiencing an emotional connection that is otherwise hard to express" (Bolman & Deal, 2013, p. 585).

CONCLUSION

Effective leaders must account for the influence we have on the journeys of others and our capacity to influence the borders we cross. Hammond's musical career exemplifies this very concept. Having begun his career in the 1980s, he has been able to transcend generations, remaining on the cutting edge of his industry. His capacity to strategically collaborate with other artists and his ability to embrace new musical trends while remaining true to his core message form lessons for school leaders. From Fred Hammond school leaders gain the lessons of significance, authorship, power, and love. Significance embodies a kind of spiritual leadership in organizations where leaders become symbols of who instills encouragement and enthusiasm (Bolman & Deal, 2008; Fullan, 2004). Authorship teaches leaders to provide guidance, yet allow space and autonomy to trust team members to accomplish group goals. Power is a part of everyday organizational existence, but it should not be misused. Fred Hammond's life is an example of how to remain humble when the ability to take advantage of power exists. Finally, love encourages a deeper caring in organizations like schools to build community, positive culture, and cohesiveness. Kouzes and Posner (2007) stated that "leadership is a relationship" (p. 24). Fred Hammond's life and music is a clear example of how leadership is enacted by forming positive relationships with other people and with a higher power. Similarly, for school leaders, the key is also relationships. "A relationship characterized by mutual respect and confidence will overcome the greatest adversities and leave a legacy of significance" (Kouzes & Posner, 2007, p. 24).

REFERENCES

Antepenko, A.H. (2008). The music connection: The positive classroom. *Educational Leadership, 66*(1). Retrieved from: http://www.ascd.org/publications/educational-leadership/sept08/vol66/num01/The-Music-Connection.aspx

Bolman, L. G., & Deal, T. E. (2008). *Reframing organizations: Artistry, choice, and leadership*. San Fransico, CA: Jossey-Bass.

Bolman, L. G., & Deal, T. E. (2013). *Reframing organizations: Artistry, choice, and leadership*. San Fransico, CA: Jossey-Bass.

Davies, M., & Dodds, G. (2011). *Leadership in the church for people of hope*. London, England: T&T Clark International.

Dempsey, M. (2000). *American visions*, December 1999/January 2000, p. 46.

Ellison, C. G. (1998). Religion, health, and well-being among African Americans. *African American Research Perspectives, 4,* 94–103.

Fred Hammond: Gospel worshipper celebrates 25th anniversary with new CD "Free to worship." (2006, October 30). *Jet.* Retrieved from https://www.highbeam.com/doc/1G1-153692207.html

Fullan, M. (2004). *Leading in a culture of change: Personal action guide and workbook.* San Francisco, CA: Jossey-Bass.

Hilliard, A. T. (2012). Practices and value of a professional learning community in higher education. *Contemporary Issues in Education Research, 5*(2), 71–74.

Holy Bible, NLT. (1996). Wheaton IL: Tyndale House.

Kouzes, J. M., & Posner, B. Z. (2007). *The leadership challenge* (4th ed.). San Francisco, CA: Wiley & Sons.

Lyons, J. E., & Chesley, J. (2004). Fifty years after Brown: The benefits and tradeoffs of African American educators and students. *The Journal of Negro Education, 73*(3), 298–313.

Minowa, Y., David S., & Glover, D. S. (2009). Consuming the black gospel culture: An interpretive study of symbolic exchanges. *Advance in Consumer Research, 36,* 266–272.

Robinson-Martin, T. (2009). Performance styles and musical characteristics of black gospel music. *Journal of Singing 5,* 595–598.

Spirit. (n.d.). In *Merriam-Webster's online dictionary* (11th ed.). Retrieved from https://www.merriam-webster.com/dictionary/spirit

Taylor, R., & Chatters, L. M. (1991). *The religious life of black Americans.* In J. S. Jackson (Ed.), *Life in black America* (pp. 105–123). Newbury Park, CA: Sage.

West, C. (2008). *Hope on a tightrope: Words and wisdom.* Carlsbad, CA: Hay House, Inc.

Why gospel music remains so popular. (1998, November 16). *Jet.* Retrieved from https://www.highbeam.com/doc/1G1-53268564.html

MAHALIA JACKSON EXEMPLIFIES LEADERSHIP THROUGH GOSPEL MUSIC AND NEGRO SPIRITUALS

Anthony H. Normore
California State University, Dominguez Hills

Gaetane Jean-Marie
University of Northern Iowa

Several years back while attending the AERA conference in New Orleans, the two of us and another colleague went to Preservation Hall, a musical venue in the French Quarter founded in 1961, to hear soulful music. Joining in with the locals, we sang the gospel spirituals played that evening. As we wrote this chapter about Mahalia Jackson, it evoked memories of that evening for each of us from different walks of life (i.e., first author is Canadian, second author is Haitian-American, and our accompanying friend is a White American male); yet, for that moment we were chanting and bopping our heads to not only the music but the meanings of the gospel words, similar to the songs and spirituals sung by Mahalia Jackson. In this chapter,

Educational Leadership and Music, pages 207–215
Copyright © 2017 by Information Age Publishing

we briefly chronicle the life of Mahalia Jackson and later connect it to educational leaders whose social justice work is soulful (i.e., activism), builds bridges, and is transformative. Much of our literature about Jackson's life and career has been drawn from wikis and primary sources (e.g., Collins, 2002; Dixon, 1997; Koster, 2002; Larkin, 1995; Lyman, 2005)

Mahalia Jackson was an American gospel singer oftentimes referred to as "The Queen of Gospel" (Collins, 2002). She became one of the most influential gospel singers in the world and was heralded internationally as a singer and a civil rights activist. Jackson was born on October 26, 1911, as Mahalia Jackson and nicknamed "Halie." She grew up in the Black Pearl section of the Carrollton neighborhood of uptown New Orleans, Louisiana. School was hardly an option for Jackson. She loved to sing, and church is where she loved to sing the most. Her Aunt Bell told her one day she would sing in front of royalty, a prediction that would eventually come true. She was baptized in the Mississippi River and eventually went back to her church to "receive the right hand of fellowship" (The Full, 2015, para. 2). By giving the right hands of fellowship, she would be invited to serve God together with her church. When one believer gives someone the right hand of fellowship, it suggests that the invitee agrees to serve God with that believer.

At the age of 16, Jackson moved to Chicago, Illinois, in the midst of the Great Migration: a movement of 6 million Blacks out of the rural South in the United States to the urban Northeast, Midwest, and West, which occurred between 1915 and 1960 (Gregory, 2005; Harrison, 1991; Henri, 1975). The movement changed forever the urban North, the rural South, African America, and in many respects the entire nation (Gregory, 2005). After her first Sunday church service where Mahalia had given an impromptu performance of her favorite song "Hand Me Down My Silver Trumpet, Gabriel," she was invited to join the Greater Salem Baptist Church Choir (The Full, 2015). She began touring the city's churches and surrounding areas with the Johnson Gospel Singers, one of the earliest professional gospel groups (Larkin, 1995). Composer Thomas Dorsey gave her musical advice, and in the mid-1930s they began a 14-year association of touring with Jackson singing Dorsey's songs in church programs and at conventions. His "Precious Lord, Take My Hand" became her signature song (Lyman, 2005); it's one of our favorites because it signifies one in search of strength during troubled times. Over the next 40 years, Jackson was signed with the Apollo label and made a popular recording that stores could not stock enough copies to meet demand (Dixon, 1997). The song, "Move on Up a Little Higher," was later honored with the Grammy Hall of Fame Award (Koster, 2002). The success of this record rocketed her to fame in the United States and in Europe soon after. During this time she toured as a concert artist, appearing more frequently in concert halls and less often in churches (The Full, 2015) taking the gospel to lay people throughout the world.

Beyond singing, Mahalia Jackson devoted much of her time and energy to helping others. She established the Mahalia Jackson Scholarship Foundation for young people who wanted to attend college. For her efforts in helping bridge international understanding among nations, she received the Silver Dove Award. She later opened a beauty parlor and a florist shop with her earnings, while also investing in real estate: her investments amounted to approximately $100,000.00 a year at her peak (The Full, 2015). At one point she was described by Harry Belafonte as the single most powerful Black woman in the United States (Whitman, 1972). She recorded about 30 albums, mostly for Columbia Records, during her career. "I sing God's music because it makes me feel free," Jackson once said about her choice of gospel adding, "It gives me hope. With the blues, when you finish, you still have the blues." (Mojo Magazine, 2003, p. 20).

At the age of 61, Mahalia Jackson died on January 27, 1972. She was considered a shining beacon for the Civil Rights Movement, one whose music truly did, as she hoped it would, break down some of the hate and fear that divided the White and Black people in the United States. Jackson's music has left a litany of lessons, lessons that educational leaders and others can learn from as they refine, extend, and challenge their own thinking. For the remainder of this chapter, we will connect Mahalia Jackson's music to the theoretical frames of resilient leadership, social justice leadership, and moral leadership.

RESILIENT LEADERSHIP

George Washington perfectly connected happiness and meaning when he said, "Happiness and moral duty are inseparably connected" (Rubin, 2011). Educational leaders who choose resilience over defeat not only gain energy to sustain change, but also gain happiness from doing meaningful work that makes a difference for students. Resilience is often described as a personal quality that predisposes individuals to bounce back in the face of loss. Resilient leaders, however, do more than bounce back, they bounce forward. With speed and elegance, resilient leaders take action that responds to new and ever-changing realities, even as they maintain the essential operations of the organizations they lead (Reeves & Allison, 2009, 2010). Not only do they quickly get their mojo back, but because they understand that the status quo is unsustainable, they also use it to move mountains.

Resilient leaders sometimes appeal with personal narratives that lead them out of oppressive conditions, or a medical or physical disability (e.g., President Franklin D. Roosevelt's paralysis from polio). In Jackson's case, at birth she suffered from "bowed legs," a condition that never stopped her from performing her dance steps for the White woman for whom her mother and her Aunt Bell cleaned house (Collins, 2002). Through her music and advocacy for civil rights in the earliest days of the U.S. movement, Jackson exemplified resilience for her career was not without challenges. With her mainstream success, she was criticized by some gospel purists who complained about her hand-clapping and foot-stomping and about her bringing "jazz into the church" (Collins, 2002). Despite her international status and having moved up to the northern states, she encountered racial prejudice. Each time she tried to buy a home, the White owners and real estate agents would turn her away, claiming the house had already been sold or they changed their minds about selling (Darden, 2004). However, such racist behavior did not stop her from overcoming barriers.

While others like Dr. Martin Luther King, Jr., fought for civil rights by speaking, Jackson fought by singing—and more. In 1956 when the Civil Rights Movement was about to ramp up and gain its first serious, nationwide attention, Dr. King contacted Jackson just a few months after the convention to ask for her help. He was planning a rally to raise money for the Montgomery bus boycott and he wanted Jackson to sing at the event. Despite death threats, Jackson agreed to sing in Montgomery. Her renditions of "I've Heard of a City Called Heaven," "Silent Night," and "Move on Up a Little Higher" raised spirits and inspired the people who were getting discouraged with the boycott (Stanford University, 2012). Through her singing, she uplifted those for social justice to hold steadfast to the purpose of the Civil Rights Movement. Two weeks after the rally, the Montgomery bus boycott achieved success as the city finally ended segregation on its buses. But the work of the Civil Rights Movement was just beginning. Jackson not only contributed to the movement through her activism, but also financially (Parachin, 1994).

In the face of current constant change and crisis in education it stands to reason that the resource we need most as educational leaders is our resilience (Allison, 2012). Issues that make way from the government offices to school district board rooms, to the administrative offices, to the classrooms seem to gain momentum on a weekly basis. These range from budget cuts, program closures, lay-offs, workforce reductions, and school closures, to changes in teacher and administrator evaluation processes, unethical behaviors, liability issues, and accountability. With the world economy in dire straits, educators and educational leaders in particular have never faced more daily changes and challenges (Allison & Reeves, 2011). As a result, thoughtful leaders in education are eager to learn how to be more resilient. Good leaders lead with open yet critical eyes. Some leaders are so risk averse that they put on blinders to avoid seeing the truth of precarious situations. Others are so pessimistic about any turn of fortune that they ignore opportunities for growth. But a leader who pays attention to relevant data recognizes both opportunities and harbingers of disaster (Fullan,

2001; Goleman, Boyatzis, & McKee, 2002). Such a leader monitors signals of flagging resilience in his or her organization and shores resilience up to counter fear and hopelessness (Collins, 2000).

Mahalia Jackson is considered a resilient leader by these authors. She was happy and doing meaningful work, and she made time for activities that revitalized her emotionally, spiritually, and intellectually. She advocated for civil rights with Dr. Martin Luther King and used her coaching skills to help him be successful. Personal renewal generates the energy that leaders need to show for demanding work. On the job, resilient leaders take advantage of good coaching, which gives them interludes for reflection during the throes of a demanding day (Reeves & Allison, 2009, 2010). Environmental activist Van Jones is credited with saying,

> Martin Luther King didn't become famous by saying, "I have a complaint." Leaders need to be polite and resilient leaders use words carefully to create a positive emotional climate in which hope prevails and individuals feel inspired to create a better future. (Allison, 2012, pp. 81–82)

Jackson stayed optimistic throughout her career both personally and professional as she faced harsh realities and brutal truths. Resilient leaders are optimistic but not naive. Optimistic leaders are quite aware of undesirable trends—when they exist. However, these leaders find negative data compelling and it inspires them to take action. Having tirelessly worked for civil rights, in addition to her own career, Jackson cultivated networks before challenges hit while she worked continuously to sustain buy-in from individuals who were currently inspired by achievements of modern organizations and the leaders who gladly provided support and resources. The time to nurture networks of support from fellow educators, community leaders, and pivotal families is before the organization begins facing threats like severe budget cutbacks or teacher shortages.

Jackson also used insights for change. Effective leaders are not in love with their own data or their own interpretation of any data (Reeves & Allison, 2009). They invite multiple perspectives and absorb relevant information from all parts of the system. Likewise, resilient leaders draw on diverse perspectives to make well-informed decisions that ultimately create new realities in organizations (Allison, 2011; Boyatzis & McKee, 2005). These decisions are almost always in response to challenges such as, "How will we reorganize the advanced placement program so more students have the opportunity to take challenging classes?" or "How will we partner with community and business organizations?" These decisions are defining moments for leaders whose reputations hinge on their impact (Allison, 2011, p. 80).

Resilience may be a highly personal characteristic, but as such it's a quality that individuals can choose to develop. Leadership coaching

(Allison & Reeves, 2009), a highly personalized strategy for developing leaders, is an ideal vehicle for doing so. Perhaps we are each born with a starting point for resilience. Perhaps events in each of our lives strengthen or compromise our resilience over time. Whether we can ever know the antecedents to resilience in human beings, one thing is certain: Each of us can choose to take action—like the ones suggested in this chapter—every day, to become resilient leaders of resilient organizations and bring about transformative change.

LEADERSHIP FOR SOCIAL JUSTICE AND MORALITY

The term social justice is evoked daily in literature and the news media; however, it can be difficult to define. According to Murrell (2006), "Social justice involves a disposition toward recognizing and eradicating all forms of oppression and differential treatment extant in the practices and policies of institutions, as well as a fealty to participatory democracy as a means of this action" (p. 81). Narrowing the definition of social justice from the world stage to the classroom does not make the task any easier. How social justice relates to and influences educational areas, such as program development, curricula, practicum opportunities, educational philosophies, and social vision is a broader conversation. What can be said is that education plays a part in promoting justice and the development of democratic citizenship (Evans, 2007; Furman & Gruenewald, 2004; Jean-Marie, Normore, & Brooks, 2009; Murrell, 2006). One might argue that this educational commitment to social justice is diminished through our current political environment of emphasizing curriculum tied to basic literacy and numeracy, and not much else.

Synthesizing the social justice discourse in educational leadership, Furman and Gruenewald (2004) offer three shared meanings of social justice embedded in various ways throughout contemporary literature: critical humanist perspective, focus on school achievement and economic well-being, and the narratives and values of the Western Enlightenment (see also Brooks & Miles, 2008; Jean-Marie, Brooks & Normore, 2009). The increased attention given to social justice brings to fore a focus on the moral purposes of leadership in schools and how to achieve these purposes (Furman & Gruenewald, 2004). As Evans (2007) observed, the scholarship of social justice supports the notion that educational leaders have a "social and moral obligation to foster equitable school practices, processes, and outcomes for learners of different racial, socioeconomic, gender, cultural, disability, and sexual orientations backgrounds" (p. 250).

Mahalia Jackson was grounded not only in resilience, but also in social justice and morality. Like many leaders (e.g., Gandhi, Mandela, King, Meier,

Chavez, Truth, Tubman), Mahalia Jackson was inspiring. She inspired numerous people through her music and through her leadership with civil rights. Examples of this inspiration (and the social justice and moral leadership [Dantley & Tillman, 2006] it reflects) are evident in the tributes made at the time of her death. Her "moral force" was praised as the main reason for her success. Of particular interest to these authors are the following: Jackson did not stop learning. When things are going well change is the last thing some educational leaders want to do, so they skimp on learning. Whenever top leaders quit learning it usually means they believe they know everything they need to know.

Jackson did not take on a litany of initiatives at the same time. Too many initiatives drain people. "Busyness" is the number one excuse people give for not getting to the most important work of an organization. Ironically, time spent putting out too many fires today undermines high-leverage action and therefore creates crisis situations tomorrow. In an article in the *Harvard Business Review,* Bruch and Menges (2010) refer to the "acceleration trap." Organizations caught in this trap load their system with too many different activities, often adopting new initiatives without discarding old ones; thus, they overload people and give them no break. The bottom line: a sense of powerlessness. Leaders who complain about being overwhelmed need to claim their priorities and let go of initiatives that don't fit those priorities. Leaders who bounce back possess a sense of self-efficacy rather than powerlessness.

In sum, during times of strife it's easy to succumb to fear. Mahalia Jackson's life exemplifies a leader who rose to the challenge and embraced success. To the latter, when leaders fail to celebrate success they lose the opportunity to learn lessons that could provide key breakthroughs that might alter current challenges. Resilient leaders celebrate even small wins—anything that shows more of what the leaders' desire—to understand how the system creates such victories. Moral and social justice leaders model positive commitment. Commitment is a powerful combination of a positive set of beliefs, coupled with an equally appropriate set of actions and behavior. When moral leaders set out to make a difference, their actions inspire others to follow and learn.

REFERENCES

Allison, E. (2012). The resilient leader. *Educational Leadership, 69*(4), 79–82.

Allison, E., & Reeves, D. (2011). *Renewal coaching field guide: How effective leaders sustain meaningful change.* San Francisco, CA: Jossey-Bass.

Boyatzis, R. E., & McKee, A. (2005). *Resonant leadership: Renewing yourself and connecting with others through mindfulness, hope, and compassion.* Boston, MA: Harvard Business School Press.

Brooks, J. S., & Miles, M. T. (2008). From scientific management to social justice and back again? Pedagogical shifts in educational leadership. In A. H. Normore (Ed.), *Leadership for social justice: Promoting equity and excellence through inquiry and reflective practice* (pp. 99–114). Charlotte, NC: Information Age.

Bruch, H., & Menges, J. I. (2010, April). *The acceleration trap.* Boston, MA: Harvard University Press.

Collins, W. (January 29, 2002). *Mahalia Jackson: St. James encyclopedia of pop culture.* Farmington Hills, MI: St. James Press.

Dantley, M. E., & Tillman, L. C. (2006). Social justice and moral transformative leadership. In C. Marshall & M. Oliva (Eds.), *Leadership for social justice: Making revolutions in education* (pp. 16–30). Boston, MA: Allyn & Bacon.

Darden, R. (2004). *People get ready! A new history of black gospel music.* New York, NY: Continuum.

Dixon, R. (1997). *Blues and gospel records: 1890–1943.* New York, NY: Oxford University Press.

Evans, A. E. (2007). Horton, highlander, and leadership education: Lessons for preparing educational leaders for social justice. *Journal of School Leadership, 17,* 250–275.

Fullan, M. (2001). *Leading in a culture of change.* San Francisco, CA: Jossey-Bass.

Furman, G. C., & Gruenewald, D. A. (2004). Expanding the landscape of social justice: A critical ecological analysis. *Educational Administration Quarterly, 40*(1), 47–76.

Goleman, D., Boyatzis, R., & McKee, A. (2002). *Primal leadership.* Boston, MA: Harvard Business School Press.

Gregory, J. M. (2005). *The southern diaspora: How the great migrations of black and white southerners transformed America.* Chapel Hill, NC: University of North Carolina Press.

Harrison, A. (1991). *Black exodus: The great migration from the American south.* Jackson, MI: University Press of Mississippi.

Henri, F. (1975). *Black migration: Movement north, 1900–1920.* Garden City, NY: Anchor Press.

Jean-Marie, G., Normore, A. H., & Brooks, J. S. (2009). Leadership for social justice: Preparing 21st century school leaders for a new social order. *Journal of Research on Leadership Education, 4*(1), 1–31.

Koster, R. (2002). *A journey from R & B to Zydeco, jazz to country, blues to gospel, cajun music to swamp pop to carnival music and beyond.* Boston, MA: Da Capo Press.

Larkin, C. (1995). *The Guinness encyclopedia of popular music.* London, England: Guinness.

Lyman, D. (2005). *Great African-American women.* New York, NY: Jonathan David.

Mojo Magazine. (2003). *The Mojo collection: The ultimate music companion* (4th ed.). Edinburgh, Scotland: Canongate Books.

Murrell, P. (2006), Toward social justice in urban education: a model of collaborative cultural inquiry in urban schools. *Equity & Excellence in Education 39*(1), 81–90.

Parachin, V. (September 1994). Mahalia Jackson. *American History, 29*(4), 42–44.

Reeves, D. B., & Allison, E. (2009). *Renewal coaching: Sustainable change for individuals and organizations.* San Francisco, CA: Jossey-Bass.

Reeves, D. B., & Allison, E. (2010). *Renewal coaching workbook.* San Francisco, CA: Jossey-Bass.

Rubin, G. (2011). *George Washington quotes.* Retrieved from https://www.brainyquote .com/quotes/authors/g/george_washington.html

The Full Wiki. (2015). *Mahalia Jackson: Wikis.* Retrieved from http://www.thefull wiki.org/Mahalia_Jackson

Whitman, A. (1972). *Mahalia Jackson, gospel singer and civil rights symbol dies.* Retrieved from https://query.nytimes.com/gst/abstract.html?res=9E02E6D716 3EE63ABC4051DFB7668389669EDE

CHAPTER 20

THE MAKING OF MATISYAHU

Music Laying the Foundation for Re-Inspiring Social Justice Work in Education

Azadeh F. Osanloo
New Mexico State University

Sometimes I lay
Under the moon
And thank God I'm breathing
Then I pray
Don't take me soon
'Cause I am here for a reason

Sometimes in my tears I drown
But I never let it get me down
So when negativity surrounds
I know some day it'll all turn around because . . .

—Matisyahu, "One Day," (2009)

Matisyahu, Hebrew for "gift of God," was born Matthew Paul Miller in Pennsylvania in 1979. In his youth he was raised as a Reconstructionist Jew. Reconstructionists define Judaism as the evolving religious civilization of the

Educational Leadership and Music, pages 217–226
Copyright © 2017 by Information Age Publishing
217

Jewish people. The notion of the religion as evolving invokes the idea that Judaism has changed over time as people and civilizations have advanced. Moreover, while the Reconstructionist philosophy distinguishes the Jewish people as unique, this uniqueness implies no sense of superiority over others. Reconstructionists believe that all people are called to the service of virtue, righteousness, and integrity, and thus welcome dialogue with people from all religious traditions (Jewish Reconstructionist Federation, 2015).

As he entered his teenage years and high school, Matisyahu rebelled against his devout Jewish upbringing. He turned to drugs and music to satiate his need for understanding, community, and culture. For many years he was a self-proclaimed "Phish-head" and followed the band Phish, a psychedelic rock band, around the country while they toured. After completing high school at a wilderness program in Bend, Oregon (where he self-identified as the "token" Jew), he returned to New York City where he began developing his eclectic sound within the musical genre of reggae. His sounds were influenced by hip-hop, giving him a unique musical amalgamation of reggae, hip-hop, beat-box, and spirituality. It was during this musical arrival that he began identifying as a Hasidic Jew and was affiliated with the Chabad-Lubavitch community in Brooklyn. For many, he was an atypical synthesis of musicality, religion, and cultural/mainstream success. His distinctive musical flares and devotional undertones garnered the attention of many different groups of listeners from reggae, rap, dance hall, and hip-hop aficionados to religious and politically-minded music lovers. Audiences were attracted to his socially conscious branding and the religio-emotional commitment to the topics he covered in song. However, this notable intersectionality came to a halt in 2011 when he posted a beardless photo of himself on his website. This caused uproar within his religious fan base as the clean-shaven face is in contradiction with the Hasidic faith. Of this revelation, he stated:

No more Chassidic reggae superstar. Sorry folks, all you get is me ... no alias. When I started becoming religious 10 years ago it was a very natural and organic process. It was my choice. My journey: to discover my roots and explore Jewish spirituality—not through books but through real life. At a certain point I felt the need to submit to a higher level of religiosity ... to move away from my intuition and to accept an ultimate truth. I felt that in order to become a good person I needed rules—lots of them—or else I would somehow fall apart. I am reclaiming myself. Trusting my goodness and my divine mission. (Read, 2011)

His 2014 album, *Akeda,* still makes references to biblical figures, Judaism, and prayer throughout; although, he has taken a deliberate, albeit delicate, step back from the fervent devoutness that peppered his earlier music. According to Matisyahu, *Akeda* is the binding and the unbinding (the story of biblical patriarch Abraham following God's demand to bind up and sacrifice his son Isaac, and then being stopped by an angel at the last moment), and the walk home. It's not just about the walk up the mountain. It's about coming back. (Cohen, 2015)

He further offered, "This stage of my life is about what you would consider the unbinding. Getting out of the religion, getting out of the marriage, the relationships" (Cohen, 2015).

As Matisyahu transitioned from the staunchly religious image he had created to a more dynamic and evolving version of himself, he encountered criticism.

> I was feeling like I was doing this very holy work actually, and all of a sudden all these people are just assuming the worst of me, saying, "Not being religious or shaving his beard is a character flaw." Just assuming that it didn't come from a holy place or a place of *avodah* (religious service), but rather that it came from some kind of weakness. It was super-intense. (Cohen, 2015)

> *Akeda* is born out of that. It comes from this place of deep feeling like Abraham, all alone up on that mountain and feeling like all of that work that I did and then having the pain of feeling misunderstood. (Cohen, 2015)

Many of us who engage in social justice work have often felt those very same things: misunderstood, weak, alone, and deep sense of pain. Yet simultaneously there was the need, nay the deep desire to trudge forward on the path that best suited the essence of our work. There is a fearlessness that comes with that type of raw, dauntless realization – a fearlessness that embodies this sort of heartening (and often heart wrenching) social justice work.

ANALYSIS OF "ONE DAY"

> *All my life I've been waiting for*
> *I've been praying for*
> *For the people to say*
> *That we don't wanna fight no more*
> *There will be no more wars*
> *And our children will play*
> *One day*

—Matisyahu, "One Day" (2009)

One of Matisyahu's greatest tracks comes from this third album, *Light.* The song "One Day" was written as a last-minute add-on to the album to garner support from the new president at Epic Records. Matisyahu told *Spinner* (U.K.) that the song "is an anthem of hope with a big beat, the kind of song that makes you bob your head and open your heart at the same time"

(Songfacts, 2016). The song was rerecorded with the additional vocals of the Senegalese hip-hop star Akon and rereleased in February 2010. During the winter of 2010, the song became the anthem for NBC's Countdown to Vancouver Olympics advertising campaign. Matisyahu explained to *MTV News* that although the song was not written expressly for the Olympic Games, the themes of the track ended up applying perfectly. "I wanted to write a song that was an accessible global anthem for hope and peace."

For me, "One Day" has often been an anthem of sadness, despair, and confusion. Saddening, despairing, and confusing because of the unfathomable and unconscionable amount of war, hatred, and violence that has become a palpable pandemic in the world today. But mostly it has been an anthem of hope. Hope that "one day, there will be no more wars, and our children will play." Not just as an educator, but also as a heart-driven person, I have always rooted my being in the ontological drive for hope. Thus, much of my work is grounded in the principle that education is a vocation of hope. Hope is an essential belief for being a social justice leader who promotes a holistic view of equity and fairness. As hooks stated: "My hope emerges from those places of struggle where I witness individuals positively transforming their lives and the world around them. Educating is always a vocation rooted in hopefulness" (hooks, 2003, p. xiv). In educational theory, Paulo Freire used the concept of hope to underlie his thoughts on the task of the progressive educator. Freire (1999) stated:

> One of the tasks of the progressive educator...is to unveil opportunities for hope, no matter what the obstacles may be. After all, without hope there is little we can do. For hope is an ontological need...the attempt to do without hope in the struggle to improve the world, as if that struggle could be reduced to calculated acts alone, or a purely scientific approach, is a frivolous illusion. (p. 9)

Freire believed that without hope, we are hopeless and cannot begin the struggle to change as hope is based on the need for truth as an ethical quality of the struggle. As such, he described hope as an ontological need; one that should be anchored in practice so that it may achieve historical concreteness (Freire, 1999, p. 9). Hope and action are inexorably intertwined for Freire, an intermingling of progressive postmodern and practice-based struggle. As Freire (1999, p. 8) stated, "The idea that hope alone will transform the world...is an excellent route to hopelessness, pessimism, and fatalism."

Central to recognizing and combating this struggle are educators who adopt a critical pedagogy. The application of a critical pedagogy is the way for many educators to act in a way that endorses hope, while simultaneously engaging in the struggle for equity. Freire argued that any curriculum that ignores the plights of the oppressed—the racialized and marginalized—merely perpetuates the status quo and reaffirms power dynamics in favor of the hegemonic elite (Freire, 1997). Critical pedagogy endorses an expansion of consciousness and favors action aimed at change. In order to challenge and question systems of domination, educators should employ techniques and tools in the classroom that engage students in critical thinking. As hooks stated, "The heartbeat of critical thinking is the longing to know, to understand how life works" (2010, p. 7). However, hooks warns, students do not become critical thinkers quickly, but rather it is a process that first includes embracing the love, power, freedom, and evolution of knowledge. She further put forth that many students "resist the critical thinking process; they are more comfortable with learning that allows them to remain passive" because passivity does not require engagement (2010, p. 10). Passivity does not require taking a position, speaking up, and standing out. It is important to acknowledge the inequities and atrocities all about us so as not to simply keep wading through the murky waters of blind passivity.

> It's not about
> Win or lose
> 'Cause we all lose
> When they feed on the souls of the innocent
> Blood-drenched pavement
> Keep on moving though the waters stay raging (Miller, 2009)

Matisyahu longs to understand how life works—that is at the heart of what he does. This understanding is comprised of a mix of hope, action, and social justice issues. For Matisyahu, the vehicle for the exploration into understanding life is music. For me, the vehicle for my exploration into the intermingling of hope, action, and social justice is education. Both endeavors cut deeply across stakeholders centralizing action as an intrinsic component, while dismantling obtuse compartmentalizations of race, class, gender, religion, and subsequent forms of otherness.

INSPIRATION AND SUGGESTIONS
FOR SOCIAL JUSTICE LEADERS

> *One day this all will change*
> *Treat people the same*
> *Stop with the violence*
> *Down with the hate*
>
> *One day we'll all be free*
> *And proud to be*
> *Under the same sun*
> *Singing songs of freedom like*
> *One day*
>
> —Matisyahu, "One Day" (2009)

The work and music of Matisyahu provides four lessons for educational leaders, specifically those who do work in the arenas of social justice, educational equity, and criticalist movements. First let me say I deliberately use the term social justice leader as opposed to leadership for social justice. For some it is lexical word play. For me, it is an indication of my edupolitical positioning and that I first and foremost am devoutly focused on social justice work whether I be a leader, teacher, instructor, or musician. The ideologies and paradigms of thought associated with social justice ground my thinking and the essence of my being. Ergo, it is imperative for me to lead with the idea of social justice first as my moniker.

The life and work of Matisyahu, in particular his song "One Day," can be viewed as inspirational for the educational leaders of today and tomorrow. Four suggestions that can be gleaned from the music of Matisyahu are: (a) exploring the vibrancy of intersectionality, (b) valuing the complexity and dynamism of the individual experience, (c) a willingness to be continuously transformed and multiculturally nurturant, and (d) the Sisyphean nature of social justice work.

EXPLORING THE VIBRANCY OF INTERSECTIONALITY

Matisyahu uses his intertwining of religion, culture, politics, and music to inspire and educate people. It is an intersection unique to his experiences. Critical theorists, to better theorize how oppression occurs in multiple spheres, often use intersectionality (Crenshaw, 2001). Generally, intersectionality explores how multiple social identities (i.e., gender, race, social class, home language, sexual orientation) in conjunction with systems of oppression coexist and make-up an individual's multifaceted identity. Educational leaders can use this same approach to influence a greater critical mass of people to work toward social justice aims. By exploring intersectionality from an asset-based stance, educational leaders can capitalize on efforts aimed at working across stakeholders toward a common social good. Social justice work is not only the work of educators, it is the work of every civic-minded, justice-orientated, critically conscious, multiculturally active, and ethical participant in a democracy (Dewey, 1916, 1938). In order for educational leaders to engage with broader audiences and increase the potential for greater social change, we must reassess the manner in which we work with and consider the contributions of those in our educational ecological systems; this means all staff, faculty, parents, families, school resource officers, and other members within the edu-community.

It is important to remember that our students are organic intellectuals. Gramsci considered all individuals to be intellectuals. And in the spirit of Gramsci (1971) students should be considered organic intellectuals, who are individuals grounded in the intellectualism of their own specific community, giving rise to social change and reform through connectivity with people, especially in terms of experiential knowledge.

> Most importantly for Gramsci, organic intellectuals of the working class not only resist hegemonic processes, but they also attempt to displace the old hegemonic order. . . . At the same time, organic intellectuals serve as role models who open the horizons of their class or popular front to secure a more equitable system of societal organization. (Fischman & McLaren, 2005, p. 434)

Within this frame, students as organic intellectuals can use their positionality to enrich their community so that collective, informed action can occur. "The role of the organic intellectual was to mediate between the good sense of subaltern groups and the formation of a counterhegemonic consciousness" (Fischman & McLaren, 2005, p. 434).

VALUING THE COMPLEXITY AND DYNAMISM
OF THE INDIVIDUAL EXPERIENCE

As a continuing and evolving learner, my personal experiences as a lifelong student are impossible to separate from my educational philosophy. As such, experiential education (Dewey, 1938) is central to my philosophy due to the fact it accesses one's educational identity, which is a constant companion in the classroom. A tenet within my philosophy is to value the learner as a unique knowing individual with a personal investment in the course. My students represent a mixture of racial and ethnic backgrounds, family construction, social and economic status, sexual orientation, and educational proclivities. Learning from these rich experiences presents extremely valuable perspectives that offer vastly different perspectives from that of solely observing the instructor, taking notes, or reading from the text. In fact, this enables a democratic community of learning in which teachers and students are, as Freire (1997) would assert, "critical co-investigators." Often, academicians impose lessons upon students as opposed to co-creating knowledge (Freire, 1997) with students. Valuing the human/individual experience is integral for educational leadership students, so that they can form a sense of agency within knowledge attainment as well as for long-term socioemotional health within social justice work. Students should be co-creators of their edupolitical world and knowledge bases (Freire, 1997). Experiential education should be valued, emphasized, and heralded. It should foment excitement in students from an otherwise desultory set of educational ideas.

Promoting the human experience encourages learners to value their own educational experience as well as become vested in the outcomes. As

Dewey asserted, learning emerges from a meaningful and growth inducing focus on the experience (Dewey, 1916). In adherence with this core value, it is important to embed real-world examples in curriculum as well as ask students to offer their helpful experiences as learning points. Co-creating this intrinsic interest promotes agency in learning and invokes power for students within the classroom. Furthermore, the emergent and meaningful discourse practiced in my classroom allows for a natural progression toward an integrated curriculum reflective of life experience and interdisciplinary lessons.

WILLINGNESS TO BE CONTINUOUSLY TRANSFORMED AND MULTICULTURALLY NURTURANT

Educators can become static in their work as it pertains to social justice. We can often become rooted in that which we know as "social justice" without being open to a new set of ideals, goals, or aims within social justice work. How do we continue to evolve, be open to and accept new ideas, and transform our thinking so that it remains inclusive? First and foremost there needs to be a willingness to be consistently and constantly transformed by our social, educational, political, and emotional environments as well as the social justice issues that emerge over time. Social justice work is neither static nor singularly defined. The world is rapidly changing and we must be prepared and willing to act within a transforming global consciousness.

Within that vein, it is important to ask: How do we not become bogged down by the "social just-us?" For me, the social just-us captures the essence of the educators who portend to put forth a salient social justice platform for issues of educational equity and critical inquiry, but they actually end up recreating the hegemonic structures of institutional oppression from which they freed themselves. It is social justice for just "us." This can animate on many different levels, in many different ways, and be conscious and/or unconscious. Academics who ground their research in social justice work, study inequalities that are routinely passed down from systemic and institutional structures. They learn to astutely name the inequity they have experienced as well as learn skillful and time-consuming ways to fight against the oppressive systems with which they engage. It is war, and often-times this war-like posturing causes them to fight with those within the same social justice sphere, especially when someone defines their work by rigid, fixed confines of what social justice work is, looks like, and should be based upon. Generally, if you are not with them constellating the war, you are against them. For me, it is an imperative to be open to different definitions and views of social justice work. No true social justice leader can live in a confined box of right and wrong. It is vital to remember that there will be times when social justice work entails issues that do not simply serve us, and we must be willing to sacrifice so that others may prosper and be nurtured.

Being multiculturally nurturant stems from the spirit of the Riddle Scale (1985), which points out that "tolerance" and "acceptance" can be seen as positive attitudes; however, the terms should actually be treated as pejoratives because they potentially mask the underlying fear or hatred, indicate that there is indeed something that needs acceptance, and (most importantly) purport that the dominant hegemonic ideologues are the ones with the power to reject or to accept. Nurturance is the ideal attitude, which sees difference as indispensable to society. In light of the Riddle's (1985) theorizing and establishing important dispositions for social justice leaders, I developed the Multiculturally Nurturant Pledge, which I use most specifically in my Multicultural Leadership course by asking students to voluntarily sign it at the beginning of the course. The first line of the pledge underscores the tone and tenor of the document. It states: "As a multicultural leader, I will accept, affirm, and nurture the differences and strengths of my students, staff, faculty, and community." This pledge harkens to the hooksian (2010) notion that a simple uniform multiculturalism does not exist; rather, multiculturalism should be viewed as a complex idea that is couched in particularism and individualism.

SISYPHEAN NATURE OF SOCIAL JUSTICE WORK

One well-known Greek myth involves the punishment of Sisyphus. After tricking the gods, Sisyphus was ordered to push a boulder uphill. But each time he reached the top of the hill, the rock rolled back to the bottom creating endless punishment for Sisyphus. The tale of Sisyphus mirrors the plight of many social justice leaders, teachers, and activists. Educational leaders who choose to conduct their work within the sphere of social justice are met with many obstacles: implicit and explicit, clandestine and blatant, opaque and transparent. While one's life purpose may be to serve in this educative capacity, it is not without venturing into emotionally, spiritually, physically, and intellectually taxing work. Social justice work can be fatiguing and devastating to one's health and happiness. How does one continue to "roll that rock up the hill," while fully cognizant that it will roll back down? For me, the effort to continue the work (the pushing of the rock up the hill) comes from two areas: camaraderie with like-minded scholars in the field and an unrelenting hope for a better future. Securing healthy and candid relationships with friends who often think and feel similarly regarding social justice issues has been a boon to my ability to continually complete this work. And then of course, hope. Without hope, social justice work would not exist. Without hope, I would not be doing this work. Without hope, we could not change the world for the better while remembering that we are here for a reason.

Don't take me soon
'Cause I am here for a reason
Sometimes in my tears I drown
But I never let it get me down
So when negativity surrounds
I know some day it'll all turn around because … (Miller, 2009)

REFERENCES

Cohen, D. (2015, March). *From Hasidism to freedom: Singer Matisyahu unbound.* Retrieved from http://www.haaretz.com/israel-news/culture/theater/1.646213

Crenshaw, K. (2001). Demarginalizing the intersection of race and sex: A black feminist critique of antidiscrimination doctrine, feminist theory and antiracist politics. In A. Green & R. Mabokela (Eds.), *Sisters of the academy: Emergent black women scholars in higher education.* (pp. 57–80). Sterling, VA: Stylus.

Dewey, J. (1916). *Democracy and education.* New York, NY: Simon and Schuster.

Dewey, J. (1938). *Experience and education.* New York, NY: Kappa Delta Pi.

Fischman, G., & McLaren, P. (2005). Rethinking critical pedagogy and the Gramscian and Freirean legacies: From organic to committed intellectuals or critical pedagogy, commitment, and praxis. *Cultural Studies–Critical Methodologies, 8*(4), 425–447.

Freire, P. (1997). *Pedagogy of the oppressed.* New York, NY: Continuum.

Freire, P. (1999). *Pedagogy of hope: Reliving pedagogy of the oppressed.* New York, NY: Continuum.

Gramsci, A. (1971). *Selections from the prison notebooks,* Q. Hoare & G. Nowell Smith (Eds. & Trans.). New York, NY: International Publishers.

hooks, b. (2003). *Teaching community: A pedagogy of hope.* New York, NY: Routledge.

hooks, b. (2010). *Teaching critical thinking: Practical wisdom.* New York, NY: Routledge.

Jewish Reconstructionist Federation (2015). *Reconstructionist Judaism: Who is a Reconstructionist Jew?* Retrieved from https://www.jewishvirtuallibrary.org/jsource/Judaism/reconstruction.html

Miller, M. (2009). One day. On *Light* [CD]. Seattle, WA: Epic Records.

Read, M. (2011). *Matisyahu shaves his beard, reminding world of his existence.* Retrieved from http://gawker.com/5867792/matisyahu-shaves-beard-reminding-world-of-his-existence

Songfacts. (2016). *One day by Matisyahu.* Retrieved from http://www.songfacts.com/detail.php?id=15894

CHAPTER 21

INTERROGATING PUNISHMENT THROUGH RACE, RAPTIVISM, AND YOUTH LEADERSHIP OF JASIRI X

Darius Prier
Duquesne University

Urban youth, if they ever were, are no longer under the illusion of a race-blind society. Their iPhones capture the murder of Black bodies in real time. Twitter responds with the hashtag Black Lives Matter, igniting a new social movement on the ground. Meanwhile, national media captures military tanks surveilling the streets of chocolate cities such as Ferguson, Missouri, and Baltimore, Maryland; and rap artists' counternarratives challenge media's criminalization of their identity. Along the way, the music, art, and the culture of hip-hop inspire youth for social and political change in their communities. These events require "a view of leadership in which educators undertake the language of social criticism, display moral courage, and connect rather than distance themselves from the most pressing

Educational Leadership and Music, pages 227–240
Copyright © 2017 by Information Age Publishing
All rights of reproduction in any form reserved.

problems and opportunities of the times" (Freire & Giroux, 1989, p. ix). In such matters, educational leaders must take stock of the political implications for what police killings of unarmed Black youth mean in media's demonization, devaluation, and punishment of their humanity, which in turn permeates our schools.

The culture of punishment on Black males in schools has a deeply rooted historical context. Discipline and control of Black male bodies through slave codes was the rule. The production and perpetuation of the Black male as a dangerous stereotype was developed between the 18th and 20th centuries, and the racial politics of such a legacy has been fomented and shaped through popular culture (e.g., media), politicians, and academia (Carter, Skiba, Arredondo, & Pollock, 2014). In addition, during the 19th century, minstrelsy of Black stereotypes in popular culture had quite an impact on negative representations of Black identities. Smiley and Fakunle (2016) argue that prior to the American Civil War, the media imaging of the Black male in popular culture was that of being comedic, buffoonish, content, happy, and overall, docile—nonthreatening.

The cultural shift from docility to the dangerousness of the Black male identity occurred after Reconstruction, when Blacks were gaining some modicum of political and economic power, and the wealthy White elite feared the political consequences (e.g., voting) of what might come with this newfound power (Smiley & Fakunle, 2016). In addition, poor Whites feared for competition over jobs. Subsequently, it was the post-Reconstruction period, along with the victory of *Plessy v. Ferguson (1896),* when a cultural shift in media occurred from Black male docility to brute/savagery.

At every turn, the racial politics of White media in popular culture controlled the public consciousness that shifted Black docility in texts such as *Uncle Tom's Cabin, Gone With the Wind,* and *Song of the South,* to Black savagery of the brute toward violence and sexual assault on White women in films such as *Birth of a Nation* in 1915 (Smiley & Fakunle, 2016). The changing social construction in media justified a hyper criminalization of Black male identity for punitive practices (e.g., lynching, incarceration; Smiley & Fakunle, 2016).

The changing sociocultural context in representation from docility to brute/savagery in the social imagination of White society has now morphed into the hidden, racist ideology of the "thug" in contemporary media that is a racially coded language, popularized in hegemonic and nonhegemonic ways in hip-hop culture. It reappropriates yesterday's old racial politics of the Black male as dangerous brute into today's thug to justify the criminalization and punishment of today's urban youth.

The changing sociocultural context in representation of the Black male as thug in media can be seen, for example, in the aftermath of Freddie Gray's death. In this media struggle over representation, the denial and

invisibility of police accountability came at the expense of all youth pro-
testers defamed as thugs by former mayor Stephanie Rawlings, President
Obama, and many political pundits in the media. Recognizing the racial
politics of such a loaded term, Baltimore City Councilman Carl Stokes said
to *CNN* we might as well call them niggers (Smiley & Fakunle, 2016). Similarly, when outspoken Seattle Seahawks cornerback and graduate of Stanford University Richard Sherman was called a thug by the media, he too
stated the term was like the new word for nigger. Both Stokes and Sherman
recognized the hidden, racially coded meanings that signified or resembled
old racial myth making of Black male savagery for punishment.

The attitudes, images, language, style, and other symbolic expressions
familiar in a supposed thug identity in hip-hop culture have become the
texts that are now read as criminality for punishment to White mainstream
society. Victor Rios would argue that today the aforementioned symbolic
expressions of racially coded criminality work alongside material expressions; both are designed in what he calls the youth control complex to pun-
ish Black and Brown males within institutions such as the media, schools,
police, and the criminal justice system (Rios, 2011).

Punitive practices of ubiquitous criminalization occur symbolically when
youth are constantly under surveillance, racially profiled, stigmatized, and
ostracized in/by institutions such as media, school, community, criminal
justice system, recreation and community centers, businesses, places of
residence, etc. (Rios, 2011). Punishment happens materially when, for example, being called a thug can materialize into zero-tolerance policies between police and schools that instigate detention, suspension, expulsion,
and incarceration practices (Rios, 2011).

The punitive practice of criminalization, symbolically and materially,
can be reflected in the racial profiling of hoodies, sagging jeans, athletic
jerseys, doo-rags, etc. that becomes symbolic expressions of criminality for
policies such as stop-and-frisk and stand-your-ground practices for police.
This also exacerbates a disproportionate rate of office referrals, detentions,
suspensions, and expulsions toward Black males in schools (Prier, 2015).
In referencing a childhood friend who was caught in the web of punitive
practices of the youth control complex between schools and police, Rios
(2011) states,

> From a young age, his teachers treated him punitively. He was seen as a prob-
> lem kid in school and spent many of his school days in the detention room.
> On the street, police often stopped him as he walked home from school, even
> before he joined the gang, because from their perspective the baggy clothes
> he wore marked him as a gang member. (pp. viii–ix)

Suffice it to say, police officers and schools officials alike consciously or
unconsciously act punitively on a history, symbolically and materially, that

sediments deeply held values in the devaluation and dehumanization of Black male life in U.S. society (Carter, Skiba, Arredondo, & Pollock, 2014).

Prophetic hip-hop texts often give expression to present day experiences of punishment in relation to the historical backdrop of slavery, Jim Crow, and segregation politics. These artists situate present tragic predicaments in relation to past racial politics to inform how they make sense of contemporary punitive measures such as police brutality, incarceration, and school-to-prison pipeline practices (Beachum & McCray, 2011; Prier, 2014).

C. P. Gause (2005) argues that popular culture is the "background noise to our daily existence" (p. 342). Subsequently, the daily existence of policing and punishment in urban society is filtered through the background noise of hip-hop. According to Paul Butler (2009), hip-hop's disproportionate and unfair entanglement with the criminal justice system situates the culture as a prime advocate in critique of the nation state. Video, lyrics, or imagery in hip-hop can offer educational leaders powerful lessons regarding youths' views of their humanity in relation to authority, such as the police and school officials. These insights build upon my previous research (see Prier, 2012) where youth rap artists said how they were viewed as "dangerous thugs" precipitated how they were targeted for punishment in streets and schools (p. 77).

Popular culture is a cultural site of struggle where hegemonic media manipulation of public consent in the targeting of blackness as "dangerous" from above, and critique and resistance of urban youth culture from below, engage in a protracted battle over disproportionate punishment practices toward Black males in urban society (Carlson & Dimitriadis, 2003; Giroux & Simon 1989). In an effort to demystify the namelessness and invisibility (Gates & West, 1996) that Black male youth experience in this dialectic, I will recruit and analyze the prophetic lyrics, images, and videos of nationally acclaimed hip-hop artist Jasiri X. I situate and foreground his critical hip-hop texts on police brutality within a larger social, political, and historical context for the lessons educational leaders might learn from how African American male youth experience and view society's punishment of their identity.

INTRODUCTION TO THE LIFE AND WORK OF JASIRI X

Jasiri X is a nationally recognized hip-hop artist and activist from Pittsburgh, Pennsylvania, who uses media to interrogate a host of societal injustices, including but not limited to gentrification, poverty, politics, and police brutality to name a few. He produces rap music and visual images in media to tell a different story about Black male youth that is not visible to the mainstream public. As founder and creative program director of 1Hood Media, Jasiri teaches youth how to produce their own stories in ways that counter negative press in the media. He specifically teaches young people the art of lyricism, media literacy, videography, photography, journalism, entrepreneurship, and a host of other 21st century skills. What separates Jasiri X from many other artists is that he could be described as what Yvonne Bynoe (2004) would call a raptivist, where one moves beyond beats and rhymes of sociopolitical awareness to intervene in matters of public policy (2004).

For several years, Jasiri has been a leading youth advocate as a staunch critic of police brutality. He has helped organize rallies and protests for local victims of police brutality in Pittsburgh—Jordan Miles and Leon Ford, who survived—as well as nationally in watershed events such as the murders of Trayvon Martin in Sanford, Florida, and Mike Brown in Ferguson, Missouri. Prior to these events, his activism helped exonerate the Jena Six, the six Black males in Central Louisiana who were charged with attempted murder over a schoolyard fight regarding nooses hanging from a tree. In addition, Jasiri has hosted community-based forums to bridge community-police relations featuring local community activists, national activists such as Uncle Bobby of the Oscar Grant family, and rap artist Tef Poe of Ferguson, Missouri.

In addition, Jasiri X serves as an organic intellectual who co-teaches particular units in social justice classes in the academy with scholars such as myself at Duquesne University. Our director of the UCEA Center for Social Justice, Gretchen Generett, has hosted Jasiri to collaborate with our Department of Educational Foundations and Leadership's DELS Conference. In this setting, we host educational leaders from across the country to develop innovative leadership strategies to work across and between the academy, school, and the community through a social justice lens. Subsequently, Jasiri has used his music to open up dialogue with school and community leaders in these learning settings to address matters of excessive discipline and punishment in schools and urban communities.

During the spring semester of 2016, Jasiri was invited by Launcelot Brown, our Distinguished Barbara A. Sizemore professor in urban education, to lecture and perform for urban youth at the School of Education's Annual Barbara A. Sizemore Youth Conference. Hundreds of young people from the Pittsburgh School District attend this conference to learn new leadership skills to take back to their communities.

Jasiri's videos have been featured on websites such Allhiphop.com and The Huffington Post. He has appeared on Duke University's online show *Left of Black*, BET's *Rap City*, *The Michael Baisden Show*, and Free Speech TV. He has blogged for the Black Youth Project, Jack and Jill Politics, and Daveyd.com. His organization, 1Hood Media, is of national acclaim garnering support from the Heinz Endowment and Pittsburgh Foundations. In addition, Jasiri has been a BMe fellow and was previously awarded the prestigious August Wilson Center for African American Culture Fellowship. He is currently an artist as activist fellow (2015–2016), an artist residency award granted by the Robert Rauschenberg Foundation.

In 2016, Jasiri was awarded an honorary doctorate by the Chicago Theological Seminary. He was also named Hip-Hop Ambassador for the State of the Black World Conference IV, hosted by the Institute of the Black World 21st Century (Jasiri X named, 2016). According to Ron Daniels, president of the organization, the institute is serious about aligning with socially conscious hip-hop artists and cultural workers such as Jasiri X who represent one of the most powerful genre's the world has ever seen (Jasiri X named, 2016). Subsequently, in this role Jasiri's leadership will wield considerable influence between the hip-hop and Pan-African social movements to cultivate radical, revolutionary change for oppressed Black people across the globe.

Finally, Jasiri is often counseled by Paradise Gray, cofounder of the legendary rap group, X-Clan, and works with his mentor Harry Bellafonte on matters related to juvenile justice reform. Jasiri uses hip-hop to (in his words) free minds "one rhyme at a time."

ANALYZING POLICE BRUTALITY THROUGH CORNEL WEST'S NAMELESSNESS AND INVISIBILITY

Jasiri X works within the prophetic tradition of the Black freedom struggle, speaking frank truths in the face of exponential levels of police brutality and vigilante violence on urban youth in U.S. society. His lyrics reflect West's notion of invisibility and namelessness, where Blacks negotiate structures of feeling and meaning in a society where Black humanity, intelligence, anguish, and pain are either questioned, ignored, denied, or rejected in the face of White supremacist ideology (Gates & West, 1996). Namelessness and invisibility suggest Black people are seen as problems and abstractions; as a monolithic group who acts, thinks, and behaves the same with no individuality to their personhood. There is also a sense of homelessness in relation to namelessness and invisibility, where Blacks feel they have no space (e.g., physical location) or place (e.g., roots of culture) to embody the presence of their humanity in an anti-Black society (Gates & West, 1996).

It is out of conditions of namelessness and invisibility where prophetic hip-hop artists provoke critical consciousness to institutional racism. They are committed to moral and political arguments, provide social and structural analysis, and express deep disappointment in absurd, tragic predicaments (Gates & West, 1996). However, they hold out a redemptive love for vulnerable communities of color, despite the malicious treatment they encumber. For example, in Jasiri X's "Oscar Grant Tribute" (2009) he states,

You seen the video man
Them cops is ruthless
I'm tired of the silence and the ... excuses/

Despite witnesses to the execution of Oscar and evidence of the video, namelessness and invisibility reminds us there is a nonrecognition of persons of color as full human beings. Therefore, to the criminal justice system accountability for how Oscar died is "inconclusive," and his death is of no consequence.

Similarly, the 2011 track "Jordan Miles" chronicles a local incident in Pittsburgh, where an honor roll high school student was brutally beaten by two police officers on his way to see his grandmother. Officers had "mistaken" his pop bottle for a gun, and they were looking for guns, drugs, and money. When urban youth are viewed as part of one monolithic group, stereotypes in namelessness and invisibility don't provide room for alternate judgments that negate all Black males as thugs/drug dealers. As Jasiri states,

but he was found guilty before a trial
cause he's a young black man in the wrong part of town
Jordan is a kid that gets good grades
not a thug bragging that he's hood raised

Miles does not represent the student who embraces a thug life mentality commonly associated with hood politics, but loves school, as demonstrated by his academic efforts. To put a face with the name and memory of Mile's bludgeoned head, Jasiri recreates the scene in the video placing his body on the concrete with a photograph of Jordan's brutalized face covering his own while reenacting/simulating the beating to his head.

"Trayvon" (Jasiri X, 2012), remixed from Kanye and Jay Z's "No Church in the Wild" (Jasiri, 2011), recounts Trayvon Martin's murder and the acquittal of George Zimmerman. When Black people are framed as problems within namelessness and invisibility, annihilation to their personhood is targeted and unquestioned. Jasiri (2012) states,

Nine milli cocking them
who's this nigga walking in my neighborhood?
He fits all the specifics of criminal statistics
he looks suspicious.

There is no name or face to Trayvon because he is already positioned as a criminal to George Zimmerman. Therefore, Jasiri paints the picture of Zimmerman's criminalization of Trayvon's blackness provoking his death. He ends the track stating, "The message is only White life is protected in America."

Jasiri's (2013) remix to Kanye's "Blood on the Leaves" represents the contradictions of perceived value between Black and White life in an anti-Black society, and the aftermath effects when police and community violence coexist. The theme of invisibility and namelessness is opened up in the video by sampling Gerardo Rivera's objectifying premise that Trayvon's hoodie provoked and justified his death as he was a "stranger" in the night. Jasiri then invokes Black invisibility, regarding media's lukewarm response to mass murder on Black life while isolated events of murder on White life are greeted with "mass hysteria."

Jasiri later argues it's only in death when Black people get a name and become visible on the canvas of t-shirts, metaphorically referenced to as galleries. However he later adds, "But after three washes those images get faded." It is as if even holding on to the memory of dead Black bodies is temporary because we don't have space and place where the affirmation of Black humanity can be permanent. Jasiri (2013) ends the track stating,

> Hold still little man let America put this noose on
> And hang you from the highest tree branch another youth gone.

Jasiri pontificates, the life of newborn Black babies metaphorically await nooses around their neck because they are given little chance to survive in a nation where no one told them their blackness was of the wrong hue at birth in a racist U.S. society.

Jasiri X remixes the beat to Drake's 2013 song "Worst Behavior" to his own track, "They Never Loved Us" (2014), addressing themes of criminalization, incarceration, and death that are transfixed on Black bodies in the matrix of police brutality. He paints vivid, painful images referencing the paralysis of Leon Ford, who was unarmed and shot several times by police in Pittsburgh; the shooting of Jordan Davis and Mike Brown; the criminalization of Black male youth as thugs in media by journalists; the herding and incarceration of Black bodies; and the historical memory of the purchasing and lynching of Black bodies as property. Toward the end of this text, there is a plea for God to "wipe the earth clean, of all the hatred in this world and let the church sing."

Finally, "The Babies" (2015) is a heartfelt plea for accountability in the compassion, caring, and redemptive love to Black youth themselves. The opening chorus repeats, "But no one stopped to think about the babies." In a U.S. culture of namelessness of Black bodies, there is "no child left behind from being profiled" in Jasiri X's words. He then states, "Imagine babies being born with a black mask; and a bullseye birthmark on our black ass."

Jasiri also critiques the American empire who sends its children to war, then treats its citizens like terrorists at home. However, Jasiri states America should not be shocked at "its babies we burying" when a culture of violence in war to get what the United States wants has been our society's way of life (2015). In addition, Cornel West's notion of namelessness and invisibility in relation to homelessness of space and place is articulated with Jasiri X's lines (2015),

> Then point to the flag
> and tell us to pledge allegiance
> To a place they still treat us like a stillborn fetus.

Toward the end of the track, there are powerful video images of children marking the names of victims of police brutality—Sandra Bland, Sam DuBose, Tamir Rice, Rekia Boyd, Aiyana Jones, and Freddie Gray—inside chalk outlines. The children and young adults then placed their bodies inside the chalk outlines where names where marked, to invoke compassion, empathy, naming, and visibility in the suffering of Black bodies. Sadly, although the video was made just last year, it is already outdated of new victims of police brutality, such as Philando Castile (St. Paul, Minnesota) and Alton Sterling (Baton Rouge, Louisiana), who could be added to the list.

If we ignore context as to why young people within popular culture express themselves in ways that reflect resistance, we misinterpret the meaning of the messages, which are intended to force the public to pay attention to a series of traumatic and unjust events Black males have experienced repeatedly over the years. To reiterate the Tupac metaphor, he mentioned he was going to continue to tell America how dirty it was in how it treated her Black children, until someone cleaned the mess up. Subsequently, the images and lyrics of Jasiri X intentionally unsettle or provoke us to think critically about whether the democratic ideals and practices of equality, liberty, and freedom are being met for all youth. As educators, critical interpretations of popular culture become important as discourses circulated within the music are heard by millions of young people who often feel or have experienced the subject matter to which the artists are speaking.

LESSONS LEARNED

Cultural expressions in Black popular culture have the power to confront the absurdity and tragedy of the Black experience within the American empire (Gates & West, 1996). According to West, "Black artists grapple with madness and melancholia, doom and death, terror and horror, individuality and identity" (p. 78). The political meanings of these emotions in art align with English and Papa's (2010) idea of restoring the shadow side of leadership, where arts and humanities encompass emotion, culture, and narratives as integral components in how leadership decisions are made.

When we move past mere verification to discovery (English & Papa, 2010), we move beyond what reality is into new questions about, for example, cultural expressions in Black popular culture, reading its signs and symbols of deep disappointment from urban youth. This approach moves us into different kinds of leadership decisions to disrupt punishment in schools and the larger society.

Beachum and McCray (2011) remind us, "encoded in the music are strife, distress, and powerful emotion" (p. 28). The music, as reflected through the Black experience, brings us to terms with struggle, joy, sorrow, hope, and the ups and downs of Black folk aspiring for the American dream in the midst of an American nightmare (Beachum & McCray, 2011, p. 28). However, to recognize prophetic voices in Black popular culture as a new kind of data/evidence to prompt decision making in educational leadership requires a shift from traditional, Taylorist, epistemological modes of inquiry in the field. Subsequently, to include the discourse of hip-hop as a cultural impetus to provoke social change and transformation in urban schools would mean rejecting one dimensional notions of efficiency, rationality, empiricism, and science—discourses void of culture, ethics, values, emotion, and narratives that are important to public life in our decision making (English & Papa, 2010).

In addition, to take into account hip-hop culture in educational leadership means one must incorporate the voices of youth, learn how they make sense of their community in relation to school through the culture, and create innovative spaces where educators can learn from students to incorporate new knowledge in the pedagogical relationship for student empowerment (Love, 2014). Importantly, Love (2014) states educators should acknowledge "to students that they actually knew very little about the languages that were spoken by youth every day, or their cultural backgrounds, but at the same time demonstrate a willingness to learn about that language and culture" (p. 448).

Furthermore, Shirley Steinberg (2014) states that youth are typically feared rather than respected, and are rarely given the authority or respect to make choices and decisions, and define their own identities in ways that are empowering to their lives. This is particularly true for Black males. What Jasiri X attempts to do as an artist is empower students to interrogate how society has come to perceive Black males, and give them tools to deconstruct problematic images he discussed in the aforementioned hip-hop texts. In a world where the Black existence is put into question by the hip-hop generation, how youth view themselves in relation to society to move toward empowerment is a crucial project for educational leaders. I close with the following lessons learned for educational leaders to consider in reflecting on my analysis of Jasiri X's lyrics on the culture of punishment toward Black male youth:

- Prophetic forms of hip-hop, rather than the culture's market-driven tendencies, can offer educational leaders critical social interpretations of how many urban youth view authority in schools and communities (West, 2004). It's the discourse of conscious minded youth; therefore, it's a mode of communication that should be studied by educational leaders. The narratives within such a discourse become valuable entry points for educational leaders to redefine, reshape, or remake pedagogical relationships with young people that are more equitable.

- Hip-hop artists such as Jasiri X are important community-based assets whose funds of knowledge, articulated through the music and culture, emerge from their everyday lived experiences. When educational leaders place value in nontraditional forms of knowledge production such as hip-hop, they can scaffold such work as culturally responsive pedagogy across and between the academy, schools, and the community (Prier, 2012).

- As I've stated elsewhere (see Prier, 2012; Prier, 2014; Prier, 2015), the political act of critical media literacy examining how the arrangement of images impact our view and differential treatment of punishment toward Black males is an indispensable skillset for educational leaders. This enables educational leaders to link the cultural work of reading signs, symbols, images, and texts in the production of popular culture, to their technical practice of challenging a culture of punishment in schools.

- There has been a significant absence in the preparation of educational leaders regarding the racial and historical context of discipline, punishment, and control on Black bodies. While I understand these discursive events are unpopular and uncomfortable conversations, statistics bear out overwhelming evidence that there is a disproportionate targeting of Black male youth, fueling school-to-prison pipeline practices (Carter, Skiba, Arredondo & Pollock, 2014; Noguera, 2008). Such a reality does not emerge from neutral, policymaking decisions. In negating how we may unintentionally act on subconscious bias, rooted in a discriminatory history, leaves void the possibility to exacerbate a historical continuum of institutional punishment on Black males.

- If we as school leaders fail to recognize the pain, despair, and despondency of Black suffering, we reproduce the invisibility and namelessness of urban youths' experiences. Subsequently, it will be difficult for educational leaders to develop empathy for Black male youth. In addition, the denial of Black suffering may sustain institutional and structural conditions that hinder democratic ideals for all of its citizens toward social transformation. Therefore, we must work through crisis in urban contexts to work outward toward social justice in education.

In closing, we as educational leaders can ill afford to be silent regarding the atrocious examples of several unarmed Black children gunned down over the past few years. These children, and the cops who killed them, were once students in our schools. We educate children to prepare them for the world. But what if that world commits intellectual, social, political, economic, and physical assault on their minds, bodies, and souls from the miseducation it has received from its defaming of Black male youth?

Jeffrey Duncan-Andrade (2009) offers that we as educators must have critical hope to confront and combat the persistent challenges of pain and suffering urban youth experience on a daily basis that permeate our classrooms. Critical hope connects the life of students to the rigorous content of subject matter being taught. It embraces a pedagogy for humanization, working through youths' pain and disappointment in ways that channel these emotions toward a more productive, hopeful, and transformative future (Duncan-Andrade, 2009). Jasiri X bears witness to the pain and suffering Black male youth experience through the art of hip-hop, where youth channel righteous rage as an innovative pedagogical space to disrupt nameless and invisibility to reconstruct more empowering narratives that affirm their humanity.

REFERENCES

Beachum, F. D., & McCray, C. R. (2011). *Cultural collision and collusion: Reflections on hip-hop culture, values, and schools.* New York, NY: Peter Lang.

Butler, P. (2009). *Let's get free: A hip-hop theory of justice.* New York, NY: The New Press.

Bynoe, Y. (2004). *Stand and deliver: Political activism, leadership, and hip-hop culture.* New York, NY: Soft Skull Press.

Carlson, D., & Dimitriadis, G. (2003). Introduction. In G. Dimitriadis & D. Carlson (Eds.), *Promises to keep: Cultural studies, democratic education, and public life* (pp. 1–35). New York, NY: RoutledgeFalmer.

Carter, P., Skiba, R., Arredondo, M., & Pollock, M. (2014). You can't fix what you don't look at: Acknowledging race in addressing racial discipline disparities. *Discipline Disparities Series: Acknowledging Race.* Retrieved from http://www.indiana.edu/~atlantic/wp-content/uploads/2014/12/Acknowledging-Race_121514.pdf

Duncan-Andrade, J. M. R. (2009). Note to educators: Hope required when growing roses in concrete. *Harvard Educational Review, 79*(2), 181–194.

English, F, & Papa, R. (2010). *Restoring human agency to educational administration: Status and strategies.* Lancaster, PA: ProActive.

Friere, P., & Giroux, H. A. (1989). Pedagogy, popular culture, and public life: An introduction. In H. Giroux & R. Simon (Eds.), *Popular culture, schooling, and everyday life* (pp. vii–xii). New York, NY: Bergin & Garvey.

Gates, H., & West, C. (1996). *The future of the race.* New York, NY: Alfred A. Knopf.

Gause, C. P. (2005). Navigating the stormy seas: Critical perspectives on the intersection of popular culture and educational leader-"ship." *Journal of School Leadership, 15*(3), 333–342.

Giroux, H. A., Simon, R. I. (1989). *Popular culture, schooling, and everyday life.* New York, NY: Bergin & Garvey.

Jasiri X named hip-hop ambassador for state of black world conference. (2016, August 10–16). *The Pittsburgh Courier,* p. B5.

Jasiri X. (2009, January 11). *OG3-Oscar Grant tribute* [Video]. Retrieved from https://www.youtube.com/watch?v=zSFs1CQYDgY

Jasiri X. (2011, July 4). *Jordan Miles* [Video]. Retrieved from https://www.youtube.com/watch?v=ONPo-wslB40

Jasiri X. (2012, April 4). *Justice for Trayvon: Jasiri X Video and Interview with ACLU* [Video]. Retrieved from https://www.youtube.com/watch?v=eEG9hYeGB7M

Jasiri X. (2013, July 22). *Blood on the Leaves Remix* [Video]. Retrieved from https://www.youtube.com/watch?v=He9dqTl4TV0

Jasiri X. (2014, July 2). *#NeverLovedUs* [Video]. Retrieved from https://www.youtube.com/watch?v=yguWeWhihAA

Jasiri X. (2015, August 9). *The babies* [Video]. Retrieved from https://www.youtube.com/watch?v=9Ba7ng26wvY

Love, B. (2014). Too young for the marches but I remember these drums: Recommended pedagogies for hip-hop-based education and youth studies. In A. Ibrahim & S. Steinberg (Eds.), *Critical youth studies reader* (pp. 444–451). New York, NY: Peter Lang.

Noguera, P. (2008). *The trouble with Black boys: And other reflections on race, equity, and the future of public education.* San Francisco, CA: Jossey-Bass.

Plessy v. Ferguson, 163 U.S. 537 (1896).

Prier, D. D. (2012). *Culturally relevant teaching: Hip-Hop pedagogy in urban schools.* New York, NY: Peter Lang.

Prier, D. D. (2014). Where do biases start? A challenge to educators. *Education Week, 34*(8), 25 & 28.

Prier, D. D. (2015). Matters of Black popular culture in educational leadership. *Teachers College Record.* Retrieved from http://www.tcrecord.org/Content.asp?ContentID=18831.

Rios, V.M. (2011). *Punished: Policing the lives of Black and Latino boys.* New York, NY: New York University Press.

Smiley, C., & Fakunle, D. (2016). From "brute" to "thug:" the demonization and criminalization of unarmed Black male victims in America. *Journal of Human Behavior in the Social Environment, 26*(3/4), 350–366. doi: 10.1080/10911359.2015.1129256

Steinberg, S. (2014). Redefining the notion of youth: Contextualizing the possible for transformative youth leadership. In A. Ibrahim & S. Steinberg (Eds.), *Critical youth studies reader* (pp. 426–433). New York, NY: Peter Lang.

West, C. (2004). *Democracy matters: Winning the fight against imperialism.* New York, NY: The Penguin Press.

CHAPTER 22

LESSONS IN LEADERSHIP FROM THE "THUNDER GOD"

Whitney Sherman Newcomb
Virginia Commonwealth University

Stephanie Blackburn
Virginia Commonwealth University

Jason Newcomb
Soulshaker Studios

> *You know me, just look in my eyes.*
> *I shed my skin, got a new disguise.*
> *My heart still beats and I'm still the same.*
> —Def Leppard, "Day After Day" (1999)

Richard John Cyril "Rick" Allen (born November 1, 1963) is an English drummer who has played for the hard rock band Def Leppard since 1978. He was born in Dronfield, Derbyshire, England and started playing the drums at the age of 9 and has performed in various local bands. When Allen was 14, his mother replied for him to an ad placed by the band Def Leppard (established in 1977) for a drummer to replace Tony Kenning who had just left the band. In 1978, Allen (just 15 at the time) joined the band and ultimately dropped out of school to concentrate on music. In 1979, Def Leppard opened for acts such as Sammy Hagar and AC/DC. The

Educational Leadership and Music, pages 241–248
Copyright © 2017 by Information Age Publishing
All rights of reproduction in any form reserved.

band released its first album *On Through the Night* in 1980 and became one of rock music's biggest bands with their album *Pyromania* in 1983.

On December 31, 1984, Allen and his then girlfriend were involved in a car accident that resulted in his arm being severed. Though doctors reattached his arm, three days later he suffered such a severe infection that doctors had to amputate his arm. At first, after losing his arm, music was only a reminder of what he was once able to do. However, after a few days the realization struck that he could still play many parts of some of his favorite songs with his feet. Jeff Rich (then *Status Quo* drummer) designed an electronic drum kit that Allen could play using only one arm. Later, an electronic drum manufacturer created a kit for Allen. He was encouraged by his band mates to continue playing the drums, and in fact Def Leppard never considered a replacement. Despite doubts, he learned to play the drums again with one hand and the use of his left leg. Allen practiced for months in a separate studio and once he felt ready to perform for an audience, he called the band together and performed the introduction to Led Zeppelin's version of "When the Levee Breaks." He received a positive emotional response from his band mates, and in 1986 they brought Jeff Rich in to play alongside Allen during their mini tour of Ireland. Def Leppard quickly realized there was no need for back up for Allen and his independent comeback was sealed. Allen had overcome physical and mental pain to return to the stage in 1986 for the European Monsters of Rock Tour. Incredibly, Def Leppard went on to achieve its greatest commercial success with the album *Hysteria* in 1987 with Allen as a one-armed drummer. Allen is known by fans as the "Thunder God" (Gold, 2009).

According to Wilkening (2014), Allen has recently dedicated himself to helping war veterans who suffer from posttraumatic stress disorder (PTSD) and injuries similar to his own. He was inspired to help others after a visit to the Walter Reed Army Medical Center in 2006. Allen told ABC News in 2012 that the time immediately following his accident was the "darkest time in my life" and that his mission is to de-stigmatize PTSD, help veterans share their stories, and learn ways to heal and recover. About a decade ago, Allen and his wife, Lauren Monroe, created the Raven Drum Foundation, which uses music as therapy to educate and empower veterans and others in crisis.

PERSONAL INSPIRATION

We, the authors, draw personal inspiration from Rick Allen's life story. Whitney is inspired by Allen's ability to accept a new/different (physical) body and way of moving through "everydayness." She is the sister of a traumatic brain injury survivor from a car accident and knows how difficult it is to recover from traumatic injuries emotionally, physically, psychologically, and spiritually. She knows acceptance is key and that openness to new/alternative ways of "doing" helps in the process of change/transformation. Whitney is also a feminist scholar who studies and teaches educational leadership, and who advocates for inclusion of all voices in knowledge making. She is acutely aware of the fact that, just as women and minorities have traditionally been silenced in the leadership education field, Rick Allen ran the risk of being silenced as a drummer because of his life changing injury. She is inspired by Allen's perseverance in overcoming the loss of an arm to remain a widely successful drummer. Allen's successful alternative drumming style has implications for anyone seeking to overcome adversity or "fit" (see Tooms, Lugg, & Bogotch, 2009) into an organization or group in some capacity.

Jason is inspired by Rick Allen's ability to heal from the physical trauma of his accident as well as from drug abuse. Jason is a burn survivor himself, who is intimately aware of the pain of recovery from a physical trauma, and a recovering addict with more than 10 years clean. He knows the destruction of addiction and the strength it takes to recover. Jason is also a musician who appreciates the time and dedication it takes to transform oneself as an artist. Music has been an integral part of the therapeutic path he has taken to recovery.

Stephanie is inspired by Allen's resilience. Having experienced significant trauma and illness at different points in her life, she knows all too well what it takes to overcome her fears and redefine the path to achieve her goals. Like Allen, having to relearn and develop new ways to play the drums, Stephanie had to relearn and develop new ways to live her life as a single mother, cancer survivor, and model for her daughters of how to be strong in the face of adversity. As the daughter of a multiple war veteran, she is moved by Allen's dedication to supporting today's veterans. His foundation provides much needed healing from the scars of war that Stephanie saw her father handle on his own, as no such opportunities were afforded him upon his return home from his deployment.

LEADERSHIP INSPIRATION

Rick Allen's transformation exemplifies numerous leadership lessons for aspiring and practicing school leaders as well as for aspiring and practicing educational leadership faculty in universities including: redefining "fit" and rethinking selection factors; resilience; and the therapeutic nature of teaching/helping others.

REDEFINING "FIT"
AND RETHINKING SELECTION FACTORS

Women and minorities often have problems attaining leadership positions in schools and districts (Sherman, 2005) for multiple reasons. One reason for their difficulties is the inaccessibility of mentoring (Sherman) due to "fit" and selection factors. While there are numerous studies on mentoring and fit, one (though now dated) easily connects to Rick Allen's struggle to maintain his successful status in rock music as a drummer. In 1987, Mertz examined mentoring for career advancement and found that four critical selection factors were identified that come into play when mentors select mentees: fit, risk, predictability, and payoff.

In regard to fit, mentors decide whether or not the mentee's goals and desires match those of the organization (philosophical fitness), and that the mentee looks similar in regard to dress and outward appearance to others in administrative positions (physical [appearance] fitness). For the second selection factor, mentors assess risk or potential harm that may result from a relationship with a mentee, because essentially the mentor is seen as responsible for the success or failure of the protégée. In regard to the third selection factor, mentors look for predictability in a mentee, meaning whether or not their future actions will be acceptable to the organization and the mentor. Last, mentors look for a payoff or potential gain from working with a mentee. Payoff to the mentor can involve recognition in the organization, access to something the mentee has access to, and future benefits as the mentee becomes more successful (Mertz, 1987).

Such highly selective factors automatically place women and minorities at a disadvantage and make mentoring a strategy that is not accessible to all who aspire to educational leadership positions. If mentors believe that only those who look and think like themselves fit organizations, neither women nor minorities will be mentored to gain leadership positions. According to Mertz (1987), "Women tend to get lower scores in fit, predictability, and payoff than similarly able and qualified men, and higher scores in risk, which is more likely to put their total scores outside the mentor's 'comfort zone'" (p. 11).

The same is directly applicable to Rick Allen's transformation from a two-armed drummer to a one-armed drummer. After his accident, Allen did not "fit" the stereotypical image for a rock and roll drummer. His predictability was low because his first attempts at drumming again were rather rocky, and at that point in time there were no other successful one-armed rock and roll drummers to mentor him. The success of his transformation was dependent upon: (a) his band members' (and other musicians') willingness to take a risk on the alternative drumming style he developed, and (b) their hope that remaining loyal to Allen would pay off in the form of future successful albums. In fact, Def Leppard went on to achieve their greatest successes after the loss of Rick Allen's arm, the lesson being that if we never take chances on people who are different from what has been defined as the "norm" and fail to conceptualize alternative ways of leading or "doing," their talents remained untapped.

RESILIENCE

When navigating change due to adversity, resilience is one of the most important factors for success. Many believe that resilience is built over time (Pankake & Beaty, 2005; Patterson, 2001; Reed & Patterson, 2007) and throughout one's lifespan (Pankake & Beaty). According to Baldwin, Maldonado, Lacey, and Efinger (2004), definitions of resilience include "having the ability to bounce back or snap back, being able to accept adversity or hardship, looking to the future, and refusing to be a victim" (p. 18). Reed and Patterson (2007) add, "Resilience means using energy productively within a school environment to achieve goals in the face of adverse conditions" (p. 89). In most all cases, the need for resiliency is instigated by a disruption to normalcy (Johnson, 2012). According to Greene (as cited in Johnson),

> Resilience can be viewed as a complex interplay between certain characteristics of individuals and their broader environments; Resilience consists of a balance between stress and the ability to cope, risk factors that stem from multiple stressful life events and protective factors that ameliorate or decrease the negative context. Resilience is developmental. Being successful strengthens a person's competence. Resilience is more important at life transitions. (p. 62)

According to Pankake and Beaty (2005), strategies that have been employed by successful educational leaders for overcoming adversity include having: a unique a knowledge and skill set; mentors to help with goals; supportive families; and remembering why you entered the profession. Patterson (2001) maintains that strategies for facing adversity include: staying upbeat, remembering what matters; tolerating ambiguity; having proactive behavior; and conserving your efforts. Patterson asserts that, "It's not so much what you do, it's how you think about what you do that makes all the difference." Reed and Patterson (2007) gleaned several strategies from interviews with women superintendents to become more resilient including: comprehensively assess past and current reality (have focus); stay positive about future possibilities (be ready for the fact that not everything will go smoothly); maintain a base of caring and support (family, colleagues, mentors); and act on the courage of your convictions (have clarity about what matters most, have courage in the face of oppression, have courage to acknowledge and learn from mistakes).

Certainly, the loss of an arm for a person in general, particularly a drummer, is a disruption to normalcy. Allen's initial reaction to his loss was a mix of depression and desire to return to drumming. His ability to accept the loss of his arm without labeling himself as a victim (assessing the intersection of past and current realities) was a first step toward bouncing back. His indisputable skill as a drummer, coupled with the support of other musicians, enabled Allen to tolerate the ambiguity of learning a different way of making music. His courage in the face of adversity led to a positive framework for imagining his future as a drummer; the lesson was that resilience, while often built over time, can be facilitated by supportive networks of people working for the success of an individual who is goal oriented, positive in the face of adversity, and skilled at coping with uncertainty. As resilience is built and outcomes are successful, the capacity for future resilience increases (Johnson, 2012).

HELPING/TEACHING OTHERS AS THERAPY

Rick Allen's interview with Beliefnet (2005) allows us to use his own words to convey to readers how his work with the Raven Drum Foundation represents the healing power of giving to others through music therapy. When asked about empowering people through drumming, Allen described the nature of a drum circle:

> The circle really is a metaphor for community. It makes the individual feel as though they're being supported in the worst times—but also in their good times. We're all on a different cycle and sometimes it takes people who are emotionally strong to help people who are feeling like the world is bearing down on them. That's really where the drum circle is so powerful. I'm sure it started out as body slaps and sort of an [ancient] form of communication and then it probably developed into a form of dance and then ritual. We can't deny the fact that we're all tribal. We all sat around a fire. We were there with the family group and then with the extended tribe. We were together because we helped each other out. That's really what the drum circle is all about.

For Allen, the drum circle represents both family and community and the support system that is needed for recovery from adversity. When asked how drumming heals, physically, Allen told Beliefnet:

> The instrument itself becomes this healing tool. For instance, when I go on stage tonight and play my drums, my intention will be for the good of everybody there and the sound that I make will go out and it will [reflect my intention].

When asked how drumming healed him personally, Allen conveyed:

> Interestingly enough, before my accident I wasn't very interested in playing drums anymore. Because like the old cliché, sex, drugs, and rock n' roll, I could do without the rock n' roll. When I got hurled out of the car and my arm got left in [it]—it was taken off by the seat belt—and I landed in a field, the first thing I said, apparently, was "I'm a drummer and I've lost my arm."

So the thing that I was really shying away from was the first thing I thought about in a time of crisis. In the hospital they tried to put my arm back on but got infected, and they had to take the thing off. For a week I was off in the anesthetic, but when I came around, the first thing I thought about was wanting to play again. They put this piece of foam at the bottom of the bed, and I started tapping my feet on [it] and all of a sudden I realized I could play all the basic rhythms that I always knew. All the information was in my head, I just needed to channel it somewhere else.

For Allen, the desire to play drums again inspired meaning for his recovery and hope for the future. His ability to recover from adversity and experience success again as a transformed drummer built within him an increased capacity for resilience, which allowed him to help others facing hardships learn to speak out about their experiences, learn self-care and healing, and find the path to resiliency and recovery themselves. His choice to help others through music therapy was defined by his specific skillset as well as his positive outlook and hope for the future.

CONCLUSION

In summary, Rick Allen's path to recovery and transformation was not only a personal journey, but a journey that, due to his public life as a musician and member of Def Leppard, inspired many others walking various paths to recovery. His acceptance of his loss was followed by an openness to alternative ways of "being" and styles of drumming that allowed him to redefine the act of drumming, as well as what a drummer looks like. Furthermore, on his path to recovery and resilience, he has made it his mission to bring along others on their own personal paths of discovery and transformation, encouraging others who have been wounded to become empowered throughout the healing process. The "Thunder God" demonstrates multiple lessons for leadership, indeed.

REFERENCES

Beliefnet (2005). *Where the magic is.* Retrieved from http://www.beliefnet.com/ Entertainment/Music/2005/09/Where-The-Magic-Is.aspx?p=1#p3dcvYPCd OkkyVOh.99

Baldwin, J., Maldonado, N. L., Lacey, C. H., & Efinger, J. (2004, April). *Resilient women leaders: A qualitative investigation.* Paper presented at the annual meeting of the American Educational Research Association, San Diego, CA.

Def Leppard. (1999). Day After Day. On *Euphoria* [LP]. Chicago, IL: Mercury.

Gold, A. (2009, August 7). Def Leppard's Rick Allen: The cream interview (updated). *Nashville Scene.* Retrieved from http://www.nashvillescene.com/

nashvillecream/archives/2009/08/07/def-leppards-rick-allen-the-cream
-interview-updated

Johnson, B. H. (2012). *African American female superintendents: Resilient school leaders.* (Unpublished dissertation). University of Minnesota, Minneapolis, MN.

Mertz, N. (1987, November). *Why women aren't mentored.* Paper presented at the annual meeting of the American Educational Research Association, Portland, OR.

Pankake, A. M., & Beaty, D. M. (2005). Stories of resiliency: Successful female educational leaders. *Journal of Women in Educational Leadership, 3*(3), 175–191.

Patterson, J. (2001). Resilience in the face of adversity. *The School Administrator, 58*(6), 18–24.

Reed, D., & Patterson, J. (2007). Voices of resilience from successful female superintendents. *Journal of Women in Educational Leadership, 5*(2), 89–100.

Sherman, W. H. (2005). Preserving the status quo or renegotiating leadership: Women's experiences with a district-based aspiring leaders' program. *Educational Administration Quarterly, 41*(5), 707–740.

Tooms, A., Lugg, C., & Bogotch, I. (2009). Rethinking the politics of fit and educational leadership. *Educational Administration Quarterly, 46*(1), 96–131.

Wilkening, M. (2014, December 31). *The day Def Leppard drummer Rick Allen lost his arm in car crash.* Retrieved from http://ultimateclassicrock.com/def-leppard
-rick-allen-car-crash-1984/

CHAPTER 23

KIRK FRANKLIN

Lessons From Gospel Music for
Transformational Educational Leadership

LaBotta Taylor
University of North Texas

Mackie V. Spradley
University of North Texas

Music is a common expression documented in many societies, cultures, and peoples (Garfias, 2004). In fact, Henry Wadsworth Longfellow (1835) declared music the "universal language of mankind" (p. 197). However, Longfellow's statement is both problematic and misleading. While it is true that all societies and cultures use music as an expression, all societies and cultures do not organize, perform, or interpret music in the same way (Harris, 2016). Each culture employs a variety of timbres, rhythms, tonal and melodic structures, harmonies, and instruments that are unique in their music making (Garfias, 2004). The function of music varies between and within cultural and social contexts. As a result, one musical expression does

Educational Leadership and Music, pages 249–258
Copyright © 2017 by Information Age Publishing
All rights of reproduction in any form reserved.

not communicate the same message or story within or across every culture (Garfias, 2004; Meeker, 2008).

Music's ability to communicate powerful messages is evident in the music of Thomas A. Dorsey, considered by many to be the father of gospel music. While Dorsey inspired thousands who were struggling during the Depression with reminiscent blues, riffs, and moans of the South, his music was also heavily criticized by Black church leaders who considered the new spiritual music form offensive and representative of a sinful lifestyle (Harris, 1992). In this instance, music both unified and divided a culture (Meeker, 2008).

Throughout history, music has preserved and reinforced the cultural beliefs and values of a society through storytelling (Center of Greek Music Tradition, 2016). For example, in biblical narratives music was used to celebrate the stages of life and share historical events, such as battles (Delcamp, 2013). In ancient Greece, people believed music could penetrate the unconscious mind, bringing healing to the soul and spirit of those who listened (Delcamp, 2013). This concept stemmed from the ideas of early Greeks, who believed music had the power to influence the listener's beliefs, behaviors, and thoughts (Center of Greek Music Tradition, 2016). Needless to say, music has a powerful place in society.

To further investigate the current social role and function of music, we must examine how music was used during critical events in history. One example of the power and influence of music was the use of songs like "Swing Low, Sweet Chariot" for runaway slaves following the Underground Railroad to freedom. In the 1960s, civil rights and freedom fighters were inspired by the words and melody of "We Shall Overcome." The song became the motivational theme in spite of the fear of lynchings and the violence of the Ku Klux Klan. Songs of protest such as "I Ain't Gonna Let Nobody Turn Me Around," motivated thousands to participate in sit-ins, bus boycotts, and marches throughout the United States (Carawan & Carawan, 2007). In the 1970s, folk music, rhythm and blues, and country music gave voice to thousands who were against the war in Vietnam and wanted peace. The cries of the people claimed, "War, what is it good for, absolutely nothin'!" Regelski (2009) poses that when music ties meaning to our experiences, it becomes a creative art form with a social function, purpose, and intent. The social role of music extends beyond its art, creativity, performance, or performer. In this sense, music can be both dynamic and complex, impacting us outwardly and inwardly. Music, although inspired by its creator also inspires its creator. The function and social role of music blurs the boundaries between beauty and power, time and space. Regelski (2009) views this as social agency as he cites the work of DeNora (2000).

> Music is in dynamic relation with social life, helping to invoke, stabilize and change the parameters of agency, collective, and individual. By the term agen-

cy here, I mean feeling, perception, cognition and consciousness, identity, energy, perceived situation and scene, embodied conduct, and comportment. If music can affect the shape of social agency, then control over music in social settings is a source of social power; it is an opportunity to structure the parameters of action. (p. 20)

The potential social influence of music can be traced as a part of leadership activity throughout history. Yet little research explores music as it relates to educational leaders, particularly those who seek to affect change.

For the purpose of this discussion we will focus on gospel music style and one gospel artist in particular, Kirk Franklin. We selected Franklin because we consider him a successful and influential artist not only in the field of gospel music, but across popular culture, including film, theater, and television. His work and presence is known internationally. Furthermore, his extensive discography includes a list of songs that portray positive messages. Our discussion will introduce the artist Kirk Franklin, then tenets of transformational leadership, and briefly discuss overlapping principles for today's educational leaders.

KIRK FRANKLIN: AN INTRODUCTION TO THE ARTIST

It is important that one of the authors openly disclose personal bias regarding Kirk Franklin. Spradley stated,

I have known Kirk Franklin for approximately 30 years. I first met him while he was a music student at Oscar Dean Wyatt High School in Fort Worth, Texas. As the primary vocal instructor for the choral department, I quickly noticed that Franklin demonstrated extraordinary giftedness as a pianist, songwriter, and choral director. His musical skills were further developed as he accompanied the gospel choir. (2016)

Born Kirk Dwayne Franklin, his teenage mother abandoned him and his father was missing in action (Brennan, 2016). He lived with his grandmother until she died. He was later adopted by his grandmother's sister, Gertrude Franklin (Franklin, 1998a). Franklin began developing his piano skills at the tender age of 4. Three years later, Franklin was offered his first musical contract, which his Aunt Gertrude turned down. By the age of 12, he became the adult choir director for the Mount Rose Baptist Church, Fort Worth, Texas. His biography describes him as a rebellious teenager as a result of his difficult teenage years.

As he persevered in life's many challenges, Franklin learned valuable lessons and gained personal, emotional, and spiritual insight. The words in his music share stories about his struggles and how his belief system helped him to overcome various obstacles (Franklin, 1998a). Now at age 46, Franklin tops the music charts with numerous awards, including seven Grammys, 13 Gospel Music Association (GMA) Dove Awards, and 15 Stellar Awards. In some ways, Franklin can be considered an inspirational leader who has transformed the field of gospel music.

Franklin exhibits leadership characteristics that reflect leadership models used in various fields, including education. Although leadership models can be conceptualized from multiple perspectives, the next section will focus on the transformative leadership model and its benefits in the field of education. The following section presents four primary tenets of transformational leadership theory. The music, message, and artistry of Kirk Franklin will serve as a means to explore the tenets of transformational leadership theory.

TRANSFORMATIONAL LEADERSHIP

Transformational leadership theory centers on the notion that leaders set higher expectations for followers, which increases the scope for improving performance (Bass, 1998). Transformational leadership can be categorized under the following four tenets: (a) charismatic leadership (or idealized influence), (b) inspirational motivation, (c) intellectual stimulation, and (d) individualized consideration. Bass goes on to explain.

> Transformational leaders behave in ways that result in their being role models for their followers. The leaders are admired, respected, and trusted. Followers identify with the leaders and want to emulate them; leaders are endowed by their followers as having extraordinary capabilities, persistence, and determination. The leaders are willing to take risks and are consistent rather than arbitrary. They can be counted on to do the right thing, demonstrating high standards of ethical and moral conduct. (Bass, 1998, p. 5)

The second tenet, inspirational motivation, focuses on how leaders inspire and motivate individuals around them by assigning purposeful tasks. More specifically,

> transformational leaders behave in ways that motivate and inspire those around them by providing meaning and challenge to their followers' work. Team spirit is aroused. Enthusiasm and optimism are displayed. Leaders get followers involved in envisioning attractive future states; they create clearly communicated expectations that followers want to meet and also demonstrate commitment to goals and the shared vision. (Bass, 1998, p. 5)

In the third tenet, intellectual stimulation, transformational leaders stimulate and inculcate innovation and creativity in followers by encouraging new approaches.

> Transformational leaders stimulate their followers' efforts to be innovative and creative by questioning assumptions, reframing problems, and approaching old situations in new ways. Creativity is encouraged. There is no public criticism of individual members' mistakes. New ideas and creative problem solutions are solicited from followers, who are included in the process of addressing problems and finding solutions. Followers are encouraged to try new approaches, and their ideas are not criticized because they differ from the leaders' ideas. (Bass, 1998, pp. 5–6)

In the final tenet, individualized consideration, leaders coach and mentor followers to their full potential.

> Transformational leaders pay special attention to each individual follower's needs for achievement and growth by acting as coach or mentor. Followers and colleagues are developed to successively higher levels of potential. Individualized consideration is practiced when new learning opportunities are created along with a supportive climate. (Bass, 1998, p. 6)

Bass (1998) points out that transformational leaders lead successful schools by creating a vision, setting goals, and fostering strong parental and community support. In another transformational leadership study, Yu, Leithwood, and Jantzi (2002) observed how the principal sets the tone for the school, sustaining an innovative climate and organizational commitment for change. Fullan (2001) further endorses the necessity of sophisticated leadership in a complex society, where transformational leaders emerge as team players, problem solvers, and escalation analysts, all in one.

ANALYSIS OF COMMON THEMES

Table 23.1 outlines the tenets of transformational leadership and the music of artist Kirk Franklin. A brief reflection proposes how the selected musical examples refine, extend, and challenge educational ideologies and practices.

IMPLICATIONS FOR EDUCATIONAL LEADERSHIP

The concepts common to the music and message of Kirk Franklin and the tenets of transformational leadership are evident in the following ways: (a) the belief system is the mechanism that informs our messaging, vision, behaviors, and daily practices; (b) the power of the belief system crosses physical boundaries and empowers the leader as well as the followers; (c) the belief system restructures our concepts of purpose, position, role, and

TABLE 23.1 Common Themes in Transformational Leadership and Kirk Franklin's Music

Transformational Leadership	Musical Evidence	Reflections
Charismatic leadership (CL) Idealized influence (II) • Leader demonstrates extraordinary capabilities such as determination, persistence and willing to take risks that are unconventional.	"Hello Fear" (Franklin, 2011, track 1) "Everyone Hurts" (Franklin, 2011, track 6) "Help me Believe" (Franklin, 2007, track 4) "You can impress people with your accomplishments, but you transform people with your struggles. I transform people when I say, "This is who I was, this is what I did, this is my struggle. I heal. And if I have a key that most people struggle with, are imprisoned with, why not use that key? Some people may say, "Keep your business to yourself." But that's also the plight of Black people: We keep the doors closed and we never heal. I heal as I reveal. The more I reveal, the more the man of God I feel like I'm becoming" (Obie, 2015, para. 7 & 8).	Great leaders throughout history have used story-telling as a means to motivate and inspire those around them. For that reason, story-telling is a very effective motivational tool (Forester, et al., 1998). His words penetrate the unconscious mind. New beliefs inform, shape, and challenge the thoughts of the listener. The music examples selected encourage listeners to persistently seek God as the answer to their problems and their fears. Franklin's music is a part of his emotional identity. It brings healing to the listener as well as the creator. The results can be transformative.
Inspirational motivation (IM) • Leader helps others to envision something better for themselves and others.	"Imagine Me" (Franklin, 2005, track 7) "Brighter Day" (Franklin, 2002, track 6) "Look at me Now" (Franklin, 2006, track 12) "I Smile" (Franklin, 2011, track 7) "Gonna be a Lovely Day" (Franklin, 1998b, track 7) "Wanna be Happy" (Franklin, 2015b, track 6) "Let it Go" (Franklin, 2005, track 5)	Inspiration is critical to effective leadership. Franklin uses common themes such as joy to convey to listeners to keep looking beyond their circumstances.

(continued)

TABLE 23.1 Common Themes in Transformational Leadership and Kirk Franklin's Music (continued)		
Transformational Leadership	**Musical Evidence**	**Reflections**
Intellectual stimulation (IS) • Stimulate innovation • There is not public criticism of individual member's mistakes.	"Losing my Religion" (Franklin, 2015b, track 1) According to Franklin, "Religion is man's systematic approach to try to keep the rules. The problem is that when man's ideology and thought process gets involved, sometimes what he does is change the rules," (Thomasos, 2015, para. 5). Franklin states, "We haven't seen God with a physical eye, so we're trying to understand him —sometimes from an academic approach, from a scientific approach, from a literal approach" (Martin, M., 2016, para. 5).	Franklin serves as a role model to others, motivates others, demonstrates empathy, and challenges innovation. His songs challenge us to reach higher levels and take risks. The artist has faced significant criticism for his decisions and behavior. For example, Dress Musical style • move from traditional gospel style to contemporary, back to traditional • mixture of and influenced by hip hop, funk, r&b, reggae, and others Collaborations and cross-overs
Individualized consideration (IC) • New opportunities are created within a supportive environment. • Interactions with others are personable.	"911" (Franklin, 2002, track 4) "Imagine Me" (Franklin, 2005, track 7) "Lean on Me" (Franklin, 1998b, track 3) "Hello Fear" (Franklin, 2011, track 1)	Franklin is honest about his failures and flaws. Willingness to collaborate with others: • Kanye West (rap/hip hop) • Papa San (reggae) • R. Kelly • Salt n Pepper • Stevie Wonder • Whitney Houston

responsibility; and (d) the belief system is constantly communicated to those around us, consciously and unconsciously. As we observed in the musical examples of Franklin, his beliefs are central to his success. Franklin's belief system shapes and informs his attitude, behavior, and practice. His music documents his personal critical reflection as he compares his action, practices, and beliefs. For example, in a television interview with Oprah Winfrey (2005), Franklin admits his addiction to porn made him "feel like a hypocrite." His actions did not align with his public confessions.

To critically reflect on one's work is never an easy task; however, educational leaders exhibit intellectualism while acting in a role of authority because they must critically reflect upon their behavior and practices while in the process of doing the work (Giroux, 1988). This process, as observed by Spradley (2013), is central to improving the effectiveness of teachers and leaders. Hence, educational leaders must work diligently to ensure that public confessions, such as action plans, mission statements, and mottos are more than empty words. Leaders should practice critically reflecting on their educational beliefs, ideologies, practices, behaviors, and policies by asking hard questions.

The beliefs and expectations of leaders inform the day-to-day decision-making processes and policies (Spradley, 2013). Therefore, transformational leaders must also critically reflect upon the motivations behind their actions. It is important to remember that every educational act is also a political one (Freire, 2000). The choices of the leader impact the lives of the students entrusted to them. These processes promote innovative thought, collaborative work, and motivated participants.

Franklin's beliefs, music, and message would transform gospel music, but not without a struggle against those considered purists, elitists, and gatekeepers of the gospel music art form. However, Franklin's struggles were not unlike those of other historical church musicians who significantly changed the performance practices of church music, such as Josquin des Prez, Palestrina, Martin Luther, Isaac Watts, and Thomas Dorsey. Franklin's goals could no longer be defined and framed by the discourses of the established organizations and institutions. In the end, Franklin's purpose and vision "to make Christ relevant within the culture" is greater than himself (Franklin, 2015a). Similarly, transformational leaders must shift mindsets in an established organization in order to relate to the culture and impact the greater community.

Many contemporary educational discourses are centered on educational reform. Unfortunately, most of what is being done to reform education has been done before in some capacity. Transformational leaders cannot look to the past for examples of how to improve our educational future or how to become more culturally relevant to their students. Transformational leaders must consciously choose to consider different solutions that may not have been commonly used practices and behaviors in the past (Taylor, 2014). Like Franklin, transformational leaders must demonstrate their willingness to take a risk, even though the risk may initiate the criticism of others (Marzano, McNulty, & Waters, 2005).

In conclusion, music is a form of storytelling. It can be used to motivate educational leaders to transform the culture. However, music can also be a personal resource to the leader, as a way to solidify ideas and shape beliefs. It can transform educational leadership, organizations, movements, thoughts, beliefs, attitudes, practices, and ideologies. Kirk Franklin's music and life are at once an inspiration and a cautionary tale, and we feel he offers importance lessons for leaders.

REFERENCES

Bass, B. M. (1998). *Transformational leadership: Industrial, military, and educational impact.* Mahwah, NJ: Lawrence Erlbaum.

Brennam, S. (2016). *Kirk Franklin.* Retrieved from http://www.allmusic.com/artist/kirk-franklin-mn0000083095/biography

Carawan, C., & Carawan, G. (2007). *Sing for freedom: The story of the Civil Rights Movement through its songs.* Louisville, KY: New South Books.

Center of Greek Music Tradition. (2016). *Music in ancient Greece.* Retrieved from http://www.lyravlos.gr/ancient-greek-music-en.asp

Delcamp, H. (2013). *An investigation of ancient Hebrew music during the time of the Old Testament, especially the role of music in the lives of Israel's first two kings, Saul and David.* (Master's thesis). Liberty University, Lynchburg, VA.

DeNora, T. (2000). *Music in everyday life.* New York, NY: Cambridge University Press.

Forester, N., Cebis, M., Majteles, S., Mathur, A., Morgan, R., Preuss, J., Tiwari, V., & Wilkinson, D. (1999). The role of storytelling in organizational leadership. [Abstract]. *Leadership & Organization Development Journal, 20*(1), 11–17.

Franklin, K. (1998a). *Church boy: My music and my life.* Nashville, TN: Word Publishing.

Franklin, K. (1998b). Lean on me. Gonna be a lovely day. On *The nu nation project* [CD]. Santa Monica, CA: Interscope Records.

Franklin, K. (2002). 911. Brighter day. On *The rebirth of Kirk Franklin* [CD]. Inglewood, CA: GospoCentric Records.

Franklin, K. (2005). Let it go. Imagine me. On *Hero* [CD]. Inglewood, CA: GospoCentric Records.

Franklin, K. (2006). Look at me now. On *Kirk Franklin presents: Songs for the storm* (Vol. 1) [CD]. Inglewood, CA: GospoCentric Records.

Franklin, K. (2011). Hello fear. I smile. On *Hello fear* [CD]. Inglewood, CA: Verity Records.

Franklin, K. (2015a). Kirk Franklin on "trap gospel" and taking heat from the church. *NPR Music.* Retrieved from http://www.npr.org/templates/transcript/transcript.php?storyId=401978156

Franklin, K. (2015b, April 26) Losing my religion. Wanna be happy? On *Losing my religion* [CD]. RCA Inspiration: Fo Yo Soul.

Freire, P. (2000). *Pedagogy of the oppressed*. New York, NY: Continuum.

Fullan, M. (2001). *Leadership in a culture of change*. San Francisco, CA: Jossey-Bass.

Garfias, R. (2004). *Music: The cultural context* (Senri Ethnological Reports No. 47). Osaka, Japan: National Museum of Ethnology. Retrieved from http://www.socsci.uci.edu/~rgarfias/aris/courses/musexprs/documents/SER47_chap-01-02.pdf

Giroux, H. A. (1988). *Teachers as intellectuals: Toward a critical pedagogy of learning*. Westport, CT: Bergin and Garvey Publishers, Inc.

Harris, M. W. (1992). *The rise of gospel blues: The music of Thomas Andrew Dorsey in the urban church*. New York, NY: Oxford University Press.

Harris, R. P. (2016). The great misconception: Why music is not a universal language. In F. Fortunato, R. P. Harris, & B. Schrag (Ed.), *Worship and mission for the global church: An ethnodoxology handbook* (pp. 84–89). Pasadena, CA: William Carey Library. Retrieved from http://www.worldofworship.org/wp-content/uploads/2016/08/Robin-Handbook-Article.pdf

Longfellow, H. W. (1835). *Outre-Mer: A pilgrimage beyond the sea*. Boston, MA: Houghton, Mifflin.

Martin, M. (2016, January). *Gospel star Kirk Franklin wants to help you lose you religion*. Retrieved from http://www.npr.org/2016/01/31/464562711/gospel-star-kirk-franklin wants-to-help-you-lose-your-religion

Marzano, R. J., McNulty, B. A., & Waters, T. (2005) *School leadership that works: From research to results*. Alexandra, VA: Association for Supervision and Curriculum Development.

Meeker, D. (2008). *Reasons why music is not a universal language and other reflections*. Retrieved from http://accounts.smccd.edu/mecklerd/MUS202/mulang.htm

Obie, B. (2015). *Kirk Franklin walks the path to "losing" his religion*. Retrieved from http://www.ebony.com/entertainment-culture/kirk-franklin-walks-the-path -t-losing-his-religion-333#axzz3ybOAnBIT

Regelski, T. A. (2009). Music education for a changing society. *Diskussion Musikpada-gogik, 38*(8), 34–42.

Spradley, M. V. (2013). *The beliefs and expectations of effective secondary choral teachers in culturally diverse schools*. (Doctoral dissertation). Retrieved from ProQuest Digital Dissertations. UMI: 3579245

Taylor, L.S. (2014). *A multiple case study of two African American female administrators in high achieving elementary schools*. (Doctoral dissertation). Retrieved from Pro-Quest Digital Dissertations. UMI: 3727238

Thomasos, C. (2015, November 14). *Kirk Franklin reveals his pride delays "Losing my religion" album*. Retrieved from http://www.christianpost.com/news/kirk-franklin-losing-my-religion-album-gospel-interview-149974/

Winfrey, O. (2005, November 30). Famous gospel singer admits addiction to porn: Interview with Kirk Franklin. In E. Rakieten (Executive producer), *Oprah Winfrey Show* [Television series episode]. Chicago, Il.: Harpo Productions, Inc.

Yu, H., Leithwood, K., & Jantzi, D. (2002). The effects of transformational leadership on teachers' commitment to change in Hong Kong. *Journal of Educational Administration, 40*(4), 368–389.

CHAPTER 24

REVOLUTION 9

Lessons in Leadership Provided
by The Beatles

Lucas Walsh
Monash University

In a world in which the popular music market has diversified in both genre and media, The Beatles continue to generate staggering revenue and sales. According to *Forbes*, in 2013 alone The Beatles earned a combined $71 million in the form of individual earnings, cash from ongoing album sales, and other revenue streams, such as DVD sales of The Beatles' films. They have sold more than 177 million albums in the United States alone and hold the title for most number one-hit records in the *Billboard* Hot 100's history (a total of 20; Angulo, 2014). Over 30 years after their original release, even the vinyl versions of *Abbey Road* (1969a) and *Sgt. Pepper's Lonely Hearts Club Band* (1967a) were in the top 10 album sales of 2014 (Nelson, 2015). And in the digital age, The Beatles sold 2 million songs within a week of being available on iTunes (Billboard, 2010).

But these sales figures do not capture the historical, cultural, and musical legacy of The Beatles, their landmark contributions to popular music,

Educational Leadership and Music, pages 259–273

their profound cultural impact on their time, and one simple, undeniable fact: They have made millions of people of happy. "The music was positive," remarked the band's drummer Ringo Starr years later, "the basic Beatles message was love" (Lennon, McCartney, Harrison, & Starr, 2000, p. 356). The Beatles continue to inspire the world through their music, their films, and their personalities.

Beneath the torrential hysteria and hyperbole of fame that surrounded them between 1963, when The Beatles first landed on the charts, and 1970 when they disbanded, there are nine lessons that educational leaders can take from their music and career that are potentially instructive. Much of the inspiration for this chapter comes from a public presentation and subsequent publication by Jeffrey Brooks (2015, 2016),[1] in which he provocatively asks the question: Is everything we know about educational leadership wrong? Brooks's critique of contemporary understandings of educational leadership as a field of practice and inquiry will be used as a launching point and touchstone throughout the following discussion, which examines the music and lives of The Beatles and explores the lessons of inspiration and caution from their story, music, and cultural impact, to rethink educational leadership. Interwoven throughout these lessons is a brief overview of their career. We start, straight-forwardly enough, at the beginning.

John Lennon started The Beatles. The seeds were planted on July 6, 1957, when Paul McCartney met Lennon for the first time after watching Lennon playing a gig with his band, The Quarrymen, at a garden fête in Liverpool (Lewisohn, 2013, p. 354). Having been invited to join the Quarrymen, McCartney then introduced George Harrison to the band as its guitarist. McCartney had shared the same (Number 86) bus to school as Harrison, which was driven by Harrison's father (Norman, 2016, p. 57). Eventually, after many changes of name and membership, Lennon, McCartney, and Harrison settled on the name "The Beatles" with Pete Best as their drummer. Richard Starkey, aka Ringo Starr, joined later in 1962 to replace Best as drummer because apparently Best lacked suitable musicality and personality-fit with the other three bandmates (Clayson, 2003, pp. 86–87). Starr, who was the oldest member of The Beatles, was to his new bandmates a seasoned drummer who added a personal style of percussion that was subtle, yet distinctive. He also meshed with his new bandmates on a social level. When The Beatles signed their first recording contract as a group on June 4, 1962, on EMI's Parlophone record label, part of the allure of the band was their collective personality and humor rather than their music (Lewisohn, 2013, p. 1276).

There was no single leader. Where the conventional wisdom for bands at the time was to have a lead singer, The Beatles' producer, George Martin, quickly realized there was none (Lewisohn, 2013, p. 1465). Even at this nascent stage of their career, The Beatles were breaking the mold of what was expected from groups at the time. There was no clear frontman; instead, the band was a tightly cohesive collective whose combination yielded a new sound that would continue to evolve throughout the decade. Mick Jagger described them as a "four-headed monster" (Lennon et al., 2000, p. 354). The Beatles were democratic to the extent that all four members had a say in determining what was released and when.

Upon entering the studio, The Beatles would soon break another convention by writing their own songs, something that was extremely rare among performers at the time. Throughout their career, the most memorable songs featured different members of the band as both writer/s and lead singer/s on microphone: from McCartney's "Yesterday" (1965d, which was covered 1,600 times during the following two decades [Guinness World Records, 1986]); Starr's "Octopus's Garden" (1969b); Lennon's "Norwegian Wood (This Bird has Flown)" (1965b); and Harrison's seminal "Something" (1969c), which Frank Sinatra famously described as "the greatest love song of the past 50 years" (MacDonald, 2008, p. 348) and which, as Harrison wryly noted, was apparently erroneously attributed by *Old Blue Eyes* to Lennon/McCartney (Lennon et al., 2000, p. 340).

LEADERSHIP IS A COLLABORATIVE EFFORT

Conventionally, educational leaders in schools are associated with principals situated on top of a hierarchical pyramid of management. But as The Beatles' example suggests, leadership need not take this form. The Beatles illustrate forms of distributed leadership in the ways that band members changed roles depending on the song, working in different combinations, and drawing inspiration from a range of people and sources to expand their musical horizons. Harrison helped Starr to write "Octopus's Garden" (1969b), while McCartney played lead guitar, as well as bass, on Harrison's "Taxman" (1966b) (MacDonald, 2008, p. 200). Lennon and McCartney would finish each other's songs. This interchangeable combination of four musicians produced an unprecedented release of musical creativity supported by a small but dedicated team of staff managed by Brian Epstein and an inventive team of engineers led by George Martin (and for one album Phil Spector).

There is a lesson here for educational leaders, one that moves beyond the typical basis of educational leadership on organizational theory (Brooks & Kensler, 2011) to one in which decision-makers, teachers, and other stakeholders interact in vibrant and inclusive ways. According to Harris (2014),

Distributed leadership means mobilizing leadership expertise at all levels in the school in order to generate more opportunities for change and to build the capacity for improvement. The emphasis is upon interdependent interaction and practice rather than individual and independent actions associated with those with formal leadership roles or responsibilities. (para. 4)

One anecdotal example was a principal that I encountered several years ago on Elcho Island, which is located off the coast of Arnhem Land in the very far north of Australia. The local school on this tiny island was plagued by incidences of sexual abuse, malnutrition, and self-harm among students who were predominantly from Indigenous backgrounds. Upon arriving at the school, the principal set about creating a team of teacher leaders with defined but malleable roles who appeared to share decision-making and responsibility for many of the challenges facing the school. As importantly, the principal linked with local communities and the students' elders on the mainland to promote inclusivity and sharing of resources. He collaborated, for example, with the local general store to ensure that food was available at breakfast time. This outward looking function of educational leadership, in which schools actively and systematically build enduring networks with external actors, such as local business, is arguably limited among many schools (Walsh, 2016). This leads to our second lesson.

LEADERS FOSTER SCHOOLS THAT ACTIVELY WORK WITH OUTSIDE ACTORS AND ORGANIZATIONS TO IMPROVE STUDENT LEARNING

Done well, distributed leadership can expand the learning opportunities for students and teachers. They can also create relationships with partners that extend beyond money to other forms of capacity building. As Michael Fullan (2000, p. 5) suggests, "Schools need the outside to get the job done."

While The Beatles were quite insular as a group, they needed others such as Epstein and Martin to realize their musical ambitions. They also collaborated with other musicians. While popular media confected a rivalry between The Beatles and The Rolling Stones, members of both groups were actually friendly (Richards, 2010, p. 141). The Beatles gave the Stones one of their first hits: "I Wanna Be Your Man" (The Rolling Stones, 1963), which reached No. 12 on the British chart. By all accounts, they all enjoyed a good relationship, with McCartney and Lennon contributing to the song "We Love You" (The Rolling Stones, 1967) that was written in support of Jagger and Richards, who were imprisoned on drug charges. The Beatles invited guitarist Eric Clapton and keyboardist Billy Preston to collaborate with them in the studio on *The Beatles* (1968a, otherwise known as "The White Album") and *Let It Be* (1970) respectively. They wrote for and produced other artists such as Mary Hopkins and Badfinger. To this day, the surviving members of The Beatles, Starr and McCartney, continue to work in collaboration with other musicians. Starr tours with his All Star Band (a highly entertaining gig if you get the chance to attend). McCartney contributed to the mash-up of "Yesterday" with Linkin Park and Jay-Z ("Numb/Encore/Yesterday," 2006) at the 2006 Grammy Awards, as well as the 2015 track, "FourFiveSeconds," with Kanye West and Rhianna (no comment).

As Brooks (2016a) suggests, educational leaders need to be collaborative in nature. A combination of factors, such as high-stakes testing, the commodification of education, and the operation of schools as closed systems, can work against effective learning. Leaders should be encouraged to share their work and promote partnerships and influences, such as those of community actors, parents and local businesses, beyond the school gates. These can have a range of potential benefits in areas such as knowledge development, professional experience, and capacity-building (Black, 2008; Walsh, 2016; see also Hannon, Patton & Temperley, 2011).

EDUCATIONAL LEADERSHIP CAN BE TRANSFORMATIONAL

Prior to leadership tensions emerging later in The Beatles' story (more to follow), leadership was shared, with the combined abilities of the band producing something transformational. A corollary of distributed leadership exemplified by The Beatles is an example of transformational leadership (Hallinger, 2003). Bush and Glover (2014) write

> Most definitions of leadership reflect the assumption that it involves a social influence process whereby intentional influence is exerted by one person [or group] over other people [or groups] to structure activities and relationships in a group or organisation (Yukl 2002, 3) . . . the central concept is influence rather than authority. Both are dimensions of power but the latter tends to reside in formal positions, such as principal or head teacher, while the former could be exercised by anyone in the school or college. (p. 554)

Arguably, Epstein as The Beatles' manager played the formal role of the principal. Epstein had absolute faith in "the boys," but also in their early days he encouraged them to clean up their act, not smoke cigarettes on stage, and present themselves as a more cohesive and less dishevelled group (Coleman, 1989). But creative decisions resided largely within the band and were made on mutual agreement, as mentioned previously (Hiatt, 2012). This democratic style of operation eroded following Epstein's sudden death by an accidental drug overdose in 1967 at the age of 32 (Coleman, 1989, p. 418). McCartney then assumed a more authoritarian role in an effort to spur the band back into the studio and film ventures, such as the critically lambasted

Magical Mystery Tour (1967c). McCartney's more controlling style of leadership led to the resentment of Lennon and Harrison (Doggett, 2009) and a more fragmented way of working that is evident on *The Beatles* double album (1968a). This has been characterized as the beginning of The Beatles' decline as a band (Lifton, 2015). Nevertheless, The Beatles continued to produce pop masterpieces, from the single "Hey Jude" (1968f) to their last recorded album, *Abbey Road* (1969a).

EDUCATIONAL LEADERS ARE OPEN TO MANY INFLUENCES

These masterpieces exhibited a range of influences, reflecting an openness to new ideas and possibilities, while building on a sound understanding of what came before. The Beatles is an interesting case study in that they altered the course of popular music while drawing on extremely diverse genres that demonstrated a sound understanding—if not mastery—of the historical legacy of those musicians who came before them. These range from blues ("Yer Blues," 1968b and "Revolution," 1968c), to Music Hall and 1920s nostalgia ("Honey Pie," 1968d), Ska ("Ob-La-Di, Ob-La-Da," 1968e) to avant-garde ("Revolution 9," 1968f), alongside conventional romantic ballads ("Michelle," 1965a).[2] The Beatles appropriated something from these different genres to make new music. As they progressed from cover-versions on their first four albums to predominantly original compositions, The Beatles went to great pains not to musically replicate the past. This constant reaching for new sounds proved to be frustrating for Starr, who would present his own "original" compositions to the band only to be informed by his (giggling) bandmates that he'd unintentionally copied an existing composition by someone else (Lennon et al., 2000).

From the use of a sitar in "Norwegian Wood" (1965b) to the music-hall references in tracks like "When I'm 64" (1967b), The Beatles sought and absorbed a variety of influences in their work. Harrison's "The Inner Light" (1968e) features a strong Indian influence, but within a catchy pop milieu. Harrison was also an early adopter of the Moog synthesiser, which is featured on *Abbey Road* (1969a). The sound of guitar feedback at the beginning of "I Feel Fine" (1964) was the result of Lennon's experimentation and is one of the first uses of feedback in recorded music (Lennon et al., 2000, p. 160). Harrison also joked that by using feedback, "In a way, [Lennon] invented Jimi Hendrix" (Harrison, 1995). This appropriation of musical discoveries, genres and unusual instruments was not done uncritically. Harrison, for example, was sceptical of McCartney and Lennon's forays into the avant-garde, referring to it as "avant-garde a clue," his tongue planted firmly in cheek (Ingham, 2003, p. 154). Listening to Lennon's sound collage, "Revolution 9" (1968f), Harrison may have a point, as this track makes for challenging listening even to this day.

Like good educational leaders, The Beatles drew on different influences without being captive to them. As Brooks (2015) suggests, much of the practice in the education field features a reliance on misplaced notions of leadership, such as the profound influence on educational leadership of dated, corporatized notions of "strategic planning" taken inappropriately out of context from discourses such as human resource management. (Brooks includes distributed leadership as one such discourse, however, following Harris [2014], I think that there is a rich understanding within educational research that can be drawn upon.) At a deeper level, and following on from Brooks's (2015) discussion, knowledge of the history and traditions of the scholarship on educational leadership can be rich and informative, but must be viewed critically and in context.

TIME AND CONTEXT PLAY IMPORTANT ROLES IN EDUCATIONAL LEADERSHIP

There is something about so much of The Beatles' catalogue that is of its time and yet timeless. "Strawberry Fields Forever" (1967d), for example, was upon its release a revolutionary new sounding multicolored evocation of 1960s psychedelia, while espousing the timeless theme of "longing for wild childhood" (MacDonald, 2008, p. 216). Timing is important to The Beatles story, particularly their arrival in the United States following the assassination of President John F. Kennedy when positive relief was welcome. Timing is also important in educational leadership, where certain beneficial characteristics of leadership (such as being collaborative) are ongoing, while others arise in response to particular educational milieus and needs, such as responding to technological change, as we shall see.

The Beatles shied away from being described as actively shaping the 1960s. As Lennon reflected in 1980, "Whatever was blowing at the time moved The Beatles, too. I'm not saying we weren't flags on the top of the ship. But the whole boat was moving" (Heylin, 2007, p. 5). Similarly, McCartney, when reflecting on The Beatles's wider cultural and social impact, has been hesitant to characterize the band as leaders per se, but more as reflections of their time (MacDonald, 2008). The Beatles were also reflective of their stages of life, as demonstrated in how their music chronicled their personal evolutions, such as Lennon's "In My Life" (1965c). Reflection is an important aspect for educational leaders. Costa and Kallick (2000) suggest that reflection "provides an opportunity for

- amplifying the meaning of one's work through the insights of others;

- applying meaning beyond the situation in which it was learned; [and]
- making a commitment to modifications, plans, and experimentation" (p. 60)

Good educational leadership arises from a reflection on experience and an acknowledgement that there are no short cuts to developing leadership. It requires hard work, feedback (not the guitar-made kind), and experience.

It has been argued that a key to The Beatles's success was that they worked hard to hone their craft before finding fame, particularly during their intensive touring in Hamburg during their early prefame years from 1960 to 1962 (Lewisohn, 2013). The Beatles played thousands of hours before appearing in the public eye. In his entertaining essay on how people such as The Beatles and Bill Gates achieved greatness, journalist Malcolm Gladwell put a figure on this effort: the "10,000 hour rule," to quantify the hours of work to produce what is sometimes erroneously conflated with natural genius (Gladwell, 2008, p. 35). By the time The Beatles were active in the popular imagination, Lennon and McCartney had honed their songwriting to a craft that could service their creative ambitions.

CREATIVITY IS A VALUABLE ASSET
FOR EDUCATIONAL LEADERS

The Beatles were constantly evolving. Their music catalogue charts massive change across 12 albums in 7 years (between 1963 and 1970). Even the songs constantly evolved during the production process. To listen to the evolution of "Strawberry Fields Forever" on The Beatles' *Love* (2006) is a masterclass in sound production and musical imagination, with the haunting demo featuring Lennon singing alone with his guitar a reminder that the final piece was founded on a reflective melody and brilliantly surrealist lyric.

As suggested at the start of this chapter, throughout their career The Beatles ignored convention, and broke many rules and accepted practices of popular music. "Hey Jude" (1968g), for example, is over seven minutes in duration, defying radio convention that songs should be less than half that length. It was released at a time when music journalists were speculating about the demise of The Beatles (a regular motif throughout their career), but which became their bestselling track (Guesdon & Margotin, 2013, p. 520).

The Beatles promoted creativity over conformity by constantly seeking new ways to communicate to their audience through musical innovation. The Beatles challenged conformity both within their own work and in popular music in general, releasing extraordinary albums such as the groundbreaking *Revolver* (1966a), with each album reflecting radical changes in direction. And as we have seen, their evolution was not without conflict or tension.

For educational leaders, too, creativity is a valuable asset. In schools, Brooks (2016) argues, conformity should not be championed over creativity. Schools are complex environments, so educational leaders need to accept that degrees of conflict are necessary if creativity is to be nurtured.

TECHNOLOGY IS A VALUABLE TOOL
THAT SHOULD BE USED IN THE SERVICE OF LEARNING

The Beatles quickly became interested in studio recording technology and pushed their studio engineers to create opportunities to extend the boundaries of what recording technology could do to meet their creative aspirations. This is abundantly evident on *Sgt. Pepper's Lonely Hearts Club Band* (1967a) and *Revolver* (1966a). On the groundbreaking "Tomorrow Never Knows" (1966c), Lennon wanted his voice "to sound like the Dalai Lama chanting from a hilltop" (Margotin & Guesdon, 2013, p. 352). Producer George Martin and his team of engineers were left to transform Lennon's abstraction to sonic reality (Miles, 1997; Spitz, 2005). To achieve this, Lennon's singing was rerecorded via a revolving speaker. Looped tape effects (popular in avant-garde music at the time) were peppered throughout the song, which unusually for that time featured nonwestern musical instruments such as sitar and tambura drone. Importantly here, The Beatles's music wasn't driven by technology, but rather technology served as a means to fulfill an artistic vision. The same applies to the educational use of technology. As Inglis, Ling, and Joosten (2000) suggest, the greatest impact of technology on students' learning arises from the way a technology is used rather the characteristics of the medium being used.

Educational leaders should at the very least seek proficiency in the basic tools of education, such as information and communication technologies (ICT). Ranging from the personal computer to the smartphone, online social networks to video-conferencing, and the app to virtual reality simulations, the opportunities for ICT to extend and enrich teaching and learning beyond the classroom continue to be enormous, but not without associated challenges. As Livingstone (2012) suggests, ICT

> converge traditionally separated educational technologies—books, writing, telephone, television, photography, databases, games, and more. In consequence, they bridge forms of knowledge and literacy, and they intersect places of learning—home, school, work and community. But these changes pose both opportunities and challenges to schools, for to embed ICT in the educational infrastructure, teacher training, curriculum structures and mate-

rials, classroom practices and modes of assessment must be redesigned at all levels. (p. 2)

Educational leaders need to be able to critically understand and negotiate these challenges and opportunities, with a particular eye on how they can be used to improve learning.

THERE IS NO ONE-SIZE FITS ALL MODEL
OF EDUCATIONAL LEADERSHIP

Infamously, when The Beatles were looking for their first record deal, they were turned down in their audition for Decca Records in 1962 under the erroneous belief by that label that "guitar groups are on the way out" (Lennon et al., 2000, p.67). Predicting what will be popular in music is arguably a fraught enterprise, but importantly, no one (outside of Epstein) could have predicted how massive The Beatles would become; such was their originality and timing. The Beatles defied existing preconceptions of what a popular music group, and indeed the music business, could be. They highlight a truism that there is no simple formula for what works in popular music.

Brooks (2015) writes that leadership cannot be reduced to a "one size fits all" approach. Models erroneously appropriated from other domains, such as business, are just some of the factors that delimit the efficacy of, or even possibility for, the illusive "magic bullet" best practice approach. Educational leadership needs to be adaptive to change in areas such as staffing and technology. Brooks (2016) rightly and passionately makes the case for leaders to reject "my way or the highway" ultimatums that are frequently made to people in organizations with alternative perspectives of how school leadership should be practiced. This opens up possibilities for leadership to come from unexpected people, situations, and places.

AND IN THE END, STUDENTS AND STUDENT LEARNING
SHOULD BE AT THE HEART IF EDUCATIONAL LEADERSHIP

The Beatles's recording career ended before any band member turned the age of 30 (excluding two recordings done in the 1990s after Lennon's assassination in 1980). As the leading pop group of their time, they were young people essentially writing music that connected with other young people. The Beatles gave a voice to young people and grew with them. They made music that ignited the imagination and pushed creative boundaries of what was possible musically. Their work was in the service of finding better ways to connect their ideas and sounds with their audience, just as teaching and learning should be at the core of educational leadership. While scholars have sought to focus on the impact of leadership on learning (e.g., Robinson, 2007), more work needs to be done in placing students and learning at the heart of leadership, such as through the models previously outlined.

Good leaders nurture student voice, while providing a vocabulary of possibility about how things can be done better. Using the voice of young people to shape what takes place in schools is something that is widely recognized, but still not done well in many schools (Black et al., 2014; Mitra & Gross, 2009). Educational leaders can drive the active and meaningful engagement of students in shaping student outcomes and the life of the school as a whole. As I have argued elsewhere with my colleagues, "traditional school leadership structures can be reimagined to promote inclusivity and . . . foster meaningful participation and experiences by modeling democratic processes and privileging student contributions in decisions about school governance, policy and pedagogy" (Black et al., 2014, p.12). As a corollary of this, leadership needs to focus on the core business of schooling as its main driver: the nature and quality of student learning.

But as suggested earlier in this chapter, this is sometimes sidelined by other models of leadership. Brooks (2016) points out that much of the literature has tended to emphasize "leadership and management" without sufficient attention to education. Keeping education at the heart of leadership continues to be a challenge for those writing about and working in the field. Rich traditions and important factors relating to educational leadership, such as curriculum, sociological dimensions of education, and educational psychology are often absent from scholarship on educational leadership. Boundaries have persisted between educational leadership as being concerned with principals and teachers as managers and workers (Brooks, 2016).

CONCLUSION

The Beatles's final message on their last recorded album, *Abbey Road* (1969), was "In the end, the love you take is equal to the love you make." The Summer of Love soon ended, and within a year The Beatles were no more. That which remains, their driving and optimistic message of love, conveyed through music, lyric and film, is what continues to matter. Similarly, educational leaders need to be driven by an ethic of social justice and moral purpose of teaching that underpin teaching and learning (Mayer & Lloyd, 2011). This purpose is associated with strong leadership (Timperley, 2011).

While The Beatles were regarded (even by themselves) as a single entity or "four headed monster," each of the four personalities seemed like leadership models: Lennon's charismatic and intellectual, McCartney's musical authority and default boss post-Epstein, Harrison's embracement of nonwestern ideas, and Starr's lovable everyman jester, who easily was the best actor of all four (there's really no contest in the films), and probably the most emotionally astute. The artistic alchemy of these four musicians produced an irreducible whole, whose timing was right and whose musical impact reverberated across successive generations.

The Beatles were four young untrained musicians from the suburbs of what was then regarded as a peripheral and unknown British city (Liverpool) who changed music, and arguably the world. So too can educational leaders, one student at a time.

NOTES

1. The author is indebted to Professor Jeffrey Brooks for sharing this book chapter in advance of its release. Thanks also to Professor Michael Leach and Emma Rujevic for their feedback.
2. All but one of these songs came from the same double album: *The Beatles* (1968a).

REFERENCES

Angulo, N. (2014, February 7). Business of the Beatles by the numbers. *FOXBusiness*. Retrieved from http://www.foxbusiness.com/features/2014/02/05/business-beatles-by-numbers.html

Billboard. (2010, November 23). Beatles sell 2 million songs in first week on iTunes. *Billboard*. Retrieved from http://www.billboard.com/articles/news/950355/beatles-sell-2-million-songs-in-first-week-on-itunes

Black, R. (2008). *Beyond the classroom: Building new school networks*. Camberwell, England: ACER Press.

Black, R., Walsh, L., Magee, J., Hutchins, L., Berman, N., & Groundwater-Smith, S. (2014). *Student leadership: A review of effective practice*. Canberra, Australia: ARACY.

Brooks, J. S. (2015, July 14). *Everything we know about educational leadership is wrong: Rethinking scholarship and practice for improved teaching and learning*. Faculty of Education Dean's Lecture Series. Monash University, Clayton, Australia. Retrieved from http://monash.edu/education/events/deans-lecture-series/jeff-brooks.html

Brooks, J. S., & Kensler, L. A. W. (2011). Distributed leadership and democratic Community. In F. W. English (Ed.), *The SAGE handbook of educational leadership: Advances in theory, research, and practice* (2nd ed., pp. 55–66). Thousand Oaks, CA: Sage.

Brooks, J. S. (2016). Everything we know about educational leadership is wrong. In G. Lakomski, C. Evers & S. Eacott (Eds.), *Questioning leadership: New directions for educational organizations* (pp. 31–44). London, England: Routledge.

Bush, T., & Glover, D. (2014). School leadership models: what do we know? *School Leadership & Management, 34*(5), 553–571. doi:10.1080/13632434.2014.9286 80

Clayson, A. (2003). *Ringo Starr.* London, England: Sanctuary.

Coleman, R. (1989). *Brian Epstein: The man who made The Beatles.* London, England: Viking.

Costa, A. L., & Kallick, B. (2000, April). Getting into the habit of reflection: Sustaining change. *Educational Leadership, 57*(7)60–62. Retrieved July 29, 2016, at: http://www.ascd.org/publications/educational-leadership/apr00/vol57/num07/Getting-into-the-Habit-of-Reflection.aspx

Doggett, P. (2009). *You never give me your money: The Beatles after the breakup.* New York, NY: HarperCollins.

Fullan, M. (2000). The three stories of education reform. *Phi Delta Kappan, 81*(8), 581–584.

Gladwell, M. (2008). *Outliers: The story of success.* London, England: Penguin Books.

Guesdon, J., & Margotin, P. (2013) *All the songs: The story behind every Beatles release.* New York, NY: Black Dog & Leventhal.

Guinness World Records. (2009). *Most recorded song.* Retrieved from http://web.archive.org/web/20060910071729/http://www.guinnessworldrecords.com/content_pages/record.asp?recordid=50867

Hallinger, P. (2003). Leading educational change: Reflections on the practice of instructional and transformational leadership. *Cambridge Journal of Education, 33*(3), 329–351.

Hannon, V., Patton, A., & Temperley, J. (2011, December). *Developing an innovation ecosystem for education: Cisco white paper.* Retrieved from http://www.cisco.com/web/strategy/docs/education/ecosystem_for_edu.pdf

Harris, A. (2014, September 29). Distributed leadership. *Teacher.* Retrieved July 25, 2016, from https://www.teachermagazine.com.au/article/distributed-leadership

Harrison, G. (1995). *The Beatles anthology* (Vol. 4). G. Wonfor and B. Smeaton (Series Directors). London, England: EMI.

Heylin, C. (2007). *The act you've known for all these years.* Edinburgh, Scotland: Canongate.

Hiatt, B. (2012, February 15). Paul McCartney: The Beatles considered reuniting. *Rolling Stone.* Retrieved from http://www.rollingstone.com/music/news/paul-mccartney-the-beatles-considered-reuniting-20120215

Ingham, C. (2003*). The rough guide to the Beatles.* London, England: Rough Guides.

Inglis, A., Ling, P., & Joosten, V. (2000). Delivering digitally. London, England: Kogan Page.

Lennon, J., McCartney, P., Harrison, G., & Starr, R. (2000). *The Beatles anthology.* San Francisco, CA: Chronicle Books.

Lewisohn, M. (2013). *The Beatles tune in.* London, England: Little Brown.

Lifton, D. (2015, November 22). *Why a self-titled album signalled the beginning of the Beatles' end.* Retrieved from http://ultimateclassicrock.com/the-beatles-white-album/?trackback=tsmclip

Linkin Park & Jay-Z (2006). (Single) "Numb/Encore/Yesterday," 48th Annual Grammy Awards, 2 February 2006.

Livingstone, S. (2012). Critical reflections on the benefits of ICT in education. *Oxford Review of Education, 38*(1), 9–24. doi: 10.1080/03054985.2011.577938

MacDonald, I. (2008). *Revolution in the head: The Beatle's records and the sixties.* London, England: Vintage.

Margotin, P., & Guesdon, J. (2013). *All the songs: The story behind every Beatles release.* New York, NY: Black Dog & Leventhal.

Mayer, D., & Lloyd, M. (2011, October). *Professional learning: An introduction to the research literature.* Melbourne, Australia: AITSL.

Miles, B. (1997). *Many years from now.* London, England: Vintage-Random House.

Mitra, D., & Gross, J. (2009). Increasing student voice in high school reform: Building partnerships, improving outcomes. *Educational Management Administration & Leadership, 37*(4), 522–543.

Nelson, K. (2015, January 21). Most of the top selling vinyl albums from 2014 were not released in 2014. *Digital Trends.* Retrieved from http://www.digitaltrends.com/music/vinyl-the-beatles-bob-marley-2014-old-records/#ixzz3g1KegsUP

Norman, P. (2016). *Paul McCartney: The biography.* London, England: Weidenfeld & Nicolson.

Richards, K. (2010). *Life.* London, England: Weidenfeld & Nicolson.

Rihanna, West, K., & McCartney, P. (2015). (Single) *FourFiveSeconds.* New York, NY: Roc Nation.

Robinson, V. (2007). *The impact of leadership on student outcomes: Making sense of the evidence.* Retrieved from http://research.acer.edu.au/research_conference_2007/5

Spitz, B. (2005). *The Beatles: The biography.* New York, NY: Little, Brown and Company.

The Beatles. (1964). I feel fine. On *Beatles '65* [LP]. Los Angeles: Capitol.

The Beatles. (1965a). Michelle. On *Rubber soul* [LP]. London, England: Parlophone.

The Beatles. (1965b). Norwegian wood (this bird has flown). On *Rubber soul* [LP]. London, England: Parlophone.

The Beatles. (1965c). In my life. On *Rubber soul* [LP]. London, England: Parlophone.

The Beatles. (1965d). Yesterday. On *Help* [LP]. London, England: Parlophone.

The Beatles. (1966a). *Revolver* [LP]. London, England: Parlophone.

The Beatles. (1966b). Taxman. On *Revolver* [LP]. London, England: Parlophone.

The Beatles. (1966c). Tomorrow never knows. On *Revolver* [LP]. London, England: Parlophone.

The Beatles. (1967a). *Sgt. Pepper's lonely hearts club band* [LP]. London, England: Parlophone.

The Beatles. (1967b). When I'm 64. On *Sgt. Pepper's lonely hearts club band* [LP]. London, England: Parlophone.

The Beatles. (1967c). *Magical mystery tour* [LP]. London, England: Parlophone.

The Beatles. (1967d). *Strawberry fields forever* [Single B-Side]. London, England: Parlophone.

The Beatles. (1968a). *The Beatles* (aka *The white album*) [LP]. London, England: Apple.

The Beatles (1968b). Yer blues. On *The Beatles* (aka *The white album*) [LP]. London, England: Apple.

The Beatles. (1968c). Revolution. On *The Beatles* (aka *The white album*) [LP]. London, England: Apple.

The Beatles. (1968d). Honey pie. On *The Beatles* (aka *The white album*) [LP]. London, England: Apple.

The Beatles. (1968e). The inner light [Single B-Side]. London, England: Parlophone.

The Beatles. (1968e). Ob-La-Di, Ob-La-Da. On *The Beatles* (aka *The white album*) [LP]. London, England: Apple.

The Beatles. (1968f). Revolution 9. On *The Beatles* (aka *The white album*) [LP]. London, England: Apple.

The Beatles. (1968g). *Hey Jude* [Single]. London, England: Apple.

The Beatles. (1969a). *Abbey road* [LP]. London, England: Apple.

The Beatles. (1969b). Octopus's garden. On *Abbey road* [LP]. London, England: Apple.

The Beatles. (1969c). Something. On *Abbey road* [LP]. London, England: Apple.

The Beatles. (1970). *Let it be* [LP]. London, England: Apple.

The Beatles. (2006). Strawberry fields forever. On *Love* [LP]. London, England: Parlophone/Apple.

The Rolling Stones. (1963). *I wanna be your man* [Single]. London, England: Decca.

The Rolling Stones. (1967). *We love you* [Single]. London, England: Decca.

Timperley, H. (2011). *A background paper to inform the development of a national professional development framework for teachers and school leaders.* Melbourne, Australia: The Australian Institute for Teaching and School Leadership.

Walsh, L. (2016). *Educating generation next: Young people, teachers and schooling in transition,* Hampshire, England: Palgrave Macmillan.

Yukl, G. A. (2002). *Leadership in organizations* (5th ed). Upper Saddle River, NJ: Prentice-Hall.

CHAPTER 25

LESSONS FOR SCHOOL LEADERS FROM SISTER SLEDGE

"We Are Family"

Terri N. Watson
The City College of New York

Debbie, 25, Joni,[1] 23, Kim, 22, and Kathy, 21, were on tour when Kim stumbled across a radio station broadcasting the 1979 World Series. During the program, and to the delight of the sisters, the announcer exclaimed: "Seventy thousand people are standing and singing 'We Are Family'!" (Robinson, 1980, p. 138). That year the Pittsburgh Pirates defeated the Baltimore Orioles to win the pennant, and Sister Sledge became international superstars. The title track from their third studio album *We Are Family* cinched first place on the rhythm & blues (R&B) chart and the album peaked at No. 2 on the U.S. *Billboard* Hot 100 (Arena, 2014).

Bernard Edwards and Nile Rodgers of the popular disco band Chic composed "We Are Family" after an initial meeting with the Sledge sisters; the siblings recorded the song in one take (Robinson, 1980). In addition to being

Educational Leadership and Music, pages 275–282
Copyright © 2017 by Information Age Publishing
All rights of reproduction in any form reserved.

the theme song for the 1979 Pittsburg Pirates, the hit single has been featured in commercials, movie soundtracks, and bids for the presidency of the United States of America (Arena, 2014). Interestingly, the practices espoused in "We Are Family" (community building, goal setting, and believing in oneself) are evident in the lived experiences of germinal Black women educational leaders.

Despite their significant contributions to the field of education and educational leadership, the perspectives of Black women are not included in traditional leadership theories (see Blake & Mouton, 1964; Burns, 1978; Fiedler, 1967; House, 1971; Stogdill, 1974). In an effort to fill this void, this chapter compares the practices posited in Sister Sledge's hit single to the lived experiences of Frances Jackson Coppin, Sarah Smith, and Anna Julia Cooper. Historical analysis such as this is an underutilized tool in educational leadership research and can be used to expand our knowledge base in meaningful ways (Horsford & D'Amico, 2015). The next section provides an overview of the early life and work of Sister Sledge.

THE SLEDGE SISTERS

We are family
I got all my sisters with me
We are family
Get up ev'ry body and sing
—Bernard Edwards and Nile Rodgers (1978)

The Sledge sisters were born in Philadelphia with talent in their lineage. Viola Williams, their maternal grandmother, was a lyric soprano opera singer and a protégé of Mary McLeod Bethune, the educationalist and civil rights activist. Edwin Sledge, their father, was part of the dance team Fred and Sledge. The duo appeared in Broadway productions and on the famed *The Ed Sullivan Show*. The girls' mother Florez (Flo) Sledge was also a dancer who once worked in the noted Club Harlem (Robinson, 1980). Unfortunately, Edwin and Flo divorced when the girls were very young. As a single mother, Flo worked two and sometimes three jobs to support her children. While she was at work, Carol, the eldest sister, was in charge of her siblings (Robinson, 1980).

With time and talent on their hands, the sisters formed a singing group. Carol elected not to be in the group; however, she taught her sisters new songs and helped them with their dance routines. Flo was happy her girls found a pastime they enjoyed, and their grandmother was thrilled to help them hone their craft. Initially known as Mrs. Williams' Granddaughters, the siblings first performed at their family's church, Williams Temple Christian Methodist Episcopal, and later in a neighborhood club where they opened for popular R&B performers, including the Pointer Sisters and Aretha Franklin (Pollen, 2014; Robinson, 1980).

Soon after their first paid performance, Sister Sledge released their first single, "Time Will Tell" (Rein, 1979; Robinson, 1980). While the siblings would record scores of hit songs throughout their career, they first experienced success with their second single, "Mama Never Told Me," in 1973. This love song was popular in the United Kingdom and in 1974 they scored their first U.S. hit, "Love Don't Go Through No Changes on Me," penned by Haras Frye and Gwendolyn "Gwen" Anthony Guthrie (Arena, 2014). By 1985 Sister Sledge were international superstars. They recorded eight albums between 1974 and 1985: *Circle of Love* (1974), *Together* (1977), *We Are Family* (1979), *Love Somebody Today* (1980), *All American Girls* (1981), *The Sisters* (1982), *Bet Cha Say That To All the Girls* (1983), and *When the Boys Meet the Girls* (1985).

While Sister Sledge sold millions of albums worldwide and were known for their record-breaking single that celebrated family unity, they experienced a rift in 1989 when Kathy Sledge decided to pursue a solo career. Currently, Debbie, Joni, and Kim still tour as Sister Sledge, and Kathy is estranged from her siblings (Arena, 2014). While the cause of the discord was never made public, in a 2014 interview with a British newspaper Debbie explained that when Kathy initially left the group they (Sister Sledge) should have issued a formal announcement. The sisters chose not to do so, which they later learned was not the best decision. Moreover, she continued, while everyone is doing great, there is still an estrangement between the siblings (Pollen, 2014). Despite their fracture, there are lessons school leaders can learn from the Sledge sisters' timeless hit "We Are Family." In the following sections the practices espoused in the classic song will be compared to the lived experiences of Frances Jackson Coppin, Sarah Smith, and Anna Julia Cooper.

COMMUNITY BUILDING

Ev'ryone can see we're together
As we walk on by
and we fly just like birds of a feather
I won't tell no lie

—Bernard Edwards and Nile Rodgers (1978)

Community building calls on all members of a group to work together for the benefit of the collective. It was surely present when the Sledge sisters embarked on their chosen careers as they dedicated their early years to developing their craft. Likewise, Frances Jackson Coppin, Sarah Smith, and Anna Julia Cooper engaged in community building as they dedicated their lives to improving the educational outcomes and life chances of African Americans.

Frances Jackson Coppin was the first Black woman to serve as a school principal in the United States (Maor, 2008). She was born into slavery and at 12 years of age, her aunt purchased her freedom. By the age of 14, Coppin was self-reliant, and in 1865 after graduating from Oberlin College she became a teacher at the Institute for Colored Youth in Philadelphia. Soon after her arrival, she established a Women's Industrial Exchange so that the wares of the young women who attended the school could be showcased. Coppin (1913) was known to persuade employers to hire her students for positions that would complement their education and better suit their personage.

Sarah Smith was born and raised in Brooklyn, New York. Her parents were wealthy farmers of mixed heritage. By the time she was 14 years old, she was a teacher's assistant at the African Free School and at the age of 32 she became New York City's first Black school leader. She served as the principal of Public School 80 from 1863 to 1900 (Maor, 2008). Smith and her school were well-known throughout the city; large crowds would often assemble to witness awe-inspiring presentations and closing exercises that showcased her students' intellectual acumen. In addition to being a successful school leader, Smith often spoke out against discriminatory hiring practices aimed at New York City's Black teachers (Maor, 2008).

Anna Julia Cooper was born a slave in Raleigh, North Carolina. At the age of 5 she decided she would be a teacher and by 9 she was a "pupil teacher" (Stewart, 2013). Like Frances Jackson Coppin, Cooper attended Oberlin College, and in 1887 she began teaching at M Street High School in Washington, DC, the nation's first public high school for Black students. She was passionate about the education of African American children, girls in particular, and would often say, "Not the boys less, but the girls more" (p. 42). In 1902 Cooper became the principal of M Street High School. Several years later, in addition to founding a small college so that African Americans could work and earn an education in tandem, she fulfilled her lifelong goal and earned a PhD at the Sorbonne.

GOAL SETTING

Living life is fun and we've just begun
To get our share of the world's delights
high hopes we have for the future
And our goal's in sight

—Bernard Edwards and Nile Rodgers (1978)

Goal setting is essential to success. When the Sledge sisters began their musical career, they prepared for stardom by practicing for hours at a time and hanging gold painted records on their bedroom walls (Rein, 1979). Relatedly in her autobiography, *Reminiscences of School Life, and Hints on Teaching,* Coppin recalled setting goals so high that she was often filled with angst. She described her thoughts as follows: "I felt that I had the honor of the whole African race upon my shoulders. I felt that, should I fail, it would be ascribed to the fact that I was colored" (1913, p. 15). Coppin was a proud Black woman and dedicated her life to the advancement of Africans in America, as well as those on the continent. Upon her retirement from the institute, she became a missionary and traveled with her husband, Levi J. Coppin (a well-known minister) to Cape Town, South Africa, where she counseled African women (Coppin, 1913).

Sarah Smith's lived experiences were filled with professional triumphs and personal tragedies. Her first husband, Samuel Tompkins, and their two children died prematurely. Smith met her second husband, Henry Highland Garnet, in 1870. They married nearly 10 years later in 1879. Sadly, he died 2 years after their union when they returned from Liberia, where he had served as a U.S. minister (Maor, 2008). Despite her personal setbacks, Smith remained committed to improving the lives of African American people. She supported the Niagara Movement (an antecedent to the National Association for the Advancement of Colored People) and helped found the Equal Suffrage Club (a Brooklyn-based organization that advocated on behalf of Black Women).

Anna Julia Cooper was a champion of Black women. In 1892 she published what many consider to be the first Black feminist manifesto, *A Voice From the South*. Unfortunately, despite her many achievements Cooper often struggled against racism and bias from her male counterparts. Further, her tenure at M Street High School was contentious. While many of the students under Cooper's tutelage went on to Ivy League institutions including Harvard, Brown, Yale, and Dartmouth, in 1905 she was brought before the board of education and charged with the following wrongdoings: (a) refusing to use a textbook authorized by the board, (b) being too sympathetic to weak and unqualified students, (c) not being able to maintain discipline (two students had been caught drinking), and (d) not maintaining a "proper spirit of unity and loyalty." (Cooper, 1988, p. 35).

Throughout the many challenges she faced, Cooper, like Sarah Smith and Frances Jackson Coppin kept her goals in sight and continued to believe in herself and her students.

BELIEVING IN ONESELF

No we don't get depressed
Here's that we call our golden rule
Have faith in you and the things you do
You won't go wrong
This is our family Jewel

—Bernard Edwards and Nile Rodgers (1978)

Believing in oneself is a central tenet of the Sledge sisters and is evident in the lived experiences of Frances Jackson Coppin, Sarah Smith, and Anna Julia Cooper. As noted, Flo, the girls' mother, often worked multiple jobs leaving Carol in charge of her younger siblings. During their free time the girls formed a group with the hopes of finding stardom. They believed in themselves as did their grandmother, Viola Williams. Likewise, Tillman (2004) found Coppin's efficacy and belief in her students to exemplify Black excellence and to "represent one of the earliest examples of the link between African American school leadership and African American student achievement" (p. 177). In 1876 Coppin wrote a letter to Frederick Douglass, the former slave turned abolitionist, and explained the source of her motivation and her ultimate aim:

> I feel sometimes like a person to whom in childhood was entrusted some sacred flame...This is the desire to see my race lifted out of the mire of ignorance, weakness and degradation; no longer to sit in obscure corners and devour the scraps of knowledge which his superiors flung at him. I want to see him crowned with strength and dignity; adorned with the enduring grace of intellectual attainments. (Coppin, n.d.)

Sarah Smith, like Frances Jackson Coppin, had a long and distinguished career as a principal. She also advocated for the rights of Black women and in the latter part of the 19th century Smith along with her sister, Dr. Susan Smith McKinney Steward, founded the Equal Suffrage League. The women's group initially met in Smith's seamstress shop in Brooklyn and worked to abolish gender and racial bias. At the age of 70, Smith traveled with her sister to London, England, where the latter delivered her paper, "Colored American Woman," at the First Universal Races Congress. The symposium lasted the four days and more than 2,000 delegates, including the Smith sisters, worked to improve race relations (Maor, 2008).

Anna Julia Cooper was a noted academic and often engaged in heated debates with Booker T. Washington (Tillman, 2004). Their exchanges epitomized long-standing ideological and class distinctions within Black America. Cooper was probably the first to oppose "teaching to the test" and remained resolute in her belief that Black educators had a distinct calling. Stewart (2013) remarked, "Anna Julia Cooper would often describe her approach to academic design this way: 'We are not just educating heads and hands, we are educating the men and women of a race'" (p. 47).

Frances Jackson Coppin like Sarah Smith and Anna Julia Cooper believed in themselves and in people of African descent. In addition, the germinal Black women educational leaders practiced community building and goal setting in their personal and professional lives. These tenets are celebrated in Sister Sledge's hit song, "We Are Family," and are applicable for tomorrow's school leaders.

In conclusion, while omitted from traditional leadership theories, Black women educational leaders have made significant contributions to the field. As a professor of educational leadership charged to prepare the next generation of school leaders, I have found it essential to look back in order to move forward. Further, while doing so it is important to make meaningful and learningful connections between theory and practice. The timeless hit "We Are Family" is a viable tool for such praxis.

NOTE

1. Joni Sledge passed away on March 11, 2017.

REFERENCES

Arena, J. (2014). *First legends of disco: 40 stars discuss their careers in classic dance music.* Bloomington, IN: AuthorHouse.

Bernard, E., & Rodger, N. (1978). We are family. On *We are family* [LP]. New York, NY: Cotillion Records.

Blake, R., & Mouton, J. (1964). *The managerial grid: The key to leadership excellence.* Houston, TX: Gulf.

Burns, J. M. (1978). *Leadership.* New York, NY: Harper & Row.

Cooper, Anna Julia (1988). *Washington, Mary Helen: A voice from the South.* New York, NY: Oxford University Press.

Coppin, Frances J. (1913). *Reminiscences of school life, and hints on teaching.* Philadelphia, PA: A.M.E. Book Concern.

Coppin State University. (n.d.). *Fanny Jackson Coppin.* Retrieved from https://www.coppin.edu/fannyjacksoncoppin

Fiedler, F. E. (1967). *A theory of leadership effectiveness.* New York, NY: McGraw-Hill.

Horsford, S. D., & D'Amico, D. (2015). The past as more than prologue: A call for historical research. *International Journal of Educational Management, 29*(7), 863–873.

House, R. J. (1971). A path-goal theory of leader effectiveness. *Administrative Science Quarterly, 16*, 321–338.

Maor, F. S. (2008). *Lifting word by word: The literacy legacy of Frances Jackson Coppin and Hallie Quinn Brown.* Germany: VDM Verlag.

Pollen, L. (2014, June 28). What happened to . . . Debbie from Sister Sledge. *Express.* Retrieved from http://www.express.co.uk/life-style/life/484965/Debbie-from-Sister-Sledge

Rein, R. K. (1979, November 5). When the Pirates hustled to Sister Sledge's 'We Are Family,' the steel city went platinum. *People, 12*, 98–106.

Robinson, S. (1980). Sister Sledge: They really are family. *Essence, 35*, 136–140.

Stewart, A. (2013). *First class: The legacy of Dunbar, America's first black public high school.* Chicago, IL: Lawrence Hill Books.

Stogdill, R. M. (1974). *Handbook of leadership: A survey of theory and research.* New York, NY: Free Press.

Tillman, L. C. (2004). African American principals and the legacy of *Brown*. *Review of Research in Education, 28,* 101–146.

EPILOGUE

"TELL THEM ABOUT THE DREAM, MARTIN"

When Homophily Happens and Music and Educational Leadership Meet Destiny

Ty-Ron M. O. Douglas
University of Missouri–Columbia

In *Borderlands: La Frontera*, Anzaldúa (2007) posits the concept of the "new mestiza consciousness," which provides geopolitical critiques that situate the complexity of U.S.-Mexico border relations; analyzes the implications of occupying a hybrid racial identity; and extends dualistic explanations to encompass the breadth of gendered, sexualized, and class-based difference. Similarly, Giroux (2005) utilizes the concept of border pedagogy to describe the power relations in educative settings that must be dismantled by leaders, educators, and students—border crossers—who are willing to challenge the "physical . . . [and] cultural borders historically constructed and socially organized within rules and regulations that limit and enable particular identities, individual capacities, and social forms" (p. 22). What we learn from scholars like Anzaldúa (2007), Giroux (2005), and Hicks (1991) is that

Educational Leadership and Music, pages 283–288
Copyright © 2017 by Information Age Publishing
All rights of reproduction in any form reserved.

voices and identities live and are silenced within, across, and on geopolitical and sociocultural boundaries and borders. Those who will be effective border crossers must account for otherization: "the process of marginalizing difference, most times through negative stigmas and stereotypes" (Villaverde, 2008, p. 42), which has been a method by which those who hold dominant positionalities have sought to silence difference and stultify subordinate groups (Bonilla-Silva, 2006; Gause, 2008; Johnson, 2006).

As a border crossing brotha-scholar (an African Bermudian/American male academician, songwriter, and singer who has had to navigate many geopolitical, cultural, and physical borders inside and outside the traditional classroom [Douglas, 2013]), I have a keen appreciation for the power and potential of music and educational leadership to both intersect with and instigate possibilities across borders. Specifically, I have become sensitive to the importance of establishing homophily—a common field of interest (Douglas, 2016), particularly when helping leaders in schools, universities and communities bridge the gap between theory and practice in our work. Music, like sport, is a common field of interest for many; a bridge that can unify and create connections amidst strangers. While definitions of leadership in educational spaces and beyond can be debated, terms and variables such as influence and communication are widely accepted as integral components or characteristics of educational leadership. It can be contended that developing homophily is a prerequisite and a byproduct of communication, and, by extension, influence. Certainly, there is a need for the development of school leaders who can effectively cross borders with a sensitivity for the nuanced and diverse terrain of space, race, and place-based variables and context (Douglas, 2016).

It is within this context of the need for models and modalities of educational leaders who can cross borders that we find Watson, Brooks, and Beachum answering Anzaldúa (2007), Giroux (2005), and Hick's (1991) call to interrupt the silence of the struggle of border crossers and to disrupt the otherization of the knowledge and ways of knowing from community-based/non-school based leaders. Who better to interrupt stultifying silence than musicians, and what better medium to interrupt the stale rehearsal of traditional leadership thought than music and an analysis of the leadership methods of those who most effectively operationalize it. At a time when academic conferences and supposedly high-impact publications struggle to transcend an exclusive academic audience, Watson, Brooks, and Beachum have assembled a dynamic array of leadership scholars who (re)introduce us to artists, albums, and anthems that transcend the limited impact factor metrics of Scopus or even the billboards. The perspectives in this timely work push the reader to consider the power of music and educational leadership, and by extension the power of music *as* educational leadership. From hip-hop artists such as Lauren Hill, Jasiri X, and Tupac, to Bono, Coltran,

Ministry, Mozart, jazz, gospel, and country music, readers are introduced to a fresh narrative, a re-cut key, an oldie-but-goodie perhaps: the reality that educational leadership is not the exclusive heir or hireling of the schoolhouse; instead, education and educational leadership transcend schooling and schoolhouse spaces (Douglas, 2016; Douglas & Witherspoon-Arnold, 2016). The best and most effective school leaders do not merely know this, they are intentional about leveraging this principle, living this reality, and leading with this ethos as a guide.

For people of color and others who have been historically and contemporarily marginalized by/in schools, Watson, Brooks, and Beachum's book is particularly important. I am reminded that the history of education reflects the legacy of struggle, sacrifice, and oppression that has also come to characterize significant race, place, and space-based elements of the Black experience (Anderson, 1988; Du Bois, 1898/1973; Morris, 2009; Ogbu, 2007; Woodson, 1911). In fact, schooling and education for Black people have historically been two separate experiences that intersect, at times, but always continue to function independent of each other (Shujaa, 1994). The notion of space not only informs our understanding of various community-based locales of learning, but there are also global and geographical implications that have impacted and continue to influence the mobilization of those engaged in freedom efforts for peoples of African descent. Moreover, across generations, geography, and genre, music is often a mouthpiece of the marginalized.

I am reminded that music forms such as jazz, spirituals, and work songs have undergirded and galvanized generations of Black people (Lovell, 1939; Manuel, Bilby, & Largey, 2006). As Stephanie Shonekan, associate professor of ethnomusicology, notes,

> The fact that each chapter of DuBois' Souls of Black Folk begins with a song speaks to the centrality of music in this icon's scholarship. It has always impressed me that he leads into each of these incredible chapters with a hymn/spiritual excerpt. (Personal communication, August 22, 2016)

Today, hip-hop music has crossed over from the urban core of neighborhood spaces to become a powerful influence on Black and other minority youth and cultures throughout the world (Emdin, 2016; Gause, 2008; Lipsitz, 1994; Love, 2012; Morrell & Duncan-Andrade, 2002). Similarly, the history and educative potency of other musical genres like Negro spirituals (Lovell, 1939) and the consciousness-raising lyrics of Afro-Caribbean reggae music (Manuel et al., 2006) affirm that education and leadership through music have been utilized across the Black diaspora as a space and vehicle for speaking truth to/with power. By centering the truths of Black and Brown musical artists alongside their White counterparts in this edited volume, the editors and contributors to this text are also validating the communities that produce the artists while simultaneously affirming the truths and leadership principles that are reflected in their songs. In this light, this text in many ways is a hymnal of excellence for educational leadership.

Often in leadership books, authors come from a business context or limiting organization models. In this project, the editors use the prism of music and its universality to extrapolate dynamic leadership principles and themes for school leaders that can transcend school contexts and organizational types. In the text, we are challenged to embrace music as both a source of knowledge and a reflection of nuanced knowledge bases and cultural nexus. It is in the intersections of lyric and leader(ship) that one begins to sense the power of the personal narrative of the artist to her/his artistry. Said differently, to the untrained ear there can appear to be a disconnect between the syncopation of a song and the stories and communities that inspired the rhythm of an artist's life, and by extension leadership through music. This book helps to make those connections explicit. For example, readers are exposed to Sister Sledge's We Are Family juxtaposed to seminal school leaders like Frances Jackson Coppin and Anna Julia Cooper.

Music has the capacity to fill a space (e.g., sound waves) and to create a space (e.g., homiphily) for connection and collaboration. Music is a language and a leader personified who can lyrically persuade, melodically modify moods, and rhythmically reinforce the ethos of a social movement. Authors in this important edited book remind us of the significance of music in uprisings like the Civil Rights Movement. I am reminded of the influence of musicians like Mahalia Jackson, who during Dr. King's address at the March on Washington is known to have encouraged King to "tell them about the dream" from behind him as he delivered his now famous speech. Record suggests that Dr. King and his advisers were actually considering leaving out the "I have a dream" portion of the speech the night before the March on Washington because he had used it previously (Willman, 2016). It was Mahalia Jackson's affirmation of "Tell them about the dream, Martin" that helped King transition from the reading of the first half of his speech to the extemporaneous rendition—at times in melodic, song-like tones—of the second half of the legendary speech. "I have a dream" is more than the embodiment of King's core message; it is an example of homophily...a chord that helped mobilize a movement that was crystallized by a moment when Mahalia and Martin were on the same proverbial song sheet in the same space at the right time.

In my latest book, *Border Crossing Brothas: Black Males Navigating Race, Place, and Complex Space* (2016), I too wrestle with the racialized, placialized, and spacialized tensions and realities of identity, education, and leadership. Music intersects with these variables; yet, in some ways, music can sometimes transcend these variables as people from diverse backgrounds connect over a melody or lyric. Rightly or wrongly, particular genres of music have come to be associated with particular racial groups, social classes, and locations. Music lovers may often remember where they were the first time they heard a particular song or may be drawn by the melody or beat of a song to revisit an emotion or location. What I love about Watson, Brooks, and Beachum's book is that it reminds us that the intersection between music and educational leadership include the stories, struggles, and successes of real people. To be an effective school leader of tomorrow, one should be in tune with the music of today.

One cannot read this text and not reflect on her/his own musical journey. I couldn't read about the singers and musicians in this text and not consider the 7 years of piano lessons my parents paid for that are imperceptible if I sit at a keyboard. From chapter to chapter, I thought about my exploits on the saxophone, singing in an all-male quintet as a teenager, and the songs I have written. I hope you reflected on your musical journey as well while reading this text, irrespective of whether you consider yourself musical or not, a shower singer, or a school practitioner with professional music ambitions. Through this text, I have been reminded that there has been an intersection between music and my educational leadership. And though gospel music is my genre of preference these days, it has been my exposure to various musical traditions that has helped me cross borders and given me a rich tapestry of language and experiences to connect and lead—homophily. Taken together, the authors and works highlighted in this text are a beautiful amalgamation of the potential of music to lead us, even as artists use music to lead others.

REFERENCES

Anderson, J. D. (1988). *Education of Blacks in the South: 1860–1935*. Chapel Hill, NC: University of North Carolina Press.

Anzaldúa, G. (2007). *Borderlands la frontera: The new mestiza* (3rd ed.). San Francisco, CA: Aunt Lute Books.

Bonilla-Silva, E. (2006). *Racism without racists: Color-blind racism and the persistence of racial inequality in the United States* (2nd ed.). Lanham, MD: Rowman & Littlefield.

Douglas, T. M. O. (2013). Confessions of a border crossing brotha-scholar: Teaching race with all of me. In D. J. Davis & P. Boyer (Eds.), *Social justice and racism in the college classroom: Perspectives from different voices* (pp. 55–67). Bingley, England: Emerald.

Douglas, T. M. O. (2016). *Border crossing brothas: Black males navigating race, place andcomplex space*. New York, NY: Peter Lang.

Douglas, T. M. O., & Witherspoon-Arnold, N. (2016). Exposure in and out of school: A black Bermudian male's successful educational journey. *Teachers College Record. 118*(6).

Du Bois, W. E. B. (1973). *The education of black people: Ten critiques, 1906–1960* (2nd ed.). New York, NY: Monthly Review Press. (Original work published 1898).

Emdin, C. (2016). *For white folks who teach in the hood . . . and all the rest y'all too: Reality pedagogy and urban education.* Boston, MA: Beacon Press.

Gause, C. P. (2008). *Integration matters: Navigating identity, culture, and resistance.* New York, NY: Peter Lang.

Giroux, H. A. (2005). *Border crossings* (2nd ed.). New York, NY: Routledge.

Hicks, D. E. (1991). *Border writing: The multidimensional text.* Minneapolis, MN: University of Minnesota Press.

Johnson, A. (2006). *Privilege, power, and difference.* New York, NY: McGraw-Hill.

Lipsitz, G. (1994). *Dangerous crossroads: Popular music, postmodernism, and the poetics of place.* New York, NY: Verso.

Love, B. L. (2012). *Hip-hop's li'l sistas speak: Negotiating hip-hop identities and politics in the new South.* New York, NY: Peter Lang.

Lovell, J., Jr. (1939). The social implications of the negro spiritual. *Journal of Negro Education, 8*(4), 634–643.

Manuel, P. L., Bilby, K., & Largey, M. (2006). *Caribbean currents: Caribbean music from rumba to reggae.* Philadelphia, PA: Temple University Press.

Morrell, E., & Duncan-Andrade, J. M. R. (2002). Promoting academic literacy with urban youth through engaging hip-hop culture. *The English Journal, 91*(6), 88–92.

Morris, J. E. (2009). *Troubling the waters.* New York, NY: Teachers College Press.

Ogbu, J. (2007). African American education: A cultural-ecological perspective. In H. P. McAdoo (Ed.), *Black families* (4th ed.; pp. 79–94). Thousand Oaks, CA: Sage.

Shujaa, M. J. (1994). Education and schooling: You can have one without the other. In M. J. Shujaa (Ed.), *Too much schooling, too little education: A paradox of black life in white societies* (pp. 13–36). Trenton, NJ: African World Press.

Villaverde, L. (2008). *Feminist primer.* New York, NY: Peter Lang.

Willman, C. (2016, January 15). *How gospel great Mahalia Jackson gave wing to MLK's 'I have a dream' Speech.* Retrieved from https://www.yahoo.com/music/how-gospel-great-mahalia-jackson-gave-wing-to-108223937471.html

Woodson, C. G. (1911). *Education of the negro prior to 1861.* New York, NY: Knickerbocker Press.

ABOUT THE EDITORS

Terri N. Watson is an assistant professor in the Department of Leadership and Special Education at The City College of New York. A Harlem native, her research examines the practices of urban school leaders and the impact of school reform initiatives on students and communities of color. Watson is currently engaged in a grant-funded longitudinal study of the leadership practices in a large predominantly Black and Latino high school. Through this research-practice partnership, she works closely with the school's leadership team to strengthen parent engagement and school-community relations in ways that support student success. Watson's scholarship may be found in *The Journal of Negro Education, Journal of School Public Relations, Journal of Cases in Educational Leadership, Journal of Ethical Educational Leadership,* and in *Leadership and Policy in Schools* wherein her 2015 article, "Reframing Parent Involvement: What Should Urban School Leaders Do Differently?" with Ira Bogotch was named Article of the Year.

Jeffrey S. Brooks is professor of educational leadership in the Faculty of Education at Monash University. He is a J. William Fulbright Senior Scholar who has conducted studies in the United States and the Philippines. His research focuses broadly on the way educational leaders influence (and are influenced by) dynamics such as racism, globalization, social justice, student learning and school reform. Brooks's research has appeared in leading academic journals and he is author of *The Dark Side of School Reform: Teaching in the Space Between Reality and Utopia* and *Black School, White School: Racism and Educational (Mis)leadership.*

Educational Leadership and Music, pages 289–290
Copyright © 2017 by Information Age Publishing
289

Floyd D. Beachum is the Bennett Professor of Urban School Leadership at Lehigh University. He is also an associate professor and program director for educational leadership in the College of Education. Beachum has a total of 21 years of experience in K–12 and higher education. His research interests include: urban school leadership, moral and ethical leadership, and social justice issues in K–12 schools. He has authored several peer-reviewed articles on these topics. His most recent coauthored book is titled, *School Leadership in a Diverse Society: Helping Schools Prepare all Students for Success.*

ABOUT THE CONTRIBUTORS

Judy A. Alston is professor/chair of the Department of Leadership Studies at Ashland University. Her research foci include Black female school superintendents, the intersections of the various isms and leadership, tempered radicals, servant leadership, spirituality, and Black LGBT issues. She holds a PhD, an MDiv, two MEds, and a BA. She is a prolific author. She is the author of *Multi-Leadership in Urban Schools*, co-author of the bestselling textbook, *School Leadership and Administration: Important Concepts, Case Studies, & Simulations* (7th, 8th, 9th editions) as well as *Herstories: Leading With the Lessons of the Lives of Black Women Activists*.

Adrian Anthony is a high school assistant principal in Florida and a doctoral candidate in educational leadership with a cognate in special education and organizational restructuring at the University of South Florida. Anthony has had a successful education career in the classroom, as a school-based administrator and as a district supervisor within the Tampa Bay area. Additionally, Anthony has had the privilege of working at the U.S. Department of Education with federal governmental policy management with the Office of Special Education [OSEP] in Washington, DC.

Kimberly Starks Berglund is a fourth year doctoral student in the Department of Educational Leadership & Policy Analysis at the University of Missouri. She is a member of the University Council for Educational Administration (UCEA), American Educational Research Association (AERA), and the National Association of Education for Young Children (NAEYC). Starks

Educational Leadership and Music, pages 291–299
Copyright © 2017 by Information Age Publishing
291

Berglund contributed to indexing the book, *Border Crossing Brothas, Black Males Navigating Race, Place, and Complex Space.* She served as second vice-president/week of the Young Child Chair of the Central Missouri Association for the Education of Young Children in mid Missouri, and is currently a Jackson Scholar (2015–2017).

Stephanie Blackburn has more than 20 years experience as a literacy specialist. She has served as a classroom teacher, instructional coach, Title I literacy specialist, Title I lead teacher, and district level consultant. Currently, Blackburn is a literacy specialist in Chesterfield County Public Schools. In addition to her position serving children during the day, she is adjunct faculty for both William & Mary and VCU teaching literacy learning courses for preK–12 preservice and in-service teachers, ELL teachers, and literacy specialists. She is a lifelong music fan and actively attends live shows from all genres. Music inspires her both professionally and personally.

Ira Bogotch is a professor of educational leadership at Florida Atlantic University. His research focuses on critical and historical methodologies in educational leadership, social justice theories and practices, and sociocultural influences on schools, communities and societies, locally, nationally, and internationally.

Christa Boske is an associate professor at Kent State University in the educational administration program. She encourages school leaders to promote humanity in schools, especially for children and families from historically disenfranchised populations. Her line of inquiry focuses on the intersections of the cognitive and affective domains of school leadership with a particular focus on how school leaders transform their sense of self to lead for social justice and equity in schools.

Leon R. de Bruin is an educator, performer, and researcher in improvised and composed music. He performs in ensembles drawing from contemporary to baroque repertoire for trumpet, and collaborates with numerous creative improvisers throughout Australasia. He is a PhD candidate in the Faculty of Education, Monash University, Australia, and his dissertation work includes the teaching and learning of improvisation, creativity and collaborative learning processes and techniques for improvisers, and musician identity. Recipient of a Monash postgraduate publications award, he has published in a number of journals concerning music, cognition, creativity and collaborative research.

James C. Coviello is a doctoral research associate at the University of Texas at El Paso in the Department of Educational Leadership and Foundations.

Coviello was a classroom teacher at the high school level for 10 years and is currently pursuing a doctoral degree in educational leadership.

Katherine Cumings Mansfield is an assistant professor of educational leadership at Virginia Commonwealth University. Mansfield graduated from the University of Texas at Austin with a PhD in educational policy and planning and a doctoral portfolio in women's and gender studies. Mansfield's scholarship examines educational policy and practice as it relates to identity intersectionalities such as gender, class, and race across P–20 contexts. Mansfield has co-edited two books: *Women Interrupting, Disrupting, and Revolutionizing Education Policy and Practice*, with Whitney Newcomb, and *Identity Intersectionalities, Mentoring, and Work-life (Im)balance: Educators (Re)negotiate the Personal, Professional, and Political* with Anjalé Welton and Pei-Ling Lee.

David E. DeMatthews is an assistant professor at the University of Texas at El Paso in the Department of Educational Leadership and Foundations. DeMatthews has worked in urban districts as a high school teacher, middle school administrator, and district administrator. He studies issues related to school leadership, urban education, special education, and social justice.

Sean L. Dickerson completed a master's degree in adult education in 2012 and is currently doctoral candidate in educational leadership and policy studies at the University of South Florida. His research interests include mentoring programs, hip-hop pedagogy, disciplinary practices in K–12 educational environments, and community-school partnerships. Dickerson also serves as the managing editor for the *Journal of Cases in Educational Leadership*, a peer-reviewed publication for use in programs that prepare educational leaders. He has presented at national conferences and has published in both the *eJournal of Education Policy* and *Curriculum and Teaching Dialogue*.

Lisa Catherine Ehrich is an associate professor in the School of Cultural and Professional Learning, Faculty of Education at Queensland University of Technology, Australia. She has worked in the higher education sector for more than 25 years and before that as a secondary teacher. In 2014, she was recognized for her long contribution to Australian leadership education when she was made a Fellow with the Australian Council for Educational Leadership (ACEL) (Queensland Branch) and awarded an ACEL Fellowship. In 2016, with Fenwick English, she published *Leading Beautifully: Educational Leadership as Connoisseurship*.

Fenwick W. English is the R. Wendell Eaves Senior Distinguished Professor of Educational Leadership in the School of Education at the University of North Carolina at Chapel Hill, a position he has held since 2001. He is a former superintendent of schools in New York, and a dean of a school of education and vice-chancellor of academic affairs in Fort Wayne, Indiana for Purdue University. He is the former president of UCEA (2006–2007) and NCPEA (2011–2012). He is the author/co-author of over 40 books, numerous book chapters and research papers. He was named a Living Legend of the profession by NCPEA in 2013.

Pedro (Dro) Genao has been part of the Mobile Moguls & Shady Records/Goliath Artists team for more than 5 years. His contributions have been primarily within the marketing, management and public relations departments.

Soribel Genao is an assistant professor at Queens College's Department of Educational Leadership. She earned her PhD from the School of Public Affairs and Administration at Rutgers University-Newark. She received her BS in mass communications from St. Johns University and her MA in urban affairs from CUNY Hunter College. She has also studied in Ghana and South Africa. Her research interests include education policy, collaborative measurement, and administrative and organizational behavior.

Stephen Jacobson is a distinguished professor at the University at Buffalo, State University of New York. His research interests include the reform of school leadership preparation and practice, and successful leadership in high poverty schools. He is currently studying schools in New Zealand and Belize. His work on school leadership has an international following and, in addition to numerous publications, he has given invited presentations around the world. He is a past president of UCEA and the Association for Education Finance and Policy (AEFP). Currently he is lead editor of *Leadership and Policy in Schools* and UCEA associate director for international initiatives.

Gaëtane Jean-Marie is dean of the College of Education and Richard 0. Jacobson Endowed Chair of Leadership in Education at the University of Northern Iowa. Jean-Marie's research focuses on educational equity and social justice in K–12 schools, women and leadership in P–20 system, and leadership development and preparation in a global context. Jean-Marie has more than 80 publications which include books, book chapters, and academic articles in peer-reviewed journals. She is the editor of the *Journal of School Leadership,* and serves on the editorial board of the *Journal of Educational Administration* and *Journal of Research on Leadership Education,* is a reviewer for several journals, and is past president of the Leadership for Social Justice AERA/SIG.

Christopher Knaus is a race scholar, critical race theory practitioner, educator, and community advocate dedicated to the overthrow of the standardization of schools. A professor of education at the University of Washington, Tacoma, Knaus examines the global impact of colonial school systems and related policies on communities of color. His work centers youth voice as key to shifting from negative schooling to education that affirms through fostering multiple voices, languages, cultures, and ways of living. Knaus focuses on educational leadership development and student-centered approaches to transforming schools.

Jay Liedel is an intervention specialist, school leader, founder of the Stark County Educational Service Center On-Site Program, and advocate for students who have been labelled with disabilities including emotional disturbance (ED). He promotes and engages in a philosophy of focusing on students' strengths to connect with students, and encourages students to be effective members of the learning environment, and their community. He integrates music and music themes within the curriculum to increase students' sense of self, and promote community values.

Ellyn Lyle embraces metaphor to untangle lived experience as a way to inform teaching and learning as autobiographical experience. She began her career in secondary English classrooms before moving toward organizational contexts where she championed critical education practices and leadership for social change. Having joined the academic community full time in 2011, she is currently associate dean in the Faculty of Education and Chair of the Leadership Department. Lyle's research interests include: praxis, the role of reflexive inquiry in practitioner development, issues of identity, leadership for social justice, and pedagogies of place.

Samuel Martin holds a doctorate in educational leadership, a master's of education in school counseling, and a bachelor of science in middle school education, each from the University of Missouri, Columbia. His research interests include the impact of race, class, and gender on school culture, student leadership development, and mentoring. Martin worked extensively with student leadership and academic support programs in his role as a school counselor in Columbia, Missouri. Currently, Martin is employed as an administrator at University City High School in St. Louis, Missouri.

Patrice A. McClellan is associate professor of business and leadership and director of the master's of organizational leadership program at Lourdes University. McClellan has published works in various journals and is also co-author of *Herstories: Leading with the Lessons of the Lives of Black Women Activists.* Her research focuses on leadership education, developing culturally competent leaders and organizational change strategies. In addition to her scholarly endeavors, McClellan is active in various community and social service organizations such as United Way's African American Leadership Council, and is also a leadership mentor for the Center for Non-Profit Resources.

Carlos R. McCray is currently a tenured associate professor and program director in the Educational Leadership Evaluation, and Organizational Development Department at the University of Louisville. Prior to McCray's arrival at the University of Louisville, he was an associate professor and department chair at Fordham University in New York. McCray is the co-author of two books titled, *Cultural Collision and Collusion: Reflection on Hip-Hop Culture, Values, and Schools* and *School Leadership in a Diverse Society: Helping Schools Prepare All Students for Success.* McCray has worked with school leaders and educators in the metropolitan areas of Atlanta, New York City, London, and Louisville. McCray was recognized by *Noodle.org*, an online magazine, as one of 67 influential educators to watch for in 2015.

Alprentice McCutchen has been a history teacher in New York since 1997, and has spent a good portion of his career using Socratic inquiry, debate, performance-based assessments, and critical writing as part of his work to help students contribute to the thinking world. McCutchen received his BA in History and African American Studies from Wesleyan University, and spent a semester at the American University in Cairo studying European imperialism and ancient near eastern history. McCutchen also holds an MA from Teacher's College, Columbia University and an MA in Islamic studies from Middlesex University. He has also co-led student trips to Egypt, Senegal, the Gambia, Spain, and Morocco. Most importantly, McCutchen is a husband and father of three girls.

Jason McKinney is a PhD student in educational policies and analysis, preK–22 (includes higher education), at the University of Missouri. He received his MEd in educational policies with an emphasis on diversity and equity issues in education at the University of Illinois, Urbana–Champaign. McKinney is a 2016–2018 Barbra L. Jackson Scholar recipient. He is an active member of the American Education Research Association (AERA), University Council Education Administration (UCEA), and the Association for the Study of Higher Education (ASHE). McKinney works with youth ministries and an educational change agent.

Jason Newcomb has been a musician and guitarist for almost 40 years in Richmond, Virginia, and Los Angeles, California. He has an eclectic understanding of and appreciation for diverse genres of music and has demonstrated this through a number of projects. Newcomb has been a member of numerous bands and is currently the lead guitarist and background vocalist for The Mashup band. He is also owner of Soulshaker Studios recording, producing, and engineering multiple music endeavors

Anthony H. Normore is professor of educational leadership, and department chair of graduate education at California State University, Dominguez Hills in the Los Angeles area. Normore's research focusses on urban school leadership development in the context of ethics and social justice. He has edited numerous books including *Handbook of Research on Communication, Leadership, and Conflict Resolution* (2016) and published a litany of book chapters, reviews, and peer-reviewed articles in numerous journals. Normore is the AERA 2013 recipient of the Bridge People Award for Leadership for Social Justice SIG, and 2015 Donald Willower Award of Excellence in Research at Penn State University. He serves on various editorial boards including *Journal of Educational Administration* and *Journal of Authentic Leadership in Education.*

Azadeh F. Osanloo is an associate professor and the Stan Fulton Endowed Chair for the Improvement of Border and Rural Schools at New Mexico State University. Her research agenda focuses on issues of educational equity; educational leadership and policy; the philosophical foundations of education; diversity, multiculturalism, and human rights; bullying interventions; and social justice. Her interconnected lines of inquiry are underscored by three co-edited books that cover the topics of urban school leadership, diversity-based bullying interventions, student and parent perceptions of bullying, and international and national social justice work. In addition, she works to increase marginalized student representation in the STEM fields via school-community garden projects with K-12 students in low-income/under-resourced areas. In collaboration with the Las Cruces Police Department she developed the Youth Leadership Academy, which is designed to increase leadership opportunities for middle-school aged youth while increasing positive relationships between police and communities of color. She has won Dean's Awards for her teaching and service and is a 2015 recipient of the American Graduate Champion Award, an award bestowed by the Corporation for Public Broadcasting.

Darius Prier is an assistant professor in the Department of Educational Foundations and Leadership, School of Education, Duquesne University. He received his PhD in educational leadership from Miami University, Oxford, Ohio. His text, *Culturally Relevant Teaching: Hip-Hop Pedagogy in Urban Schools* (2012) was nominated for a Critics Choice Award by the American Educational Studies Association (AESA). Prier has published in academic journals such as the *International Journal of Qualitative Studies in Education* (QSE), *Urban Education, Teachers College Record, Equity & Excellence in Education,* and *Education Week.* He is also a consultant and national speaker on youth leadership.

Rosa L. Rivera-McCutchen is an assistant professor in the educational leadership program at CUNY Lehman College. She began her career in education as a high school teacher in Bronx, NY, before earning her doctorate at New York University. Rivera-McCutchen's teaching and research focus on the theory and practice of leadership in small schools in order to create socially just and equitable schools for Black and Latin@ students in urban settings. Her research has appeared in *Urban Education, The Urban Review, Journal of School Leadership, Journal of Cases in Educational Leadership* and in an edited book entitled *Critical Small Schools: Beyond Privatization in New York City Urban Educational Reform.*

Louis "Marty" Ruccolo is the Supervisor for Transition Services for Broward County Public Schools, creating and implementing programs which transition students with disabilities into adult life and living. Before that, Marty was a middle school math teacher who would bring his drums to school and play for his students, saying: "music is numbers in your ears." Marty has been a professional musician for over 40 years playing all genres, including; Rock, Jazz, R&B, Funk and Fusion. Marty still plays professionally with several bands, including his brother Jimi's groups in the Fort Lauderdale and Miami-Dade, Florida area.

Omar J. Salaam is a PhD candidate in the educational leadership and policy studies program at the University of South Florida with a completed cognate in evaluation. He is a product of the American urban school environment with further nurturing from the environment of a historically Black college/university in preparation for his career as an educator. His 20-plus years of K–12 experience include: music teacher and band director in Florida, Michigan, and Malaysia; assistant principal in multiple Florida school districts; teacher of English, geography, physical education, and principal in Malaysia; and now an instructor at the University of South Florida.

Whitney Sherman Newcomb is a professor and interim chair of the Department of Educational Leadership at Virginia Commonwealth University. Newcomb teaches courses in social justice and equity in leadership, ethical leadership, and leadership presence. She is the author of more than 50 published journal articles, book chapters, and three books. Newcomb has received awards for her teaching and scholarship and was presented with the Emerald Literati Award for Excellence for her work as guest editor of

"Globalization: Expanding Horizons in Women's Leadership," a special issue of the *Journal of Educational Administration*. She is a vocalist and avid music lover.

Mackie V. Spradley is an adjunct professor in the Department of Teacher Education and Administration, College of Education, University of North Texas (UNT), Denton, Texas. She received the BM in voice from UNT and her MA in vocal pedagogy from Texas Woman's University, Denton. She received her PhD in curriculum and instruction with an emphasis in anthropology from UNT. Spradley has published in academic journals, such as the *National Forum of Multicultural Issues Journal* and the *Texas Music Educators Conference Connections*. She is a national speaker on music education, culturally responsive pedagogy, and social justice.

LaBotta Taylor is an adjunct professor in the Department of Teacher Education and Administration, College of Education, University of North Texas (UNT) at Dallas. She received her BBA in marketing, MEd in educational administration, and a PhD in curriculum and instruction from UNT, Denton, Texas. Taylor has published in the *Journal of the Texas Alliance of Black School Educators* (JTABSE). She has served as a peer reviewer for organizations, such as the *American Educational Research Association* (AERA) and the *American Association for Teaching and Curriculum* (AATC). Taylor is also an educational consultant and national speaker on educational leadership.

Lucas Walsh is an associate dean (academic staff) in the Faculty of Education at Monash University in Victoria, Australia. Walsh has worked in government, corporate, and not for profit sectors including the International Baccalaureate program. He has been invited to advise local, state and federal governments, such as the National Curriculum Board and Australian Institute for Teaching and School Leadership. His latest book is *Educating Generation Next: Young People, Teachers and Schooling in Transition.*

Heather Wayne is a practicing school psychologist in Westchester, New York. She holds national and state certifications in the tri-state area. She attended Fordham University in the Lincoln Center Campus for her PhD in School Psychology and MSEd in Educational Psychology: Educational Evaluation and Intervention. Dr. Wynne has published and presented on a variety of topics including: achievement goals, positive behavior interventions, educational leadership, resiliency, and social justice issues.

9 781681 238555